D0713743

DISCARD

ENCYCLOPEDIA OF AMERICAN INDIAN REMOVAL

Volume 2   PRIMARY DOCUMENTS

Daniel F. Littlefield, Jr.
and James W. Parins, Editors

GREENWOOD

AN IMPRINT OF ABC-CLIO, LLC
Santa Barbara, California • Denver, Colorado • Oxford, England

Library of Congress Cataloging-in-Publication Data

Encyclopedia of American Indian removal / Daniel F. Littlefield Jr. and James W. Parins, Editors.
    p. cm.
  Includes bibliographical references and index.
  ISBN 978-0-313-36041-1 (set hardcopy : alk. paper) — ISBN 978-0-313-36042-8 (set ebook) — ISBN 978-0-313-36043-5 (v. 1 hardcopy : alk. paper) — ISBN 978-0-313-36044-2 (v. 1 ebook) — ISBN 978-0-313-36045-9 (v. 2 hardcopy : alk. paper) — ISBN 978-0-313-36046-6 (v. 2 ebook)
  1. Indian Removal, 1813–1903—Encyclopedias. 2. Indian Removal, 1813–1903—Sources. I. Littlefield, Daniel F. II. Parins, James W. III. Title.
  E98.R4E63   2011
  970.004′97003—dc22   2010037598

ISBN: 978-0-313-36041-1
EISBN: 978-0-313-36042-8

15 14 13 12 11   1 2 3 4 5

This book is also available on the World Wide Web as an eBook.
Visit www.abc-clio.com for details.

Greenwood
An Imprint of ABC-CLIO, LLC

ABC-CLIO, LLC
130 Cremona Drive, P.O. Box 1911
Santa Barbara, California 93116-1911

This book is printed on acid-free paper (∞)

Manufactured in the United States of America

CONTENTS

Volume 2, Primary Documents   1

Part I: Policy   1
1. Articles of Agreement and Cession [The Georgia Compact]
   (1802)   1
2. Message from the President of the United States [President
   James Monroe] (January 27, 1825)   4
3. Letter from the Secretary of War to the Chairman of the
   Committee on Indian Affairs, accompanied by a Bill for the
   Preservation and Civilization of the Indian Tribes within the
   United States (1826)   7
4. Removal of the Indians Westward: Disposition of the Several
   Tribes of Indians to Emigrate West of the Mississippi (1826)   14
5. An Act to add the Territory lying within the limits of this State,
   and occupied by the Cherokee Indians, to the counties of
   Carroll, DeKalb, Gwinnett, Hall and Habersham; and to
   extend the laws of this State over the same, and for other
   purposes (1828)   23
6. Report of the Georgia Committee on the State of the Republic
   (1829)   24
7. An Act to provide for an exchange of lands with the Indians
   residing in any of the states or territories, and for their removal
   west of the river Mississippi (1830)   27
8. Excerpt from President Andrew Jackson's Second Annual
   Message (1830)   29
9. An Act to prevent the exercise of assumed and arbitrary power,
   by all persons under pretext of authority from the Cherokee
   Indians, and their laws, and to prevent white persons from
   residing within that part of the chartered limits of Georgia,
   occupied by the Cherokee Indians, and to provide a guard for
   the protection of the gold mines, and to enforce the laws of
   the State within the aforesaid territory (1830)   31

10. Excerpt from the Report of the Secretary of War [Lewis Cass]
    (1831)   34
11. First Annual Message of President Martin Van Buren (1837)   43

Part II: Responses to Policy   46
12. Statement of Menominees Concerning Treaties Ceding Lands
    in Wisconsin to the Indians of New York (1824)   46
13. For the *Cherokee Phoenix*: Indian Emigration (1828)   47
14. Elias Boudinot [Editorial] (January 28, 1829)   50
15. Elias Boudinot [Editorial] (June 17, 1829)   52
16. Elias Boudinot [Editorial] (June 19, 1830)   53
17. William Penn: Excerpt from "On the Present Crisis in the
    Condition of the American Indian" (1830)   55
18. Letter from Chickasaw Chiefs to Andrew Jackson (1835)   71
19. Excerpt from Memorial and Protest of the Cherokee to
    the Honourable the Senate and House of Representatives
    of the United States of North America, in Congress
    Assembled (1836)   75
20. Letter from John Ross, Principal Chief of the Cherokee
    Nation of Indians, in Answer to Enquiries from a Friend
    Regarding the Cherokee Affairs with the United States (1836)   86
21. Excerpt from Letters and Other Papers Relating to Cherokee
    Affairs Being a Reply to Sundry Publications by John Ross (1837) 97
22. Potawatomis of the Wabash Respond to A. C. Pepper (1838)   107
23. Address on the Present Condition and Prospects of the
    Aboriginal Inhabitants of North America with Particular
    Reference to the Seneca Nation. Delivered at Buffalo, New
    York, by M. B. Pierce, A Chief of the Seneca Nation, and a
    Member of Dartmouth College (1839)   113
24. Appeal to the Christian Community on the Condition and
    Prospects of the New-York Indians in Answer to a Book,
    Entitled The Case of the New-York Indians, and Other
    Publications of the Society of Friends by Nathaniel T. Strong,
    A Chief of the Seneca Tribe (1841)   126

Part III: Removals   168
25. Escaped Slave Advertisements (1830–1837)   168
26. Letters of Henry C. Brish about Removal of the Senecas of
    Ohio (1832)   175
27. Journal of a Party of Choctaws Proceeding with Horses in
    Charge of Lieut. J. Van Horne, United States Disbursing
    Agent for the Removal of Indians from Vicksburgh Mi. to Join
    the Main Party of Choctaws Emigrating West of the Mississippi
    River on the Road Leading to Fort Towson. Also Journal of a
    party of Upwards of Six Hundred emigrating Choctaws on
    their Way from Little Rock, Ar. Ter. to their New Country
    Near Fort Towson (1832)   179

28. Journal of Occurrences Kept by the Conductors of the
    Lewistown Detachment of Emigrating Ohio Indians, Senecas
    and Shawnees; Commencing on the 20th of August, 1832,
    and Ending on the 13th of December, 1832 (1832)   186
29. Excerpt of a Letter from J. J. Abert to Lewis Cass (1833)   194
30. Journal of a Party of Seminole Indians Conducted by Lieut. J.
    Van Horne U.S. Army Disbursing Agent Indian Removal from
    McLain's Bottom Arkansas, to the Seminole Country West, on
    the Canadian (1836)   196
31. Journal of My Journey with Two Thousand Creek Indians
    Emigrating to Arkansas, Tuck-e-batch-e hadjo Principal Chief
    (1836)   203
32. Journal of Occurrences on the Route of a Party of Emigrating
    Creek Indians Kept by Lieutenant Edward Deas, U.S. Army
    Disbursing Agent in the Creek Emigration, in Charge of the
    Party (1837)   219
33. George H. Proffit's Removal Journal (1837)   224
34. A Journal of occurrences in conformity with the Revised
    Regulations No 5. Paragraph 8. Kept by B. B. Cannon,
    Conductor of a Party of Emigrating Cherokee Indians, put in
    his charge, at the Cherokee Agency East, by Genl. N. Smith,
    Superintendent of Cherokee removals, on the 13th day of
    October 1837   229
35. Journal of Occurrences in the Route of Emigration of a Party
    of Cherokee Indians, Kept by Lieut. Edward Deas, U.S. Army,
    Conductor of the Party, from Waterloo, Alabama, to the New
    Country West of the Mississippi River (1838)   238
36. Excerpt from the Journal of Rev. Daniel S. Butrick, May 19,
    1838–April 1, 1839: Cherokee Removal (1838)   245
37. The Drane Contingent of Cherokees (1838)   261
38. Journal of an Emigrating Party of Pottawattomie Indians,
    From Twin Lakes, in Marshall County, Ia., to Their Homes on
    the Osage River in the W[ester]n Territory. Conducted by
    Wm. Polke, Esq. (1838)   263

Annotated Bibliography   281

Index   295

About the Editors   309

PRIMARY DOCUMENTS

PART I: POLICY

1. Articles of Agreement and Cession (The Georgia Compact) (1802)

During the national debate on removal, the cession agreement reprinted below, commonly known as the Georgia Compact, became Georgia's legal and political base for insisting that the federal government remove the Indians from within the state's borders as it promised to do in the Compact. After passage of the Indian Removal Act in 1830, the Compact became the convenient excuse given to the Creeks and Cherokees for not protecting them from incursions by Georgia.

Articles of Agreement and Cession

Articles of agreement and cession entered into on the twenty-fourth day of April, one thousand eight hundred and two between the Commissioners appointed on the Part of the United States by virtue of an act entitled "An act for an amicable settlement of limits with the State of Georgia, and authorizing the establishment of a Government in the Mississippi territory," and of the act supplemental to the last mentioned act, on the one part; and the commissioners appointed on the part of the State of Georgia by virtue of an act entitled "An act to carry the twenty-third section of the first article of the Constitution into effect," and of the act to amend the last mentioned act, on the other part.

Article I. The State of Georgia cedes to the United States all the right, title, and claim, which the said State has to the jurisdiction and soil of the lands situated within the boundaries of the United States, south of the State of Tennessee and west of a line beginning on the western bank of the Chattahoochee river, where the same crosses the boundary line between the

United States and Spain; running thence up the said river Chattahoochee and along the western bank thereof to the great bend thereof next above the place where a certain creek or river called "Uchee" (being the first considerable stream, on the western side, above the Cussetas and Coweta towns) empties into the said Chattahoochee river; thence in a direct line to Nickajack on the Tennessee river; then crossing the said last mentioned river, and thence running up the said Tennessee river and along the western bank thereof to the southern boundary line of the State of Tennessee: upon the following express conditions, and subject thereto, that is to say:

First,—That out of the first net proceeds of the sales of the lands thus ceded, which net proceeds shall be estimated by deducting from the gross amount of sales the expenses incurred in surveying, and incident to the sale, the United States shall pay, at their Treasury, one million two hundred and fifty thousand dollars, to the State of Georgia; as a consideration for the expenses incurred by the said State, in relation to the said Territory; and that, for the better securing as prompt a payment of the said sum as is practicable, a land office, for the disposition of the vacant lands thus ceded to which the Indian title has been or may hereafter be extinguished, shall be opened within a twelvemonth after the assent of the State of Georgia to this agreement, as hereafter stated, shall have been declared.

Secondly,—That all persons, who on the twenty-seventh day of October one thousand seven hundred and ninety-five were actual settlers within the territory thus ceded, shall be confirmed in all the grants legally and fully executed prior to that day by the former British Government of West Florida, or by the Government of Spain, and in the claims which may be derived from any actual survey or settlement made under the act of the State of Georgia entitled "An act for laying out a district of land situate on the River Mississippi, and within the bounds of this State, into a county to be called Bourbon," passed the seventh day of February one thousand seven hundred and eighty-five.

Thirdly,—That all the lands ceded by this agreement to the United States, shall, after satisfying the abovementioned payment of one million two hundred and fifty thousand dollars to the State of Georgia, and the grants recognized by the preceding condition, be considered as a common fund, for the use and benefit of the United States, Georgia included, and shall be faithfully disposed of for that purpose and for no other use or purpose whatever: Provided, however, that the United States for the period and until the end of one year after the assent of Georgia to the boundary established by this agreement shall have been declared, may, in such manner as not to interfere with the abovementioned payment to the State of Georgia, nor with the grants hereinbefore recognized, dispose of or appropriate a portion of the said lands not exceeding five millions of acres, or the proceeds of the said five millions of acres, or of any part thereof, for the purpose of satisfying, quieting, or compensating, for any claims other than those herein before recognized, which may be made to the said lands or to any part thereof: it being fully understood, that if an act of Congress making such disposition or appropriation shall not be passed into a law within the above mentioned period of one year, the United States shall not be at liberty thereafter to cede any part of the said lands on account of claims which may be laid to the same, other than those recognized by the preceding condition, nor to compensate for the same; and, in case of any such cession or compensation, the present cession of Georgia to the right of soil over the lands thus ceded or compensated for shall be considered as null and void; and the lands thus ceded or compensated for shall revert to the State of Georgia.

Fourthly,—That the United States shall, at their own expense, extinguish for the use of Georgia, as early as the same can be peaceably obtained on reasonable terms, the Indian title to the county of Talassee, to the lands left out by the line drawn with the Creeks in the Year one thousand seven hundred and ninety-eight, which had been previously granted by the State of Georgia; both which tracts had formerly been yielded by the Indians; and to the lands within the forks of Oconee and Oakmulgee rivers; for which several objects the President of the United States has directed that a treaty should be immediately held with the Creeks: and that the United States shall, in the same manner, also extinguish the Indian title to all the other lands within the state of Georgia.

Fifthly,—That the territory thus ceded shall form a State, and be admitted as such into the Union, as soon as it shall contain sixty thousand free inhabitants, or at an earlier period if Congress shall think it expedient, on the same conditions and restrictions, with the same privileges, and in the same manner as is provided in the ordinance of Congress of the thirteenth day of July one thousand seven hundred and eighty-seven for the government of the Western Territory of the United States; which ordinance shall, in all its parts, extend to the territory contained in the present act of cession, that article only excepted which forbids Slavery.

Article II. The United States accept the cession abovementioned, and on the conditions therein expressed: and they cede to the State of Georgia whatever claim, right or title they may have to the jurisdiction or soil of any lands lying within the United States, and out of the proper boundaries of any other State, and situated south of the southern boundaries of the States of Tennessee, North Carolina and South Carolina, and east of the boundary line herein above described as the eastern boundary of the Territory ceded by Georgia to the United States.

Article III. The present act of cession and agreement shall be in full force as soon as the Legislature of Georgia shall have given its assent to the boundaries of this cession; provided that the said assent shall be given within six months after the date of these presents; and provided that Congress shall not, during the same period of six months, repeal so much of any former law as authorizes this agreement and renders it binding and conclusive on the United States. But if either the assent of Georgia shall not be thus given, or if the law of the United States shall be thus repealed within the said period of six months, then, and in either case, these presents shall become null and void.

In faith whereof the respective commissioners have signed these presents, and affixed hereunto their seals. Done at the City of Washington, in the District of Columbia, this twenty-fourth day of April, one thousand eight hundred and two.

James Madison
Albert Gallatin
Levi Lincoln [Commissioners on the Part of the United States]
James Jackson
Abraham Baldwin
John Milledge, Commissioners on the Part of the State of Georgia
J. Franklin, Senator U.S. from North Carolina, Witness
Sam A. Otis, Secretary of the Senate of the United States, Witness
John Beckley, Clerk of the House of Representatives of the United States, Witness

Source: American State Papers: Public Lands 1:114.

2. Message from the President of the United States (President James Monroe) (January 27, 1825)

This letter introduces a report from Secretary of War John C. Calhoun in which he summarizes data from the Office of Indian Affairs that outline the names and numbers of tribes in the states and territories that have not been removed. The data identify the quantity of land claimed by each tribe as well as an estimate of the appropriation needed to remove all remaining tribes to the West. President James Monroe comments on these data while making the case for removal for all the Indians east of the Mississippi.

To the Senate of the United States:
Being deeply impressed with the opinion, that the removal of the Indian tribes from the lands which they now occupy within the limits of the several states and territories, to the country lying westward and northward thereof, within our acknowledged boundaries, is of very high importance to our Union, and may be accomplished, on conditions, and in a manner, to promote the interest and happiness of those tribes, the attention of the Government has been long drawn, with great solicitude, to the object. For the removal of the tribes within the limits of the state of Georgia, the motive has been peculiarly strong, arising from the compact with that state, whereby the United States are bound to extinguished the Indian title to the lands within it, whenever it may be done peaceably and on reasonable conditions. In the fulfillment of this compact I have thought that the United States should act with a generous spirit, that they should omit nothing which should comport with a liberal construction of the instrument, and likewise

be in accordance with the just rights of those tribes. From the view which I have taken of the subject, I am satisfied, that, in the discharge of these important duties, in regard to both the parties alluded to, the United States will have to encounter no conflicting interests with either; on the contrary, that the removal of the tribes, from the territory which they now inhabit, to that which was designated in the message at the commencement of the session, which would accomplish the object for Georgia, under a well digested plan for their government and civilization, which should be agreeable to themselves, would not only shield them from impending ruin, but promote their welfare and happiness. Experience has clearly demonstrated, that, in their present state, it is impossible to incorporate them, in such masses, in any form whatever, into our system. It has also demonstrated, with equal certainty, that, without a timely anticipation of, and provision against, the dangers to which they are exposed, under causes which it will be difficult, if not impossible, to control, their degradation and extermination will be inevitable.

The great object to be accomplished is, the removal of those tribes to the territory designated, on conditions which shall be satisfactory, and honorable to the United States. This can be done only by conveying to each tribe a good title to an adequate portion of land, to which it may consent to remove, and by providing for it there, a system of internal government, which shall protect their property from invasions, and, by the regular progress of improvement and civilization, prevent that degeneracy which has generally marked the transition from the one to the other state.

I transmit, herewith, a report from the Secretary of War, which presents the best estimate which can be formed from the documents in that Department, of the number of Indians within our states and territories, and of the amount of lands held by the several tribes within each: of the state of the country lying northward and westward thereof, within our acknowledged boundaries; of the parts to which the Indian title has already been extinguished, and of the conditions on which other parts, in an amount which may be adequate to the object contemplated may be obtained. By this report, it appears, that the Indian title has already been extinguished to extensive tracts in that quarter, and that other portions may be acquired to the extent desired, on very moderate conditions. Satisfied, I also am, that the removal proposed is not only practicable, but that the advantages attending it, to the Indians, may be made so apparent to them, that all the tribes, even those most opposed, may be induced to accede to it, at no very distant day.

The digest of such a government, with the consent of the Indians, which should be endowed with sufficient power to meet all the objects contemplated, to connect the several tribes together in a bond of amity, and preserve order in each: to prevent intrusions on their property; to teach them, by regular instructions, the arts of civilized life, and make them a civilized people, is an object of very high importance. It is the powerful consideration, which we have to offer these tribes as an inducement to relinquish the lands on which they now reside, and to remove to those which are designated. It is not doubted, that this arrangement will present considerations of sufficient force to surmount all their prejudices in favor of the soil of their nativity, however strong they may be. Their elders have sufficient intelligence to discern the certain progress of events, in the present train, and sufficient virtue, by yielding to momentary sacrifices, to protect their families and posterity from inevitable destruction. They will also perceive that they may thus attain an elevation, to which, as communities, they could not otherwise aspire.

To the United States, the proposed arrangement offers many important advantages in addition to those which have been already enumerated. By the establishment of such a government over these tribes, with their consent, we become, in reality, their benefactors. The relation of conflicting interests, which has heretofore existed between them and our frontier settlements, will cease. There will be no more wars between them and the United States. Adopting such a government, their movement will be in harmony with us, and its good effect be felt throughout the whole extent of our territory, to the Pacific. It may fairly be presumed, that, through the agency of such a government, the condition of all the tribes inhabiting that vast region, may be essentially improved; that permanent peace may be preserved with them, and our commerce be much extended.

With a view to this important object, I recommend it to Congress to adopt, by solemn declaration, certain fundamental principles, in accord with those above suggested, as the basis of such arrangements as may be entered into with the several tribes, to the strict observance of which the faith of the nation shall be pledged. I recommend it, also, to Congress, to provide, by law, for the appointment of a suitable number of Commissioners, who shall, under the direction of the President, be authorized to visit, and explain to the several tribes, the objects of the Government, and to make with them, according to their instructions, such arrangements as shall be best calculated to carry those objects into effect.

A negotiation is now depending with the Creek nation for the cession of lands held by it within the limits of Georgia, and with a reasonable prospect of success. It is presumed, however, that the result will not be known during the present session of Congress. To give effect to this negotiation, and to the negotiations which it is proposed to hold, with all the other tribes within the limits of the several states and territories, on the principles and for the purposes stated, it is recommended, that an adequate appropriation be now made by Congress.

JAMES MONROE

Washington, 27th January, 1825.

Source: 18th Cong., 2nd sess., in *Compilation of the Messages and Papers of the Presidents, 1789–1897,* ed. J. D. Richardson (Washington, DC: U.S. Government Printing Office, 1897), 2: 180–283.

3. Letter from the Secretary of War to the Chairman of the Committee on Indian Affairs, accompanied by a Bill for the Preservation and Civilization of the Indian Tribes within the United States (1826)

In the following selection, James Barbour sets forth a rationale for a bill that would remove the Indians from east of the Mississippi to west of that river. He acknowledges that the government is feeling pressure from white people living in proximity to Indian communities to extinguish the Indian land titles in the East and to open those areas to settlement by whites. He also outlines a plan to establish a territory in the West in which the Indians would live, based on the territorial models already in place in various regions of the United States. Barbour's piece sets out many of the familiar arguments in favor of removal, including how proximity to whites degrades the Indians and places them in danger of extinction. It also attempts to discredit the policies currently in place to "civilize" the Indians.

**Department of War,
February 3d, 1826.**

The condition of the aborigines of this country, and their future destiny, have long engaged the attention of the philosopher and statesman, inspiring an interest correspondent to the high importance of the subject. The history of the past presents but little on which the recollection lingers with satisfaction. The future is not more cheering, unless resort be speedily had to other councils than those by which we have heretofore been governed. From the first discovery of America to the present time, one master passion, common to all mankind, that of acquiring land, has driven, in ceaseless succession, the white man on the Indian. The latter reluctantly yielding to a force he could not resist, has retired from the ocean to the mountains, and from the mountains to more inhospitable recesses, wasting away by sufferings, and by wars, foreign and intestine, till a wretched fragment only survives, of the numerous hordes once inhabiting this country, whose portion is to brood in grief over their past misfortunes, or to look in despair on the approaching catastrophe of their impending doom.*

It were now an unprofitable task to inquire, on what principle the nations of Europe were justified in dispossessing the original proprietor of his birth right. They brought with them their own maxims, which recognized power as the only standard of right, and fraud and force as perfectly legitimate in the acquisition of territory. It has been done, and time has confirmed the act.

In the contest for dominion, the milder qualities of justice and clemency were disregarded. But that contest has long since ceased, especially in the United States, where, on the one side are seen a great people, familiar with

---

*The whole number of Indians within the United States is estimated, in round numbers, at 300,000 of which 120,000 reside in the States and Territories.

arts and arms, whose energies are increased by union, and directed by an efficient government: on the other, a few ignorant and divided tribes of barbarians. It is necessary only for the former to express its will, to receive or enforce immediate submission from the latter. The suggestions of policy or necessity should no longer stifle the claims of justice and humanity. It is now, therefore, that a most solemn question addresses itself to the American people, and whose answer is full of responsibility. Shall we go on quietly in a course, which, judging from the past, threatens their extinction, while their past sufferings and future prospects, so pathetically appeal to our compassion? The responsibility to which I refer, is what a nation owes to itself, to its future character in all time to come. For, next to the means of self-defence, and the blessings of free government, stands, in point of importance, the character of a nation. Its distinguishing characteristics should be, justice and moderation. To spare the weak is its brightest ornament. It is, therefore, a source of the highest gratification, that an opportunity is now offered the United States to practice these maxims, and give an example of the triumph of liberal principles, over that sordid selfishness which has been the fruitful spring of human calamity.

It is the province of history to commit to its pages the transactions of nations. Posterity look to this depository with the most intense interest. The fair fame of their ancestors, a most precious inheritance, is to them equally a source of pride, and a motive of continued good actions. But she performs her province with impartiality. The authority she exercises in the absence of others, is a check on bad rule. The tyrant and the oppressor see, in the character of their prototypes, the sentence posterity is preparing for them. Which side of the picture shall we elect? for the decision is left to ourselves. Shall her record transmit the present race to future generations, as standing by, insensible to the progress of the desolation which threatens the remnant of this people: or shall these unfriendly characters give place to a generous effort which shall have been made to save them from destruction. While deliberating on this solemn question, I would appeal to that high Providence, whose delight is justice and mercy, and take council from the oracles of his will, revealed to man, in his terrible denunciations against the oppressor.

In reviewing the past, justice requires that the humane attempts of the Federal Government, coeval with its origin, should receive an honorable notice. That they have essentially failed, the sad experience of every day but too strongly testifies. If the original plan, conceived in the spirit of benevolence, had not been fated to encounter that as yet unabated desire, to bereave them of their lands, it would, perhaps, have realized much of the hopes of its friends. So long, however, as that desire continues to direct our councils, every attempt must fail. A cursory review is all that is necessary to show the incongruity of the measures we have pursued, and the cause of their failure.

Missionaries are sent among them to enlighten their minds, by imbuing them with religious impressions. Schools have been established by the aid of private, as well as public donations, for the instruction of their youths. They have been persuaded to abandon the chase—to locate themselves, and become cultivators of the soil—implements of husbandry, and domestic, have been presented them, and all these things have been done, accompanied with professions of a disinterested solicitude for their happiness. Yielding to these temptations, some of them have reclaimed the forest, planted their orchards, and erected houses, not only for their abode, but for the administration of justice, and for religious worship. And when they have done, *you* send *your* Agent to tell them they must surrender their country to the white man, and re-commit themselves to some new desert, and substitute as the means of their subsistence the precarious chase for the certainty of cultivation. The love of our native land is implanted in every human bosom, whether he roams the wilderness, or is found in the highest state of civilization. This attachment increases with the comforts of our country, and is strongest when these comforts are the fruits of our own exertions. We have imparted this feeling to many of the tribes by our own measures. Can it be matter of surprise, that they hear, with unmixed indignation, of what seems to them our ruthless purpose of expelling them from their country, thus endeared. They see that our professions are insincere—that our promises have been broken; that the happiness of the Indian is a cheap sacrifice to the acquisition of new lands: and when attempted to be soothed by an assurance that the country to which we propose to send them is desirable, they emphatically ask us, what new pledges can you give us that we shall not again be exiled when it is your wish to possess these lands? It is easier to state, than to answer this question. A regard to consistency, apart from every other consideration requires, a change of measures. Either let him retain and enjoy his home, or, if he is to be driven from it, abstain from cherishing illusions, we mean to disappoint, and thereby make him to feel more sensibly the extent of his loss.

Having pointed out the incongruities of this system, so unhappily organized, that it contains within itself the causes of its own abortion, I proceed to review the more modern plans of removing the different tribes from the East to the West of the Mississippi. That this plan originated in that benevolence for which its author is so distinguished, is cheerfully admitted: but that *it* too, is obnoxious to many objections, I fear, is no less true. The first objection is the impracticability of its execution, if that is to depend on treaties alone. Some of the tribes in whose removal we are most deeply concerned, have peremptorily refused to abandon their native land. Those who may be persuaded to emigrate, will carry with them the same internal feuds which are so destructive to their kind, and for which no remedy is proposed. Different tribes are to be placed in juxtaposition without a *controlling* power, between which, hereditary and implacable hostilities have raged, and which are not likely to be appeased, till the one or the other is exterminated. But these difficulties surmounted, in what relation are they to stand to the United States? The history of every age teaches us how difficult it has been to maintain tranquillity between conterminous and independent states—though civilized. How must that difficulty be increased when one of the parties is Savage? Thefts and murders, and numberless causes of discord, must inevitably precipitate collisions which cannot but prove fatal to the weaker party. And the same propensity which has conducted the white population to the remote regions they now occupy, will continue to propel the tide, till it is arrested only by the distant shores of the Pacific. Before this resistless current, the Indian must retire till his name will be no more. It would be, however, worse than useless to waste *your* time in multiplying objections to existing plans—I have therefore, supposing it to be within the duty assigned me by the Committee, submitted the project of a bill, with such provisions as I think, under all the circumstances, are best calculated to effect the desired object.

In performing the service assigned by the Committee, whose wishes alone would have been a sufficient inducement on my part to render a cheerful compliance, I have a further reason—a desire to comply with the requests of the People of the United States residing in the neighborhood of Indian settlements. The Department is continually pressed with applications, from New York to Arkansas, to adopt measures to extinguish the Indian titles to their lands, and remove the Indians. An unavailing attempt to obtain a cession of their lands is sometimes ascribed by the disappointed to ignorance, or a want of zeal, or some worse motive on the part of Agents employed—and new attempts to negotiate are solicited with unabated importunity. The obstinacy of the Indians, arising from their partial civilization, whose removal we most wish, fully equals the zeal of those who wish to procure their lands—and hence, an insuperable difficulty presents itself of effecting, by *treaties,* the object which is so desirable, of putting an end to this fruitful source of collision.

I am not arrogant enough to suppose that it is free from all objections. For I am aware that no plan, which human ingenuity could suggest, would be altogether exempt, as the subject is encompassed on every side with difficulties. The utmost reach of my hopes is limited to a diminution of these difficulties, both in number and extent. It is only by comparison I am satisfied that my scheme can solicit a preference. I submit the outlines of the bill, the principles of which are the following:

First. The country West of the Mississippi, and beyond the States and Territories, and so much on the East of the Mississippi as lies West of Lakes Huron and Michigan, is to be set apart for their exclusive abode.

Secondly. Their removal by individuals, in contradistinction to tribes.

Thirdly. A Territorial Government to be maintained by the United States.

Fourthly. If circumstances shall eventually justify it, the extinction of tribes, and their amalgamation into one mass, and a distribution of property among the individuals.

Fifthly. It leaves the condition of those that remain unaltered.

In offering a few remarks upon these different heads, I beg to call the attention of the committee to the leading principle of the bill, namely: That nothing is proposed to be done, in reference to the Indians, *without their own consent.* In making this a preliminary to our acting, I have been influenced rather by a desire to relieve the proposed plan from objections, than from any settled conviction of its necessity. The relations between the United States and the Indians are so entirely peculiar, that it is extremely difficult to refer to any well settled principles by which to ascertain the extent of our authority over them. Our ancestors, as well as every European nation that seized upon their country, denounced them as Heathens, utterly out of the pale of civil society, and as a consequence, disposed of them according to their will and pleasure. From the adoption of the Federal Government, however, they were regarded, to some extent, as an independent people. Hence, treaties were made with them for a surrender of the usufruct of their lands. On the other hand, they were denied the exercise of this right as it respects other nations, and were even restrained from selling their lands to our own citizens. And beside regulating their trade, Congress went so far as to punish, by the decisions of our own courts, for offences committed within or without their own territories. In forbearing to go further, it is left to conjecture, whether it arose from a want of authority, or the expediency of exercising it. To avoid, therefore, any difficulty which different opinions might produce on this point, their consent has been *made necessary* by the bill, as a requisite to its operation.

The first provision looks to the procurement of a country for future residence beyond the settlements of the whites. Fortunately, that object can be easily effected. In adopting the limits prescribed in the bill, I have pursued the plan heretofore proposed. In including the lands as a part lying between Lakes Michigan and Huron, and the River Mississippi, I have been governed as well by the above consideration, as the fact that it is now in the occupancy of the Indians, and, from its natural features, is not desirable at present for the habitation of our citizens.

The principal recommendation of this plan, next to the advantages to be gained by ourselves, is, that the future residence of these people will be forever undisturbed—that there, at least, they will find a home and a resting place. And being exclusively under the control of the United States, and, consequently, free from the rival claims of any of the States, the former may plight its most solemn faith that it shall be theirs forever, and this guaranty is therefore given.

The second provision referred to is that of effecting their removal by portions less than whole tribes, when the latter is impracticable. Some of the tribes, in whose immediate removal we are particularly interested, have expressed a fixed determination against an exchange of their lands. This difficulty is said to arise from the influence of their chiefs, who have appropriated the most fertile lands to themselves, and have become wealthy. *Their* consent to remove cannot be obtained; but the majority, or large portions of the tribe who have no such inducement to remain, it is asserted by those who know, or pretend to know their wishes, may be persuaded to emigrate. By the proposed plan the fact can be ascertained, and whatever portion may be willing to go, will, under this provision, be removed.

The third object of the bill is, the establishment of a Territorial Government by the United States for their protection and their civilization. The bill proposes a Governor, three Judges, and a Secretary, to be appointed by the

President, with the advice and consent of the Senate, and such modifications in detail as the President shall ordain, subject to the approbation of Congress.

I have already intimated, in a former part of this report, the consequences of sending the Indians to the country destined for their final abode, without some controlling authority. Without this they will be exposed to endless mischiefs. It is not necessary to prescribe particularly in the bill their government. Its organization may safely be deposited in the hands of the President, subject to the control of Congress. I will, nevertheless, suggest, that, as soon as the civilization of the Indians would admit of it, I would give them a legislative body, composed of Indians to be selected in the early stages by the President, and eventually to be elected by themselves, as well for the purpose of enacting such laws as would be agreeable to themselves, as for the purpose of exciting their ambition. Distinction being the object of universal pursuit with man, whether barbarous or civilized, it is presented to the Indians in this scheme. They will be taught, that there is another road to it than through blood and slaughter. The objection on the part of the most intelligent, to an amalgamation with the whites, is, that they can never rise to offices of trust and profit. Here this difficulty will be removed. In time, let us indulge the hope, that they will be competent to self government, when they may be left entirely to themselves, and when, in consequence, their ambition will find its proper theatre, and be gratified; then none will have any adequate motive to remain among the whites.

A fourth object of the bill is, the division of their lands in such manner, and at such times, as the President may think proper. The object of this provision is, to give the power to the President, when, in his judgment, circumstances will justify it, to distribute the land among the individuals by metes and bounds, in contradistinction to its being held in common by a tribe. Nothing, it is believed, has had a more injurious influence on our efforts to improve the condition of the Indians, than holding their land in *common*. Whether such a system may succeed on a very limited scale, when under a beneficent patriarchal authority, is yet to be ascertained. Past experience has left the strongest evidence against its practicability under less favorable auspices. The attempt of that kind in the first settlement of Virginia, and, I believe, in the early settlements elsewhere, conducted the colonists to the very brink of ruin, from which they were rescued only by abandoning it. The distribution of the soil, and the individuality imparted to the avails of its cultivation, history informs us, instantly gave a new and favorable aspect to their condition. How far the strong motives of human action may be modified by education and habit, may be left in the hands of the speculative philanthropists. The only safe rule for governments is, to act on human nature as it is, and conform its changes of policy to new, but well ascertained developments. If, therefore, the position be a just one, that every attempt at a community of property has eventuated unsuccessfully, even with civilized man, it is no matter of wonder that it should have been equally so with the savage. To the lands thus granted, add liberally all that is necessary to enable them effectually to succeed in their new condition—implements of husbandry, mechanics for repairing them, domestic animals, and supplies of food. By directing a part of the funds at present paid for annuities, judiciously, under proper Agents, to be appointed by the United States, and as long as necessity required it, the Indians might be brought, by degrees, to a love of civilized life, and be reconciled to the performance of its duties. And although the difficulty of inducing him to labor, is duly appreciated, yet, when its benefits are once realized in the individuality of its productions, and by increasing his comforts, the hope can scarcely be deemed desperate which places him under the same influences as the white man. I refer to the document B as disclosing interesting information on this branch of the subject. The principal fixed, the time of its application to different tribes might be left to the discretion of the President, who, in its exercise, would conform to circumstances, commencing with those most convenient and most civilized, and cautiously extending its application till the whole be embraced. The money we annually expend on our Indian relations, and frequently not very profitably to them, from the manner of their appropriating it, would furnish an ample fund to meet any probable expense arising from the execution of this plan. By reference to document A, it will be seen that this year we have had to pay for this object $781,827.14.

To those advantages may be added the consideration, that, after an individual distribution, the effort of the whites to dispossess them of their lands thus held must cease. The individual appropriation of land gives a sanctity to the title which inspires respect in nations the most barbarous. It would repress, with us, any thought of disturbing it. When this is effected, their distinction of tribes may easily be abolished, and the whole consolidated into one great family. And lastly, the bill leaves those that remain to the wisdom and justice of posterity. If, as is believed, the number disposed to emigrate is comparatively great, those that remain will be so few that their condition may be regulated without committing violence on their wishes or their interests, and yet reconciling their residence with the prosperity of the whites. It is obvious, from causes that need not be enumerated, they must soon surrender their distinction of race for the resemblance of the white man, and accept, as an equivalent, the blessings which that resemblance cannot fail to bring with it—a peaceful but sure remedy, which may be safely left to time along to produce.

I will add, that the end proposed is the happiness of the Indians—the instrument of its accomplishment—their progressive, and finally, their complete civilization. The obstacles to success are their ignorance, their prejudices, their repugnance to labor, their wandering propensities, and the uncertainty of the future. I would endeavor to overcome these by schools: by a distribution of land in individual right; by a permanent social establishment which should require the performance of social duties, by assigning them a country of which they are never to be bereaved, and cherishing them with parental kindness.

In looking to the possible results of this plan, I am cheered with the hope, that much good may be effected with comparatively little injury. Our difficulties in their present form, will be diminished, or entirely removed. The desire to acquire Indian lands will cease, and no longer produce collisions. The Indians will at last know their lot with certainty. That many will avail themselves of this arrangement so as to arrive at the blessings of civilization, I think there can be no reasonable doubt; that all will not, I readily admit. The imprudent of our own people are equally beyond the reach of legislative protection.

To this may be added the consolation furnished by the recollection, that, in the efforts we have made, we had acquitted ourselves of a debt of justice and humanity; and if they should even fail by the overruling influence of an inscrutable destiny, whose fulfillment requires their extinction, however it may fill us with sorrow, we shall be relieved from remorse.

Respectfully submitted,

JAMES BARBOUR

Source: U.S. Congress. House. *Preservation and Civilization of the Indians.* 19th Cong., 1st sess., 1826. H. Doc. 102, pp. 5–12.

4. Removal of the Indians Westward: Disposition of the Several Tribes of Indians to Emigrate West of the Mississippi (1826)

The commissioner of Indian affairs, Thomas L. McKenney, describes the southern tribes and their disinclination to remove, blaming it on a lack of understanding on the Indians' part as to the government's removal plan. He goes on to consider tribes from the Ohio Valley and Old Northwest, their numbers, and removal plans for them. McKenney touches on the Indian groups west of the Mississippi into whose territory the eastern tribes would be removed and gives scanty plans for the government of the new territory to be established for the Indians in the West.

Department of War
Office of Indian Affairs, 27th Dec. 1826

To the Hon. James Barbour,
Secretary of War:

Sir: I have the honor, in compliance with your directions, to make to you the following report on the several points embraced in the resolution of the House of Representatives, of the 20th inst. relating to "the disposition of the several tribes of Indians within the United States to emigrate West of the Mississippi," &c.

Of the disposition of those tribes to emigrate, no *certain* information can be given. It is true, of the four principal tribes, two of them, the Choctaws and Chickasaws, have recently, and to the Commissioners appointed to negotiate with them in reference to this subject, given a decided negative;

and from the other two, the Creeks and Cherokees, we have the most decided indications of a like determination. But these answers have been given under the same mode of application, and which it is respectfully suggested is not only the most exceptionable in their view of the subject, but will continue to be, as it has been in regard to those tribes, unsuccessful. I mean *the mode of treating with them.*

The exceptions on the part of those Indians to this mode, arise out of preconceived prejudices, and out of the circumstance of making the proposition direct to the enlightened among them, who, if they happen not to be chiefs, have an influence over those who are, which they exert, and which has been, and in my opinion will continue to be effectual, in defeating such propositions made in this form for the future. Those prejudices, it must be conceded, are natural. They arise out of a review of the past. Those enlightened half-breeds, from whom the opposition to emigration generally comes, read in the history of the past the effects of this mode of acquiring lands. They see the entire country of the East has been swept of their brethren who once inhabited there; and that, as the chiefs in the Middle and Northern States have listened to proposals to treat with them, they also have disappeared, until only a remnant of their once mighty race is left. They moreover enjoy the preciousness of domestic life; and in the absence of game, have, to a very great extent, at least, turned their attention to the soil, and to manufacturing. They dread a rupture of those ties; and, from the moment a proposition is made in the Congress to appropriate the means to treat with either of those tribes, those intelligent and lettered Indians exert an influence over the head men, and over as many of the body of their people as they can reach, which has resulted, as we have seen, in their refusal to acquiesce in the terms proposed to them. "The obstacles to their removal" are, in my opinion, in great part those which arise out of *the mode* of approaching them.

In support of this opinion, I beg leave respectfully to add an extract from a letter addressed to the Department by the Hon. John McKee, of the 13th of September last—a period, it will be remarked, but little anterior to that in which the Commissioners met the Choctaws in council.

"I have recently," writes this correspondent, "been in the Choctaw nation, and at a council of the chiefs, where the subject of their migration to the West, and of *the approaching treaty,* was much spoken of. Considerable opposition to *both* was publicly expressed; though I found some of the old and best informed were of opinion, that they could not long subsist where they now are, and that an early march to the West would be most favorable to a judicious selection of a new residence, and the formation of friendly associations with the Indians in that quarter."

Col. McKee having been once the Agent to the Choctaws, and having enjoyed their confidence in an eminent degree, may be considered as having given a correct view of their dispositions. Their opposition was to *both*— to the treaty, as well as to a removal. To their dislike of the former may be attributed, in great part, their objection to the latter.

"The methods best calculated to overcome this obstacle," and which I esteem to be, in regard to the great body of at least three of the tribes enumerated, the only one of consequence, would be to assemble at some suitable and central place, the enlightened and influential half-breeds of those tribes, for the purpose of explaining to them, by persons to be appointed for that object, and who should carry with them, not only the full instructions of the Government, and *its pledges,* but also, an influence arising out of their known friendship to the Indians, what are the *real views* of the Government in relation to them, and especially those which have been indicated in the plans that have been proposed for their location on lands West of the Mississippi. It is not my opinion that all those who might assemble at such a council would return from it with sentiments and purposes favorable to a removal *themselves,* but I do believe the most of them would perceive that, if their *own* interests would be promoted by remaining on the lands they now occupy, and suitable and liberal portions of them should be given to them individually, the interests of the great body of their people would be promoted by emigration. The effect of such convictions would disembarrass the question of removal of its chief difficulty, when the simultaneous appointment of suitable persons to go among the Indians, to advise them, men of character and fidelity, and who should be known to the Indians as such, and suitable provisions in presents being made, in rifles, kettles, blankets, and the establishment of depots at suitable points, and of ferries; in a word, all the facilities of transportation established, the obstacles which are now in the way of emigration, in so far as it regards the great body of the Indians, might be considered as being removed.

There will remain one other obstacle to be removed, and which I will remark upon when I come to the query in the resolution which is connected with it.

"The Teachers of Schools now in operation among the Indians," are, it is believed, with but one exception,[*] favorable to the removal of the Indians; and it is believed that the previous arrangements which it is essential to adopt, and to some of which I have referred, and to the remainder reference will be made in the proper place, these teachers, who have, and so deservedly, the confidence of the Indians, would exercise the most efficient agency in carrying the plan of removal into effect.

It is proper to state, that when the general removal of the Indians was first discussed as a measure of policy and humanity, some of those who had made large investments in buildings, and in other branches of the necessary provision for schools, apprehended not only a probable loss of those investments, but that the Indians would be so circumstanced in their new home, as to put it out of their power to follow them, with any prospect of success, in their benevolent aim to enlighten and instruct them, and to introduce them into the benefits and blessings of the civilized and Christian state. But when these objections were answered in the further development of the

---

[*]Mr. Findley of Ohio.

plan for the collocation of the Indians, and these humane teachers were informed that their labors would be required under it; and that the money they had laid out where they now are, would doubtless be reimbursed in the erection, by the Government, of schools West of the Mississippi, upon suitable plans, they were satisfied with the measure; and, in one instance, a proposition has been made by a teacher to go and explore the country, and open the way for the removal of the Indians who are particularly within his charge. There are "reasons, therefore, to authorize the belief that the teachers will co-operate in the measure," should "an appropriation be made to defray the expense of such removal and settlement."

Some estimate may be formed of "the progress which has been made in civilization," from the fact that, within the last eight years, when there were not, it is believed, in the United States or Territories, *fifty* Indian children deriving instruction of any sort, there are now upwards of *twelve hundred* enjoying the benefits of a system of education, which combines, with the customary methods of teaching, a knowledge of farming and the mechanic arts, and the various branches of domestic economy, in weaving, spinning, knitting, &c. But the best illustration of the state of improvement may be had by a reference to the volume of Indian Treaties, pages 479, 480, 481, and part of 482. The paper referred to contains a detailed account of the employments, improvements, and population, and laws of the Cherokees—the most improved of the four Southern tribes.

"In the plains and valleys," says the writer, who is himself a native, "the soil is generally rich, producing Indian corn, cotton, tobacco, wheat, oats, Indigo, sweet and Irish potatoes. The natives carry on considerable trade with the adjoining States, and some of them export cotton in boats down the Tennessee to the Mississippi, and down that River to New Orleans. Apples and peach orchards are quite common, and gardens are cultivated, and much attention is paid to them. Butter and cheese are seen on Cherokee tables. There are many public roads in the nation, and houses of entertainment are kept by natives. Numerous and flourishing villages are seen in every section of the country. Cotton and woollen cloths are manufactured here. Blankets, of various dimensions, are manufactured by Cherokee hands. Almost every family in the nation grows cotton for its own consumption. Industry and commercial enterprize are extending themselves in every part. Nearly all the merchants in the nation are native Cherokees. Agricultural pursuits (the most solid foundation of our national prosperity,) *engage the chief attention of the People,*" &c. &c. The population is about 14,000.

Of the other three tribes, the Creeks, Choctaws, and Chickasaws, it may be said, they are following in the steps of the Cherokees; but are not so far advanced. The precise state of advancement of which, and of other tribes, is not known, but all of them, where the game has grown scarce, are more or less cultivators of the ground.

Of the tribes that have "manifested a disposition to emigrate," may be named the Cherokees and Choctaws, in part; the Shawnees, and, in part, the Creeks.

Of the Cherokees, there have gone over from Tennessee and Georgia, and now occupy lands in Arkansas, some six thousand; and part of the Choctaws are also there, and upon lands (as are the Cherokees,) which have been ceded to them by treaty. Of the Choctaws, Colonel McKee writes, in his letter of the 13th of September last: "Many of the Indians (Choctaws) are disposed to emigrate, but are ignorant of the route, or the means by which they can reach the contemplated settlement, that they are deterred from making an effort; but, with an active, intelligent conductor, who could inform them where and how they could obtain such aids as the Government will furnish them on the route, *many* would, in my opinion, soon set out for a country so much better adapted to their wants and habits, than where they now are."

I know no way of reconciling the late decided rejections of the proposals made by the Commissioners to the Choctaws, with the statements of Colonel McKee, except upon the grounds assumed, viz: their settled antipathy to *the mode* of negotiation with them. That Colonel McKee is correct in his report of the disposition of the Choctaws, there can be no doubt, as every year, even with the uncertainty of the ways and means to subsist upon, adds more or less to the number of those who have settled in Arkansas. It is reasonable to suppose that, with the facilities of removal, and the inducements which have been suggested, the number would be greatly augmented.

The Shawnees are *pressing* to the West. The Agent, falling in with what he esteems to be the policy of the Government, has, to provide the emigrants with the necessary outfits, there being no specific provision for such expenditures, actually incurred a personal responsibility to the amount of some four thousand dollars. How far it may be proper for the Agents to encourage emigration will depend on the provision which the Congress may make to defray the cost of it. Should it be decided proper to withhold the means, there will remain no alternative but to inform the Agents that there are no means applicable to the object, except the very limited amount which has generally been furnished towards it, from the contingent fund.

Of the Creeks, the last accounts received from the Agent state, that upwards of eight hundred had enrolled for emigration. For the cost of their removal, provision has been made by the Congress.

I have confined my remarks chiefly to the four Southern tribes. They are those to whom, as to policy, the greater portion of the remaining tribes in our States and Territories look; and, whatever measures the body of those tribes may adopt, it is believed would be followed by the others. The whole number of Indians in the several States and Territories, exclusive of that portion of the Michigan Territory which lies West of Lake Michigan, and North of the State of Illinois, is about 97,000. Of this number, about 58,000 reside in North Carolina, Georgia, Tennessee, Alabama, and Mississippi; these are Cherokees, Creeks, Choctaws, and Chickasaws. Any movement of these that should indicate that a portion of those tribes, even if that should not exceed one half, it is believed would operate upon the 3000 Wyandots, Shawnees, Senecas, Delawares, Kaskaskias, Miami, and Eel Rivers, who reside in Ohio, and the 5000 Seminoles, and fragments of other tribes, in Florida.

But such a movement in these four principal tribes is not esteemed to be indispensable to the removal of the rest, if the proper measures are adopted to secure it, and these are in addition to what has been suggested, and this will have a direct bearing, also, on the four great tribes, the selection and location of a suitable country, and which I esteem to be no less necessary as *a first step*, to secure the object of removal, than a just and humane one to those Indians who are now emigrating. They go, they know not whither. Their object is a greater range of country and subsistence. They follow, as well as they are able, in the tracks of others who have preceded them; and crossing the Mississippi, get involved in difficulties with the stronger bands, or settle upon, or roam over lands from which, in a short time afterwards, they will be, as some have been, compelled *again* to remove.

Those tribes who are "unwilling" to emigrate, so far as these are known to the Government, and, judging of their dispositions from the result of the negotiations which have been attempted, are the Creeks, in part, the Cherokees, in part, the Choctaws and Chickasaws, in part, and, indeed, nearly all the tribes, *as such,* in Georgia, Tennessee, Alabama, and Mississippi, and Ohio; although a gradual emigration is making from all of them. But this expressed "unwillingness," as has been stated, is believed to be the result, more of hostility to the mode of ascertaining their dispositions, than to any fixed purpose, on their part, not to emigrate. The gravest exception to removal, it is believed, applies to the Cherokees; and, of this tribe, a larger portion, under *any* arrangements that may be adopted for their removal, will remain, than of all the other tribes together: and for the reason that they are more enlightened, and have more comforts, and are more prosperous, than are any others. And just in proportion as these advances may be made by the other tribes, will be the difficulties of obtaining their consent to remove. One of the principal inducements that could be offered to the Cherokees, in addition to that of compensation for their land, would be that arising out of a disposition to impart to their brethren, in their new homes, the benefits of the civilized state; and to enjoy, under the form of Government which it has been proposed to adopt for them, some of its rewards and honors.

"The objections," to removal are, first, those which arise out of attachment to their soil, and its improvements; and the uncertainty as to the nature of the country to which they are invited to emigrate. Could this be examined, and should it prove suitable, and should it be so esteemed by a deputation of their own People, (and they should be permitted to judge and report for themselves,) it is not unreasonable to believe, pressed, as they are, on all sides, and feeling, as they advance in improvement, the galling effects of the division which separates them from the emoluments and honors of the civilized state, that they would gladly escape from such a condition to one more free and independent.

The Indians are not "acquainted" with either "the nature or situation of the country, to which it is proposed to remove them."

The "particular district of country" which has been looked to, for the permanent home of the Indians, who should emigrate West of the Mississippi, is that which lies North of the river Arkansas, and West of the State of Missouri; but, as no examination of it has been made, with a view to its occupancy by the tribes now in the States East of the Mississippi, it cannot be known "what particular district or districts of country West of the Mississippi they ought to occupy."

It is not known how far the Indians are "willing to abandon the chase, and depend for their subsistence upon the pursuits of agriculture, and the arts of civilized life;" but, it is presumed, that, under the form of Government, which it has been proposed to establish for them, that some would pursue the game, should the country possess it, and others agriculture; and that their dependence upon the latter would supersede their reliance on the former, in proportion as they might become enlightened, and made to feel, by an interest in the soil, and the right of property, the superior benefits which a cultivation of the soil confers over those which are to be derived from the mere hunter state. And in regard to their present views on this subject, they would emigrate, should they emigrate at all, carrying with them, and in the same proportions, the habits which they now indulge in their present locations; and which may be estimated, as two to five, the larger number even yet depending and preferring to depend upon the precarious subsistence which they derive from hunting. It is also true, that this proportion applies to the older, and, in general uninstructed, Indians. And, however the greater facilities of taking game might operate to draw some aside from the cultivation of the soil, their places would be filled, and the ratio assumed diminished, by the force of education, which is now felt by so many hundreds of the rising generation, and by an interest in the soil, and the influence of a Government suited to their state of improvement.

It is believed the Indians have not been made clearly to understand the nature and form of Government proposed to be instituted over them. It is believed, also, that just in proportion as they shall be made to comprehend it, will their objections to it be lessened. I derive this belief, in part, from my own intercourse with some of these People. I found, in the few with whom I conversed on this subject, the most decided objections to the plan, which, however, on its being fully explained, were given up, with the acknowledgment that it had not been understood by them.

For like reasons, it is not known "whether the chiefs, head men, and people, of the tribes, are willing to dissolve their existing political relations; or whether they are willing the United States should create a government over, and make laws for, them; or whether they are willing to change the tenure of their lands, and hold them in severalty, or whether the tribes West of the Mississippi are willing the Indians in the States and Territories should be concentrated in their country." These are points of information that can be had only on a satisfactory account being given of the soil and salubrity of the country, to which they may be invited to go; and this cannot be known, until it shall be examined; nor until a form of government be established, and clearly and fully explained, and submitted to them. It is believed, however, that, these two preliminaries being attended to, there is enough of the love of property in the most of the Indians in the States, to induce them to prefer a government suited to their condition, as to the simple elements of which it would be composed, and to hold lands in severalty, in preference to the present, and as many of them believe, very uncertain tenure by which they hold them at all.

The dispositions of the tribes West of the Mississippi, so far as this has been ascertained, is favorable to receive their brethren on this side. A deputation came over in 1825, to invite the Ohio Indians to go and join them, and it is doubtless in consequence of that union of feeling which these People cherish, and which distance it appears cannot separate, that the Shawnees are now going over.

"The intentions and objects of the Government," have not been made known except in a general way, to any of the tribes, although the intelligent among them appear in some instances to understand them, so far at least as these relate to removal. No expression of a "willingness to come into the measures has been made," because perhaps no measures have been taken in regard to this particular question which could lead to an answer either way.

Whether "the Indians now in the States and Territories will upon removal be able to provide for themselves the means of subsistence without the aid of the Government," cannot be known until the quality of the soil to which they may be transferred is known, or how far they may be induced to seek a subsistence out of it. It is highly probable, however, that aid will be required to be extended to them by the Government, but to what extent it is not possible to know until their numbers shall be ascertained, as well as their dispositions for agricultural pursuits, and the quality of the soil upon which they may settle.

Assuming however that the country is examined, and shall turn out to be well suited to the condition, and abundant in resources to supply the wants of the emigrants; and that an extinction of the Osage and Kanzas titles may be necessary to secure a suitable country, and this has been in part accomplished, it is believed that ten thousand dollars may be required to purchase the right to the country, for the purposes contemplated, and to cover the expenses attending the negotiation. To this may be added the cost of removing the Piankeshaws, Weas, Shawnees, Kickapoos and Delawares; also, the Wyandotts, Senecas, Miamis, and Eel Rivers, and the Kaskaskias, which may be estimated at twenty dollars for each Indian; suppose that each one receives a rifle and blanket, and kettle, and some powder and lead, and in addition an average cost of supplies from the depots, of ten dollars more, making thirty dollars a head, will make, there being about 2500 Indians of those tribes, $75,000. Upon the supposition that the entire body of Indians in the States and Territories consent to emigrate, there being of these about 97,000, the cost may be estimated for *removing them*, at $30 a head, which, including the tribes above named, will amount to $291,000.

It is not possible to estimate with any certainty the price which they would require for these lands, of which they own nearly 77,000,000 of acres, but it is believed that the proceeds of these lands will not only cover all the cost of providing a new country for them, and transporting them to it, but supply all their wants in the incipient periods of their settlement, and also all the implements of agriculture, and the preliminary expenses attending a division of lands, and providing stock, and leave a surplus afterwards for the support of the kind of Government which it may be esteemed best to adopt and place them under, and as long as that Government may require to be assisted by that of the Union.

The present "annual expense" to the Government in educating upwards of 1200 children, is $10,000. It is presumed an additional sum of $10,000 more would sustain the system under the proposed plan of removal.

"The annual expense of the Government proposed to be instituted over them," it is difficult to estimate, but it may be assumed at nearly the same which it costs the United States to support the Government of the Territories, of Michigan for example, which is something short of ten thousand dollars.

It is believed that a proper attention to the location of congenial tribes may not only avert the calamities of war to which these People are liable, but strengthen and perpetuate the peace under the auspices of which they would doubtless assemble. One of the chief causes of war among them will have been removed by the fixing of limits and settlement of boundaries; and by the change in their habits which a cultivation of the soil, a multiplication of schools, and a consequent increase of intelligence, will not fail to produce.

It is believed that a hundred United States' Troops, seconded as it is presumed they would be by corps of educated young men, would be sufficient to maintain the peace, and ensure the execution of the laws, and protect the colony from any outrage, from without; and that, in a few years, as the emigrants should become still more enlightened, and the term of a generation only *need* be required to civilize them all, no aid will be required from the military of the United States, any more than is now required to keep the peace between the Choctaws and Chickasaws. They would soon become one People, and combine as such for the general safety. What the cost of a hundred United States' Troops would be, I have no certain means of ascertaining: nor for how many years their services would be required.

To commence this work of removal, I would respectfully suggest that for the first year thirty thousand dollars would be sufficient, exclusive of the cost of assembling the council of educated and influential chiefs, and for the pay of agents who might be appointed to go among the Indians, to explain to them the views and objects of the Government; and to point out the ways that might be opened, and to name the depots and crossing places, and for others to accompany them.

But I am of opinion that the first step, and without which it would be fruitless to attempt a removal, is to ascertain, by actual examination, whether a suitable country can be had; and if so, where located, and within what limits, and which should be clearly defined in all that relates to its extent and fitness for a last home for the most unfortunate of human beings. And have they not a right to expect of the Government of the United States, that they will not be asked to abandon the homes they now occupy without the certainty of having others provided for them?

All which is respectfully submitted,

THO. L. McKENNEY.

Source: U.S. Congress. House. *Removal of the Indians Westward,* 19th Cong., 2nd sess., 1826. H. Doc. 28, pp. 5–13.

5. An Act to add the Territory lying within the limits of this State, and occupied by the Cherokee Indians, to the counties of Carroll, DeKalb, Gwinnett, Hall and Habersham; and to extend the laws of this State over the same, and for other purposes (1828)

Emboldened by the election of Andrew Jackson to the presidency in 1828, Georgia acted immediately to extend its laws over the Cherokee Nation, adding Cherokee lands in Georgia to five existing counties to provide the legal entities necessary for the extension and enforcement of state laws. Georgia also extinguished Cherokee laws. Between the election of 1828 and Jackson's inauguration in early 1829, Mississippi and Alabama also passed laws similar to the Georgia law (reprinted below). This law began a legal battle that culminated in *Cherokee Nation v. Georgia*, in which the U.S. Supreme Court avoided the question regarding the constitutionality of Georgia's act by ruling that the Cherokees were not a foreign nation under the language of the Constitution.

Be it enacted by the Senate and House of Representatives of the State of Georgia, in General Assembly met, and it is hereby enacted by the authority of the same, That from and after the passing of this act, all that part of the territory, within the limits of this state, and which lies between the Alabama line, and the old path leading from the Buzzard Roost, on the Chattahoochee river, to Sally Huse's, where the said path strikes the Alabama road, thence with said road, to the boundary line of Georgia, be and the same is hereby added to, and shall become a part of the county of Carroll.

Sec. 2. And be it enacted, by the authority aforesaid, That all that part of the said territory, lying and being north of the last mentioned line, and south of the road, running from Charles Gates ferry, on Chattahoochee river, to Dick Roes, to where it intersects with the path aforesaid be, and the same is hereby added, and shall become a part of the county of DeKalb.

Sec. 3. And be it further enacted, That all that part of said territory lying north of the last mentioned line, and south of the old Federal Road be, and the same is hereby added, and shall become a part of the county of Gwinnett.

Sec. 4. And be it further enacted, That all that part of the said territory, lying north of said last mentioned line, and south of a line to begin on the Chestertee river, at the mouth of Yoholo creek, thence up said creek, to the top of the Blue ridge, thence to the head waters of Notley river, thence down said river, to the boundary line of Georgia be, and the same is hereby added to, and shall become a part of the county of Hall.

Sec. 5. And be it further enacted, That all that part of the said territory, lying north of the last mentioned line, within the limits of Georgia be, and the same is here by added to, and shall become a part of the county of Habersham.

Sec. 6. And be it further enacted, That all the laws of this State be, and the same are hereby extended over said territory, and all white persons residing within the same, shall immediately after the passage of this act, be subject and liable to the operation of the said laws, in the same manner as other citizens of the state, or the citizens of said counties respectively.

Sec. 7. And be it further enacted, That after the first day of June, 1830, all Indians then, and at that time, residing in said territory, and within any one of the counties as aforesaid, shall be liable and subject to such laws and regulations, as the legislature may hereafter prescribe.

Sec. 8. And be it further enacted, That all laws, usages, and customs made, established and in force, in the said territory, by the said Cherokee Indians be, and the same are hereby on, and after the first June, 1830, declared null and void.

Sec. 9. And be it further enacted, That no Indian, or descendant of Indian, residing within the Creek or Cherokee nations of Indians, shall be deemed a competent witness, or a party to any suit, in any court created by the constitution, or laws of this state, to which a white man may be a party.

Irby Hudson, Speaker of the House of Representatives
Thomas Stocks, President of the Senate
Assented to, Dec. 20, 1828
John Forsyth, Governor

Source: Acts of the General Assembly of the State of Georgia, Passed in Milledgeville at an Annual Session in November and December, 1828. Milledgeville, GA: Camak & Ragland, 1829, pp. 88–89.

6. Report of the Georgia Committee on the State of the Republic (1829)

The report reprinted below, besides putting forth Georgia's alleged humanitarian reasons for insisting that the Indians remove, presents a core argument used by Georgia throughout the removal controversy: that the Indians are merely "occupants," not owners, of the land. It also recognizes that the Indians are caught in the middle of "collisions of rival sovereignty," that is, the nullification debate.

House of Representatives,
Saturday, 12th December, 1829.

The Committee on the State of the Republic, to whom was referred the talk of the President of the United States to the Creek Indians, and the letter of the Secretary of War to the Cherokee Delegation, together with other documents developing the policy of the Executive Government of the United States, concerning the Aborigines of this country, Report, That this is a subject full of interest to the politician and to the Christian. A concise review of this policy may be productive of some good, and cannot be productive of any harm.

All experience has shown that the association of the white man with the red has generally, if not uniformly, proved injurious to both. This fact is deemed conclusive as to the propriety of a separation.

But if any thing more were necessary to demonstrate the necessity of a separation, it would be found in the fact that neither the General Government nor missionary societies can prosecute their benevolent purposes concerning the Indians, without serious obstacles, so long as there may be a free association of Indians and white men. It is too manifest to escape observation, that white men of abandoned characters are most apt to associate with Indians, and to exert a baleful influence on their morals and their counsels. The strength of the reasoning on this head is greatly increased when it is recollected that many of the Indians occupy positions in which they will be always exposed to collisions with the state authorities; indeed, it may be assumed as a fact, that the State Governments never will consent that any tribe of Indians shall exercise the powers of sovereignty within the chartered limits of the States; that they will have to submit to the State laws, or remove beyond their limits.

Much may be said on original principles concerning the rights of the States in this regard, but these are considered as questions no longer open for discussion: they have been settled by the usages of Europe and America—by judicial decisions, and Legislative enactments. The Supreme Court of the United States long since decided that "the Legislature of Georgia, in 1715, had the power of disposing of the unappropriated lands within its own limits." At a subsequent period it decided that titles to lands in this country rested on the right of discovery. This right residing (with some modification perhaps,) at the time of the American revolution, in the government of Great Britain, was conquered from that country, by the American arms. Subsequent to that period, it has been strengthened, in a number of instances, by conquests over different tribes of Indians; for instance, the Cherokees in 1791, and the Creeks at a later period. These tribes, with others, have been permitted to enjoy a mere occupancy of their lands, chiefly for the purpose of hunting, and have been taken under the guardianship of the United States; but this occupancy, merely permissive, and this guardianship, merely gratuitous, have in no wise destroyed the rights of the States, individually or collectively. If some of the States have accepted or engaged the aid of the General Government, for the purpose of extinguishing Indian titles, this may enable them to avoid the trouble and expense attending the extinguishment, but does not destroy their own right to extinguish.

One of the best illustrations of civil or political right, in relation to Indian lands, is obtained from a compilation made by the Rev. Dr. Jedediah Morse, acting as an agent of the General Government, in his report and appendix to Mr. Secretary Calhoun. From this it appears, more especially from the authority of an eminent lawyer, cited at page 279, that the Indians are entitled to a limited or qualified property in the soil, a right to occupy and enjoy, under certain modifications, but with no power to convey, nor indeed to do any other act of ownership. The right of soil, or the absolute property, and the jurisdiction over it, belong to the State. The interest in the soil carries with it the right to buy off, or otherwise remove, the encumbrance of Indian occupancy. This right of the State is full and absolute. Even if the hunter State should be changed for the agricultural, the Indians are entitled to no more of their territories, after the change, than is requisite to give them, from cultivating the earth, a support equal to that which they derived from their whole territory, in the hunter State.—Morse *Report, p.* 68. Such is a substantial statement of some of the leading principles of customary law as it bears upon the situation of the Indians.

Should it be said that the right of disposing of their soil; the right of jurisdiction or of prescribing the rule of action in their territories; and the right of removing their occupancy, constituting the sovereignty over their territories, belong to the Union, and that the Indians have not been left at the mercy of the individual States; it may be answered that the sovereignty over the Indians and Indian lands in the territories of the United States, if not in the new States, formed as they are from the territory of the Union, may be accorded to the General Government; but the rights of the old thirteen, sustained as they are by law and by adjudication, will never be abandoned.

The Committee on the State of the Republic, reserving the right of giving, in another report, if necessary, a more full exposition of the laws and usages concerning Indians, have, on the present occasion, only given such a brief view of those usages as will place the policy of the General Government far stronger relief before the nation.

Such being the usages concerning Indians, the policy adopted by the General Government is clearly proper, at least so far as it is intended to induce them to remove, beyond the limits of the States, or to withdraw from those limits; and to extend to them, in some favorable position, the aid and protection of the government. The advantages resulting from a location beyond the limits of the States depend on an exemption from the mischievous intercourse of bad white men, and from the collisions of rival sovereignty, and upon the unobstructed exertions of the government, and various benevolent associations, for their benefit. In this view of the subject, it is not wonderful that the religious public are beginning to use their exertions to promote emigration to the delightful region beyond the Mississippi; for however the son of the forest may be entitled to the rights of humanity, and however the States may be disposed to avoid collision with the General Government, in relation to Indian affairs, a dependent situation within the States is attended with evils too obvious and too serious to be overlooked. These evils to the Indians might be greatly enhanced by the manner of exercising the power, entering into the composition of sovereignty, of buying *off*, or otherwise removing, the permissive occupancy of the territory claimed by them: for although the President of the United States has given a guarantee of this occupancy, it is not perceived that this guarantee rests on any valid foundation; and it may therefore be presumed that it will ultimately be withdrawn, when the President shall have reviewed the whole ground, including the exposition of Indian titles, made by an authorised agent, with the apparent sanction of a late administration of the General Government.

In view of the premises, the committee recommend the adoption of the following resolution, viz:

Resolved by the Senate and House of Representatives of the State of Georgia, in General Assembly met, That they approve the policy of the General Government towards the Indians, so far as it is calculated to induce them to remove beyond the operation of those causes which evidently tend to retard their improvement, and to extend to them, in a favorable position, the fostering protection and assistance of the country.

Resolved, That copies of this report and resolution be transmitted to the President of the United States, and to the delegation in Congress from this State.

Approved, Dec. 18, 1829.

Source: Acts of the General Assembly of the State of Georgia, Passed in Milledgeville at an Annual Session in November and December, 1829. Milledgeville, GA: Camak & Ragland, 1830, pp. 167–169.

7. An Act to provide for an exchange of lands with the Indians residing in any of the states or territories, and for their removal west of the river Mississippi (1830)

Indian removal became a divisive issue in American politics after the election of Andrew Jackson. The congressional act known as the Indian Removal Act was intensely debated in the national press and Congress before it barely passed and became law on May 28, 1830. The act empowered the president to negotiate with the tribes for their removal from their lands east of the Mississippi to lands west of the river. The Jackson administration used the law as a coercive threat and transformed the voluntary removal policies of earlier administrations to generate removal treaties and to force removal. Although the act was brief and simple in its language in comparison to much congressional legislation, it was devastating to the tribes to which it was applied.

Be it enacted by the Senate and House of Representatives of the United States of America, in Congress assembled, That it shall and may be lawful for the President of the United States to cause so much of any territory belonging to the United States, west of the river Mississippi, not included in any state or organized territory, and to which the Indian title has been extinguished, as he may judge necessary, to be divided into a suitable number of districts, for the reception of such tribes or nations of Indians as may choose to exchange the lands where they now reside, and remove there; and to cause each of said districts to be so described by natural or artificial marks, as to be easily distinguished from every other.

SEC. 2. *And be it further enacted,* That it shall and may be lawful for the President to exchange any or all of such districts, so to be laid off and described, with any tribe or nation within the limits of any of the states or territories, and with which the United States have existing treaties, for the whole or any part or portion of the territory claimed and occupied by such tribe or nation, within the bounds of any one or more of the states or territories, where the land claimed and occupied by the Indians, is owned by the United States, or the United States are bound to the state within which it lies to extinguish the Indian claim thereto.

SEC. 3. *And be it further enacted,* That in the making of any such exchange or exchanges, it shall and may be lawful for the President solemnly to assure the tribe or nation with which the exchange is made, that the United States will forever secure and guaranty to them, and their heirs or successors, the country so exchanged with them; and if they prefer it, that the United States will cause a patent or grant to be made and executed to them for the same: Provided always, That such lands shall revert to the United States, if the Indians become extinct, or abandon the same.

SEC. 4. *And be it further enacted,* That if, upon any of the lands now occupied by the Indians, and to be exchanged for, there should be such improvements as add value to the land claimed by any individual or individuals of such tribes or nations, it shall and may be lawful for the President to cause such value to be ascertained by appraisement or otherwise, and to cause such ascertained value to be paid to the person or persons rightfully claiming such improvements. And upon the payment of such valuation, the improvements so valued and paid for, shall pass to the United States, and possession shall not afterwards be permitted to any of the same tribe.

SEC. 5. *And be it further enacted,* That upon the making of any such exchange as is contemplated by this act, it shall and may be lawful for the President to cause such aid and assistance to be furnished to the emigrants as may be necessary and proper to enable them to remove to, and settle in, the country for which they may have exchanged; and also, to give them such aid and assistance as may be necessary for their support and subsistence for the first year after their removal.

SEC. 6. *And be it further enacted,* That it shall and may be lawful for the President to cause such tribe or nation to be protected, at their new residence, against all interruption or disturbance from any other tribe or nation of Indians, or from any other person or persons whatever.

SEC. 7. *And be it further enacted*, That it shall and may be lawful for the President to have the same superintendence and care over any tribe or nation in the country to which they may remove, as contemplated by this act, that he is now authorized to have over them at their present places of residence.

SEC. 8. *And be it further enacted*, That for the purpose of giving effect to the provisions of this act, the sum of five hundred thousand dollars is hereby appropriated, to be paid out of any money in the treasury, not otherwise appropriated.

Source: Statutes at Large 4 (1830): 411–412.

8. Excerpt from President Andrew Jackson's Second Annual Message (1830)

Andrew Jackson's second annual message to Congress on December 6, 1830, contained a progress report on Indian removal since passage of the Indian Removal Act the previous May. He reported the successful negotiation of the first two removal treaties: the Treaty of Franklin with the Chickasaws and the Treaty of Dancing Rabbit Creek with the Choctaws. Later, to his disappointment, the Chickasaws would fail to find a suitable land in the West, thereby making their treaty invalid. His speech makes clear his reasons for focusing on removal of the southern tribes first: to blunt the nullification movement, to populate the South with whites as a bulwark against foreign invasion, and to "save" the Indians by removing them. His ethnocentrism is evident in his balancing images of "savagery" against those of "civilization."

It gives me pleasure to announce to Congress that the benevolent policy of the Government, steadily pursued for nearly thirty years, in relation to the removal of the Indians beyond the white settlements is approaching to a happy consummation. Two important tribes have accepted the provision made for their removal at the last session of Congress, and it is believed that their example will induce the remaining tribes also to seek the same obvious advantages.

The consequences of a speedy removal will be important to the United States, to individual States, and to the Indians themselves. The pecuniary advantages which it promises to the Government are the least of its recommendations. It puts an end to all possible danger of collision between the authorities of the General and State Governments on account of the Indians. It will place a dense and civilized population in large tracts of country now occupied by a few savage hunters. By opening the whole territory between Tennessee on the north and Louisiana on the south to the settlement of the whites it will incalculably strengthen the southwestern frontier and render the adjacent States strong enough to repel future invasions without remote aid. It will relieve the whole State of Mississippi and the western part of Alabama of Indian occupancy, and enable those States to advance rapidly in population, wealth, and power. It will separate the Indians from immediate contact with settlements of whites; free them from the power of the States; enable them to pursue happiness in their own way and under their own rude institutions; will retard the progress of decay, which is lessening their numbers, and perhaps cause them gradually, under the protection of the Government and through the influence of good counsels, to cast off their savage habits and become an interesting, civilized, and Christian community.

What good man would prefer a country covered with forests and ranged by a few thousand savages to our extensive Republic, studded with cities, towns, and prosperous farms embellished with all the improvements which art can devise or industry execute, occupied by more than 12,000,000 happy people, and filled with all the blessings of liberty, civilization and religion?

The present policy of the Government is but a continuation of the same progressive change by a milder process. The tribes which occupied the countries now constituting the Eastern States were annihilated or have melted away to make room for the whites. The waves of population and civilization are rolling to the westward, and we now propose to acquire the countries occupied by the red men of the South and West by a fair exchange, and, at the expense of the United States, to send them to land where their existence may be prolonged and perhaps made perpetual. Doubtless it will be painful to leave the graves of their fathers; but what do they more than our ancestors did or than our children are now doing? To better their condition in an unknown land our forefathers left all that was dear in earthly objects. Our children by thousands yearly leave the land of their birth to seek new homes in distant regions. Does Humanity weep at these painful separations from everything, animate and inanimate, with which the young heart has become entwined? Far from it. It is rather a source of joy that our country affords scope where our young population may range unconstrained in body or in mind, developing the power and facilities of man in their highest perfection. These remove hundreds and almost thousands of miles at their own expense, purchase the lands they occupy, and support themselves at their new homes from the moment of their arrival. Can it be cruel in this Government when, by events which it can not control, the Indian is made discontented in his ancient home to purchase his lands, to give him a new and extensive territory, to pay the expense of his removal, and support him a year in his new abode? How many thousands of our own people would gladly embrace the opportunity of removing to the West on such conditions! If the offers made to the Indians were extended to them, they would be hailed with gratitude and joy.

And is it supposed that the wandering savage has a stronger attachment to his home than the settled, civilized Christian? Is it more afflicting to him to leave the graves of his fathers than it is to our brothers and children? Rightly considered, the policy of the General Government toward the red man is not only liberal, but generous. He is unwilling to submit to the laws of the States and mingle with their population. To save him from this alternative, or perhaps utter annihilation, the General Government kindly offers him a new home, and proposes to pay the whole expense of his removal and settlement.

Source: www.ourdocuments.gov/doc.php?doc=25&page=transcript.

9. An Act to prevent the exercise of assumed and arbitrary power, by all persons under pretext of authority from the Cherokee Indians, and their laws, and to prevent white persons from residing within that part of the chartered limits of Georgia, occupied by the Cherokee Indians, and to provide a guard for the protection of the gold mines, and to enforce the laws of the State within the aforesaid territory (1830)

In its annual session of 1830, the Georgia General Assembly continued to tighten its grip on the Cherokee Nation. In the sweeping act reprinted below, Georgia not only outlawed the Cherokee government, which the law called "the exercise of assumed and arbitrary power," but also required whites living in the Cherokee Nation on March 1, 1831, to obtain a license to remain and to swear an oath of allegiance to the state of Georgia. It also created the Georgia Guard to protect the confiscated Cherokee gold fields and to enforce Georgia laws within the Cherokee lands.

Be it enacted by the Senate and House of Representatives of the State of Georgia, in General Assembly met, and it is hereby enacted by the authority of the same, That after the first day of February, eighteen hundred and thirty-one, it shall not be lawful for any person, or persons, under colour or pretence, of authority from said Cherokee tribe, or as head men, chiefs, or warriors of said tribe, to cause or procure by any means the assembling of any council, or other pretended Legislative body of the said Indians, or others living among them, for the purpose of legislating, (or for any other purpose whatever.) And persons offending against the provisions of this section, shall be guilty of a high misdemeanor, and subject to indictment therefor, and on conviction, shall be punished by confinement at hard labour in the Penitentiary for the space of four years.

Sec. 2. And be it further enacted by the authority aforesaid, That after the time aforesaid, it shall not be lawful for any person or persons under pretext of authority from the Cherokee tribe, or as representatives, chiefs, headmen, or warriors of said tribe, to meet, or assemble as a council, assembly, convention, or in any other capacity, for the purpose of making laws, orders, or regulations for said tribe. And all persons offending against the provisions of this section, shall be guilty of a high misdemeanor and subject to an indictment, and on conviction thereof, shall undergo an imprisonment in the Penitentiary at hard labour for the space of four years.

Sec. 3. And be it further enacted by the authority aforesaid, That after the time aforesaid, it shall not be lawful for any person or persons, under colour, or by authority, *of* the Cherokee tribe, or any of its laws or regulations, to hold any court or tribunal whatever, for the purpose of hearing and determining causes, either civil or criminal; or to give any judgment in such causes, or to issue, or cause to issue any process against the person or property of any of said tribe. And all persons offending against the provisions of this section, shall be guilty of a high misdemeanor, and subject to indictment, and on conviction thereof shall be imprisoned in the Penitentiary at hard labor for the space of four years.

Sec. 4. And be it further enacted by the authority aforesaid, That after the time aforesaid, it shall not be lawful for any person or persons, as a ministerial officer, or in any other capacity, to execute any precept, command, or process, issued by any court or tribunal in the Cherokee tribe, on the persons or property of any of said tribe. And all persons offending against the provisions of this section, shall be guilty of a trespass and subject to indictment, and on conviction thereof shall be punished by fine and imprisonment in the jail or in the Penitentiary not longer than four years, at the discretion of the court.

Sec. 5. And be it further enacted by the authority aforesaid, That after the time aforesaid, it shall not be lawful for any person, or persons, to confiscate, or attempt to confiscate, or otherwise to cause a forfeiture of the property or estate of any Indian of said tribe, in consequence of his enrolling himself and family for emigration, or offering to enroll for emigration, or any other act of said Indian in furtherance of his intention to emigrate. And persons offending against the provisions of this section, shall be guilty of high misdemeanor, and on conviction, shall undergo an imprisonment in the Penitentiary at hard labor for the space of four years.

Sec. 6. And be it further enacted by the authority aforesaid, That none of the provisions of this act, shall be so construed as to prevent said tribe, its headmen, chiefs, or other representatives from meeting any agent or commissioner, on the part of this State or the United States, for any purpose whatever.

Sec. 7. And be it further enacted by the authority aforesaid, That all white persons residing within the limits of the Cherokee nation, on the first day of March next, or at any time thereafter, without a license or permit, from his Excellency the Governor, or from such agent as his Excellency the Governor, shall authorise to grant such permit or license, and who shall not have taken the oath hereinafter required, shall be guilty of an high misdemeanor, and upon conviction thereof, shall be punished by confinement in the Penitentiary at hard labour, for a term not less than four years: Provided, that the provisions of this section shall not be so construed, as to extend to any authorised agent or agents, of the government of the United States, or of this State, or to any person or persons, who may rent any of those improvements, which have been abandoned by Indians, who have emigrated West of the Mississippi: Provided nothing contained in this section, shall be so construed as to extend to white females, and all male children under twenty-one years of age.

Sec. 8. And be it further enacted by the authority aforesaid, That all white persons, citizens of the State of Georgia, who have procured a license in writing, from his Excellency the Governor, or from such agent as his Excellency the Governor, shall authorise to grant such permit or license, to reside within the limits of the Cherokee nation, and who have taken the following oath, viz:—"I, A. B. do solemnly swear (or affirm, as the case may be,) that I will support and defend the Constitution and laws of the State of Georgia, and uprightly demean myself as a citizen thereof, so help me God," shall be, and the same are hereby declared, exempt and free from the operation of the seventh section of this act.

Sec. 9. And be it further enacted, That his Excellency the Governor, be, and he is hereby authorised to grant licenses to reside within the limits of the Cherokee nation, according to the provisions of the eighth section of this act.

Sec. 10. And be it further enacted by the authority aforesaid, That no person shall collect, or claim any toll from any person for passing any turnpike gate or toll bridge, by authority of any act or law of the Cherokee tribe, or any chief or headman or men, of the same.

Sec. 11. And be it further enacted by the authority aforesaid, That his Excellency the Governor, be, and he is hereby empowered, should he deem it necessary, either for the protection of the mines, or for the enforcement of the laws of force within the Cherokee nation, to raise and organise a guard, to be employed on foot, or mounted as occasion may require, which shall not consist of more than sixty persons, which guard shall be under the command of the commissioner or agent appointed by the Governor, to protect the mines, with power to dismiss from the service, any member of said guard, on paying the wages due for services rendered, for disorderly conduct, and make appointments to fill the vacancies occasioned by such dismissal.

Sec. 12. And be it further enacted by the authority aforesaid, That each person who may belong to said guard, shall receive for his compensation at the rate of fifteen dollars per month when on foot, and at the rate of twenty dollars per month when mounted, for every month that such person is engaged in actual service, and in the event that the commissioner or agent herein referred to, should die, resign or fail to perform the duties herein required of him, his Excellency the Governor, is hereby authorised and required to appoint in his stead, some other fit and proper person to the command of said guard, and the commissioner or agent, having the command of the guard aforesaid, for the better discipline thereof, shall appoint three sergeants who shall receive at the rate of twenty dollars per month, while serving on foot, and twenty-five dollars per month, when mounted, as compensation whilst in actual service.

Sec. 13. And be it further enacted by the authority aforesaid, That the said guard, or any member of them, shall be, and they are hereby authorised and empowered to arrest any person legally charged with or detected in, a violation of the laws of this State, and to convey as soon as practicable, the person so arrested before a Justice of the Peace, Judge of the Superior or Justice of Inferior Court, of this Slate, to be dealt with according to law and the pay and support of said guard be provided out of the fund, already appropriated for the protection of the gold mines.

ASBURY HULL, Speaker of the House of Representatives.
THOMAS STOCKS, President of the Senate.
Assented to, 22d Dec. 1830.

GEORGE R. GILMER, Governor.

Source: Acts of the General Assembly of the State of Georgia, passed in Milledgeville at an Annual Session in October, November, and December 1830. Milledgeville, GA: Camak & Ragland, 1834, pp. 114–117.

10. Excerpt from the Report of the Secretary of War (Lewis Cass) (1831)

As Andrew Jackson's secretary of war, Lewis Cass played a major role in implementing the Indian Removal Act. In this report, he discusses some important aspects of removal policy, including the limitations of treaties, the power of the federal government vis-à-vis that of the states, and the claim of exemption by the tribes in their attempt to parry attempts to extend state laws over Indian nations, as well as the claim of sovereignty by the Indians. He also proposes conditions for removed tribes and reports on the recent land cessions by Ohio tribes.

Lewis Cass
November 21, 1831

The condition and prospects of the aboriginal tribes within the limits of the United States are yet the subjects of anxious solicitude to the Government. Circumstances have occurred within a few years, which have produced important changes in the intercourse between them and us. In some of the States, they have been brought within the operation of the ordinary municipal laws, and their regulations have been abrogated by legislative enactments. This procedure renders most of the provisions of the various acts of Congress upon this subject inoperative; and a crisis in our Indian affairs has evidently arrived, which calls for the establishment of a system of policy adapted to the existing state of things, and calculated to fix upon a permanent basis the future destiny of the Indians. Whatever change may be contemplated in their condition or situation, no one will advocate the employment of force or improper influence in effecting it. It is due to the character of the government and the feelings of the country, not less than to the moral and physical imbecility of this unhappy race, that a spirit of kindness and forbearance should mark the whole course of our intercommunication with them. The great object, after satisfying ourselves what would best ensure their permanent welfare, should be to satisfy them of the integrity of our views, and of the wisdom of the course recommended to them. There is enough in the retrospect for serious reflection on our part, and for unpleasant recollection on theirs; and it is only by a dispassionate examination of the subject, and by prudent and timely measures, that we can hope to repair the errors of the past by the exertions of the future.

The Indians, who are placed in immediate contact with the settled portions of the United States, have now the alternative presented to them, of remaining in their present positions, or of migrating to the country west of the Mississippi. If they are induced to prefer the former, their political condition becomes a subject of serious consideration. They must either retain all those institutions, which constitute them a peculiar people, both socially and politically, or they must become a portion of that great community which is gathering round them, responsible to its laws, and looking to them for protection.

Can they expect to maintain that *quasi* independence they have heretofore enjoyed? and could they so maintain it, would the privilege be beneficial to them?

The right to extend their laws over all persons, living within their boundaries, has been claimed and exercised by many of the States. The Executive of the United States has, on full consideration, decided that there is no power in that department to interpose any obstacle to the assumption of this authority. As upon this co-ordinate branch of the government devolves the execution of the laws, and particularly many of the most important provisions in the various acts regulating intercourse with the Indians, it is difficult to conceive how these provisions can be enforced, after the President has determined they have been abrogated by a state of things inconsistent with their obligations. How prosecutions can be conducted, trespassers removed by military power, and other acts performed, which require the co-operation of the Executive, either in their initiation or progress.

I do not presume to discuss this question. I find it determined, and the settled policy of the Government already in operation. Whatever diversity of opinion there may be upon the subject, those who are most opposed to their views will probably admit, that the questions is a doubtful one, complicated in its relations, and pregnant with serious consequences. The claims of exemption from the operation of the State laws, which is presented in favor of the Indians, must rest upon the Constitution of the United States, upon natural right, or upon conventional engagements. If upon the former, it may be doubted whether that instrument contain any grant of authority to the General Government, which necessarily divests the State Legislatures of their jurisdiction over any class of people, living within their respective limits. The two provisions, which can alone bear upon the subject, seem to have far different objects in view. If the claim rest upon natural right, it may be doubted whether the condition and institutions of this rude people do not give to the civilized communities around whom and among whom they live, the right of guardianship over them; and whether this view is not fortified by the practice of all other civilized nations under similar circumstances—a practice, which, in its extent and exercise, has varied from time to time, as the relative circumstances of the parties have varied, but of whose limitation the civilized communities have been and must be the judges. And, besides, if the Indian tribes are independent of the State authorities, on account of the natural and relative rights of both, there tribes are equally independent of the authorities of the United States. The claim, upon this ground, places the parties in the attitude of entire independence; for the question then is not how we have divided our political power between the confederated Government and its members, and to which we have entrusted the exercise of this supervisory authority, but whether the laws of nature give to either any authority upon the subject. But, if the claim rest upon alleged conventional engagements, it may then be doubted whether in all our treaties with the Indian tribes there is any stipulation, incompatible with the exercise of the power of legislation over them. For if there were, the legislative power of Congress, as well as that of the respective States, would be annihilated, and the treaties alone would regulate the intercourse between the parties. But, on a careful investigation, it will probably be found, that, in none of our treaties with the Indian tribes, is there any guaranty of political rights incompatible with the exercise of the power of legislation. These instruments are generally either treaties of peace or of cession. The former restore and secure to the Indians interest of which they were deprived by conquests, and the latter define the boundaries of cessions or reservations, and prescribe the terms and consideration, and regulate generally the principles of the new compact. In both, every sound rule of construction requires, that the terms used should be expounded agreeably to the nature of the subject-matter, and to the relations previously subsisting between the parties. If general expressions are not controlled by these principles, then the term "their land," or, as it is elsewhere called, "their hunting grounds," instead of meaning what our own negotiators and the Indians themselves understood, that possessory right, which they have heretofore enjoyed, would at once change our whole system of policy, and leave them as free to sell, as it would individuals or nations to buy, those large unappropriated districts, which are rather visited than possessed by the Indians.

It may be remarked that all rights secured by treaty stipulations are wholly independent of this question of jurisdiction. If the Indians are subject to the legislative authority of the United States, that authority will no doubt be exercised so as not to contravene those rights. If they are subject to the respective States, such, too, will be the course of legislation over them. An if, unadvisedly, any right should be impaired, the Indians have the same resort as our own citizens to the tribunals of justice for redress; for the law, while it claims their obedience, provides for their security. The supremacy of the State Governments is neither inconsistent with our obligations to the Indians, nor are these necessarily impaired by it. It may be difficult to define precisely the nature of their possessory right, but no one will contend that it gives them the absolute title of the land with all its attributes; and every one will probably concede that they are entitled to as much as is necessary to their comfortable subsistence. If we have entered into any stipulations with them, of which, however, I am not aware, inconsistent with the limited powers of the Government, or interfering with paramount obligations, the remedy is obvious. Let ample compensation be made to them by the United States, in a spirit of good faith and liberality. The question would be one, not of pecuniary amount, but of national character and national obligations.

That we may neither deceive ourselves nor the Indians, it becomes us to examine the actual state of things, and to view these as they are, and as they are likely to be. Looking at the circumstances attending this claim of exemption on the one side, and of supremacy on the other, is it probable that the Indians can succeed in the establishment of their pretensions? the nature of the questions, doubtful, to say the least of it; the opinion of the Executive; the practice of the older States, and the claims of the younger ones; the difficulties which would attend the introduction into our system of a third government, complicated in its relations, and indefinite in its principles; public sentiment, naturally opposed to any reduction of territorial extent or political power; and the obvious difficulties, inseparable from the consideration of such a great political question, with regard to the tribunal, and the trial, the judgment, and the process; present obstacles which must be overcome before this claim can be enforced.

But could the tribes, and the remnants of tribes, east of the Mississippi, succeed in the prosecution of this claim, would the issue be beneficial to them, immediately or remotely?

We have every reason to believe it would not; and this conclusion is founded on the condition and character of the Indians, and on the result of the efforts, which have been made by them, and for them, to resisted the operation of the causes that yet threaten their destruction.

I need not stop to illustrate these positions. They are connected with the views, which will be found in the sequel of this report. And it is not necessary to embarrass a subject already too comprehensive.

A change of residence, therefore, from their present positions to the regions west of the Mississippi, presents the only hope of permanent establishment and improvement. That it will be attended with inconveniences and sacrifices, no one can doubt. The associations, which bind the Indians to the land of their forefathers are strong and enduring; and these must be broken by their migration. But they are also broken by our citizens, who every day encounter all the difficulties of similar changes in the pursuit of the means of support. And the experiments, which have been made, satisfactorily show, that, by proper precautions, and liberal appropriations, the removal and establishment of the Indians can be effected with little comparative trouble to them or us. Why, then, should the policy of this measure be disputed, or its adoption opposed? The whole subject has materially changed, even with a few years; and the imposing considerations it now presents, and which are every day gaining new force, call upon the Government and the country to determine what is required on our part, and what course shall be recommended to the Indians. If they remain, they must decline, and eventually disappear. Such is the result of all experience. If they remove, they may be comfortably established, and their moral and physical condition meliorated. It is certainly better for them to meet the difficulties of removal, with the probability of an adequate and final reward, than, yielding to their constitutional apathy, to sit still and perish.

The great moral debt we owe to this unhappy race is universally felt and acknowledged. Diversities of opinion exist respecting the proper mode of discharging this obligation, but its validity is not denied. And there certainly are difficulties which may well call for discussion and consideration:

For more than two centuries we have been placed in contact with the Indians. And if this long period has been fruitless in useful results, it has not been so in experiments, having in view their improvement. Able men have been investigating their condition, and good men attempting to improve it. But all these labors have been as unsuccessful in the issue, as many of them were laborious and expensive in their progress.

The work has been aided by Governments and communities; by public opinion, by the obligations of the law, and by the sanction of religion. But its history furnishes abundant evidence of entire failure, and every thing around us upon the frontiers confirms its truth. The Indians have either receded as our settlements advance, and united their fragments with some kindred tribe, or they have attempted to established themselves upon reservations, in the vain hope of resisting the pressure upon them, and of preserving their peculiar institutions. Those, who are nearest to us, have generally suffered most severely by the debasing effects of ardent spirits, and by the loss of their own principles of restraint, few as these are, without the acquisition of ours; and almost all of them have disappeared, crushed by the onward course of events, or driven before them. Not one instance can be produced in the whole history of the intercourse between the Indians and the white men, where the former have been able, in districts surrounded by the latter, to withstand successfully the progress of those causes, which have elevated one of these races and depressed the other. Such a monument of former successful exertion does not exist.

These remarks apply to the efforts, which have been heretofore made, and whose history and failure are known to us. But the subject has been lately revived with additional interest, and is now prosecuted with great zeal and exertion; whether with equal effect, time must show. That most of those engaged in this labor are actuated by pure and disinterested motives, I do not question. And, if in their estimate of success, they place too high a value upon appearances, the error is natural to persons zealously engaged in a task calculated to enlist their sympathies and awaken their feelings, and has been common to all, who have preceded them in this labor of philanthropy, and who, from time to time, have indulged in anticipations of the most signal success, only to be succeeded by disappointment and despondency.

That these exertions have recently been productive of some advantage, may well be admitted. A few have probably been reclaimed from abandoned habits, and some, perhaps, have really appreciated the inestimable value of the doctrines which have been taught them. I can speak from personal observation only of the northern and northwestern tribes. Among them, I am apprehensive the benefits will be found but few and temporary. Of the condition of the Cherokees, who are said to have made greater advances than any of their kindred race, I must judge from such information as I have been able to procure. Owing to the prevalence of slavery and other peculiar causes among them, a number of the half-breeds and their connexions, and perhaps a few others, have acquired property, and with it some education and information. But I believe the great mass of the tribe is living in ignorance and poverty, subject to the influence of the principal men, and submitting to a state of things, with which they are dissatisfied, and which offers them no rational prospect of stability and improvement.

The failure, which has attended the efforts heretofore made, and which will probably attend all conducted upon similar principles, may be attributed partly to the inherent difficulty of the undertaking, resulting from characteristics peculiar to the Indians, and partly from the mode in which the operations have been conducted.

Without entering into a question which opens a wide field for inquiry, it is sufficient to observe that our primitive people, as well in their habits and opinions as in their customs and pursuits, offer obstacles almost insurmountable to any considerable and immediate change. Indolent in his habits, the Indian is opposed to labor; improvident in his mode of life, he has little foresight in providing, or care in preserving. Taught from infancy to reverence his own traditions and institutions, he is satisfied of their value, and dreads the anger of the Great Spirit, if he should depart from the customs of his fathers. Devoted to the use of ardent spirits, he abandons himself to its indulgence without restraint. War and hunting are his only occupations. He can endure, without complaining, the extremity of human suffering; and if he cannot overcome the evils of his situation, he submits to them without repining. He attributes all the misfortunes of his race to the white man, and looks with suspicion upon the offers of assistance that are made to him. These traits of character, though not universal, are yet general; and the practical difficulty they present, in changing the condition of such a people, is to satisfy them of our sincerity and the value of the aid we offer; to hold out to them motives for exertion; to call into action some powerful feeling, which shall counteract the tendency of previous impressions. It is under such circumstances, and with these difficulties in view, that the Government has been called upon to determine what arrangements shall be made for the permanent establishment of the Indians. Shall they be advised to remain or remove? If the former, their fate is written in the annals of their race; if the latter, we may yet hope to see them renovated in character and condition by our example and instructions, and by their exertions.

But, to accomplish this, they must first be placed beyond the reach of our settlements, with such checks upon their disposition to hostilities as may be found necessary, and with such aid, moral, intellectual, and pecuniary, as may teach them the value of our improvements, and the reality of our friendship. With these salutary precautions, much should then be left to themselves, to follow such occupations in the forest or the field as they may choose, without too much interference. Time and prosperity must be the great agents in their melioration. Nor have we any reason to doubt but that such a condition would be attended with its full share of happiness; nor that their exertions would be stimulated by the security of their position, and by the new prospects before them. By encouraging the severalty of soil, sufficient tracts might be assigned to all disposed to cultivate them; and, by timely assistance, the younger class might be brought to seek in their farms a less precarious subsistence than is furnished by the chace [*sic*]. Their physical comforts being increased, and the desire of acquisition brought into action, a moral stimulus would be felt by the youthful portion of the community. New wants would appear, and new means of gratifying them; and the great work of improvement would thus commence, and, commencing, would go on.

To its aid, the truths of religion, together with a knowledge of the simpler mechanic arts and the rudiments of science, should then be brought; but if our dependence be first placed upon these, we must fail, as all others have failed, who have gone before us in their field of labor. And we have already fallen into this error of adapting our efforts to a state of society, which is probably yet remote among the Indians, in withdrawing so many of the young men from their friends, and educating them at our schools. They are there taught various branches of learning, and, at some of these institutions, in partial knowledge of the mechanic arts, and of the principles of agriculture. But after this course of instruction is completed, what are these young men to do? If they remain among the whites, they find themselves the members of a peculiar caste, and look round them in vain for employment and encouragement; if they return to their countrymen, their acquirements are useless; these are neither understood nor valued; and, with the exception of a few articles of iron, which they procure from the traders, the common work of our mechanics is useless to them. I repeat, what is a young man, who has been thus educated, to do? He has no means of support, no instruments of agriculture, no domestic animals, no improved farm. Taken in early life from his own people, he is no hunter; he cannot find in the chace [*sic*] the means of support or exchange; and that, under such circumstances, he should abandon himself to a life of intemperance, can scarcely excite our surprise, however it must our regret. I have been earnestly asked by these young men, how they were to live; and I have felt that a satisfactory answer was beyond my reach. To the Government only can they look for relief, and if this should be furnished, though in a moderate degree, they might still become useful and respectable; their example would be encouraging to others, and they would form the best instructors for their brethren.

The general details of a plan for the permanent establishment of the Indians west of the Mississippi, and for their proper security, would require much deliberation; but there are some fundamental principles, obviously arising out of the nature of the subject, which, when once adopted, would constitute the best foundation for our exertions, and the hopes of the Indians.

1. A solemn declaration, similar to that already inserted in some of the treaties, that the country assigned to the Indians shall be theirs as long as they or their descendants may occupy it, and a corresponding determination that our settlements shall not spread over it; and every effort should be used to satisfy the Indians of our sincerity and of their security. Without this indispensable preliminary, and without full confidence on their part in our intentions, and in our abilities to give these effect, their change of position would bring no change of circumstances.

2. A determination to exclude all ardent spirits from their new country. This will no doubt be difficult, but a system of surveillance upon the borders, and of proper police and penalties, will do much towards the extermination of an evil, which, where it exists to any considerable extent, is equally destruction of their present comfort and their future happiness.

3. The employment of an adequate force in their immediate vicinity, and a fixed determination to suppress, at all hazards, the slightest attempt at hostilities among themselves.

   So long as a passion for war, fostered and encourage as it is, by their opinions and habits, is allowed free scope for exercise, it will prove the master spirit, controlling, if not absorbing, all other considerations. And if in checking this evil some examples should become necessary, they would be sacrifices to humanity, and not to severity.

4. Encouragement to the severalty of property, and such provision for its security, as their own regulations do not afford, and as may be necessary to its enjoyment.

5. Assistance to all who may require it in the opening of farms, and in procuring domestic animals and instruments of agriculture.

6. Leaving them in the enjoyment of their peculiar institutions, as far as may be compatible with their own safety and ours, and with the great objects of their prosperity and improvement.

7. The eventual employment of persons competent to instruct them, as far and as fast as their progress may require, and in such manner as may be most useful to them.

Arrangements have been made upon fair and equitable terms with the Shawnees and Senecas of Lewistown, with the Shawnees of Wapaghkonetta, and with the Ottowas [sic] of Blanchard's fork, and the Maumee, all within the State of Ohio, for the cession of their reservations in that State, and for their migration to the region assigned for the permanent residence of the Indians. A similar arrangement was made with the Senecas in the early part of the year, and they are already upon their journey to their new country. A deputation from the Wyandots has gone to examine the district offered to them; and the general outlines of an arrangement for a cession have been agreed upon, to be formally executed, if the report of the exploring party should prove satisfactory.

It has been suggested that a considerable portion of the Cherokees in Georgia are desirous of availing themselves of the provisions of the treaty, May 6th, 1828, for their removal. With a view to ascertain this fact, and to afford them the aid offered by that treaty, if they are inclined to accept it, a system of operations has been adopted, and persons appointed to carry it to effect. Sufficient time to form a judgment of the result of this measure has not yet elapsed.

But if all the efforts, which may be made, the subject will be fully and fairly explained to the Indians, and they will be left to judge for themselves. The agents are prohibited from the exertion of any improper influence, but are directed to communicate to the Indians the views of the President, and his decided convictions, that their speedy removal can only preserve them from the serious evils which environ them. It is to be hoped, that they will accept this salutary advice, and proceed to join their countrymen in the district appropriated for their permanent residence.

If the seeds of improvement are sown among them, as many good men assert and believe, they will ripen into an abundant harvest—profitable to themselves in the enjoyment, and to all the members of this dispersed family in the example.

The details of an outrage committed by a party of Fox Indians upon a number of Menomonies [*sic*] at Prairie du Chien, while encamped under the protection of our flag, will be found in the report of the officer having charge of the bureau of Indian affairs. The alleged motive for this wanton aggression was some previous injury of a similar nature, stated to have been committed by the Menomonies [*sic*] upon the Fox Indians—a justification, which can never be wanting, where neither time nor treaties, as in this case, are permitted to cancel the offence.

This aggression, together with the difficulties at Rock island with the Sac Indians, of which the same report furnishes the particulars, shows the necessity of employing upon the frontiers a corps of mounted men, to be stationed at the most exposed points, and to be always prepared to follow every party, that may attempt to interrupt the peace of the border by attacking either our citizens, or other Indians. These predatory bands strike a stroke, and disappear. And there is in the institutions of the Indians such a strong tendency to war, that we shall long be liable to these outrages. Military prowess and success form their principal road to distinction. And the interminable forests and prairies of the West offer them the means of shelter and escape. No infantry force can expect to overtake them; and if we are not provided with mounted troops, who can prevent or punish these aggressions, we shall frequently be compelled to adopt measures more expensive and inconvenient to us, and more injurious to the Indians.

> Very respectfully, sir,
> I have the honor to be,
> Your obedient servant,
>
> LEWIS CASS

To the President of the United States

Source: U.S. Congress. House. *Report of the Secretary of War.* 22nd Cong., 1st sess, November 21, 1831. H. Doc. 2. Serial 216.

11. First Annual Message of President Martin Van Buren (1837)

Martin Van Buren, as president, inherited the policy of Indian removal as it had been shaped by his predecessor, Andrew Jackson. As his first annual message to Congress indicates, he embraced the policy wholeheartedly. The section of his message on Indian removal is reprinted below. Pleased with the "happy results" of removal by the end of 1837, he presents it, like his predecessors did, as a humanitarian venture aimed at saving the Indians, who, in time, will enjoy the fruits of white U.S. "civilization." Two of his points have dire implications for the future. First, he believes (incorrectly) that Indian removal has provided a solution to the legal jurisdictional dispute between the states and the federal government. Second, he supports the War Department's call for construction of a line of forts along the western frontier to protect American settlements. As events of subsequent years proved, the forts gave a sense of security to Americans who were attracted to the frontier and laid the groundwork for the next major assault on Indians and their lands in the trans-Mississippi West.

The system of removing the Indians west of the Mississippi, commenced by Mr. Jefferson in 1804, has been steadily persevered in by every succeeding President, and may be considered the settled policy of the country. Unconnected at first with any well-defined system for their improvement, the inducements held out to the Indians were confined to the greater abundance of game to be found in the West; but when the beneficial effects of their removal were made apparent, a more philanthropic and enlightened policy was adopted, in purchasing their lands east of the Mississippi. Liberal prices were given, and provisions inserted in all the treaties with them, for the application of the funds they received in exchange to such purposes as were best calculated to promote their present welfare, and advance their future civilization. These measures have been attended thus far with the happiest results.

It will be seen, by referring to the report of the Commissioner of Indian Affairs, that the most sanguine expectations of the friends and promoters of this system have been realized. The Choctaws, Cherokees, and other tribes that first emigrated beyond the Mississippi, have, for the most part, abandoned the hunter state, and become cultivators of the soil. The improvements in their condition has been rapid, and it is believed that they are now fitted to enjoy the advantages of a simple form of government, which has been submitted to them and received their sanction; and I cannot too strongly urge this subject upon the attention of Congress.

Stipulations have been made with all the Indian tribes to remove them beyond the Mississippi, except with the bands of the Wyandots, the Six Nations in New York, the Menomonees [*sic*], Munsees, and Stockbridges, in Wisconsin, and Miamies in Indiana. With all but the Menomonees, it is expected that arrangements for their emigration will be completed the present year. The resistance which has been opposed to their removal by some of the tribes, even after treaties had been made with them to that effect, has arisen from various causes, operating differently on each of them. In most instances, they have been instigated to resistance by persons to whom the trade with them and the acquisition of their annuities were important; and in some, by the personal influence of interested chiefs. These obstacles must be overcome; for the Government cannot relinquish the execution of this policy without sacrificing important interests, and abandoning the tribes remaining east of the Mississippi to certain destruction.

The decrease in numbers of the tribes within the limits of the States and Territories has been most rapid. If they be removed, they can be protected from those associations and evil practices which exert so pernicious and destructive an influence over their destinies. They can be induced to labor, and to acquire property; and its acquisition will inspire them with a feeling of independence. Their minds can be cultivated, and they can be taught the value of salutary and uniform laws, and be made sensible of the blessings of free government, and capable of enjoying its advantages. In the possession of property, knowledge, and a good Government, free to give what direction they please to their labor, and sharers in the legislation by which their persons and the profits of their industry are to be protected and secured, they will have an ever-present conviction of the importance of union and peace among themselves, and of the preservation of amicable relations with us. The interests of the United States would also be greatly promoted by freeing the relations between the General and State Governments from what has proved a most embarrassing encumbrance, by a satisfactory adjustment of conflicting titles to lands, caused by the occupation of the Indians, and by causing the resources of the whole country to be developed by the power of the State and General Governments, and improved by the enterprise of a white population.

Immediately connected with this subject is the obligation of the Government to fulfill its treaty stipulations, and to protect the Indians thus assembled "at their new residences from all interruptions and disturbances from any other tribes or nations of Indians, or from any other person or persons whatsoever;" and the equally solemn obligation to guard from Indian hostility its own border settlements, stretching along a line of more than one thousand miles. To enable the Government to redeem this pledge to the Indians, and to afford adequate protection to its own citizens, will require the continual presence of a considerable regular force on the frontier, and the establishment of a chain of permanent posts. Examinations of the country are now making, with a view to decide on the most suitable points for the erection of fortresses and other works of defence, the results of which will be presented to you by the Secretary of War at an early day, together with a plan for the effectual protection of the friendly Indians, and the permanent defence of the frontier states.

Martin Van Buren
December 5, 1837

Source: Message from the President of the United States to the Two Houses of Congress, at the Commencement of the Second Session of the Twenty-fifth Congress. Washington, DC: Thomas Allen, 1837.

12. Statement of Menominees Concerning Treaties Ceding Lands in Wisconsin to the Indians of New York (1824)

This statement is a good example of the difficulties that arose for many of the Indian nations when making treaties and after. For a variety of reasons, including lack of facility in English, incompetent or dishonest translators, or inadequate explanations, the Indians did not fully comprehend a treaty's assertions or realize the implications for the future. Many times, concepts central to a treaty's tenets, for example, land ownership, were completely foreign to the Native culture. Other factors, such as the signing of treaties by "treaty chiefs," which often meant those who were recognized by the whites but not by the Indians as authorized to act for the Nation, presented difficulties as well. The following statement refers to treaties of 1821 and 1822 in which the Oneidas, Stockbridge-Munsees, and Brothertons purchased land to settle in Wisconsin.

The memorial and petition of the undersigned chiefs and principal men of the Menominie nation of Indians, residing within the Michigan Territory, represents:

That when the New York Indians, or Nautoways, first came to this country, they asked the Menomonies to sell to them a small piece of their land. That the Menomonies replied to them, they had no land to sell; that their country was already too small for their numbers, and that they were themselves compelled to hunt upon other Indians' lands. That, notwithstanding this answer, the Nautoways held a treaty with some of the men of the Menomonie nation, at which none of the principal chiefs attended, and purchased, or pretended to purchase, a part of the Menomonies' country, the boundaries of which they knew nothing about. That the old men of this nation, who have any right to the country claimed by the nation, which extends from Lake Michigan to the upper part of the Wisconsin river, *now sign this paper*; not one of whom was present at that treaty; and that as soon as their backs were turned, some of their men, who had no right to dispose of the land, held the treaty; and whatever consideration was then paid, or has since been paid, they know not, having received no portion of the same. And as an evidence of the fact, that they knew nothing of that treaty, not one of the old inhabitants of this place was called upon, as is usual, to attend at the making of the same: and they are not accustomed to transact so important a business as this would have been, without asking their advice.

They state the same facts, or objections, to the second, or last treaty which is said to have been held; and their object now is, to, and they do, *protest* against any further settlements being made upon their lands by the Nautoways. "If any more should come here, what shall we do with our wives and children, whom we can now scarcely support? We beg of our great father to prevent any more of them from coming to this country. With the Winnebagoes we are united by kindred, yet it is with great difficulty that we can live upon terms of friendship even with them. We are satisfied with the settlement made here by the whites, *but we cannot admit any nation of Indians to settle in the country.*"

Green Bay, June 16, 1824
MENOMINIES
OASH-KOSH, the Brave
JOSEPH CORRON, son of Thomas,
KETS-KAN-NO-NIEN
PE-WAY-TINENT
SAY-KEE-TOAK
AMABLE CORRON
MUK-KAY-TAY-WET

Source: U.S. Congress. Senate. *Correspondence on the Emigration of Indians, 1831–1833,* 23rd Cong., 1st sess., 1834. S. Doc. 512. 2:536.

13. For the *Cherokee Phoenix:* Indian Emigration (1828)

This letter is an example of the thinking of literate Cherokees as the pressure to remove was building because of the Georgia legislature's actions in extending state jurisdiction over the Creek and Cherokee nations. Although many officials in Washington and elsewhere regarded the Indians as savages who didn't understand their circumstances, this Cherokee is all too aware of the situation and its dangers.

MR. EDITOR:—I have seen published in one of your late papers the treaty between the United States and Cherokees west of the Mississippi, and am pleased to see the anxiety manifested by the Government to secure for them a *permanent* home. This blessing it seems will even be extended to those East of the Mississippi, *provided* they accede to the propositions of the Government. But the offer of a few such paltry articles as a brass kettle, a few pounds of Tobacco &c. is too insignificant to be thought of, as an inducement for us to abandon our cultivated possessions, and join our wilder brethren in the west. It is too late to think we can be so much allured by *soft words* and *smooth promises* as to sell our birth-right for a few dried leaves of a noxious weed. Those who may entertain an opinion of our speedy removal, and that too to be effected by such trifling inducements as above, will be lost in the labyrinth of their speculations; and ere long the splendid mansions which their imaginations have builded upon the plains of Look Out and Coosa will vanish before reality, like darkness before the rising sun.

The subject of emigration is indeed one of great importance, and claims the peculiar attention of every citizen. If we direct our eyes to Arkansas, we shall see our brethren in distress, in consequence of their removal; we see them walking in grosser darkness than ourselves. If we look back, scenes which have befallen them are presented to our view, which cause our hearts to throb with brotherly sympathy. How many honest and innocent fathers and brothers have been laid low by the ruthless hands of more ignorant and vicious neighbors. Avarice and barbarity have deprived their social circles of many worthy members, who would yet have added to our number, had a unanimity of sentiment prevailed, and had they not been duped to wander in search of a mere phantom. Who will dare to raise with the spirit of murder the tomahawk at our door? or who will dare to molest us as we pursue the windings of our paths in peace through our fertile vallies? None. But can our brethren say in truth this is the case with them? With us the war club is only associated with scenes which have long since passed, but is ever suspended over the heads of our more unfortunate brothers. Let us weigh well this momentous subject ere we act, perhaps an age might not undo that which may have been the work of a day. We know the value of our lands, and we know how to appreciate the comforts of life. We know what has transpired, and we are aware of the possibility of what might again happen. We know the lands which our brethren have given up were very poor and we are certain those which they have got in exchange must be far more barren and sterile, since the face of the treaty has discovered it, and the sum of $50,000 given them "on account of the *reduced value* of a *great portion* of the lands ceded." The aborigines are not accustomed to the culture of a barren soil, but select the choicest spots, to open their farms; and to be honest in the matter, we have now as much poor land, as we have any use for, without undertaking long journeys, undergoing new trials, and making experiments on a broad scale to acquire more.

It is said, "they (the Cherokees,) have by the exchange freed themselves from the harrassing and ruinous effects consequent upon a location amidst a white population." But time will soon prove the contrary; Difficulties of a new and more serious nature await them. It has been pretty well ascertained here, that the Delegates violated, and transcended the authority vested in them by the Nation, in entering into a treaty. And it is not improbable but we may see another McIntosh tragedy played all over again. But independent of this; when the game becomes scarce, by being killed up, or driven farther westward, how will they support themselves? penetrate farther into the forest, or turn their attention to agricultural pursuits? suppose the latter, and where will they have a sufficiency of good lands for cultivation? In the event we were to remove and be united with them, our laws would clash with theirs, we would have our own peculiar partialities and prejudices, and they would have theirs; in consequence of this difference, perhaps a few avaricious speculating individuals would solicit from the General Government, a set of laws, as stipulated in the 6th article of the treaty. Imagine, then how our internal affairs would be regulated, *harrassed* on the one side, and *embarrassed* on the other; Repentance then for the past would be too late. A difference in sentiment would produce a division of parties, and rebellion, dispersion, and extinction would soon follow up in succession. We would be loth to meditate upon the gloomy prospects of bettering our condition by a removal, far less hazard a *ruinous experiment.*

An attempt has been made to enforce upon us the belief that if we *were* to emigrate, it would facilitate our civilization, and we would sooner become an enlightened people. But any man of moral capacity who will divest himself of all unnatural prejudices, and view the subject, will at once perceive the fallacy of this doctrine. Our present location possesses greatly the ascendancy in every point of view. Our improvement is as rapid as can reasonably be expected, and we are much farther advanced in the arts and sciences than our brethren at Arkansas. Now, I would ask to be informed by the votaries of this '*doctrine of policy,*' how it happens that those who live at the "paradise of the west," which affords such powerful means to propel them onward in improvement, are so far behind us? The examples of the surrounding states possess a great influence over us. Our political Government keeps pace by gradual changes, as we imbibe new principles of legislation, with our domestic advancement. Our population is not on the wane in consequence of our situation amidst the whites, but is rapidly increasing—the implements of husbandry have been substituted for the bow and quiver. In short we possess all the enjoyments adequate to the support of common life. Now why deprive us of all our comforts, tear us from all we hold dear, and drag us from the soil which gave us birth, rendered doubly precious, as the bones of our fathers have been deposited here from time immemorial, to accomplish that which is now in rapid progression? Why disregard our prayers for justice, cruelly sport with our feelings, and trample under foot our best interests? Will a glimpse of the blue summit of the Rocky Mountains inspire us with a moral aptitude to learn anthems of adoration to the Great Father of the universe? Will an association with bears and buffaloes give a new spring and vigor to our efforts, and thereby enhance our civil and moral improvement? or will the examples of more ignorant and barbarous tribes act as a great incentive for us to train up our children after the manner of enlightened communities, that they may become adept in the sciences, and dive into the deep recesses of nature, and finally become a renowned people? No. Remove us west of the Mississippi and what will be the result? In our earlier days we were accustomed to follow the chase for support; we found it an easy life; but we were entreated to abandon it as a preparatory step for the reception of instruction; the game has at length become scarce, and we no longer depend upon it for support, but upon the cultivation of the earth; and those who have not imbibed this laudable spirit from habits of industry, have been actuated by necessity; and now, while we are prospering under the exhilarating rewards of agriculture, the rifle is again put into our hands, and brass kettle swung to our backs, and we are led into the deep forest where game is plenty, by the hands of those who would once have had us abandon the chase. Admirably consistent.—Men brought up to the engagement of some certain pursuit are not easily detracted therefrom, when surrounding circumstances invite continuance,—Were we not settled in the 'paradise of the West,' the chase would become our favorite pursuit, to follow which we should neglect other avocations.—The principle which we have imbibed of governing ourselves after enlightened republics would again be subverted into the chase, and we should degenerate from our present eminence, lower, and lower, until degradation with its concomitant train of evils should close up the rear.

Notwithstanding the inattention paid by the Government to the solemn resolution of the General Council never again to cede one foot more of land, it is to be hoped and in justice expected, that the Cherokees are to be regarded as free agents in the disposal of their Territory, and upon a refusal to yield compliance no coercive measures will be used. The Government has acknowledged and guaranteed to us our possessions, and bound herself to protect us in our rights, an observance of which is all the Cherokees will ask. She was not unmindful of her own interest at the time when those treaties were made, but justice and humanity had a voice in her councils, and we trust at this late day, when the eyes of the civilized world are directed to the great American republic, for examples worthy of the high eminence to which she has arrived, she will never suffer herself to be so much influenced by *interest* as to lose sight of justice, and cruelly despoil a tribe of innocent Indians of their most sacred rights and privileges.

YOUNG BEAVER

Source: Cherokee Phoenix, September 17, 1828.

14. Elias Boudinot (Editorial) (January 28, 1829)

This editorial argues that the Cherokees have reached a state of civilization as evidenced by the facts that they have adopted religion, are printing in English and Cherokee, and have abandoned hunting and gathering for herding and farming. The piece argues for the preservation of Cherokee nationhood. It believes that foes aim to "disorganize" the Nation by erasing Cherokee law and replacing it with Georgia law or by removing the Cherokees. Both actions, Boudinot asserts, would lead to the extinction of Cherokees as a people.

It is frequently said that the Indians are given up to destruction, that it is the will of heaven, that they should become extinct and give way to the white man. Those who assert this doctrine seem to act towards these unfortunate people in a consistent manner, either in neglecting them entirely, or endeavoring to hasten the period of their extinction. For our part, we dare not scrutinize the designs of God's providence towards the Cherokees. It may suffice to say that, his dealings have been merciful and very kind. He inclined the heart of GEORGE WASHINGTON, when we were in a savage state, to place us under the protection of the United States, by entering into a treaty of peace and friendship with our forefathers, on the second day of July, in the year of our Lord one thousand seven hundred and ninety one; in which treaty is the following provision.

That the Cherokee Nation may be led to a greater degree of civilization, and to become herdsmen and cultivators, instead of remaining hunters, the United States will, from time to time, furnish gratuitously, the said nation with useful implements of husbandry.

He furthermore inclined that illustrious man, and his successors in office, and the Agents of the United States, to carry the foregoing provision into execution. By his overruling providence, a door was opened for the introduction of those implements of husbandry; and at this day, were Washington living, he would find that his expectations and wishes were realized. He would rejoice, and those who compassionated the Indians with him would rejoice to see that the Cherokees have in great measure become herdsmen and cultivators—they are no more hunters and gatherers. Where they were accustomed to hunt the deer, the bear and the beaver, are seen their farms, & they labor peaceably, for the troubles of warfare do not now molest them.

We cannot enumerate all the dealings of God towards us in a temporal point of view. They are gracious, and in our minds would convey the belief that he has mercy still in store for us. But what are his dealings in a spiritual point of view? "If the Lord were pleased to destroy us he would not have shewed us all these things nor would, as at this time, have told us such things as these." We have heard great things indeed, salvation by Jesus Christ. To what purpose has God opened the hearts of Christians of different denominations to commiserate, not only the Cherokees, but all the other tribes? To what purpose are contributions freely made to support missionaries and Schools? To what purpose is it that these missionaries meet with such remarkable success, and that preachers are rising from among the Cherokees themselves? To what purpose is it that hundreds have made a public profession of religion, and that the number is rapidly increasing? To what purpose is it that, that the knowledge of letters has been disseminated with a rapidity unknown heretofore, and that eight hundred copies of a Cherokee HYMN BOOK is now issuing from our press? What do all these indicate? Do they indicate the displeasure of God against us, and the certainty of our extinction? It is not for man to pry into the designs of god where he has not expressly revealed them, but from his past blessings we may hope for future mercies.

The causes which have operated to exterminate the Indian tribes that are produced as instances of the certain doom of the whole Aboriginal family appear plain to us. These causes did not exist in the Indians themselves, nor in the will of heaven, nor simply in the intercourse of Indians with civilized man, but they were precisely such causes as are now attempted by the state of Georgia—by infringing upon their rights—by disorganizing them, and circumscribing their limits. While he possesses a national character, there is hope for the Indian. But take his rights away, divest him of the last spark of national pride, and introduce him to a new order of things, invest him with oppressive laws, grievous to be borne, he droops like the fading flower before the noon day sun. Most of the Northern tribes have fallen a prey to such causes, & the Catawbas of South Carolina, are a striking instance of the truth of what we say. There is hope for the Cherokee as long as they continue in their present situation, but disorganize them, either by removing them beyond the Mississippi, or by imposing on them "heavy burdens," you cut a vital string in their national existence.

Things will no doubt come to a final issue before long in regard to the Indians, and for our part, we care not how soon. The State of Georgia has taken a strong stand against us, and the United States must either defend us in our rights, or leave us to our foe. In the former case, the General Government will redeem her pledge solemnly given in treaties.—In the latter, she will violate her promise of protection, and we cannot, in future, depend consistently, upon any guarantee made by her to us, either here or beyond the Mississippi.

Source: Cherokee Phoenix, January 28, 1829.

15. Elias Boudinot (Editorial) (June 17, 1829)

This editorial was written in response to Secretary of War John Eaton's comments to the Cherokee delegation, chastising them for writing a constitution, which Eaton saw as an affront to the state of Georgia. It is also in response to President Andrew Jackson's address to the Creeks, in which he asserts that if the tribe remains in Alabama, it will be subject to the laws of the state.

From the documents which we this day lay before our readers, there is not a doubt of the kind of policy, which the present administration of the General Government intends to pursue relative to the Indians. President Jackson has, a neighboring editor remarks, "recognized the doctrine contended for by Georgia in its full extent." It is to be regretted that we were not undeceived long ago, while we were hunters and in our savage state. It appears now from the communication of the Secretary of War to the Cherokee Delegation, that the illustrious Washington, Jefferson, Madison, and Monroe were only tantalizing us, when they encouraged us in the pursuit of agriculture and Government and when they afforded us the protection of the

United States, by which we have been preserved to this present time as a nation. Why were we not told long ago, that we could not be permitted to establish a government within the limits of any state? Then we could have borne disappointment much easier than now. The pretext for Georgia to extend her jurisdiction over the Cherokees has always existed. The Cherokees have always had a government of their own. Nothing, however, was said when we were governed by savage laws, when the abominable law of retaliation carried death in our midst, when it was a lawful act to shed the blood of a person charged with witchcraft, when a brother could kill a brother with impunity, or an innocent man for an offending relative. At that time it might have been a matter of charity to have extended over us the mantle of Christian laws and regulations. But how happens it now, after being fostered by the U. States, and advised by great and good men to establish a government of regular law; when the aid and protection of the General Government have been pledged to us; when we, as dutiful "children" of the President, have followed his instructions and advice, and have established for ourselves a government of regular law; when everything looks so promising around us, that a storm is raised by the extension of tyrannical and unchristian laws, which threatens to blast all our rising hopes and expectations?

There is, as would naturally be supposed, a great rejoicing in Georgia. It is a time of "important news"—"gratifying intelligence"—"The Cherokee lands are to be obtained speedily." It is even reported that the Cherokees have come to the conclusion to sell and move off to the west of the Mississippi—not so fast. We are yet at our homes, at our peaceful firesides, (except those contiguous to Sandtown, Carroll, &c.) attending to our farms and useful occupations.

We had concluded to give our readers fully our thoughts on the subject, which we, in the above remarks, have merely introduced, but upon reflection & remembering our promise, that we will be moderate, we have suppressed ourselves, and have withheld what we had intended should occupy our editorial column. We do not wish, by any means, unnecessarily to excite the minds of the Cherokees. To our home readers we submit the subject without any special comment. They will judge for themselves. To our distant readers, who may wish to know how we feel under present circumstances, we recommend the memorial, the leading article in our present number. We believe it justly contains the views of the nation.

Source: Cherokee Phoenix, June 17, 1829.

16. Elias Boudinot (Editorial) (June 19, 1830)

In this editorial, Elias Boudinot writes that the Indian Removal Act is closer to passage. He finds the bill's language illogical when it states that the act will violate treaties yet declares that they are inviolable. The editor, however, seems to sense that the outcome is inevitable, and that in spite of strong allies in Congress, the Indians will lose their cases to retain their homelands.

In our last was given the proceedings of the House of Representatives on the Indian bill, to the time when it was ordered to a third reading. In this day's paper will be found the final proceedings, and the adoption of the amendment by the Senate. We stated last week that if the amendment was adopted, or the bill failed, by the refusal of the Senate to adopt it, our fears would not be realized in their full extent. But since, upon mature reflection, and after reading the doings of the Senate which the reader can see for himself, we are constrained to say, the formal acknowledgment of the validity of treaties is but a mock show of justice. This is evident from the fact that the very men who have all along contended for the unconstitutionality of treaties with the Indians, were the first to agree to the amendment of the House, & to reject the amendments offered by Messrs. Frelinghuysen, Sprague and Clayton. The bearing of the bill then on the interests of the Indians will be the same as if it had passed in its original shape.

We confess our ignorance, our utter ignorance, of the views of the majority of the members of Congress, so far as they have been developed, on the rights of the Indians, and the relation in which they stand to the United States, on the score of treaties; nor can we discern the consistency of contending for the unconstitutionality of these treaties, and yet at the same time, declaring that *they shall not be violated*, which a man of common sense would take to be the meaning of the amendment. If a treaty is unconstitutional, it is of course null and void, and cannot be violated. If a treaty *may not be violated*, it is taken for granted that it is binding; and if it is binding, the parties to it have a right to demand its enforcement. How are we then to understand the decision of the Senate on this important subject? What do they mean by adopting the proviso, and at the same breath deliberately refusing to enforce the provisions of the existing treaties? We can find no suitable answer but this, *palpable injustice is meditated against the poor Indians!*

It is somewhat surprising that many well meaning persons, who would never in other circumstances, lend their aid and influence to do injustice to the Indians should be perfectly blinded by this bill. They believe, as its advocates represent to them, that it is harmless, and that its operation cannot be otherwise than highly beneficial. But they are greatly deceived—the bill is not harmless, nor was it ever intended to be harmless. For the truth of this assertion, look at the decision of the Senate, rejecting the several amendments for the protection of the Indians! This 500,000 dollars is intended to co-operate with any other expedient, which will play at our backs like a flaming sword, while this sum will address itself to our fears and avarice. Compulsion behind, while the means of escape are placed before. Go or perish. And this is said when treaties are declared to be binding, and in them ample provisions are made for the protection of the Indians. Who would trust his life and fortune to such a faithless nation? No Cherokee *voluntarily* would.

At this time of much distress and darkness, the Cherokees can have some consoling thoughts—they have been ably and most manfully defended to the last, and although self-interest and party and sectional feelings have triumphed over justice, yet it has been only by a pitiful majority, and against the known will and feelings of the good people of these United States. Those worthy advocates of Indian rights in the Senate and House of Representatives will be remembered while there is a living Cherokee—and notwithstanding oppression and power may crush us and utterly destroy us, yet their laudable efforts to save us, will be estimated in their proper light, and held in pleasing recollection by the Christian and Philanthropist of future ages, and of all countries.

Source: Cherokee Phoenix, June 19, 1830.

17. William Penn: Excerpt from "On the Present Crisis in the Condition of the American Indian" (1830)

Jeremiah Evarts, preacher, writer, and editor, wrote 24 essays under the pseudonym William Penn that were published between August and December 1829 in the *National Intelligencer*, a widely read publication of the time. The pieces attempted to do two things: establish the integrity of treaties made by the Cherokee Nation with Great Britain and the United States, and demolish the arguments of the pro-removal forces that were gaining momentum since the election of Andrew Jackson in 1828. Evarts chose the Cherokees as his example to show the progression of treaties that guaranteed that Nation possession of its lands in perpetuity. The 1st and 24th essays given here argue against the pro-removal position, and the 19th is an example of how Evarts examines the pacts between the dominant society and the Indians.

No. I

Contents of this Number—Information needed—Great interests at stake—The character of our country involved—The world will judge in the case—Value of national character—Apprehension of the divine displeasure—Statement of the controversy.

Every careful observer of public affairs must have seen, that a crisis has been rapidly approaching, for several years past, in reference to the condition, relations, and prospects, of the Indian tribes, in the southwestern parts of the United States. The attention of many of our most intelligent citizens has been fixed upon the subject with great interest. Many others are beginning to inquire. Several public documents, which have recently appeared in the newspapers, serve to awaken curiosity, and to provoke investigation.

Still, however, the mass of the community possess but very little information on the subject; and even among the best informed, scarcely a man can be found, who is thoroughly acquainted with the questions at issue. Vague and inconsistent opinions are abroad; and however desirous the people may be of coming at the truth, the sources of knowledge are not generally accessible. Some persons think, that the Indians have a perfect right to the lands which they occupy, except so far as their original right has been modified by treaties fairly made, and fully understood at the time of signing. But how far such a modification may have taken place, or whether it has taken place at all, these persons admit themselves to be ignorant. Others pretend, that Indians have no other right to their lands, than that of *a tenant at will;* that is, the right of remaining where they are, till the *owners of the land* shall require them to remove. It is needless to say, that, in the estimation of such persons, the white neighbours of the Indians are the real owners of the land. Some people are puzzled by what is supposed to be a collision between the powers of the general government and the claims of particular States. Others do not see that there is any hardship in bringing the Indians under the laws of the States, in the neighbourhood of which they live; or, as the phrase is, within the limits of which they live. Some consider it the greatest kindness that can be done to the Indians to remove them, even without their consent and against their will, to a country where, as is supposed, they will be in a condition more favourable to their happiness. Others think, that if they are compelled to remove, their circumstances will be in all respects worse than at present; and that, suffering under a deep sense of injury, and considering themselves trodden down by the march of inexorable oppression, they will become utterly dispirited, and sink rapidly to the lowest degradation, and to final extinction.

So great a diversity of opinion is principally owing to want of correct information. It is my design, Messrs. Editors, to furnish, in a few numbers of moderate length, such materials, as will enable every dispassionate and disinterested man to determine where the right of the case is.

In the mean time, I would observe, that the people of the United States owe it to themselves, and to mankind, to form a correct judgment in this matter. The questions have forced themselves upon us, as a nation:—*What is to become of the Indians? Have they any rights?* If they have, *What are these rights? and how are they to be secured?* These questions must receive a practical answer; and that very soon. What the answer shall be, is a subject of the deepest concern to the country.

The number of individuals, who are interested in the course now to be pursued, is very great. It is computed, that there are within our national limits more than 300,000 Indians; some say 500,000; and, in the southwestern States, the tribes whose immediate removal is in contemplation, have an aggregate population of more than 60,000. The interests of all these people are implicated, in any measure to be taken respecting them.

The character of our government, and of our country, may be deeply involved. Most certainly an indelible stigma will be fixed upon us, if, in the plentitude of our power, and in the pride of our superiority, we shall be guilty of manifest injustice to our weak and defenceless neighbours. There are persons among us, not ignorant, nor prejudiced, nor under the bias of private interest, who serious apprehend, that there is danger of our national character being most unhappily affected, before the subject shall be fairly at rest. If these individuals are misled by an erroneous view of facts, or by the adoption of false principles, a free discussion will relieve their minds.

It should be remembered, by our rulers as well as others, that this controversy, (for it has assumed the form of a regular controversy,) will ultimately be well understood by the whole civilized world. No subject, not even war, nor slavery, nor the nature of free institutions, will be more thoroughly canvassed. The voice of mankind will be pronounced upon it;—a voice, which will not be drowned by the clamor of ephemeral parties, nor silenced by the paltry considerations of local or private interest. Such men as the Baron Humboldt and the Duc de Broglie, on the continent Europe, and a host of other statesmen, and orators, and powerful writers, there and in Great Britain, will not be greatly influenced in deciding a grave question of public morality, by the excitements of one of our elections, or the selfish views of some little portions of the American community. Any course of measures, in regard to the Indians, which is manifestly fair, and generous, and benevolent, will command the warm and decided approbation of intelligent men, not only in the present age, but in all succeeding times. And with equal confidence it may be said, if, in the phraseology of Mr. Jefferson, the people of the United States should "feel power, and forget right;"—if they should resemble a man, who abounding in wealth of every kind, and assuming the office of lawgiver and judge, first declares himself to be the owner of his poor neighbour's little farm, and then ejects the same neighbour as a troublesome encumbrance;—if, with land enough, now in the undisputed possession of the whites, to sustain ten times our present population, we should compel the remnants of tribes to leave the places, which, received by inheritance from their fathers and never alienated, they have long regarded as their permanent homes;—if, when asked to explain the treaties, which we first proposed, then solemnly executed, and have many times ratified, we stammer, and prevaricate, and complete our disgrace by an unsuccessful attempt to stultify, not merely ourselves, but the ablest and wisest statesmen, whom our country has yet produced;—and if, in pursuance of a narrow and selfish policy, we should at this day, in a time of profound peace and great national prosperity, amidst all our professions of magnanimity and benevolence, and in the blazing light of the nineteenth century, drive away these remnants of tribes, in such a manner, and under such auspices, as to insure their destruction;—if all this should hereafter appear to be a fair statement of the case;—then the sentence of an indignant world will be uttered in thunders, which will roll and reverberate for ages after the present actors in human affairs shall have passed away. If the people of the United States will imitate the ruler who coveted Naboth's vineyard, the world will assuredly place them by the side of Naboth's oppressor. Impartial history will not ask them, whether they will feel gratified and honored by such an association. Their consent to the arrangement will not be necessary. The revolution of the earth in its orbit is not more certain.

It may be truly said, that the character which a nation sustains, in its intercourse with the great community of nations, is of more value than any other of its public possessions. Our diplomatic agents have uniformly declared, during the whole period of our national history, in their discussions with the agents of foreign powers, that we offer to others the same justice which we ask from them. And though, in times of national animosity, or when the interests of different communities clash with each other, there will be mutual reproaches and recriminations, and every nation will, in its turn, be charged with unfairness or injustice, still among nations, as among individuals, there is a difference between *the precious and the vile;* and that nation will undoubtedly, in the long course of years, be most prosperous and most respected, which most sedulously cherishes a character for fair dealing, and even generosity, in all its transactions.

There is a higher consideration still. The Great Arbiter of Nations never fails to take cognizance of national delinquencies. No sophistry can elude his scrutiny; no array of plausible arguments, or of smooth but hollow professions, can bias his judgment; and he has at his disposal most abundant means of executing his decisions. In many forms, and with awful solemnity, he has declared his abhorrence of oppression in every shape; and especially of injustice perpetrated against the weak by the strong, *when strength is in fact made the only rule of action.* The people of the United States are not altogether guiltless, in regard to their treatment of the aborigines of this continent; but they cannot as yet be charged with any *systemic legislation* on this subject, inconsistent with the plainest principles of moral honesty. At least, I am not aware of any proof, by which such a charge could be sustained.

Nor do I, in these preliminary remarks, attempt to characterize measures now in contemplation. But it is very clear, that our government and our people should be extremely cautious, lest, in judging between ourselves and the Indians, and carrying our own judgment into execution with a strong hand, we incur the displeasure of the Most High.—Some very judicious and considerate men in our country think, that our public functionaries should stop where they are; that, in the first place, we should humble ourselves before God and the world, that we have done so much to destroy the Indians, and so little to save them; and that, before another step is taken, there should be the most thorough deliberation, on the part of all our constituted authorities, lest we act in such a manner as to expose ourselves to the judgments of Heaven.

I would have omitted this topic, if I thought that a majority of readers would regard its introduction as a matter of course, or as a piece of affectation, designed for rhetorical embellishment. In my deliberate opinion, it is more important, and should be more heeded, than all other considerations relating to the subject; and the people of the United States will find it so, if they should unhappily suppose themselves above the obligation to *do justly, love mercy, and walk humbly with their God.*

I close this introductory number, by stating what seems to be the present controversy between the whites and the Indian tribes of the southwestern States: I say the *whites*, (that is our country generally,) because certain positions are taken by the government of the United States, and certain claims are made by the State of Georgia, and certain other claims by the States of Alabama and Mississippi. The Indians do not admit the validity of any of these positions or claims; and if they have a perfect original title to the lands they occupy, which title they have never forfeited or alienated, their rights cannot be affected by the charters of kings, nor by the acts of provincial legislatures, nor by the compacts of neighbouring states, nor by the mandates of the executive branch of our national government.

The simple question is: *Have the Indian tribes, residing as separate communities in the neighbourhood of the whites, a permanent title to the territory, which they inherited from their fathers, which they have neither forfeited nor sold, and which they now occupy?*

For the examination of this question, let the case of a single tribe or nation be considered; for nearly the same principles are involved in the claims of all the Indian nations.

The Cherokees contend, that their nation has been in possession of their present territory from time immemorial; that neither the king of Great Britain, nor the early settlers of Georgia, not the state of Georgia after the revolution, nor the United States since the adoption of the federal constitution, have acquired any title to the soil, or any sovereignty over the territory; and that the title to the soil and sovereignty have been *repeatedly guaranteed to the Cherokees, as a nation,* by the United States, in treaties which are now binding on both parties.

The government of the United States alleges, as appears by a letter from the Secretary of War, dated April, 1829, that Great Britain, previous to the revolution, "*claimed* entire sovereignty within the limits of what constituted the thirteen United States;" that 'all the rights of sovereignty which Great Britain had with said states became vested in said states respectively, as a consequence of the declaration of independence, and the treaty of 1783;' that the Cherokees were merely 'permitted' to reside on their lands by the United States; that this permission is not to be construed so as to deny to Georgia the exercise of sovereignty; and that the United States has no power to guarantee any thing more than a right of possession, till the state of Georgia should see fit to legislate for the Cherokees, and dispose of them as she should judge expedient, without any control from the general government.

This is a summary of the positions taken by the Secretary of War; and, though not all of them expressed in his own language, they are in strict accordance with the tenor of his letter.

In my next number, I shall proceed to inquire, *What right have the Chero-kees to the lands which they occupy?*

No. XIX

Statement of important positions on this subject—Other treaties with Georgia—Treaty-making power of the general government—Are the Indians capable of making a treaty?—Are engagements with them to be called agreements?—The Supreme court cannot pronounce a treaty void—Supposed case of Mr. Girard—Whether the national government can cede the territory of a State.

In the postscript to my last number, I proposed to suspend my communications for some weeks, announcing, at the same time, several topics, which remained to be discussed. This annunciation seems not have been sufficiently explicit. I must be permitted, therefore, to state, in the use of different phraseology, the points, which ought still to be examined, before the strength of the Cherokee cause can be justly estimated.

Unless I am mistaken, it can be clearly shown,

That the original right of the Cherokees, confirmed and guaranteed by so many treaties, was not, and could not be, affected by the compact of 1802, between Georgia and the United States:

That Georgia so understood the matter, for a quarter of a century after the year 1802, as appears by numerous acts of her legislature:

That the proposed plan for removing the Indians is visionary, and derives no support from experience:

That the proposed guaranty of a new country would not be entitled to confidence; and that the offer of a guaranty, in present circumstances, would be esteemed by the Cherokees a cruel insult:

That the actual removal of the southwestern tribes, would, in all probability, be followed by great evils to them, without any corresponding benefit to them, or to others; and That a conscientious man will be very cautious how he advises the Indians to yield their unquestionable rights, and to commit all their interests to the issue of a mere theoretical experiment, which, to say the least, is very likely to fail, and for the failure of which there can be neither remedy nor indemnity.

It has appeared, that the colony of Georgia, (with the cognizance of the British government,) and the State of Georgia, in the days of her youthful independence, negotiated with the Creeks and Cherokees on the undisputed basis, that these Indians were nations; that they had territorial and personal rights; that their territory was in remain in their possession, till they should voluntarily surrender it: and that treaties with them are as truly binding, as treaties are between any communities whatever. Such is the aspect of all the transactions, in relation to this subject; and no candid reader of history can avoid these conclusions. Seven formal treaties, all possessing these general characteristics, have been already mentioned. The last of them was dated in the year 1783, just fifty years from the first settlement of the colony. It is probable, that, within this period, many subordinate negotiations were held.

The treaty of Galphinton was formed in the year 1784, and is not unfrequently referred to. The next year, a treaty of peace was made between Georgia and the Creeks. I have not been able to find these two documents, nor to ascertain the provisions which they contain. Quotations made from them on the floor of Congress by a representative of Georgia, leave no room to doubt, that they are of the same general character, as the treaties which preceded them.

In 1787 the federal constitution was formed, by which the power of making treaties was conferred on the President and Senate of the United States. As this was a subject of great importance, the framers of the constitution not only took care (Art. III. section 2) to assign the treaty-making power of the general government, but to inhibit (Art. I. section 10) the several States from entering into "any treaty, alliance, or confederation." Since the constitution was adopted, no State has negotiated with Indians. All public measures respecting them have fallen within the scope of the powers vested in the general government.

Georgia, in her character of a sovereign and independent State, adopted the constitution, and thus became a member of the Union. She must be bound, therefore, by all acts of the President and Senate, which are performed by virtue of powers conferred in the constitution. Very recently, some of her public men have asserted, that the United States have neither the power to make treaties with Indians, nor to cede any part of the territory of a State.

The power to make treaties with Indians is denied on the ground, that treaties can be made with *nations only*; and that communities of Indians are not *nations.* Unfortunately for this theory, it was notoriously invented to answer a particular purpose. It is not, and cannot be, entitled to the least degree of credit. Communities of Indians have been called nations, in every book of travels, geography, and history, in which they have been mentioned at all, from the discovery of America to the present day. Treaties have been made with them, (uniformly under the *name* of treaties,) during this whole period. The monarchs of Europe, and the colonies of Europeans, were perpetually making treaties with Indians, in the course of the 17th and 18th centuries. The colony of Georgia always spoke of the Creek and Cherokee *nations*; and the compacts, which she made with them, she called *treaties*. The framers of the constitution must be supposed to have used language in its ordinary acceptation. When the constitution speaks of a *treaty*, it certainly embraces every sort of compact, which the universal voice of mankind had designated by that name.

It would seem, according to the present doctrine of Georgia politicians, that civilized people may be called nations and can make treaties; but uncivilized people are to be called savages, and public engagements with them are to be denominated—*what* such engagements are to be denominated, we are not as yet informed. There must be a new code of national law, and a new set of writers upon it, in order to help Georgia out of her present imagined difficulties—I say *imagined,* because there is no real difficulty; not the slightest. What are the distinctive marks of a civilized people, and who is to decide whether these marks are found in a given case, are matters unexplained. Nor are we told in what respects treaties between civilized nations are to be interpreted differently from public engagements with an uncivilized people.

A representative from Georgia said in his place last winter, that these "agreements with the Indians had improperly been called treaties." (Let it be borne in mind, that Georgia herself *always called them treaties*.) In a subsequent part of his speech, he spoke of the "bad faith" of the Creeks, in not observing the stipulations, which they had made in these "agreements;" and to this alleged *bad faith*, he gave the additional hard names of "*fraud and perfidy*." We may gather, therefore, the conclusion, that savages are bound by their *agreements*, though these agreements must not be called treaties. It is contended, however, that the United States are not bound by their agreements with the Cherokees, because the United States cannot in their federal capacity, make agreements with savages, although the general government has the exclusive power of making treaties with civilized nations: the whole of which philosophy and logic, when thoroughly digested and concocted, amounts to this;—that treaties between civilized nations bind both the parties; but that agreements with savage tribes, while they bind the savages, on the penalty of extermination, to observe every one of their engagements, leave civilized parties to break every one of their engagements, or "agreements," whenever it suits their pleasure, or their interest, to do so. This is the morality to be incorporated into the new code of national law, with another section declaring, that all parties to an agreement, even though it be called a treaty, have the perfect right to decide whether they are themselves civilized, or not, and whether other parties are uncivilized or not.

It is by no means favorable to this theory, that Washington, Hamilton, and Jefferson had the temerity, (following the uninterrupted current of example and authority, which had come down from the discovery of America,) to treat with Indians as nations, and to consider engagements with them as being treaties, within the meaning of the constitution. From the origin of our general government to the present day, every President of the United States, not excepting the present incumbent, has used the words treaty and nation, in precisely the same manner; and every Senate has confirmed the universal use.

Besides, the President and Senate must decide, from the nature of the case, what is a treaty, and what is not. Even the Supreme Court cannot pronounce a document not to be a treaty, which the President and Senate have pronounced to be one; for the constitution expressly declares treaties to be "the supreme law of the land, and the judges, in every State, to be bound thereby." If treaties are the supreme law, they cannot surely be pronounced null and void by any judicial tribunal.

Again, if the President and Senate should be justly chargeable with a mistake, in extending the treaty-making power to a subject, to which it was not properly applicable; and if the Supreme Court might decide, that a certain document, purporting to be a treaty, is only an agreement between the President and Senate of the United States and another party, although both parties had long understood it to be a treaty, and had observed it as such;—in such a case, what would honor and justice require? Should the people of the United States take advantage of a blunder made by their highest functionaries, and long acquiesced in? especially if the other party had reposed entire confidence in the validity of the proceeding, and had made important sacrifices in fulfilling his stipulations?

Suppose, for instance, that an agent of the United States had bought ships of Mr. Girard, for public purposes, to the amount of $100,000, and the contract had been sent to the Senate and ratified as a treaty. Here would have been a great blunder, no doubt; but is Mr. Girard to suffer by it? When he applies for payment, is he to be told, that the contract with him has improperly been called a treaty; that the President and Senate have no power to make treaties on such subjects; and that, therefore, he cannot be paid for his ships? Mr. Girard would be not a little amazed at this; and might naturally enough exclaim, that, in all his intercourse with mankind, he had never before met with so impudent, and so foolish, an attempt to cheat. As he grew cooler, he might say: "You have had my ships and sent them to sea. You engaged to pay me for them. If you called the contract a *treaty*, the name is one of your own choosing. Nor had I any thing to do with sending it to the Senate. I sold my ships to an authorized agent of the government, and he engaged that I should be paid for them. If the transaction is not a treaty, it is at least a *fair bargain*; and that is enough for me. I expect honest men, whether public or private, willingly to execute their bargains; and, as to dishonest men, I shall do all in my power to *hold them to their bargains*, whether they are willing, or not."

So the Cherokees may plead, that it was not for them to judge, as to the extent of the treaty-making power. They made an agreement with men, who represented their Father, the President. They supposed the President to know the extent of his own powers. At any rate, they relinquished land, and gave up many advantages, for the sake of a solemn guaranty in return. If the agreement which they made, was not a treaty, it was an *obligatory contract*; and they have a right to expect, and to demand, that the contract shall be fulfilled.

The politicians of Georgia contend, that, even if the United States have power to make treaties with Indians, still, they have no power to cede away the territory of a State. This objection cannot be supported, in any sense. But it is plausible; and the whole plausibility rests in a mere sophism. The United States have never ceded, not attempted to cede, any part of the territory of Georgia. They simply guaranteed to the Indians their original title; or, in other words, the United States solemnly engaged to the Indians, that no human power should deprive them of their hereditary possessions, without their own consent. This was no encroachment upon the rights of Georgia; nor did it relate at all to the territory of Georgia; which territory embraced those lands only, that had been previously obtained from the Indians. If the treaty of Holston were an encroachment upon the rights of

Georgia, why was there no complaint made at the time? The senators from Georgia were in their seats; and the citizens of Georgia were never charged, I believe, with passively surrendering their rights. Why, then, was no complaint made for more than thirty-five years?

But it is perfectly clear, that the United States *may* cede the territory of any State in the Union by treaty. Such an event may be very improbable; I care not if you say it is morally impossible, that the President and Senate should ever cede any part of what is really, and truly, the territory of a State. Yet, if such an event should take place, the transaction would not be void for want of constitutional power. The general government has the power to make treaties without limitation. Of course, treaties may be made by the United States, on all subjects which are frequently found in treaties of other nations. But there is scarcely a more common subject of treaties, in every part of the world, than a cession of territory. How are foreign nations to know the extent of our treaty-making power? If our President, and two-thirds of our Senators, will cede any part of our territory, there is no help for it. Our security lies, not in their want of power to do this; but in their want of inclination.

If the United States had ceded to England, all that part of the State of Maine, which was in possession of the British forces at the close of the last war, how can it be pretended that the treaty would not be binding? Indeed, at this very moment, there is a dispute about the boundaries of Maine. If the king of the Netherlands should egregiously mistake, in deciding the question now referred to him, which I admit to be very improbable;—still, if he should mistake, the State of Maine will lose 7,000,000 acres of land; and all this will be lost by the operation of the treaty of Ghent.

Proud nations have often been mortified, by being obliged to cede some part of their territory. It is not probable that our mortifications will come from that quarter. We have, however, not a few permanent causes of severe mortification. If it should be said, five hundred years hence, that in the middle of the nineteenth century the United States were compelled, by an overwhelming force, to cede State Island to a foreign power, the fact would not be a thousandth part so disgraceful, as to have it truly said that the United States adopted from Georgia, the maxim, that power is right; and, in pursuance of that maxim, despoiled an unoffending and suffering people, of those very possessions, which WE HAD SOLEMNLY GUARANTEED TO THEM FOREVER.

William Penn

No. XXIV

Plan for the removal of the Indians—Objections to it—invented for the benefit of the whites—It speaks too much of generosity, too little of justice—It is visionary—The Indians unwilling to remove—No good place can be found for them—Government cannot fulfill its promises—There can be no guaranty—Privations of a removal, and quarrels afterwards—Where shall they remove next?—If removed, the Indians will not confide in the government—Conclusion.

I have now arrived at my closing number; in which I propose to examine the plan for the removal of the Indians beyond the Mississippi.

This plan, so far as its principles have been developed and sanctioned by the government, is as follows:—

Congress will set apart a tract of country west of the Arkansas territory, perhaps 150 miles long and 100 miles broad, and will guaranty it as a perpetual residence of Indians. Upon this tract will be collected numerous tribes, now resident in different States and Territories. The land will be divided among tribes and individuals, as Congress shall direct. The Indians, thus collected, will be governed by white rulers; that is, by agents of the United States; till the time shall arrive, when they can be safely trusted with the government of themselves. At present they are to be treated as children, and guarded with truly paternal solicitude. The United States will bear the expense of a removal; and will furnish implements of agriculture, the mechanical arts, schools and other means of civilization. Intruders will be excluded. Ardent spirits will not be allowed to pass the line of demarcation. And, as a consequence of all these kind and precautionary measures, it is supposed that all the Indians will rise rapidly in various respect; that they will be contented and happy in their new condition; and that the government will merit and receive the appellation of benefactors. This is the plan; and the following considerations appear to my mind in the light of objections to it:—

1. It is a suspicious circumstance, that the wishes and supposed interests of the whites, and not the benefit of the Indians, afford all the impulse, under which Georgia and her advocates appear to act. The Indians are in the way of the whites; and this is at bottom of the plan. But if the Cherokees had been cheerfully admitted, by the inhabitants of Georgia, to possess an undoubted right to the permanent occupation of their country; and if this admission were made in terms of kindness, and with a view to good neighborhood, according to Mr. Jefferson's promise embodied in a treaty;—if such had been the state of things, we should have heard nothing of the present scheme. Is it likely that a plan conceived in existing circumstances, and with the sole view of yielding to unrighteous and unreasonable claims, can be beneficial in its operation upon the Indians? A very intelligent member of Congress from the west declared to the writer of these numbers, that the design of the parties most interested was, to destroy the Indians, and not to save them. I do not vouch for the accuracy of this opinion; but it is an opinion not confined to one, or two, or twenty of our public men. At any rate there is no uncharitableness in saying, that Georgia is actuated by a desire to get the lands of the Cherokees; for she openly avows it. As little can it be doubted, that the plan in question is suited to accomplish her desires. It is not common, for a party deeply interested, to devise the most kind and benevolent way of treating another party, whose interests lie in a different direction.

2. The plan is to be distrusted, because its advocates talk much of future generosity and kindness; but say nothing of the present obligations of honor, truth, and justice. What should we say, in private life, to a man, who refused to pay his bond, under hand and seal,—a bond, which he did not dispute,

and which he had acknowledged before witnesses a hundred times over,—and yet should ostentatiously profess himself disposed to make a great many handsome presents to the obligee, if the obligee would only be so discreet as to deliver up the bond? Would it not be pertinent to say, "Sir, *be just before you are generous*;—first pay your bond, and talk of presents afterwards?"

Let the government of the United States follow the advice given by Chancellor Kent to the State of New York. Let our public functionaries say to the Cherokees; "The United States are bound to you. The stipulations are plain; and you have a perfect right to demand their literal fulfillment. Act your own judgment. Consult your own interests. Be assured that we shall never violate treaties." If this language were always used; if *acknowledged obligations* were kept in front of every overture; there would be less suspicion attending advice, professedly given for the good of the Indians. It is not my province to question the motives of individuals, who advise the Cherokees to remove. No doubt many of these advisers are sincere. Some of them are officious; and should beware how they obtrude their opinions, in case of which they are profoundly ignorant, and in a manner calculated only to weaken the righteous cause. All advisers, of every class, should begin their advice with an *explicit admission of present obligations.*

3. The plan in question appears to me entirely visionary. There has been no experience among men to sustain it. Indeed, theoretical plans of government, even though supposed to be founded on experience gained in different circumstances, have uniformly and utterly failed. So wise and able a man as Mr. Locke was totally incompetent, as the experiment proved, to form a government for an American colony. But what sort of a community is to be formed here? Indians of different tribes, speaking different languages, in different states of civilization, are to be crowded together under one government. They have all heretofore lived under the influence of their hereditary customs, improved, in some cases, by commencing civilization; but they are now to be crowded together, under a government unlike any other that ever was seen. Whether Congress is to be employed in digesting a municipal code for these congregated Indians, and in mending it from session to session; or whether the President of the United States is to be the sole legislator; or whether the business is to be delegated to a civil or military prefect, we are not told. What is to be the tenure of land;—what the title to individual property;—what the rules of descent;—what the modes of conveyance;—what the redress for grievances;—these and a thousand other things are entirely unsettled. Indeed, it is no easy matter to settle them. Such a man as Mr. Livingston may form a code for Louisiana, though it requires uncommon talents to do it. But ten such men as he could not form a code for a heterogeneous mixture of Indians.

If this embarrassment were removed, and a perfect code of aboriginal law was formed, how shall suitable administration be found? Is it probable that the agents and sub-agents of the United States will unite all the qualifications of Solon and Howard? Would it be strange if some of them were indolent, unkind, partial, and dissolute? and if the majority were much more intent on the emoluments of office, than on promoting the happiness of the Indians? One of the present Indian agents, a very respectable and intelligent man, assured me, that the plan for the removal of the Indians was altogether chimerical, and, if pursued, would end in their destruction. He may be mistaken; but his personal experience in relation to the subject is much greater than that of any person who has been engaged in forming or recommending the plan.

4. The four southwestern tribes are unwilling to remove. They ought not to be confounded with the northern Indians, as they are in very different circumstances. The Cherokees and Choctaws are rapidly improving their condition. The Chickasaws have begun to follow in the same course. These tribes, with the Creeks, are attached to their native soil, and very reluctant to leave it. Of this the evidence is most abundant. No person acquainted with the actual state of things can deny, that the feelings of the great mass of these people, apart from extraneous influence, are decidedly and strongly opposed to a removal. Some of them, when pressed upon the subject, may remain silent. Others, knowing how little argument avails against power, may faintly answer, that they will go, *if they must* and *if a suitable place can be found for them.* At the very moment, when they are saying this, they will add their strong conviction, that no suitable place can be found. In a word, these tribes will not remove, unless by compulsion, or in the apprehension of force to be used hereafter.

5. The Indians assert, that there is not a sufficient quantity of good land in the contemplated tract, to accommodate half their present numbers; to say nothing of the other tribes to be thrust into their company. Even the agents of the United States, who have been employed with a special view to make the scheme popular, admit that there is a deficiency of wood and water. Without wood for fences and buildings, and for shelter against the furious northwestern blasts of winter, the Indians cannot be comfortable. Without running streams, they can never keep livestock; nor could they easily dig wells and cisterns for the use of their families. The vast prairies of the west will ultimately be inhabited. But it would require all the wealth, the enterprise, and the energy of Anglo-Americans, to make a prosperous settlement upon them. Nor, if the judgment of travelers is to be relied on, will such a settlement be made, till the pressure of population renders it necessary. The most impartial accounts of the country, to the west of Missouri and Arkansas, unite in representing it as a boundless prairie, with narrow stripes of forest trees, on the margin of rivers. The good land, including all that could be brought into use by partially civilized men, is stated to be comparatively small.

6. Government cannot fulfill its promise to emigrating Indians. It is incomparably easier to keep intruders from the Cherokees where they now are, than it will be to exclude them from the new country. The present neighbours of the Cherokees are, to a considerable extent, men of some property, respectable agriculturists, who would not think of any encroachment, if the sentence of the law were promoted firmly in favor of the occupants of the soil. Stealing from the Indians is by no means so common, as it was fifteen years ago. One reason is, that the worst class of white settlers has migrated farther west. They are stated, even now, to hover around the emigrant Creeks, like vultures. It may be laid down as a maxim, that so long as Indians possess any thing, which is an object of cupidity to the whites, they will be exposed to the frauds of interested speculators, or the intrusions of idle and worthless vagrants; and the farther removed Indians are from the notice of the

government, the greater will be their exposure to the arts, or the violence, of selfish and unprincipled men.

Twenty years hence, Texas, whether it shall belong to the United States or not, will have been settled by the descendants of Anglo-Americans. The State of Missouri will then be populous. There will be great roads through the new Indian country, and caravans will be passing and repassing in many directions. The emigrant Indians will be *denationalized*, and will have no common bond of union. Will it be possible, in such circumstances, to enforce the laws against intruders?

7. If the Indians remove from their native soil, it is not possible that they should receive a satisfactory guaranty of a new country. If a guaranty is professedly made by a compact called a *treaty*, it will be done at the very moment that treaties with Indians are declared not to be binding, and for the very reason that existing treaties are not strong enough to bind the United States. To what confidence would such an engagement be entitled?

It is now pretended that President Washington, and the Senate of 1790, had no power to guaranty to Indians the lands on which they were born, and for which they were then able to contend vigourously, at the muzzle of our guns. Who can pledge himself, that it will not be contended, ten years hence, that President Jackson, and the Senate of 1830, had no constitutional power to set apart territory for the permanent residence of the Indians? Will it not then be asked, where is the clause in the constitution, which authorized the establishment of a new and anomalous government, in the heart of North America? The constitution looked forward to the admission of the New States into the Union: but does it say any thing about Indian States? Will the men of 1840, or 1850, be more tender of the reputation of President Jackson, than the men of the present day are of the reputation of President Washington? Will they not say, that the pretended treaty of 1830, (if a treaty should now be made,) was an act of sheer usurpation? that it was known to be such at the time, and was never intended to be kept? that every man of sense in the country considered the removal of 1830, to be one of the few steps, necessary to the utter extermination of the Indian? That the Indians were avowedly considered as children, and the word *treaty* was used as a plaything to amuse them, and to pacify grown up children among the whites?

If the design is not to be accomplished by a treaty, but by an act of Congress, the questions recurs, Whence did Congress derive the constitutional power to make an Indian State, 150 miles long and 100 miles broad, in the heart of this continent? Besides, if Congress has the constitutional power to pass such an act, has it not the power of repealing the act? Has it not also the power of making a new State of whites, encircling the Indian community, and entitled to exercise the same power over the Indians, which the State of Alabama and Mississippi now claim the right of exercising over the four southwestern tribes? Will it be said, that the contemplated Indian community will have been first established, and received its guaranty, and that therefore Congress cannot inclose the Indians in a new State? Let it be remembered, that the Creeks and Cherokees received their guaranty about thirty years before the State of Alabama came into existence; and yet that State claims the Indians within its chartered limits, as being under its proper jurisdiction; and has already begun to enforce the claim. Let not the government trifle with the word guaranty. If the Indians are removed, let it be said, in an open and manly tone, that they are removed because we have the power to remove them, and there is a political reason for doing it; and that they will be removed again, whenever the whites demand their removal, in a style sufficiently clamorous and imperious to make trouble for the government.

8. The constrained migration of 60,000 souls, men, women, and children, most of them in circumstances of deep poverty, must be attended with much suffering.

9. Indians of different tribes, speaking different languages, and all in a state of vexation and discouragement, would live on bad terms with each other, and quarrels would be inevitable.

10. Another removal will soon be necessary. If the emigrants become poor, and are transformed into vagabonds, it will be evidence enough, that no benevolent treatment can save them, and it will be said that they may as well be driven beyond the Rocky Mountains at once. If they live comfortably, it will prove that five times as many white people might live comfortably in their places. Twenty-five years hence, there will probably be 4,000,000 of our population west of the Mississippi, and fifty years hence not less than 15,000,000. By that time, the pressure upon the Indians will be much greater from the boundless prairies, which must ultimately be subdued and inhabited, than it would ever have been from the borders of the present Cherokee country.

11. If existing treaties are not observed, the Indians can have no confidence in the United States. They will consider themselves as paupers and mendicants, reduced to that condition by acts of gross oppression, and then taken by the government, and stowed away in a crowded workhouse.

12. The moment a treaty for removal is signed by any tribe of Indians, on the basis of the contemplated plan, that moment such tribe is *denationalized*; for the essence of the plan is, that all the tribes shall come under one government, which is to be administered by whites. There will be no party to complain, even if the pretended treaty should be totally disregarded. A dead and mournful silence will reign; for the Indian communities will have been blotted out forever. Individuals will remain to feel that they are vassals, and to sink unheeded to despondency, despair, and extinction.

But the memory of these transactions will not be forgotten. A bitter roll will be unfolded, on which *Mourning, Lamentation, and Woe, to the people of the United States* will be seen written in characters, which no eye can refuse to see.

Government has arrived at the bank of the Rubicon. If our rulers now stop, they may save the country from the charge of bad faith. If they proceed, it will be known by all men, that in a plain case, without any plausible plea of necessity, and for very weak and unsatisfactory reasons, the great and boasting Republic of the United States of North American, *incurred the guilt of violating treaties*; and that this guilt was incurred when the subject was fairly before the eyes of the American community, and had attracted more attention than any other public measure since the close of the last war.

In one of the sublimest portions of Divine Revelation, the following words are written:

Cursed be he, that removeth his neighbour's landmark: and all the people shall say, Amen.

Cursed be he, that maketh the blind to wander out of the way; and all the people shall say, Amen.

Cursed be he that perverteth the judgment of the stranger, fatherless, and widow; and all the people shall say, Amen.

Is it possible that our national rulers shall be willing to expose themselves and their country to these curses of Almighty God? Curses uttered to a people, in circumstances not altogether unlike our own? Curses reduced to writing by the inspired lawgiver, for the terror and warning of all nations, and receiving the united and hearty *Amen* of all people to whom they have been made known?

It is now proposed to remove the landmarks, in every sense;—to disregard territorial boundaries, definitely fixed, and for many years respect;—to disregard a most obvious principle of natural justice, in accordance with which the possessor of property is to hold it, till some one claims it, who has a better right;—to forget the doctrine of the law of nations, that engagements with dependent allies are as rigidly to be observed, as stipulations between communities of equal power and sovereignty;—to shut our ears to the voice of our own sages of the law, who say, that Indians have a *right to retain possession of their land, and to use it according to their discretion,* antecedently to any positive compacts; and finally, to dishonor Washington, the Father of his country,—to stultify the Senate of the United States during a period of thirty-seven years,—to burn 150 documents, as yet preserved in the archives of State, under the denomination of treaties with Indians, and to tear out sheets from every volume of our national statute-book and scatter them to the winds.

Nothing of this kind has ever yet been done, certainly not on a large scale, by Anglo-Americans. To us, as a nation, it will be a new thing under the sun. We have never yet acted upon the principle of seizing the lands of peaceable Indians, and compelling them to remove. We have never yet declared treaties with them to be mere waste paper.

Let it be taken for granted, then, that *law will prevail.* "Of law," says the judicious Hooker, in strains which have been admired for their beauty and eloquence ever since they were written,—"Of law there can be no less acknowledged, than that her seat is the bosom of God; her voice the harmony of the world. All things in heaven and earth do her homage; the very least as feeling her care, and the greatest as not exempted from her power. Both angels and man, and creatures of what condition soever, each in different sort and order, yet all with uniform consent, admiring her as the mother of their peace and joy."

Source: William Penn [Jeremiah Evarts]. *On the Present Crisis in the Condition of the American Indian.* Philadelphia: Thomas Kite, 1830.

18. Letter from Chickasaw Chiefs to Andrew Jackson (1835)

A common complaint by Indians regarding treaties their tribes had made with the United States was—and still is—that the treaties, as explained by federal spokesmen, said something different from what the Indians understood the treaties to say. So it was with removal treaties. For the Chickasaws, it was a misunderstanding by federal officials of what the Chickasaw negotiators meant by the term *head of household*. As the following letter from the Chickasaw chiefs to Andrew Jackson on December 24, 1835, demonstrates, the meaning of the term as the Americans understood it in their application of the Treaty of Pontotoc (1832) and the Articles of Convention and Agreement (1834) not only created an inequality in the distribution of Chickasaw land but also undermined the matrilineal practice of descent and inheritance.

To His Excellency, Andrew Jackson
    President of the United States of America
    The undersigned, a portion of the Chickasaw Nation of Indians, respectfully entreat the attention and consideration of the President, to the construction which has been placed, upon a most important clause of the last Treaty between their Nation and the United States.
    The clause of the Treaty, to which they refer, is a part of the Fifth Article of the treaty made at Washington and ratified on the first day of July 1834, and is in these words—"It is agreed that the fourth article of the 'Treaty of Pontitock' be so changed that the following reservations be granted in fee:—To heads of families, being Indians, or having Indian families, consisting of ten persons, and upwards, four sections of land are reserved. To those who have five and less than ten persons, three sections. Those who have five and less than ten persons, three sections. Those who have less than five, two sections. Also those who own more than ten slaves, shall be entitled to one additional section; and those owning ten and less than ten to half a section."
    Under that clause, it has been held, that where an Indian had at the time of the ratification of the Treaty, two or more wives, in all cases such wives and their respective children, shall be numbered together as one family, each wife being counted, and that the husband as the head of such family shall be entitled to a reservation accordingly.
    The undersigned have been induced to submit this subject to the consideration of the President, from a belief that such a construction is different from the intention of those who made the Treaty on the part of their Nation, from a fear that it will deprive many families of that provision which it was the object of the Treaty to secure, and from an anxious desire to prevent future jealousies and dissensions, which will not be so apt to arise if those, whose rights are implicated in this question, shall know that it has been decided by the highest authority, and upon a full consideration of all the circumstances by which it is attended.

The undersigned respectfully submit, that it was the primary object of the Treaty, to secure a provision for every Indian family, without exception, and that in pursuance of that object a reservation in fee of a certain number of sections of land was granted to the head of every such family: That the question "What is an Indian family?" ought to be decided except so far as it may be controlled by the words of the Treaty, by reference to what is considered 'a family' according to the Customs and manners of life among the Chickasaws.

The undersigned believe that as well the Treaty of the first of March 1833 made at Pontitock, as the Treaty of the first of July 1834 made at Washington, is entirely silent in relation to the case of an Indian having a plurality of wives; that such case is not expressly provided for in either Treaty, and indeed, does not seem to have entered into the contemplation of those by whom they were penned; for had it been otherwise, a case so likely to produce embarrassment and difficulty would not have been left to conjecture.

The undersigned submit to the consideration of the President, whether there be any expressions in the Treaties above referred to, which warrant the conclusion that the several wives of an Indian and their respective children are to be considered, with reference to the grant of reservations as one family? And they suggest, that, in the absence of any express intention, it would be wrong to construe any particular words or clauses of the said Treaties so as to disappoint any of the proper objects of the grant contained therein, and especially where such words and clauses are inserted for another object, and may have another and more proper effect. For instance, there is a clause in the fourth article of the 'Treaty of Pontitock' in these words;—"If any person shall now occupy two places and wish to retain both, they may do so, by taking a part at one place and a part at the other." Now it frequently happens, that an Indian has several wives living at different places, and from the clause last quoted, it might be inferred to be the intention of the Treaty, that such Indian with his several wives was only entitled to one reservation, to be taken a part at the residence of one and a part at the residence of the other. But when it is considered, that many among the more opulent of the Chickasaws have plantations and stock-farms at a distance from their main residence, the latter frequently being situated in a poor but healthy section of the country, it is obvious that the clause was inserted to meet such cases. And, yet, this is the strongest and perhaps the only clause in either of the Treaties, in support of the construction under consideration.

On the contrary, it may be said, that in the event of the death of an Indian having several wives a considerable difficulty may occur under the present construction. It is provided by the sixth article of the Treaty of Washington, that when a party owning a reservation "shall die, the interest in the same shall, belong to the wife, or to the wife and children." A rule which is to endure for five years or until the Chickasaws leave their present home. Now, in what manner would one reservation be divided, among several wives and their respective children? Would all the wives be considered as one, or would each take a child's part? Again, about ten persons seem to be considered by the Treaty, as the probable number in the largest family, which is usually as many as are the children of one mother, but an Indian, from several wives, has often many more. The late distinguished chief Levi Colbert, for instance, left upwards of twenty children, the offspring of his several wives. And, thus, a reservation that would be an ample provision for a family of ten persons, might be very inadequate for a family of twenty or thirty.

Admitting, that the question 'What is an Indian family?' is not answered by the Treaties, and depends on the meaning to be given to the word 'family' as it is therein used, the undersigned contend, that according to the customs of the Chickasaws and their manner of life, the several wives of an Indian, and their respective children, do not constitute one family, in the proper sense of that word.

The matrimonial connection among the Chickasaws is slight, it is contracted without formality, and dissolved at the pleasure of either party. From that cause and the allowance of a plurality of wives, it follows as a natural consequence, that a descent is always traced through the maternal line, the succession of their Kings ever having been determined in that way. The father is not considered to be under any obligation to support his children, the care and nurture of them is exclusively the duty of the mother, and after her death is devolved on her female relations, the father frequently taking no further concern in their welfare. On the death of the father, the children do not inherit his property, but his oldest collateral relations; and it frequently happens, that by them the wife and children are stripped of all his property.

It is an ancient and universal law among the Chickasaws, that the wife has a separate estate in all her property, whether derived to her from her relations or acquired by her, with full liberty to dispose of it in any manner she may please. Where an Indian has several wives, they generally keep separate establishments, often at a distance from each other, and very rarely, if ever except when they are sisters, living together in the same house. The home of each is regarded as her own, and is generally so known and distinguished by the community. Their respective children claim no relationship, but are to each other as strangers.

The undersigned forbear to mention more of the Indian laws and customs having a reference to this subject from a conviction that they are by no one better known and understood than by the President, and they confidently submit to his determination, whether each of the several wives of an Indian with her children, does not constitute a separate family, and by consequence, a distinct object of the grant made by the Treaty?

It may be said, that a difficulty will arise, in such cases, in deciding whether the reservations are to vest in the wives as heads of their respective families, or whether the husband shall take distinct reservations in right of his several wives. Admitting, that one reservation is vested in the husband, with the expectation that he will dispose of it for the support and benefit of one family, the undersigned can perceive no reason, why several reservations may not be vested in him with the expectation that he will dispose of them, for the support and benefit of several families. It is true, such husband may dissolve his connection with one of his wives, and thereby cut off her and her children from any provision, but it is equally true, and just as likely to happen, that an Indian husband may dissolve his connection with an only wife, and the same consequence would follow. It may be objected, that an Indian having several wives would receive an undue share of the land, considering him as an individual, this may be true, but regarding the rights of the several families which he represents, there is only an apparent not a real inequality; and although the share which he would receive might be large, so might be the number of those for whose benefit it was intended. From these reasons, the undersigned have been brought to the conclusion, that where an Indian had at the date of the ratification of the Treaty two or more wives all residing together with him, or having separate residences, he had resided with, and treated them, equally as wives, distinct reservations have vested in the husband according to the number of the several families of which he is the head.

But there are some cases, in relation to which it might be proper to draw a different conclusion from a correct construction of the Treaty, and say, that reservations have vested in the wives as heads of their respective families. It frequently happens that an Indian has two or more wives, with one of whom he almost exclusively resides, and only occasionally visits the others. The latter cannot be considered as having any thing more than the name of wives, but that has been deemed sufficient to make them part of the family of their nominal husband, and virtually excluded them from any benefit under the Treaty. Although they may be known among the Indians by the same common appellation the undersigned believe that it would be in perfect accordance with the spirit of the Treaty to consider them not as wives, but as distinct heads of families and entitled to reservations accordingly.

There is another class of these claimants whose case is attended by peculiar circumstances, if the change produced in the domestic relations of the Indians, by the extension of the laws of the State over them, is to be regarded in the construction of the Treaty.

By the Fourth section of an act passed by the Legislature of the State of Mississippi on the nineteenth day of January 1830, it is enacted "That all marriages, matrimonial connections or associations entered into by virtue of any 'usage or custom of the said Indians, and by them deemed valid, be, and the same are hereby declared to be as binding and obligatory, as if the same had been solemnized according to the laws of this State.'" There is no provision in the act in relation to marriages among the Indians to be contracted after its date; such marriages seem to have been left to the general laws of the State, to the operation of which the Indians are expressly subjected. By those laws a second marriage, being a former wife, is null and void, with whatever legal formalities it may have been contracted.

Now, where an Indian, after the passage of the act above referred to, and before the date of the ratification of the Treaty of Washington, has formed a matrimonial connection under the Indian custom with a woman, and had at the same time a wife or wives living, the undersigned submit to the determination of the President, whether she is not entitled to a reservation in her own name as the head of a family, or as a claimant under the sixth article of the Treaty of Washington, according to the situation in which she stood, when that Treaty was ratified.

In conclusion, the undersigned respectfully suggest, that no consideration of policy should prevent a construction of the Treaty so liberal as to embrace every object within the true spirit and meaning of its provision, for it is now generally conceded, that, after defraying all charges, a fund of several millions of dollars will be obtained from that part of the Chickasaw lands not taken by the reservations.

The undersigned, therefore, most respectively request, that the subject of this memorial may receive the examination of the President, and that, so far as any of the claimants, in whose behalf it is presented, have rights which ought to be allowed, the proper directions may be given for that purpose; but if their claims should appear to the President not to be valid, then, that his decision may be communicated, through the Agent of the Chickasaw Indians, for the satisfaction of those concerned, thereby showing to them, that though they may be disappointed, they have not been forgotten.

Ishtahotopa, King X mark
Martin Colbert
Pistalatubba X mark
Capt. Mcgilbry X mark
Emubba X mark
Stemullucky X mark
Stemoker X mark
Mahulatubba X mark
Karohar X mark
George Colbert X mark
Isaac Alberson X mark
James Colbert

Source: Ishtehotopa et al. to Andrew Jackson, December 24, 1835, National Archives Microfilm, Microcopy M234, Roll 136, Frames 608ff.

19. Excerpt from Memorial and Protest of the Cherokee to the Honourable the Senate and House of Representatives of the United States of North America, in Congress Assembled (1836)

The leadership of the anti-removal majority of the Cherokee Nation filed this protest of the Treaty of New Echota six months after its signing. At the time, representatives of both parties were in Washington lobbying officials. This document, along with "John Ross's Letter to a Friend," was published as a pamphlet and reprinted in sympathetic journals and newspapers. It also elicited the response of Elias Boudinot, writing for the Treaty Party.

The undersigned representatives of the Cherokee nation, east of the river Mississippi, impelled by duty, would respectfully submit, for the consideration of your honourable body, the following statement of facts: It will be seen, from the numerous subsisting treaties between the Cherokee nation and the United States, that from the earliest existence of this government, the United States, in congress assembled, received the Cherokees and their nation into favour and protection; and that the chiefs and warriors, for themselves and all parts of the Cherokee nation, acknowledged themselves and the said Cherokee nation to be under the protection of the United States of America, and of no other sovereign whatsoever; they also stipulated, that the said Cherokee nation will not hold any treaty with any foreign power, individual state, or with individuals of any state: that for, and in consideration of, valuable concessions made by the Cherokee nation, the United States solemnly guaranteed to said nation all their lands not ceded, and pledged the faith of the government, that "all white people who have intruded, or may hereafter intrude on the lands reserved for the Cherokees, shall be removed by the United States, and proceeded against," according to the provisions of the act, passed 30th March, 1802, entitled "An act to regulate trade and intercourse with the Indian tribes, and to preserve peace on the frontiers." It would be useless to recapitulate the numerous provisions for the security and protection of the rights of the Cherokees, to be found in the various treaties between their nation and the United States. The Cherokees were happy and prosperous under a scrupulous observance of treaty stipulations by the government of the United States, and, from the fostering hand extended over them, they made rapid advances in civilization, morals, and in the arts and sciences. Little did they anticipate, that when taught to think and feel as the American citizen, and to have with him a common interest, they were to be *despoiled by their guardian*, to become strangers and wanderers in the land of their fathers, forced to return to the savage life, and to seek a new home in the wilds of the far west, and that without their consent. An instrument purporting to be a treaty with the Cherokee people, has recently been made public by the president of the United States, that will have such an operation, if carried into effect. This instrument, the delegation aver before the civilized world, and in the presence of Almighty God, is fraudulent, false upon its face, made by unauthorized individuals, without the sanction, and against the wishes, of the great body of the Cherokee people. Upwards of fifteen thousand of those people have protested against it, solemnly declaring they will never acquiesce. The delegation would respectfully call the attention of your honourable body to their memorial and protest, with the accompanying documents, submitted to the senate of the United States, on the subject of the alleged treaty, which are herewith transmitted.

If it be said that the Cherokees have lost their national character and political existence, as a nation or tribe, by state legislation, then the president and senate can make no treaty with them; but if they have not, then no treaty can be made for them, binding, without and against their will. Such is the fact, in reference to the instrument entered into at New Echota, in

December last. If treaties are to be thus made and enforced, deceptive to the Indians and to the world, purporting to be a contract, when, in truth, wanting the assent of one of the pretended parties, what security would there be for any nation or tribe to retain confidence in the United States? If interest or policy require that the Cherokees be removed, without their consent, from their lands, surely the president and senate have no constitutional power to accomplish that object. They cannot do it under the power to make treaties, which are contracts, not rules prescribed by a superior, and therefore binding only by the assent of the parties. In the present instance, the assent of the Cherokee nation has not been given, but expressly denied. The president and senate cannot do it under the power to regulate commerce with the Indian tribes, or intercourse with them, because that belongs to congress, and so declared by the president, in his message to the senate of February 22, 1831, relative to the execution of the act to regulate trade and intercourse with the Indian tribes, &c. passed 30th of March, 1802. They cannot do it under any subsisting treaty stipulation with the Cherokee nation. Nor does the peculiar situation of the Cherokees, in reference to the states, their necessities and distresses, confer any power upon the president and senate to alienate their legal rights, or to prescribe the manner and time of their removal.

Without a decision of what ought to be done, under existing circumstances, the question recurs, is the instrument under consideration a contract between the United States and the Cherokee nation? It so purports upon its face, and that falsely. Is that statement so sacred and conclusive that the Cherokee people cannot be heard to deny the fact? They have denied it under their own signatures, as the documents herein before referred to will show, and protested against the acts of the unauthorized few who have arrogated to themselves the right to speak for the nation. The Cherokees have said they will not be bound thereby. The documents submitted to the senate show, that when the vote was taken upon considering the propositions of the commissioner, there were but seventy-nine for so doing. Then it comes to this: could this small number of persons attending the New Echota meeting, acting in the individual capacity, dispose of the rights and interests of the Cherokee nation, or by any instrument they might sign, confer such power upon the president and senate?

If the United States are to act as the guardian of the Cherokees, and to treat them as incapable of managing their own affairs, and blind to their true interests, yet this would not furnish power or authority to the president and senate, as the treaty-making power, to prescribe the rule for managing their affairs. It may afford pretence for the legislation of congress, but none for the ratification of an instrument as a treaty made by a small faction against the protest of the Cherokee people.

That the Cherokees are a distinct people, sovereign to some extent, have a separate political existence as a society, or body politic, and a capability of being contracted with in a national capacity, stands admitted by the uniform practice of the United States from 1785, down to the present day. With them have treaties been made through their chiefs, and distinguished men in primary assemblies, as also with their constituted agents or representatives. That they have not the right to manage their own internal affairs, and to regulate, by treaty, their intercourse with other nations, is a doctrine of modern date. In 1793, Mr. Jefferson said, "I consider our right of pre-emption of the Indian lands, not as amounting to any dominion, or jurisdiction, or paramountship whatever, but merely in the nature of a remainder, after the extinguishment of a present right, which gives us no present right whatever, but of preventing other nations from taking possession, and so defeating our expectancy. That the Indians *have the full, undivided, and independent sovereignty as long as they choose to keep it, and that this may be for ever.*" This opinion was recognized and practised upon, by the government of the United States, through several successive administrations, also recognised by the supreme court of the United States, and the several states, when the question has arisen. It has not been the opinion only of jurists, but of politicians, as may be seen from various reports of secretaries of war—beginning with Gen. Knox, also the correspondence between the British and American ministers at Ghent in the year 1814. If the Cherokees have power to judge of their own interests, and to make treaties, which, it is presumed, will be denied by none, then, to make a contract valid, the assent of a majority must be had, expressed by themselves or through their representatives, and the president and senate have no power to say what their will shall be, for from the laws of nations we learn that "though a nation be obliged to promote, as far as lies in its power, the perfection of others, it is not entitled forcibly to obtrude these good offices on them." Such an attempt would be to violate their natural liberty. Those ambitious Europeans who attacked the American nations, and subjected them to their insatiable avidity of dominion, in order, as they pretended, for civilizing them, and causing them to be instructed in the true religion, (as in the present instance to preserve the Cherokees as a distinct people,) these usurpers grounded themselves on a pretence equally unjust and ridiculous. It is the expressed wish of the government of the United States to remove the Cherokees to a place west of the Mississippi. That wish is said to be founded in humanity to the Indians. To make their situation more comfortable, and to preserve them as a distinct people. Let facts show how this *benevolent* design has been prosecuted, and how faithfully to the spirit and letter has the promise of the president of the United States to the Cherokees been fulfilled—that "*those who remain may be assured of our patronage, our aid, and good neighbourhood.*" The delegation are not deceived by empty professions, and fear their race is to be destroyed by the mercenary policy of the present day, and their lands wrested from them by physical force; as proof, they will refer to the preamble of an act of the general assembly of Georgia, in reference to the Cherokees, passed the 2d of December, 1835, where it is said, "from a knowledge of the Indian character, and from the present feelings of these Indians, it is confidently believed, that the right of occupancy of the lands in their possession should be withdrawn, *that it would be a strong inducement to them to treat with the general government, and consent to a removal to the west;* and whereas the present legislature openly avow that their primary object in these measures intended to be pursued, *are founded on real humanity to these Indians,* and with a view, in a distant region, to perpetuate them with their old identity of character, *under the paternal care of the government of the United States;* at the same time frankly disavowing *any selfish or sinister motives towards them in their present legislation."* This is the profession. Let us turn to the practice of *humanity,* to the Cherokees, by the state of Georgia. In violation of the treaties between the United States and the Cherokee nation, that state passed a law requiring all white men, residing in that part of the Cherokee country, in her limits, to take an oath of allegiance to the state of Georgia. For a violation of this law, some of the ministers of Christ, missionaries among the Cherokees, were tried, convicted, and sentenced to hard labour in the penitentiary. Their case may be seen by reference to the records of the supreme court of the United States.

Valuable gold mines were discovered upon the Cherokee lands, within the chartered limits of Georgia, and the Cherokees commenced working them, and the legislature of that state interfered by passing an act, making it penal for an Indian to dig for gold within Georgia, no doubt "*frankly disavowing any selfish or sinister motives towards them.*" Under this law many Cherokees were arrested, tried, imprisoned, and otherwise abused. Some were even shot in attempting to avoid an arrest; yet the Cherokee people used no violence, but humbly petitioned the government of the United States for a fulfillment of treaty engagements, to protect them, which was not done, and the answer given that the United States could not interfere. Georgia discovered she was not to be obstructed in carrying out her measures, "*founded on real humanity to these Indians;*" she passed an act directing the Indian country to be surveyed into districts. This excited some alarm, but the Cherokees were quieted with the assurance it would do no harm to survey the country. Another act was shortly after passed, to lay off the country into *lots.* As yet there was no authority to take possession, but it was not long before a law was made, authorizing a lottery for the lands laid off into lots. In this act the Indians were secured in possession of all the lots touched by their improvements, and the balance of the country allowed to be occupied by white men. This was a direct violation of the fifth article of the treaty of the 27th of February, 1819. The Cherokees made no resistance, still petitioned the United States for protection, and received the same answer that the president could not interpose. After the country was parceled out by lottery, a horde of speculators made their appearance, and purchased of the "fortunate drawers," lots touched by Indian improvements, at reduced prices, declaring it was uncertain when the Cherokees would surrender their rights, and that the lots were encumbered by their claims. The consequence of the speculation was that, at the next session of the legislature, an act was passed limiting the Indian right of occupancy to the lot upon which he resided, and his actual improvements adjoining.

Many of the Cherokees filed bills, and obtained injunctions against dispossession, and would have found relief in the courts of the country, if the judiciary had not been prostrated at the feet of legislative power. For the opinion of a judge on this subject, there was an attempt to impeach him, then to limit his circuit to one county, and when all this failed, equity jurisdiction was taken from the courts, in Cherokee cases, by acts passed in the years 1833 and 1834. The Cherokees were then left at the mercy of an interested agent. This agent, under the act of 1834, was the notorious William N. Bishop, the captain of the Georgia Guard, aid to the governor, clerk of a court, postmaster, &c., and his mode of trying Indian rights is here submitted:

Murray Country, Georgia, Feb. 26, 1835.

Mr. John Martin,

Sir: the legal representative of lots of land [here lot descriptions appear] has called on me, as state's agent, to give him possession of the above described lots of land, and informs me that you are the occupant upon them. Under the laws of the state of Georgia, passed in the years 1833 and 1834, it is made my duty to comply with his request; you will, therefore, prepare yourself to give entire possession of said premises, on or before the 20th day of February next, fail not under the penalty of the law."

"Wm. N. Bishop, State's Agent."

Mr. Martin, a Cherokee, was a man of wealth, had an extensive farm, large fields of wheat growing, and was turned out of house and home, and compelled, in the month of February, to seek a new residence within the limits of Tennessee. Thus Mr. Bishop settled his rights according to the notice he had given. The same summary process was used towards Mr. John Ross, the principal chief of the Cherokee nation. He was at Washington city, on the business of his nation. When he returned, he travelled till about ten o'clock at night, to reach his family; rode up to the gate; saw a servant, believed to be his own; dismounted, ordered his horse taken; went in, and to his utter astonishment, found himself a stranger in his own house, his family having been, some days before, driven out to seek a new home. A thought then flitted across his mind, that he could not, under all the circumstances of his situation, reconcile it to himself to tarry all night under the roof of his own house as a stranger, the new host of that house being the tenant of that mercenary band of Georgia speculators, at whose instance his helpless family had been turned out and made homeless.

Upon reflecting, however, that "man is born unto trouble," Mr. Ross at once concluded to take up lodgings there for the night, and to console himself under the conviction of having met his afflictions and trials in a manner consistent with every principle of moral obligation towards himself and family, his country and his God. On the next morning he arose early, and went out into the yard, and saw some straggling herds of his cattle and sheep browsing about the place. His crop of corn undisposed of. In casting a look up into the wide-spread branches of a majestic oak, standing within the enclosure of the garden, and which overshadows the spot where lie the remains of his dear babe, and most beloved and affectionate father, he there saw, perched upon its boughs, that flock of beautiful pea-fowls, once the matron's care and delight, by now left to destruction and never more to be seen. He ordered his horse, paid his bill, and departed in search of his family: after travelling amid heavy rains, he had the happiness of overtaking them on the road, bound for some place of refuge within the limits of Tennessee. Thus have his houses, farm, public ferries, and other property, been seized and wrested from him. Mr. Richard Taylor was also at Washington, and in his absence his family was threatened with expulsion, and compelled to give two hundred dollars for leave to remain at home for a few months only. This is the "*real humanity*" the Cherokees were shown by the real or pretended authorities of Georgia, "disavowing any selfish or sinister motives towards them."

Mr. Joseph Vann, also a native Cherokee, was a man of great wealth, had about eight hundred acres of land in cultivation; had made extensive improvements, consisting, in part, of a brick house, costing about ten thousand dollars, mills, kitchens, negro houses, and other buildings. He had fine gardens, and extensive apple and peach orchards. His business was so extensive, he was compelled to employ an overseer and other agents. In the fall of 1833, he was called from home, but before leaving, made a conditional contract with a Mr. Howell, a white man, to oversee for him in the year 1834, to commence on the first of January of that year. He returned about the 28th or 29th of December 1833, and learning Georgia had prohibited any Cherokee from hiring a white man, told Mr. Howell he did not want his services. Yet Mr. Bishop, the state's agent, represented to the authorities of Georgia that Mr. Vann had violated the laws of that state, by hiring a white man, had forfeited his right of occupancy, and that a grant ought to issue for his lands. There were conflicting claims under Georgia for his possessions. A Mr. Riley pretended a claim, and took possession of the upper part of the dwelling-house, armed for battle. Mr. Bishop, the state's agent and his party came to take possession, and between them and Riley a fight commenced, and from twenty to fifty guns were fired in the house. While this was going on, Mr. Vann gathered his trembling wife and children into a room for safety. Riley could not be dislodged from his position up stairs, even after being wounded, and Bishop's party finally set fire to the house. Riley surrendered and the fire was extinguished.

Mr. Vann and his family were then driven out, unprepared, in the dead of winter, and snow upon the ground, through which they were compelled to wade, and to take shelter within the limits of Tennessee, in an open log cabin, upon a dirt floor, and Bishop put his brother Absalom in possession of Mr. Vann's house. This Mr. Vann is the same who, when a boy, volunteering as a private soldier in the Cherokee regiment, in the service of the United States in the Creek war, periled his life in crossing the river at the battle of the Horse Shoe. What has been his reward?

Hundreds of other cases might be added. In fact, near all the Cherokees in Georgia who had improvements of any value, except the favourites of the United States' agents, under one pretext or other, have been driven from their homes. Amid the process of expulsion, the Rev. John F. Schermerhorn, the United States commissioner, visited the legislatures of Tennessee and Alabama, and importuned those bodies to pass laws, prohibiting the Cherokees who might be turned out of their possessions from within the Georgia limits, taking up a residence in the limits of those states.

In the month of May, 1835, the general council of the Cherokee nation passed a resolution, appointing agents to ascertain the value of improvements taken by white men, and also the amount of all claims against the United States for spoliations upon the Cherokees. It was believed full justice could not be done in a treaty, otherwise than by ascertaining the injuries they had sustained. This resolution looked to a treaty with the United States, so soon as arrangements therefore could be made. Numbers of Cherokees had been forced from their houses and farms, particularly by the authorities of Georgia, and the citizens of the United States being in possession of the improvements, if they were not valued in a short time, daily undergoing alterations and additions, they could not be identified as Cherokee improvements. These agents were required to register all claims for improvements and spoliations, in books to be kept for that purpose; to proceed forthwith and to report to the principal chief, to be submitted to the next general council of the nation, which was to commence in October following, when the commissioner of the United States was to appear for the purpose of making a treaty. Messrs. J. J. Trott, Robert Rogers, Elijah Hicks, Walter S. Adair, and Thomas F. Taylor, were appointed as agents, and in the latter part of July proceeded to the duties assigned them. After having made some progress, Messrs. Trott and Hicks were arrested by a part of the Georgia Guard. The officer commanding deprived them of all their books and papers, marched them off sixty miles, tied with ropes to Spring Place, the station of the guard, and there kept them, with Messrs. Taylor and Adair, who had also been arrested, in close confinement, in a guard-house, built to keep Indians in, for nine or ten days. A writ of habeas corpus was obtained, to bring the prisoners before a judge, but the guard evaded the service of the writ, by running the prisoners from place to place. The prisoners were required by Bishop, the captain of the guard, to give bond and surety to the state of Georgia, in the sum of one thousand dollars each, to appear at court, and to desist from valuing Cherokee improvements. They appeared at court, but no further steps were taken against them. The books and papers have never been returned. This arrest was stated to be at the instance of Messrs. Schermerhorn and Currey, agents for the United States, who, it is said, corresponded with the governor of Georgia and the secretary of war on the subject, and that a part of this correspondence may be seen in the war department.

Joseph M. Lynch, an officer in the Cherokee nation, for executing the laws of the nation, was arrested by the Georgia guard, lodged in jail, and bail for his appearance at a court of justice refused. His negroes were also seized and committed to jail, and there continued until they broke jail and made their escape. Not less barbarity has been practiced towards the Cherokees by Benjamin F. Currey, the agent of the United States for Cherokee emigration, openly alleging it to be the policy of the United States to make the situation of the Indians so miserable as to drive them into a treaty, or an abandonment of their country, as may be seen by his letter to Messrs. Brazleton and Kennedy of 14th September, 1835. A few instances will be given as illustration of his mode of operation and general conduct.

Wahka and his wife were natives of, and residents in, the Cherokee nation east of the Mississippi. The agents of the United States prevailed upon the wife to enrol for emigration, against the remonstrances of the husband, and they afterwards, by force, separated her from her husband, and took her and the children to Arkansas, leaving the husband and father behind, because he would not enrol. The improvements upon which he resided were valued in the name of the wife, and he turned out of possession.

Atalah Anosta was prevailed upon to enrol when drunk, contrary to the wish and will of his wife and children; when the time arrived for him to leave for Arkansas, he absconded. A guard was sent after him by B. F. Currey, which arrested the woman and children, and brought them to the agency about dark, in a cold rain, shivering and hungry. They were detained under guard all night and part of the next day, and until the woman agreed to enrol her name as an emigrant. The husband then came in, and he and his wife and their children were put on board a boat and taken to Arkansas. There they soon lost two or three of their children, and then returned on foot to the Cherokee nation east of the Mississippi.

Sconatachee, when drunk, was enrolled by Benjamin F. Currey; when the emigrants were collected, he did not appear, and Currey and John Miller, the interpreter, went after him. Currey *drew a pistol*, and attempted to drive the old man to the agency, who presented his gun and refused to go. Currey and Miller returned without him. He made the facts known to Hugh Montgomery, the Cherokee agent, who gave him a certificate that he should not be forced away against his will. So the matter rested till the emigrants were collected the next year, and then Currey sent a wagon and guard for him. He was arrested, tied, and hauled to the agency, leaving some of his children behind in the woods, where they had fled on the approach of the guard. Richard Cheek enrolled for emigration, but before the time of departure, he hired to work on the Tuscumbia rail-road, in Alabama. When the emigrants started, Currey had Cheek's wife taken, put on board a boat, and started to Arkansas. She was even denied the privilege of visiting her husband as she descended the river. He was left behind, and never saw her more. She died on the way.

Such outrages, and violations of treaty stipulations, have been the subject of complaint to the government of the United States on the part of the Cherokees for years past: and the delegation are not surprised that the American people are not now startled at those wrongs, so long continued, for by habit men are brought to look with indifference upon death itself. If the government of the United States have determined to take the Cherokee lands without their consent, the power is with them; and the American people can "reap the field that is not their own, and gather the vintage of his vineyard whom by violence they have oppressed."

There is no ground for the pretended necessity under which the authorities of the United States have acted, for at the time of the formation and

ratification of the pretended treaty, the Cherokee people had their delegation and representatives in Washington city, with instructions and full
powers to negotiate a treaty. This delegation were importuning the government for an opportunity to do so, as their correspondence with the war
department will show. It will further show, they were at first received and
recognized as the proper party with which to make a treaty, and then
rejected, unless they would adopt the act of the faction at New Echota,
which in them would have been a violation of the express will of their constituents. They were willing to act under their authority for the Cherokee
people, but the opportunity to do so was refused. Then there is no force in
the argument for the ratification of a fraudulent treaty, that it was necessary
something should be done. There is as little in the assertion, that the Cherokees were in a distressed and starving condition, and that it was therefore
necessary to ratify the New Echota instrument, as a treaty for their benefit
and preservation, as the best that could be done. This position denies to the
Cherokees the right to think for themselves.

Their distresses have not been denied, but the argument comes with a bad
grace from the agents of the United States, who have produced them avowedly
for the purpose of forcing a treaty. The Cherokees have not asked, but refuse
the proffered relief, and are surely the best judges of their own true situation,
can properly appreciate the motives for the offer, as also the expressed sympathy for their misfortunes, and the avowed benevolence towards the Indian
race, all of which amounts simply to this: "We want, and intend to take your
lands, and are sorry you are unwilling for us to do so in our own way."

The delegation will call to the recollection of the members of the house,
the arguments and predictions of the opponents to the passage of "An act
to provide for an exchange of lands with the Indians, residing in any of the
states or territories, and for their removal west of the Mississippi." While that
measure was under discussion in the house of representatives in 1830, the
members opposed insisted its passage would be an encouragement to the
states to press upon the Indians, and to force them from their homes; that it
was the secret design to make their situation so wretched and intolerable,
that they would be forced to abandon their country. This was expressly
denied by the friends of the measure, by none more earnestly than the
members from Georgia, who insisted the measure was founded in humanity
to the Indians. Who was right, let subsequent facts decide. That law, though
not so designed by congress, has been the source from which much of the
Cherokee sufferings has come. . . .

The present is the third attempt to make a treaty with a few unauthorized
Cherokees, against the will of their nation. In the year 1834, a treaty was made
at Washington with Andrew Ross, James Starr, Thomas J. Pack, and John
West, which the senate refused to ratify. . . . On the 14th of March, 1835,
another was concluded with John Ridge, Archilla Smith, Elias Boudinot, S. W.
Bell, John West, William A. Davis, and Ezekiel West. It was never submitted to
the senate, but by the president directed to be submitted to the Cherokees
for their consideration and approbation, which was done, with an address

from the president himself. The propositions were rejected with great unanimity by the Cherokee people. . . . [*The memorial goes on at some length to
describe the interactions of Schermerhorn and the Treaty Party in drafting the Treaty of
New Echota.*] By this treaty all the lands, rights, interests, and claims of whatsoever nature of the Cherokee people east of the Mississippi, are pretended
to be ceded to the United States for the pittance of $5,600,000! Let us take a
cursory view of the country and other rights of the Cherokees professed to be
surrendered to the United States under the provisions of the fraudulent
treaty. The Cherokee territory, within the limits of North Carolina, Georgia,
Tennessee and Alabama is estimated to contain ten millions of acres. It
embraces a large portion of the finest lands to be found in any of the states;
and a salubrity of climate unsurpassed by any. . . . [The memorial describes
the amenities of the Cherokee lands, demonstrating their value as well above
the thirty cents per acre on offer under the treaty.]

The faith of the United States being solemnly pledged to the Cherokee
nation for the guarantee of the quiet and uninterrupted protection of their
territorial possessions for ever; and it being an unquestionable fact, that the
Cherokees love their country; that no amount of money could induce them
voluntarily to yield their assent to a cession of the same. But when, under all
the circumstances of their peculiar situation and unhappy condition, the
nation see the necessity of negotiating a treaty for the security and future welfare, and having appointed a delegation with full powers for that purpose, is
it liberal, humane, or just, that a fraudulent treaty, containing principles and
stipulations altogether objectionable, and obnoxious to their own sense of
propriety and justice, should be enforced upon them? The basis of the
instrument, the sum fixed upon, the commutation of annuities, and the general provisions of the various articles it contains, are all objectionable. Justice
and equity demand, in any final treaty for the adjustment of the Cherokee
difficulties, that their rights, interests, and wishes should be consulted; and
that the individual rights of the Cherokee citizens, in their possessions and
claims, should be amply secured; and, as freemen, they should be left at liberty to stay or remove where they please. Also, that the territory to be ceded
by the United States to the Cherokee nation west of the Mississippi, should
be granted to them by a patent in fee simple, and not clogged with the conditions of the act of 1830; and the national funds of the Cherokees should be
placed under the control of their national council.

The delegation must repeat, the instrument entered into at New Echota,
purporting to be a treaty, is deceptive to the world, and a fraud upon the
Cherokee people. If a doubt exist as to the truth of their statement, a committee of investigation can learn the facts, and it may also learn that if the
Cherokees are removed under that instrument, it will be by force. This declaration they make in sincerity, with hearts sickening at the scenes they may
be doomed to witness; they have toiled to avert such a calamity; it is now with
congress, and beyond their control; they hope they are mistaken, but it is
hope against a sad and almost certain reality. It would be uncandid to conceal
their opinions, and they have no motive for expressing them but a solemn

sense of duty. The Cherokees cannot resist the power of the United States, and should they be driven from their native land, then will they look in melancholy sadness upon the golden chain presented by President Washington to the Cherokee people as emblematical of the brightness and purity of the friendship between the United States and the Cherokee nation.

Jno. Ross
John Martin
James Brown
Joseph Vann
John Benge
Lewis Ross
Elijah Hicks
Rich'd Fields
Representatives of the Cherokee Nation
Washington City, 21 June, 1836

Source: U.S. Congress. House. *Memorial of the Cherokee Representatives, Submitting the Protest of the Cherokee Nation against the Ratification, Execution, and Enforcement of the Treaty Negotiated at New Echota, in December 1835.* 24th Cong., 1st sess., June 22, 1836. H. Doc. 286.

20. Letter from John Ross, Principal Chief of the Cherokee Nation of Indians, in Answer to Enquiries from a Friend Regarding the Cherokee Affairs with the United States (1836)

John Ross's letter, along with a memorial and protest from the Cherokee delegation to the U.S. Senate and House of Representatives dated June 1836, was printed as a pamphlet and widely distributed in the East. According to the editor of *The Friend*, where it was subsequently republished, Ross's "object was to effect the extensive circulation of these documents, by means of the public journals and otherwise, with the view of eliciting the sympathies of the public." Ross's words prompted a reply by Elias Boudinot that took the form of not only a rejoinder to Ross but also a rationale for the Treaty Party's actions.

Washington City
July 2, 1836
My Dear Sir,
    Your interest in relation to our fortunes is very kind and liberal, and I sincerely thank you for it. You say you hope I shall not be offended at your questions, and that I will believe you have no sinister views in writing me, to clear up certain doubts which have been forced upon you, concerning my movements in Cherokee affairs. Instead of being annoyed, I thank you for the opportunity which you have given me, through these doubts, of

endeavouring, briefly, to explain, not only our position, but some portions of my own conduct connected with it, which have been grossly, but purposely, misrepresented.

I wish I could acquiesce in your impression that a Treaty has been made, by which every difficulty between the Cherokees and the United States has been set at rest; but I must candidly say, that I know of no such Treaty. I do not mean to prophesy any similar troubles to those which have, in other cases, followed the failure to adjust disputed points with Indians; the Cherokees act on a principle preventing apprehensions of that nature—their principle is, "endure and forbear;" but I must distinctly declare to you that I believe, the document signed by unauthorized individuals at Washington, will never be regarded by the Cherokee nation as a Treaty. The delegation appointed by the people to make a Treaty, have protested against that instrument "as deceptive to the world and a fraud upon the Cherokee people." You say you do not see my name appended to the paper in question, but that you regard the omission as a typographical mistake, because you do find my name among those who are mentioned in it as the future directors of Cherokee affairs.

I will answer these points separately: and, first,

My name is not, by mistake, omitted among the signers of the paper in question; and the reasons why it is not affixed to the paper, are the following:—

Neither myself nor any other member of the regular delegation to Washington, can, without violating our most sacred engagements, ever recognize that paper as a Treaty, by assenting to its terms, or the mode of its execution. They are entirely inconsistent with the views of the Cherokee people. Three times have the Cherokee people formally and openly rejected conditions substantially the same as these. We were commissioned by the people, under express injunctions, not to bind the nation to any such conditions. The delegation representing the Cherokees, have, therefore, officially rejected these conditions themselves, and have regularly protested before the Senate and House of Representatives, against their ratification. The Cherokee people, in two protests, the one signed by twelve thousand two hundred and fifty persons, spoke for themselves against the Treaty, even previous to its rejection by those whom they had selected to speak for them.

With your impressions concerning the advantages secured by the subtle instrument in question, you will, no doubt, wonder at this opposition. But it possesses not the advantages you and others imagine; and that is the reason why it has encountered, and ever will encounter opposition. You suppose we are to be removed through it from a home, by circumstances rendered disagreeable and even untenable, to be secured in a better home, where nothing can disturb or dispossess us. *Here is the great mystification.* We are not secured in the new home promised to us. We are exposed to precisely the same miseries, from which, if this measure is enforced, the United States' power professes to relieve us, but does so entirely by the exercise of that power, against our will.

If we really had the security you and others suppose we have, we would not thus complain. But mark the truth and judge for yourself. White men obtain their title to property, between one and another, by what is called *fee simple*. I have discovered that many of those who have voted in favour of his presented Treaty, have done so under the impression that they were voting lands to us in *fee simple*—especially as we are to be compelled to pay for those lands the sum of five hundred thousand dollars—having already paid for a portion of them, by exchange, what is equivalent to the full amount of their intrinsic value. But the difference between the right by which the state of Georgia and other states hold lands, is a very, very material difference from that which the Cherokees shall have paid, according to this arrangement, at the smallest estimate, calculating the valuation of the exchange at government prices, and adding it to the sum to be paid in money—*seven millions of dollars!* Seven millions for lands without a real title! For this sum, I admit, the United States do promise that they will "cause a patent, or grant, to be made and executed" to us for the aforesaid tract of land, but it is always on the proviso, "that such land shall *revert* to the United States, if the Indians become extinct, or abandon the same." Now, the use of this very phrase, allotted to the Indians, in payment for their valuable country; the United States retains the absolute property in her own hands, only allowing to the Indians a far inferior right of occupancy to that which they have ever been admitted to possess where they now are, and where they were born. The pretended Treaty expressly avows that it is under the law containing the cause above quoted, and other similar laws, that the transfer is made; and the Indian title is to subject, not only to these laws already existing, but to such laws as may be made hereafter; and to which laws, present and prospective, the Indian regulations for self-government must be subordinate. Now, in addition to the inconveniences and insecurity inevitable, from the vagueness of the submission, may entirely extinguish, not only the right of occupancy, but of self-government. For example, suppose it should suit the policy of the United States, hereafter, to pass a law organizing a territorial government upon the Cherokee lands, west? That law necessarily destroys the character of the Cherokee nation as a distinct community; the nation becomes legally extinct; the lands revert to the United States, and the Cherokee people are bound, by assenting to the conditions of the pretended Treaty, to acquiesce in this law providing a plausible pretext for their annihilation. And should they demur, what is the result? An article in the pretended Treaty expressly stipulated, that military posts, and military roads may, anywhere, and at any time, be established by the United States, in the new country, set apart for the Indians. Hence, any one who might complain of any act of the United States as unauthorized by the right construction of the pretended Treaty, would be as liable to ejectment for the purpose of creating a military post at the malcontent's abode in the Cherokee country west—as now he actually is, and long has been, under similar circumstances, in the Cherokee part of Georgia:—and were vexations to become universal, as they have in Georgia, the region might, in the same manner, be filled with soldiers, and the existence of the Cherokee nation become at once extinguished by laws to which the people will be said themselves to have assented. That there is no disposition ever to interfere thus, is attempted to be proved by reference to an article of the pretended Treaty, excluding intruders and white men; but this very article is clogged with a worse than neutralizing condition—a condition pregnant with sources of future disquiet—a condition that it is not to prevent the introduction of useful farmers, mechanics, and teachers, under which denomination some future Executive of the United Sates may find it convenient, hereafter, to overwhelm the original population, and bring about the Territorial Government, by which the Cherokees will be regarded as legally extinguished, and the country of their exile as *reverting* to its real proprietor, the United States. Thus will the favourite theory, which has been ascribed to the President, be fully realized. This policy will *legislate the Indians off the land.*

That all these things are possible, is proved by the present posture of affairs in the region of our birth, our sacred inheritance from our fathers. It is but a few years, since the apprehension of scenes like those from which the United States acknowledges her incompetency to protect us, even under the pledge of Treaties, would have been regarded as a morbid dream. But a State has already been created on the boundary of the retreat set apart for the exile of the Indians—The State of Arkansas; another State, and an independent one—a new republic, made up of many of the old foes of the Indians—Texas, is rising on another boundary; and who shall say how soon these, and other new bordering states, may become as uneasy from the Indian neighbourhood, as the old ones are now? It was at one time thought that the United States never could declare she was unable to keep the Treaties of former days. Is it less possible that she may hereafter experience the same difficulty in keeping those of the days in which we live? especially, as in the present instance, she may be called upon, not only to defend those Treaties from violation by her own citizens, but by the people, though of the same origin, belonging to a new, a warlike, and independent republic.

To proceed to your second remark: that you find my name among those enumerated in the pretended Treaty, who are to form a Committee for the Regulation, under that instrument, of Cherokee affairs.

It is true, my name is on that list, and at the head of the thirteen members named by the United States Government; but it was never placed there with my sanction. I disclaim the act, as I disclaim the instrument which contains the act. If ever I hold an office in the Nation of my compatriots, it must be from *their* election, not the nomination of the executive of another country; and the insertion of my name among the thirteen in question, ranks with the other unauthorized proceedings of an irresponsible and self-constituted opposition to the legalized authorities of the nation. If I have objected to the pretended Treaty, not only as made with persons whom the Nation will not recognize as made with persons whom the nation will not recognize as its representatives, but as exchanging relations in some degree defined, for those utterly and dangerously undefined; as rendering a distressed people entirely dependent upon the policy or the caprices of successors to a government which has not respected that people's dearest rights;

I certainly would not render myself the accomplice of what I look upon as wronging those whose interests are more precious to me than my own.

I will now turn to portions of your letter, more immediately touching my own character; and at the head of these I find what you call, on the misrepresentation of Mr. Schermerhorn, my having agreed to bind "my people" to sell the Cherokee nation, on certain terms, from which I afterwards capriciously departed.

I must here beg leave to observe that I have never yet been placed in a position which could render my individual decision conclusive upon any matters of this nature, nor could I ever wish for such responsibility. The Cherokee people are not "my people;" I am only one of their agents and their elected chief: It is I who serve under them, not they under me. At the time of the transaction to which you allude, the delegation, of which I was a member, had ample powers to make a treaty for a partial cession of the country, with security in the residue; but we had no authority for the extension of our discretionary power to any treaty for an entire sale of the country; such a suggestion was not contemplated by the people and it would consequently be impossible for us to decide upon such, without a reference to those who sent us. I myself was only one among many. I could not, by my single act, bind even my associates to any promise of an entire sale, nor of course to any *award*, even had such an *award* been made, for the amount to be paid for an entire sale; I could only, with them, submit such an offer, if made to the people. The facts of the case to which you allude, however, are these:—

During the congressional session of term before last, (1834–5) while the legally constituted delegation from the Cherokee nation was at Washington, an unauthorised delegation, consisting mostly of the same members who appeared there, equally unauthorised, last winter, and signed the paper pretending to be a treaty, were intriguing to be admitted into secret negotiations with the United States Government, while the delegation of which I was a member, were conducting theirs openly. It was said the party first mentioned came at the instance of the government, but of this there was no proof. Mr. Schermerhorn, at the same time, was seeking to obtain a promise from the regular delegation, that they would meet him as a commissioner; affirming that he was in the confidence of the President, and if such a promise were given, he was certain to be appointed. Receiving no encouragement from the legal delegation, he is understood to have gone over to Mr. Ridge and his friends, and to have opened negotiations with them.—Soon after, it was understood that the President refused to entertain the proposition for which we had discretionary power, namely, that for a partial cession of the country, with security in the residue. It was understood, too, that he would not only require an absolute sale, to which our discretionary power did not extend; but that he also refused, on the score of the alleged extravagance of the sum demanded, to entertain our proposition of an absolute sale for twenty millions, in the event of its approval by the people, for whom, on this particular point, we had no authority to act finally. An impression had already got abroad that Mr. Ridge and his friends had, anterior to this, signified to the

Executive their readiness to make a treaty at four millions of dollars, or less. But the President had repeatedly said that he would go as far as the Senate would permit. The negotiation being about to fail, the legal delegation concluded to ask that the President would submit the whole matter to the Senate and take their advice as to what ought to be done, under all the circumstances. It appeared to me and my associates that the Senate on adequately investigating the value of the country, would do us justice. The delegation was hence impelled to comply with a sudden oral request that they would sign a promise on the spot, to abide by the "*award*" of the Senate and to submit that "*award*" for the approval of the nation; but the promise, on our part, was given under an express understanding, through the Secretary of War, that the Executive would submit the case for the consideration of the Senate, and, had he done so fully and *fairly*, we should have had nothing to object, whatever might have been the result: because the United States Executive, in thus referring the matter to the Senate, would have laid before the people for their decision; and we are confident that a result thus obtained must have been grounded upon proper examination, not only into the real value of the country, but all the attending circumstances. But we waited and waited and waited and nothing was attempted. We heard, indeed, that immediately after the signature by us of the paper in question, conferences were held by Messrs. Ridge, Currey, Boudinot, and Schermerhorn, at the White House, which led to changes in the views of the Executive. We also heard that the President had been advised, at one time, to meet the Senate and consult with them, (as was done by President Washington in reference to the former Cherokee Treaty of Holston,) and thus fix upon the sum to be paid for our country; and when we heard that, we felt satisfied there would be a fair examination, and justice might be expected; but we afterwards were told, that the President had been induced to abstain from communicating with the Senate at all in relation to the matter, under the impression, if the Indian question were settled in consequence of such conference, that the opposition would ascribe the settlement, not to the president, but to the Senate, the majority of whom then differed with him in politics. When we were given reason to fear the question had been made to degenerate into a mere party question, we were, indeed, apprehensive that our hopes of a speedy settlement would be defeated. The session was now drawing to a close. On the 3d of March, 1835,—the morning of the 4th being the time for adjournment—hearing nothing more from the Executive, we found ourselves compelled, late at night, to memorialize the Senate. Our memorial was referred to the Committee on Indian Affairs. This Committee made a sudden and a brief report, recommending the purchase of the Cherokee country, upon such terms as should cover its intrinsic value. It has before this been communicated to the Senate, by the Secretary of War, that Mr. Ridge and his party, had agreed to treat for four millions, or less. A resolution was submitted, at midnight, just as the Senate were about to separate, that, in their opinion, the President ought to allow a sum not exceeding five millions. This resolution, proposed in a hurry, was carried in as great a hurry, and, though a *mere opinion*, not pledging

either of the President or the Senate to any consequent action, it was represented to us as an "*award*," and we were told we had engaged ourselves to be
bound by it, notwithstanding we knew it would not be considered as binding
on any one else. Nevertheless, though so far from an "*award*"—nevertheless,
though it was even *less than an opinion*, because it was given without evidence
or reflection—we thought fit to lay it before the people as distinctly as if it
had really been the "*award*" which we had been induced to promise we would
lay before them. Accordingly, at the next Council, I submitted the proceedings to the convened nation, who unanimously protested, in open assembly,
against any Treaty on the basis of the five millions, under any circumstances;
and, therefore, had I been ever so much disposed to regard the *opinion* as an
award, the VETO OF THE NATION settled the matter finally, and would have
nullified any proceedings of mine to the contrary.

I will simply add, that the pretended Treaty, executed last session, is substantially on the terms, and made with the irresponsible party, of which I
have here sketched the origin. The sketch I have given, I hope, explains to
your satisfaction, the truth concerning the often repeated slander against
me, of having actually made a Treaty, upon certain conditions, from which I
afterwards receded.

I will now proceed to the other charge against me, which you mention as
having been made by Mr. Schermerhorn, namely, that I have no right to
interfere in Cherokee affairs, because I once accepted a reservation on
terms which made me a citizen of the United States, and thus disqualifying
me for office in the Cherokee country, rendered my continuance there in
power as Principal Chief, an usurpation. You observe that it is also asserted
by Mr. Schermerhorn that I actually expatriated myself from the nation, by
quitting the place of my birth to reside in the United States, and hence lost
my privileges as a Cherokee.

It would be enough, perhaps, for me to mention the fact, that this silly
pretence has been put on and put off so frequently by the government
agents, as it happened to suit their purposes to consider me a chief or no
chief, that an abandonment of the charge can always be produced as an off-
set against every assertion of it. But it is more satisfactory to me to go fully
into it and to show its shallowness as well as its malevolence.

There was a tract of land given to my ancestors by the Cherokee nation.
In the year 1819 the United States thought proper to secure six hundred
and forty acres of that tract to me, as a *special* reservation. Some other grants
were made at the same time, under express conditions, but mine, (as were
one or two others,) was *untrammelled by conditions*, and hence denominated
"*special*." I did not reside on it when granted. It was known that I did not. It
was known I never had resided on it. My residence had, for some time, been
at Rossville, near the Lookout Mountain, within the charter limits of
Georgia; a part of the nation which the United States aver is beyond the
jurisdiction of any United States Treaty. The Treaty conveying away these
lands, contained a condition that all persons to whom *reservations* were made
should give notice that they would *continue to reside* on the lands secured to

them. As it was so well known that I did not reside at the reservation in question, and never had resided there, it was therefore obvious that I could not *continue* what I had never *begun.* As a point of etiquette, however, I was advised that some communication in reference to my reservation might be expected; and finding all my neighbours were writing to the Agent—to comply with forms, and to prevent any disturbance from the subtleties of technical distinctions, I followed their example, and gave notice, *not* that I meant *to continue to reside* on the reservation where I had never resided, but that it was my intention to continue to *occupy and enjoy permanently* the land reserved to me by the Treaty of 1819. I considered myself as standing nearly in the position of an alien, especially authorized to hold lands in a foreign country, without forfeiting his allegiance to his own. I distinctly stated, at the same time, that I was "fully convinced the condition of the same Treaty did not immediately apply to special reservations;" and that I only gave this notice to comply with forms, and forms not understood by me as affecting the spirit in which that treaty had conveyed mine and one or two others. In so doing, I made no change of residence. It did not remove out of the nation, and become a citizen of the United States. I never have left the limits of the Cherokee nation, excepting when sent to school as a boy, and engaged in business in early youth and manhood, first in the situation of clerk to a merchant, and afterwards on my own account. Since then, whenever I have left the nations, it has been to transact the affairs of the nation. Nevertheless, Mr. Schermerhorn thinks he has succeeded in proving something against me, when he quotes one of our laws, where it is stated "the authority and claim of our common property, shall cease with the persons who shall think proper to remove themselves without the limits of the Cherokee nations." The reverend politician then triumphantly says, Mr. John Ross complied with the condition of the Treaty of 1819; how could he comply with that condition and retain lands withdrawn from his country unless he ceased to live in his country? In ceasing to live in his country, he forfeited his rights of citizenship there, and, by so doing he ceased to be a Cherokee, and necessarily became a citizen of the United States! This is splendid reasoning, no doubt; but supposing the circumstances assumed as facts, to be true, how does the case then stand? To those who took reservations under the article which Mr. Schermerhorn says, made them, by implication, citizens of the United States, the United States found it inconvenient to confirm the rights which they promised. The United States were pledged to protect the reservees from intruders; and yet intruders came and forcibly drove many of the reservees from their reservations, and the marauders were sustained by the authority of a border state! Hence the reservees became homeless. They had no resource but to return to the domain of their brother Indians; and thither they did return, and they were welcomed. In the meantime, they instituted suits before the Circuit Courts of Georgia for the recovery of their lands. The appeal succeeded. But Georgia, instead of reinstating them, memorialized Congress for an appropriation *to buy out the reservees,* because she had already *lotteried away* these very lands, assuming them to be hers under a promise of prospective possession from the United States. An appropriation was made and the entire spirit of the arrangement was changed by the capricious legislation of alleged *expediency!* and thus, to alter the application of a remark by Mr. Schermerhorn, the relations between the United States and the reserves, "became resolved into their original elements," by the non-compliance of the United States with the conditions under which a modification of those relations with some, at least, might have been intended.

Thus you will perceive that Mr. Schermerhorn has made an inference of his own from a treaty article, to suit his own purposes; and assuming that purposely erroneous inference to be a fact, has then proceeded to try us by it, as though it were a fact; and, tried under such a law, and such a judge, what true Cherokee could look to be acquitted?

Of another attempt—the attempt of which you speak to deny the authority of the Cherokee government, because, when the intolerance of Georgia rendered the observance of the letter of the Cherokee laws a penal offence in that part of the Cherokee country coming within the charter limits of Georgia—certain changes in the forms defined by our Constitution became necessary, I shall say but little. That attempt to divide and slander us has also emanated from the Reverend Mr. Schermerhorn. It was intended to break down our chiefs and government. The people saw and understood it, and determined to preserve both without changing the spirit of our laws, though they were forced to modify the mode of their fulfillment. In troubled times, this has so often been done everywhere, that for precedents it is not necessary to look very deeply into history. Nor is it any novelty in collisions between states or individuals, to attempt the crushing of the individual by whom either may be thwarted. In the United States this has occurred even in reference to its greatest man. Some measures of the Ambassador of the French Republic, being opposed by Washington, Mr. Genet, and the vain and wrong-headed Ambassador in question, endeavoured to break down the great Washington himself, and that in the very bosom of his own country. The American people laughed at Genet, and loved Washington all the better for his contempt of the impertinence. It is unnecessary to enlarge upon the ridiculous and unworthy figure which Schermerhorn will make in future history, as a reverend clergyman going with a pious, though somewhat rubicund face, upon a political embassy into an Indian country, and there attempting to gain in his purpose by dividing the nation against itself, and getting up a party to overthrow the constituted authorities and meet his particular views. He was imitating Genet in a smaller sphere; a Genet in clerical robes, with a military guard, alternately preaching honesty and intriguing to mystify a plain people by the subtleties of political negotiation. In reference to us, however, Mr. Schermerhorn has rendered his own arts impotent, and that by his own acts. Though he has sometimes disavowed our authority, he and his associates have generally immediately afterwards treated with us under a formal acknowledgement of that authority, and they have done so up to a very recent date, extending far beyond that of their latest disavowal.

I will here take occasion to touch upon two points in reference to our negotiations, which do not seem to be understood by the American people. One impression concerning us, is, that though we object to removal, as we are equally averse to becoming citizens of the United States, we ought to be forced to remove; to be tied hand and foot and conveyed to the extreme western frontier, and then turned loose among the wild beasts of the wilderness. Now, the fact is, we never have objected to become citizens of the United States and to conform to her laws; but in the event of conforming to her laws, we have required the protection and the privileges of her laws to accompany that conformity on our part. We have asked this repeatedly and repeatedly it has been denied.

The other point to which I would advert is this: a charge that the whole scope of my policy has been to get the money of the nation into my own hands. *This is a monstrous misrepresentation.* The funds of the nation never have been in my hands. They have been with the councils of the nation, as the funds of the United States are with the representatives of her people. For the propriety of *this* course we have always contended—for nothing more. We have wondered when we have heard objections made against our opposition to the policy of the United States in wishing to take our own funds away from our own councils and to place them under the entire control of agents of the American Government—*a policy at length accomplished by the pretended treaty of this spring!* So far from ever wishing the control of our national funds, I would not take such control, even were it offered to me, which, by the laws of the nation, it never can be. But I will maintain to the last, that the United States ought not to give our money into the hands of frontier agents—often, in all countries, more deserving suspicion, and more liable to temptation, because less under surveillance, than any other public officers whatever, can be. The funds of the nation are our own funds—they consist of money paid for the purchase of our own lands, and that on forced and speculative, and consequently very inadequate terms;—and being the property of the nation, and property remaining after severe sacrifices on our part—as the property of the nation it is right that those funds should be under the control of the councils of the nation.

I must bring my letter to a close. I fear it has already wearied you. But it gratifies me to find any one desirous of looking earnestly into the true state of the Cherokee question, and I wish to afford all such enquirers every satisfaction. You have already perceived that the singular attitude into which our affairs have been thrown by the mere trickery of party, emanated entirely from the subserviency of irresponsible Cherokees to the policy, backed by the power of the administration. It is a remarkable fact that even so lately as February 9, 1836, Mr. John Ridge joined the regular delegation in a solemn protest against the dishonesty of this course, although three days previous, February 6, 1836, his father Major Ridge, who had arrived at the head of the counterfeit delegation of the got-up party, had communicated under it to the real representatives of the people; and yet, with no new facts before him, on the 25th of March, 1836, this same Mr. John Ridge, in a letter of condolence to the reverend politician, Mr. Schermerhorn, returns to the opposition, and violently vituperates his recent associates and the *whole course* of their proceedings and their policy; a vituperation in which he necessarily must be understood as including himself; this being only his fourth entire revolution in politics within as many months: varying as often as the moon, without the excuse of lunacy for his changes.

In conclusion I would observe, that I still strongly hope we shall find ultimate justice from the good sense of the administration and of the people of the United States. I will not even yet believe that either the one or the other would wrong us with their eyes open. I am persuaded they have erred only in ignorance, and an ignorance forced upon them by the misrepresentation and artifices of the interested. You yourself are aware to what an extent these artifices have been carried. You are aware that the Seminole outbreak and the Creek troubles, have been insidiously spoken of as connected with our condition; and although I myself never saw a Seminole Indian, and there is not intercourse whatever between our nation and theirs; although with the Creeks, also, we have far less communication than the state of New York has with Canada, nevertheless there have been some persons malevolent enough to wish the Cherokees extirpated because the Creeks and Seminoles have risen, and very many others uninformed enough to join the war cry against us, under the sweeping denunciation that being all Indians, we ought alike to suffer!—The Cherokees, under any circumstances, have no weapon to use but argument. If that should fail, they must submit, when their time shall come, in silence; but honest argument they cannot think will be forever used in vain. The Cherokee people will always hold themselves ready to respect a *real* treaty and bound to sustain any treaty which they can feel that they are bound to respect. But they are certain not to consider the attempt of a very few persons to sell the country for themselves, as obligatory upon them, and I and all my associates in the regular delegation still look confidently to the effect of a sense of justice upon the American community, in producing a real settlement of this question, upon equitable terms and with competent authorities. But, on one point, you may be perfectly at rest. Deeply as our people feel, I cannot suppose they will ever be goaded by those feelings to any acts of violence. No, sir. They have been too long inured to suffering without resistance, and they still look to the sympathies and not to the fears, of those who have them in their power. In certain recent discussions in the representative hall at Washington, our enemies made it an objection against me and against others, that we were not Indians, but had *the principles of white men*, and were consequently unworthy of a hearing in the Indian cause. I will own that it has been my pride, as principal chief of the Cherokees, to implant in the bosoms of the people, and to cherish in my own, *the principles of white men*! It is to this fact that our white neighbours must ascribe their safety under the smart of the wrongs we have suffered from them. It is in this they may confide for our continued patience. But when I speak of *the principles of white men*, I speak not of such principles as actuate those who take thus to us, but of those mighty principles to which the United States owes her greatness and her liberty. To principles like these even yet we turn with confidence for redemption from our miseries. When congress shall be less overwhelmed with business, no doubt, in some way, the matter may be brought to a reconsideration, and when the representatives of the American people have leisure to see how little it will cost them to be just, we are confident they will be true to themselves, in acting with good faith towards us. Be certain that while the Cherokees are endeavouring to obtain a more friendly consideration from the United States, they will not forget to show by their circumspection how well they merit it; and though no doubt there are many who will represent them otherwise, for injurious purposes, I can assure you that the white people have nothing to apprehend, even from our sense of contumely and unfairness, unless it be through the perverse and the treacherous maneuvers of such agents as they themselves may keep among us.

I have the honour to be Dear Sir, Most truly yours,

John Ross

Source: The Friend Vol. 9, no. 44 (August 6, 1836), pp. 350–352, 357–359.

21. Excerpt from Letters and Other Papers Relating to Cherokee Affairs Being a Reply to Sundry Publications by John Ross (1837)

From the time in 1832 when Elias Boudinot and other members of the Treaty Party became convinced that resistance to removal was futile until the time actual removal was carried out, they exchanged a number of charges with Ross's party. Here, Boudinot responds to some of Ross's charges and, in so doing, lays out the rationale for the Treaty of New Echota. He also comments on Ross's attempts to treat with the United States for a removal on more "favorable terms" than those of the 1835 treaty. Specifically, Boudinot's response here is to Ross's "Letter to a Friend," which was widely distributed in the East in pamphlet form.

What is termed the "Cherokee question" may be considered in two points of view: the controversy with the States and the General Government, and the controversy among the Cherokees themselves. The first has been agitated in so many ways, and before so many tribunals, that it is needless, for any good purpose, to remark upon it at this place. The latter is founded upon the question of a remedy, to extricate the Cherokees from the difficulties, in consequence of their conflict with the States. Upon this point, less has been said or known before the public but it has not been the less interesting to the Cherokees. It is here where different views and different feelings have been excited.

"What is to be done?" was a natural inquiry, after we found that all our efforts to obtain redress from the General Government, *on the land of our fathers*, had been of no avail. The first rupture among ourselves was the moment we presumed to answer that question. To a portion of the Cherokee people it early became evident that the interest of their countrymen and the happiness of their posterity, depended upon an entire change of policy. Instead of contending uselessly against superior power, the only course left, was, to yield to circumstances over which they had no control.

In all difficulties of this kind, between the United States and the Cherokees, the only mode of settling them has been by treaties; consequently, when a portion of our people became convinced that no other measures would avail, they became the *advocates of a treaty*, as the only means to extricate the Cherokees from their perplexities; hence they were called *the treaty party*. Those who maintained the old policy, were known as *the anti-treaty party*. At the head of the latter has been Mr. John Ross.

It would be to no purpose now to describe these Indian political parties, or to enter into a particular history of the rise, progress, and the present state of the dissensions which have distracted the Cherokees. It is enough to say that our parties have been similar to other political parties found among the whites. They have been characterized by high feeling, and not unfrequently, by undue asperity. It is easy to conceive of the disadvantages under which the first mentioned party must have labored. To advocate a treaty was to declare war against the established habits of thinking peculiar to the aborigines. It was to come in contact with settled prejudices—with the deep rooted attachment for the soil of our forefathers. Aside from these natural obstacles, the influence of the chiefs, who were ready to take advantage of the well known feelings of the Cherokees, in reference to their lands, was put in active requisition against us.

It is worthy of notice that, in this contest, we have had to bear no small share of obloquy, arising from our very principles, from our opposition to the views and measures of what is termed the *constituted authorities* of the nation, and from the illusive appearance of having a vast majority opposed to us. That obloquy was increased by the manner in which we were represented to our people. Traitors, land sellers, interested persons, &c., were terms calculated to stir up prejudice and opposition. To represent us in the various lights to our own people, we supposed to be a matter of course, judging from the nature of all political contests. But we have lately been arraigned before the American public—a tribunal to which we, as Cherokees, are not properly amenable in this affair—in our own family disputes. Mr. Ross has made sundry publications of late, by the aid of writers whom he has employed for the purpose, which have arraigned us to that tribunal. He has called upon the public to award its judgment against us. He has represented us as a disaffected faction, opposed to him, the constituted chief of this nation. He represents us as a small minority opposed to the will of the people; that we have ceded their lands without their authority, and against their expressed injunctions. These are matters which the Cherokees themselves, the result of which must be left to their posterity to judge.

Without replying to these charges in this place, we will state what are supposed to be the great cause of our present difficulties—our present dissensions. *A want of proper information among the people.* We charge Mr. Ross with having deluded them with expectations incompatible with and injurious to, their interest. He has prevented the discussion of this interesting matter, by systematic measures, at a time when discussion was of the most vital importance. By that means the people have been kept ignorant of their true condition. They have been taught to feel and expect what *could not* be realized, and what Mr. Ross himself must have known *would not* be realized. This great delusion has lasted to this day. Now, in view of such a state of things, we cannot conceive of the acts of a *minority* to be so reprehensible or unjust as are represented by Mr. Ross. If one hundred persons are ignorant of their true situation, and are so completely blinded as not to see the destruction that awaits them, we can see strong reasons to justify the action of a minority of fifty persons to do what the majority *would do* if they understood their condition—to save a nation from political thraldom and moral degradation. It is not intended to discuss the question here, but simply to show that a great deal may be said on both sides; besides, the reader will recollect that it is in reference to an Indian community, and to very extraordinary circumstances.

The original error was in the refusal of the leaders and advisers of this nation to discuss the question which is now agitated only in the last extremity, and in closing every avenue by which the people might be reached with correct information. That was an error which cannot now be retrieved, and which has thrown us into inextricable difficulties. The *treaty party* is not to blame for this. We sounded the alarm in time; we called upon the *authorities of the nation* to see to what these matters were tending—to save the nation by timely action; we asked, we entreated, we implored. But we were met at the very threshold as enemies of our country. The same system of opposition has been waged against us to this day. . . . [*Here follows correspondence between Boudinot and Ross, some of it concerning the freedom of a tribal editor to express his view versus the authority of the tribal leaders to censor those remarks, among other things.*]

Resolutions

[*Resolutions made by members of the Treaty Party after they were excluded from the council at Red Clay.*]

Whereas a crisis of the utmost importance in the affairs of the Cherokee people has arrived, requiring from every individual the most serious reflection, and the express of views as to the present condition and future prospects of the nation; and whereas a portion of the Cherokees have entertained opinions which have been represented as hostile to the true interest and happiness of the people, merely because they have not agreed with the chiefs and leading men: and as these opinions have not heretofore been properly made known, therefore,

Resolved, That it is our decided opinion, founded upon the melancholy experience of the Cherokees within the last two years, and upon facts which history has furnished us in regard to other Indian nations, that our people cannot exist amidst a white population, subject to laws which they have no hand in making, and which they do not understand; that the suppression of the Cherokee Government, which connected this people in a distinct community, will not only check their progress in improvement and advancement in knowledge, but, by means of numerous influences and temptations which this new state of things has created, will completely destroy every thing like civilization among them, and ultimately reduce them to poverty, misery, and wretchedness.

Resolved, That, considering the progress of the States' authorities in this country, the distribution and settlement of the lands, the organization of counties, the erection of county seats and court-houses, and other indications of a determined course on the part of the surrounding States, and considering, on the other had, the repeated refusal of the President and Congress of the United States to interfere in our behalf, we have come to the conclusion that this nation cannot be reinstated in its present location, and that the question left to us and to every Cherokee, is, whether it is more desirable to remain here, with all the embarrassments with which we must be surrounded, or to seek a country where we *may* enjoy our own laws, and live under our own vine and fig tree.

Resolved, That in expressing the opinion that this nation cannot be reinstated, we do it from a thorough conviction of its truth; that we never will encourage our confiding people with hopes that can never be realized, and with expectations that will assuredly be disappointed; that however unwelcome and painful the truth may be to them, and however unkindly it may be received from us, we cannot, as patriots and well-wishers of the Indian race, shrink from doing our duty in expressing our decided convictions; that we scorn the charge of selfishness and a want of patriotic feelings alleged against us by some of our countrymen, while we can appeal to our consciences and the searcher of all hearts for the rectitude of our motives and intentions.

Resolved, That, although *we love the land* of our fathers, and should leave the place of our nativity with as much regret as any of our citizens, we consider the lot of the *exile* immeasurably more to be preferred that a submission to the laws of States, and thus becoming witnesses of the ruin and degradation of the Cherokee people.

Resolved, That we are firmly of the opinion, that a large majority of the Cherokee people would prefer to remove, if the true state of their condition was properly made known to them. We believe that if they were told that they had nothing to expect from further efforts to regain their rights as a *distinct community*, and that the only alternatives left to them is either to remain amidst a white population, subject to the white man's laws, or to remove to another country, where they *may* enjoy peace and happiness, they would unhesitatingly prefer the latter.

Resolved, That we were desirous to leave to our chiefs and leading men to seek a country for their people, but as they have thought proper not to do anything towards the ultimate removal of the nation, we know of none to which the Cherokees can go as an asylum but that possessed by our brethren west of the Mississippi; that we are willing to unite with them under a proper guaranty from the United States that the lands shall be secured to us, and that we shall be governed by our own laws and regulations.

Resolved, That we consider the policy pursued by the Red Clay council, in continuing a useless struggle from year to year, as destructive to the present peace and future happiness of the Cherokees, because it is evident to every observer that while this struggle is going on, their difficulties will be accumulating, until they are ruined in their property and character, and the only remedy that will then be proposed in their case will be, *submission to the laws of the States* by taking reservations.

Resolved, That we consider the fate of our poor brethren, the Creeks, to be a sufficient warning to all those who may finally subject the Cherokees to the laws of the States by giving them reservations.

Resolved, That we will never consent to have our own rights and the rights of our posterity, sold "*prospectively*" to the laws of the States by our chiefs, in any compact or "compromise" into which they may choose to enter with the Government; that we cannot be satisfied with any thing less than a release from State legislation; but, while we do not intend to have our own political interests compromised, we shall not oppose those who prefer to remain subject to State laws.

Resolved, That we were disposed to contend for what we considered to be our own rights, as long as there was any hope of relief *to the nation,* but that we never can consent to the waste of our public moneys in instituting and prosecuting suits which will result only to individual advantage.

Resolved, That it is with great surprise and mortification we have noticed the idea attempted to be conveyed to the minds of our people, that the nation can be relieved by the courts of Georgia; that we regard the appealing to those courts, *by the nation,* for redress, as an entire departure from the true policy maintained by the Cherokees in their struggle for national existence.

November, 1834.

[*The following is a communication from Boudinot to John Ross.*]

Among the many charges that have been made against me and my associates during this unhappy controversy, is that of being *interested persons.* This has been often repeated, and some have gone so far as to say that we have been *bought* or *bribed,* and hence our *subserviency* to the Government in this matter. I perceive, in your communications, you employ the term *interested,* which you evidently intend to apply to us. We do not deny that we are deeply interested in the result of this question: as Cherokees, and in common with other Cherokees, we cannot but be deeply interested. To represent us in any other light, is an unprovoked assault upon our reputation.

But the charge, that we have been actuated, in all our efforts to effect a treaty for the removal of the Cherokees, by interested motives, has so often been made, you have finally undertaken to endorse it, and it is in that light you attempt to represent me. I do not now particularly refer to what you have said in your communication, but to what you have repeatedly alleged to these confiding people. What is the nature of those interested motives? Are they political or pecuniary? The former is too insignificant to deserve notice. That you mean the latter, in other words, that, by the consummation of a treaty, I am to be benefited in a pecuniary point of view, or to receive some special advantage, it is easy to surmise. I may here content myself by denying the allegation and throwing the burden of proof upon you, according to the maxim of all civilized nations, that the accuser must prove his charges before the accused can be accounted guilty.

And where is your proof in support of this grave charge? You are acquainted with Indian treaties, and you understand the mode of forming them, and securing special advantages. You have made such treaties, and you have seen such *special advantages* secured in them. Are they not found upon the very face of the instruments themselves? and are not the names of the persons to be thus benefited broadly inscribed upon them? *You know it is so*, universally so, where special reservations are given. Where, then, can you find, in the treaty which you so much oppose, and which you allege has been the result of self-interest, my name identified with anything that will give me any pecuniary advantage over my fellow-countrymen? Perhaps you will answer, that my name is found among the committee of thirteen to transact all the business of the Indians, and hence I have secured to myself a lucrative office. It so happens, however, which will be sufficient for my defence in this respect, that not one cent is provided, under the treaty, even for the *expenses* of the committee.

It may be said, perhaps, that notwithstanding I have taken precaution to prevent any showing of self-interest upon the face of the treaty, I am, nevertheless, to reap some great pecuniary advantage under its execution or operation. The execution of the treaty has now sufficiently progressed either to conform or refute that assertion; and how is it? Instead of *I* being benefited over my fellows, it is *you*. Any person need but look to the lists of valuations, to be convinced upon this point. And how is it possible that I can receive any extra pecuniary advantage under the present treaty? To be sure, I might have had the same opportunities with some of my countrymen to speculate upon the ignorance and credulity of our citizens; I could as easily have taken advantage of their weakness, and ingratiated myself into their good favor, by pretending to be a land lover, and deluding them in hopes and expectations which I myself did not believe would be realized; and under that deep delusion into which our people have been thrown, I could have purchased their possessions and claims for a trifle, and thus have enriched myself upon the spoils of my countrymen; but I have detested that vile speculation. I have seen others engaged in it, and those, too, who were understood to be your friends, and consequently opposed to a treaty. What speculation have I made, then, which you might allege the treaty was made to confirm to me?

Again: It is well known that while you were adding one farm after another, and stretching your fences over hills and dales, from river to river, and through swamps and forests, no doubt, (for I can conceive no other substantial reason for such unusual conduct,) with a view to these very times; I say, while you were making these great preparations, which have not turned out to be a pecuniary advantage to you, I was here, toiling, at the most trying time of our difficulties, for the defence of our rights, in an arduous employment, and with a nominal salary of three hundred dollars only, entirely neglecting my own pecuniary interest. You know it is so; it is too notorious to call for denial; and yet you would present me as being actuated, in this affair, by interested motives! . . .

Another of your defences is in reference to the charge that your policy has been to get the money of the nation into your hands. The extent that I have intended to charge you is, that your policy has been to get the money into the hands of what you call the *constituted authorities*. I need not spend time to prove that, for you avow it yourself in your letter, and you contend for its propriety. While you justify that policy, you make a "monstrous misrepresentation" when you say that the treaty throws our money into the hands of frontier agents. You will find *no such provision* in the treaty. It seems that you have been hard run to find real objections, so that you have been compelled to make imaginary objections. The only agent known in the treaty, and the only one responsible to the Cherokees for the disbursement of the money, according to the provisions of the treaty, is the United States. This is in accordance with the universal practice established in all our past treaties with the Government.

Now what is your wish—what is your policy? You would place the five millions in the hands of the *authorities of the nation*; their receipt, of course, would discharge the United States. Let the least reflecting mind think, for a moment, of the operation of such a policy. Responsibility is an essential ingredient in all money operations. And where is the responsibility of the Red Clay council equal to the proper disbursement of $5,000,000? A bare statement will show your policy to be consummately ridiculous. Will you say that the *authorities* of the nation is a sufficient security? What do you mean by that oft repeated word, when you know there is no authority of the nation?. . . .

"If ever I hold an office in the nation of my compatriots, it must be from *their election*, not the nomination of an executive of another country." "I am only one of their agents, and their *elected* chief." And again: "*The people* saw and understood it, and determined to preserve both without changing the spirit of our laws, though they were forced to modify the mode of their fulfilment." With what scrupulous fidelity you make the assertions in these extracts will be seen from the following short and simple statement of facts, which you cannot gainsay:

According to a provision of the Cherokee constitution, the office of the principal chief and the members of the council are to be filled, the latter by election of the people, for two years, and the former by the general council, for four years. The last election held was in the month of August, of 1830, and the next was to have been held in 1832. In the same year, in the month of October, came the election, by the council, for the principal chief. On account of a law of the State of Georgia, there was no election held in

August, 1832; and consequently, the members of the council, who were, according to the constitution, to elect the principal chief in the month of October following, were not elected. In this state of things, the members of the council, whose term of service was about to expire, took the following measures, at a called council, held, I think, in the month of August. I will be short. They passed a resolution appointing twenty-four men, selected (by the council) from the Cherokee people then on the ground, the aggregate number of which did not *exceed* two hundred. These twenty-four men were required to meet, as the resolution expressed it, in *convention*. I claim to know something of this matter, because I was a member of the convention. Two propositions were introduced: 1. That the Cherokee Government should be continued, *as it was*, for two years. This was my proposition. 2. That the Cherokee government should be continued, as it was, *while our difficulties lasted*. The latter prevailed, and it was sent to the council as the *advice* of the *convention*, which the council very gravely *accepted*, and referred to the people *on the ground* for their confirmation. The members of the council, the chiefs, and all, accordingly retained their seats after the expiration of their term of office prescribed in the constitution, and have retained them ever since.

Such is the simple history of this matter. For aught I know, this may be only a *modification* of the mode of fulfilling the Cherokee laws, although it has seemed to me to be an entire change of the principles of the Government. And by some new kind of construction it may be considered by *you* as an act *of the people*, although I can safely venture in the assertion that three out of five do not even know, *to this day*, that such transactions ever transpired. And for aught I know you may hold your office by *the election of the people*, and may be their "elected chief," although there has been no *election* since the constitution, under which you cannot pretend to hold your present office. . . .

It is a little singular that while you declare the new Echota treaty to be "deceptive to the world, and a fraud upon the Cherokee people," although it was made in the face of day, and in the eye of the nation, to prove your assertion, you resort to matters which are deceptive and fraudulent. It is deceptive to say that the great body of the Cherokees are opposed *understandingly* to the New Echota treaty, and they have *understandingly* authorized you to make another, with which they would be better pleased. The fact is, these Cherokees, perhaps, have never spent one moment's thought beyond that of *loving* and *securing* the land upon which they live; their whole instruction has tended to that point. According to that instruction, and the impressions produced in their minds by your want of candor and plain dealing, a portion of the Cherokees may be opposed to the new Echota treaty, but not more than they would be to any other, *as long as they understood you as trying to reinstate them in the country*. This is the whole secret of this much talked of opposition. Is it right to humor this delusion? Be candid with them; tell them that their country cannot be saved, and that you want their authority to sell, yes, *to sell* it, an authority which you have alleged to the Government you have received, and you will see to where this opposition against a removal will go.

Again, it is a "fraud upon the world" to say that "upwards of fifteen thousand Cherokees have protested against the treaty, solemnly declaring they will never acquiesce," and to produce before the world a paper containing that number of signatures. Let us see how this matter is. I will quote another sentence. "The Cherokee people, in two protests, the one signed by twelve thousand seven hundred and fourteen persons, and the other by three thousand two hundred and fifty persons, spoke for themselves against the treaty." In order to illustrate these, I take another term from your memorial. "The Cherokee population has recently been reported by the War Department to be 18,000." Of these 18,000, there are upwards of 1,000 blacks, who, you will not allege, have been among the signers. Of the remaining sixteen or seventeen thousand, (for I have not the census before me,) upwards of 1,000, at the lowest estimate, had been registered for removal, none of whom, it is likely, would have signed any protest. Here are then about 15,000, probably less, to do what? To "*protest*," "SOLEMNLY DECLARE," to "sign," to SPEAK FOR THEMSELVES against the treaty! I must confess my impotency to unravel such a mystery as this. A *population* of 15,000 furnishes 15,000 who are able and competent *to declare and to speak for themselves!* I suppose, however, we are required to believe it implicitly. This must indeed be a wise and precocious nation. Well may you say, "that owing to the intelligence of the Cherokee people, they have a correct knowledge of their own rights." ...

I will trouble you with one more topic, and then I will close this letter.

It is with sincere regret that I notice you say little or nothing about the moral condition of this people, as affected by present circumstances. I have searched in vain, in all your late communications, for some indication of your sensibility upon this point. You seem to be absorbed altogether in the pecuniary aspect of this nation's affairs; hence your extravagant demands for the lands we are compelled to relinquish; your ideas of the value of the gold mines, which, if they had been peaceably possessed by the Cherokees, would have ruined them as soon as the operation of the State laws have done; of the value of our marble quarries, our mountains and forests. Indeed, you seem to have forgotten that your people are a community of moral beings, capable of an elevation to an equal standing with the most civilized and virtuous, or deterioration to the level of the most degraded, of our race. Upon what principle, then, could you have made the assertion that you are reported to have made, "that the Cherokees had not suffered one-half what their country was worth," but upon the principle of valuing your nation in dollars and cents? If you meant simply the physical sufferings of this people, your assertion may be listened to with some patience; but can it be possible that you, who have claimed to be their leader and guardian, have forgotten that there is another kind of suffering which they have endured, and will endure as long as they are kept in these perplexities, of *a far more important nature?* Can it be possible that you consider the mere pains and privations of the body, and the loss of a paltry sum of money, of a paramount importance to the depression of the mind and the degradation and pollution of the soul? That the difficulties under which they are laboring, originating from the operation of the State laws, and their absorption by a white population, *will* affect them in that light, I need not here stop to argue with you: that they have *already* affected them, is a fact too palpable, too notorious, for us to deny it: that they will *increase* to affect them, in proportion to the delay of applying the remedy, we need only judge from past experience. How, then, can you reconcile your conscience and your sense of what is demanded by the best interest of your people, first with your incessant opposition to *a* treaty, and then your opposition to *the* treaty, because circumstances, which had calculated upon the nation by your delays, had compelled, if your please, a minority to make it; and forsooth it does not secure just such a title to the western lands as you may wish; and because a sufficient sum of *money* is not obtained for the "invaluable" gold mines, marble quarries, mountains, and forests of our country! How can you persist in deluding your people with phantoms, and in your opposition to that which alone is practicable, when you see them dying a moral death?

To be sure, from your account of the condition and circumstances of the Cherokees, the public may form an idea different from what my remarks may seem to convey. When applied to a portion of our people, confined mostly to whites intermarried among us, and the descendants of whites, your account is probably correct, divesting it of all the exaggeration with which you have encircled it; but look at the mass, look at the entire population as it now is, and say, can you see any indication of a progressing improvement, anything that can encourage a philanthropist? You know that it is almost a dreary waste. I care not if I am accounted a slanderer of my country's reputation; every observing man in the nation knows that I speak the words of truth and soberness. In the light that I consider my countrymen, not as mere animals, and to judge of their happiness by their condition as such, which, to be sure, is bad enough, but as moral beings, to be affected for better or for worse by moral circumstances, I say their condition is wretched. Look, my dear sir, around you, and see the progress that vice and immorality have already made! see the spread of intemperance, and the wretchedness and misery it has already occasioned! I need not reason with a man of your sense and discernment, and of your observation, to show the debasing character of that vice to our people; you will find an argument in every tippling shop in the country; you will find its cruel effects in the bloody tragedies that are frequently occurring in the frequent convictions and executions for murders, and in the tears and groans of the widows and fatherless, rendered homeless, naked, and hungry, by this vile curse of our race. And has it stopped its cruel ravages with the lower or poorer classes of our people? Are the higher orders, if I may so speak, left untainted? While there are honorable exceptions in all classes—a security for a future renovation under other circumstances—it is not to be denied that, as a people, we are making a rapid tendency to a general immorality and debasement. What more evidence do we need, to prove this general tendency, that the slow but sure insinuation of the lower vices into our female population? Oh! it is heart-rending to think of these things, much more to speak of them; but the world *will* know them, the world *does* know them, and we need not try to hide our shame.

Now, sir, can you say that in all this the Cherokees had not *suffered* one half what their country was worth? Can you presume to be spending your whole time in opposing *a* treaty, then in trying, as you say, to make a *better* treaty, that is to get more money, a full compensation for your gold mines, your marble quarries, your forests, your water courses—I say, can you be doing all this while the canker is eating the very vitals of this nation? Perish your gold mines and your money, if, in the pursuit of them, the moral credit of this people, their happiness and their existence, are to be sacrificed!

If the dark picture which I have here drawn is a true one, and no candid person will say it is an exaggerated one, can we see a brighter prospect ahead? In another country, and under other circumstances, there is a *better* prospect. Removal, then is the only remedy, the only *practicable* remedy. By it there *may be* finally a renovation; our people may rise from their very ashes, to become prosperous and happy, and a credit to our race. Such has been and is now my opinion, and under such a settled opinion I have acted in all this affair. My language has been: "fly for your lives;" it is now the same. I would say to my countrymen, you among the rest, fly from the moral pestilence that will finally destroy our nation.

What is the prospect in reference to *your* plan of relief, if you are understood at all to have any plan? It is dark and gloomy beyond description. Subject the Cherokees to the laws of the States in their present condition? It matters not how favorable those laws may be, instead of remedying the evil you would only rivet the chains and fasten the manacles of their servitude and degradation. The final destiny of our race, under such circumstances, is too revolting to think of. Its course *must* be downward, until it finally becomes extinct or is merged in another race, more ignoble and more detested. Take my word for it, it is the sure consummation, if you succeed in preventing the removal of your people. The time will come when there will be only here and there those who can be called upon to sign a protest, or to vote against a treaty for their removal; when the few remnants of our once happy and improving nation will be viewed by posterity with curious and gazing interest, as relics of a brave and noble race. Are our people destined to such a catastrophe? Are we to run the race of all our brethren who have gone before us, and of whom hardly any thing is known but their name, and, perhaps, only here and there a solitary being, waking, "as a ghost over the ashes of his fathers," to remind a stranger that such a race *once* existed? May God preserve us from such a destiny.

Source: U.S. Congress. Senate. *Documents in Relation to the Validity of the Cherokee Treaty of 1835.* 25th Cong., 2nd sess., 1838 S. Doc. 121, pp. 1–43.

22. Potawatomis of the Wabash Respond to A. C. Pepper (1838)

In July 1838, Superintendent of Emigration Abel C. Pepper met with the Potawatomis of the Wabash in Indiana, who had refused to gather for removal to the West. The patronizing talk Pepper gave provides an excellent example of the arguments Andrew Jackson and, later, Martin Van Buren instructed their commissioners to use in advocating removal: the tribes were once great but have dwindled and are now weak, the whites are growing in number and will intrude on the Indians' lands, the Indians who remain east of the Mississippi River will no longer be paid annuities and will have to submit to the laws of the state, and, finally, the United States will have to resort to force if the tribes do not remove. A version of the proceedings of the meeting between Pepper and others and the Potawatomis in 1838 is reprinted below. The Potawatomis' brief response to Pepper's long-winded talk is to the point but at the same time subtle in its reference to the Potawatomis' and Pepper's common relationship to the Great Spirit, their willingness to listen, and the need for a reasoned response.

At a Council held near Plymouth, Indiana, July 17, 1838. Present:
A. C. Pepper, Superintendent,
A. Morgan, Assistant Superintendent,
J. B. Duret, Enrolling Agent,
George M. Jerolaman, Atten'dng Physician,
And the Chiefs and Warriors of the Pottawattamies of the Wabash.
Col. Pepper arose, and addressed the Council as Follows:
Chiefs, Warriors, and Young men of the Pottawattamies of the Wabash.

My Children—We ought to thank the Great Spirit for the enjoyment of life and health—for the privilege of meeting together in peace and friendship and to implore his aid and protection while we sit in council.

My children—My heart has been heavy, and the spirit within me sorrowful for many days, because I have been told that you have listened to the songs of bad birds—that you have been advised not to come to your Great Father's council—that your hearts were getting weak; and that you were almost persuaded no longer to hold the chief of the 26 fires by the hand.

My children—My heart begins to be glad, because your presence here gives the lie to part of those bad stories; I therefore hope they are all untrue.

My children—I have many things to say to you, and as it may be the last council in which we shall ever meet, I want you to open your ears and incline your hearts to hear and receive the advice of your Great Father.

My children—When we get into trouble and difficulties we naturally look around us to discover, if we can, the causes which have produced them, as well as the remedies for the evils complained of. To impress upon your minds the importance of guarding against the consequences which have resulted from your habits, customs and mode of living, it is necessary to direct your attention to what you have been and what you are now.

My children—When the pale faces first came over the big waters towards the sun rise, they were a little handful; you were a great nation of brave warriors—all this great island from the seat to the East, to the great ocean where the sun sets, and from the big lakes where the water freezes, to the gulph of Mexico, where the sun falls on the top of the head, was yours. This handful of white men asked you for a place to build a fire: you gave them what they asked and took them by the hand as friends. They immediately met in council and made laws to protect the weak from the violence of the strong and wicked amongst them—to punish the man who should raise his hand to strike another; to inflict death upon the murderer who should slay his brother; to imprison others for less offences and make them work for the benefit of the people whose peace should be disturbed by their wicked acts. This council decreed, that the little piece of land you gave them should be divided into fields; that each man should raise and eat his own corn; should build his own house and feed his own children. Under these wise laws the little handful has prospered and grown into a mighty nation, while you have dwindled down to a handful.

My children—Has it never occurred to your minds that all this has happened because your councils made laws different from those of the white man? You allowed your people to strike each other for slight offences. If death was the consequence, the murderer was to be slain by the friends of the deceased; and this friend himself must be slain by the hands of the avenger, and so on, until the vengeance practised under your laws, has caused the earth to flow with the blood of the red man. You allowed your people to make fields and plant corn where they pleased, but did not secure the right to individuals to eat the fruit of their own labor; all was common. The idle and worthless were permitted to eat the corn produced by the labor of the industrious and prudent. You made war with each other and with the white man, the history of which you know as well as I do; and thus you have become less and less until you are now like a little tree in the middle of a thick forest of tall pines.

My children—Your Great Father thinks if you will remove to your own country and make laws like his, you may grow up again and become strong and happy. He believes that nothing else will save you as a nation. But some of you, I understand, say that the country to which your Great Father wishes you to go, is not good—that the small pox will attack and destroy you there—and if you should escape from its ravages, other tribes of Indians will kill you, and that your Great Father only wishes to send you there to have you destroyed.

My children—You know your great Father too well to believe seriously, in the absence of bad advice, any such evil stories of his intentions towards you. These words have been put into your mouths by your enemies and the enemies of the government, which has fed and protected you in kindness and mercy for more than forty winters. Will you believe the words of these enemies to your happiness who only seek to be rewarded with money, rather than listen to your Great Father whose goodness has been manifested towards you by all his acts for so long a time?

My children—Do not, I beseech you, let go the hand of your Great Father and listen to the bad counsel of men who would sacrifice your happiness for ever for a few pitiful dollars.

My children—I am informed you say you have not sold this land where you live. This is wrong, and you should not say so, and you would not if you were not advised to it by those who intend you no good. Your land has been sold and you know it. The treaty has been ratified and is in force, you have received every dollar of the consideration and receipted for it, and the fraud which you say has been practiced upon you consists in this only, that you received one dollar per acre for 22 sections, instead of fifty cents per acre for eleven sections of the same land at which price you had sold it by your treaty with Gen. Marshall. I repeat, you have received your money; your treaty has been ratified, and you cannot break it. Whatever your advisers may tell you to the contrary, be assured that treaties can only be broken by making war, and then the strong arm conquers the weak and makes its own terms. You have been advised, I am told, to petition Congress to restore you back this land. Do not listen to this advice. Two branches of the three, which form the council of the 26 fires, have examined and ratified the treaty. They did not consider the absence of Menomonie's name to the treaty furnished any grounds for an argument against its ratification.

My children—Listen to me, I speak the words of your Great Father, the chief of the 26 fires.

By the treaty at Greenville, 44 winters ago, you buried the tomahawk which had been raised by the advice of the King of Great Britain, then the enemy of the great Chief of the 26 fires. This was done in the presence of the Great Warrior, Gen. Wayne.

By that treaty you promised to acknowledge no other father than the President of the U.S.; never to listen to the proposition of any foreign nation, the ill councils of whose subjects might be calculated to foment dissatisfaction between the members of your own nation, and between your Great Father and yourselves.

You promised in the sight of the Great Spirit who heard it, that you would live in peace and friendship with the Americans.

This treaty contained many valuable things beneficial to all the tribes of red people who were parties to it. Your great Father promised you many things for your own good; and especially to pay you a certain amount of goods or money every year.

Which of these promises has your Great Father broken? Has he not kept every one of them with the strictest good faith? But have you always held fast to this chain of peace? Have you performed all those promises in good faith—or rather have you not opened your ears to hear the bad advice of those who persuade you not to listen to your Great Father?

My children—Let us turn our eyes back to events that are past. Have you not several times, by the instigation of the enemies of your Great Father, broken the chain of peace established between the United States and your nation by General Wayne and the brave chiefs of your tribe? Have you not raised the tomahawk against the white children of your Great Father? thereby forfeiting all your land, and severing the ties that bound him to protect with his strong arm, advise you by his wise counsels, and supply bread and blankets for your hungry and naked children?

My children—Did your Great Father take advantage of your disobedience as he might justly have done? Did he take your lands from you, and force you over the great lake, as his powers enabled him to do? Did he withhold from you his good counsel, his friendship, or the necessary supplies to comfort your warriors, your wives and children? No! I answer No! You will remember that he did none of those things which his just anger authorized him to do. No, my children, he pitied and deplored your unhappy condition—he invited you back to your duty—he gave you back your land and your warriors who were his prisoners—he presented to you the hand of friendship—he extended over you the strong arm of protection, and reestablished the wampum of peace which you had violated.

My children—You know every word that I have spoken is true; and still some of you appear restless and dissatisfied with your Great Father, after all the good he has done for you.

My children—What do you want? Have I not often told you that I would always listen to your complaints and supply your wants, agreeably to the provisions of your treaties, and punish the misconduct of white men towards you as far as the law would allow me to do?

My children—My heart grieves me and my eyes are watered with tears to hear that some of you have determined to refuse the good counsel of your Great Father, and threaten to cross the Great Lake and take your British Father by the hand again.

If you reject the good offer of a country provided for you west of the Mississippi by your Great Father, you cannot receive the benefits provided for in the treaties which you have entered into. By them you have agreed to remove, and to receive your annuity west of the great river. In that country only have the laws of the Grand Council of your Great Father provided for you the protection and support adequate to the wants and peculiar condition of your nation. Here your Great Father can no longer give you the aid and protection stipulated for and promptly rendered to all the tribes located west of the Mississippi.

My children—your fire is extinguished in this country. If you wish to renovate the feeble energies of a once great and brave nation, you must go to your own country and build a new fire there, where you will be out of the way of your deadly enemy the "liquid fire," which makes fools of your wise men, moral monsters of your warriors, imbeciles of your young men, and the whole earth to weep with the blood of your nation.

My children—If you comply with your treaties you may yet be happy; but if you refuse to listen to the counsels of your Great Father your destruction as a nation of as brave and good men as ever lived, is inevitable. It will overtake you soon; and the few winters allowed you before its consummation, must be spent in degraded misery and want.

My children, listen—Your Great Father is strong; you are weak; you must listen to him. He has required me to say to you, that altho' he will not force you to emigrate now, yet, if you refuse to go, he will no longer recognise you in your present position; he will pay you no more annuity; he will no longer consider you under his protection; he will leave you to the laws of the white man.

My children—It requires no great skill to explain to you your situation if you refuse to fulfill your treaties; it must be plain to the mind of every one, that such refusal will be a manifest violation of the obligations entered into with your Great Father, and would justify him in resorting to force to drive you from this country; but this he will not do now, if you live peaceably with your white neighbors—he never was first to raise the tomahawk, and he never will be. Persisting in the refusal to live up to your treaties will produce consequences so serious to yourselves, that I hope sincerely no one will assume the awful responsibility of advising you to it. If any one shall so advise you, he will have a terrible and solemn account to settle with the government whose humane laws he will violate—with the suffering hundreds of your people—and last, and greatest of all, with Him who knows, and tries, and searches the hearts of all men.

My children—You have heard what I had to say. I hope you will give me a good answer—an answer that may show a disposition to listen to the advice of your Great Father, and make his heart glad.

Mac-kah-tah-mo-ah then arose, and said—

My Father—We have heard what you said, and will give you an answer to-morrow.

The Council then adjourned; and having met again on Wednesday, the 18th inst.—

I-o-wa, the Principal Chief of the Indiana Pottawattamies, arose and said—

My Father—We have appointed San-go-aw to speak for us. We do not give him the power of Chief; but the words he will speak will be the voice of the Chiefs.

San-go-aw then arose, and said—

My Father—You told us yesterday to listen to you—to open our ears and incline our hearts to what you had to say. I now request you to open your ears, and your heart, and hear what I shall say.

My Father—My Chiefs were glad to hear you appeal to the Great Spirit for the truth of what you said. We are glad to hear you speak of the President. The Almighty is pleased with much of what you told us yesterday, and we agree in many things. He is always pleased to see us live together in peace and friendship. My chiefs have all heard and considered upon what you told us, and you shall hear what they now say. When you asked my chiefs an expression of their opinion relative to removal, they were glad and appointed this day to give you an answer.

My father—You have asked my chiefs and all present to go west of the Mississippi—they have all told me to say they would not go. The

Great Spirit desires us to live in peace with all men. We want the United States to pay us our annuity, and we don't know but that we will get our land back again, and this is the reason my chiefs are not willing to go west of the Mississippi. We were glad when you mentioned our Great Father the President. He does not wish to be at variance with any one, and neither do we.

My father—We heard what you said yesterday, and you have heard what we have just said. We do not want you to say any more on the subject, for if you do, we will not listen to it.

The Indians than immediately arose and departed from the Council.

Source: The Logansport Telegraph, July 21, 1838, p. 2, c. 1–4.

23. Address on the Present Condition and Prospects of the Aboriginal Inhabitants of North America with Particular Reference to the Seneca Nation. Delivered at Buffalo, New York, by M. B. Pierce, A Chief of the Seneca Nation, and a Member of Dartmouth College (1839)

After the Revolutionary War, both New York and Massachusetts claimed the Iroquois lands in New York. In 1786, New York was given jurisdiction over the land, but Massachusetts was granted the preemptive right to purchase the land should the Iroquois decide to sell. This right was sold three times over the next few years, during which tracts of land were purchased from the Senecas. The people ended up on several small reservations in western New York. The Senecas soon became demoralized, their social structures decayed, and traditional rituals became less vital due to reservation life.

The Senecas were split into two factions known as the Christian and Pagan parties. The Christian Party welcomed the missionaries and their efforts by adopting the lifestyles and institutions of the white people. The Pagans rejected this missionary influence, and many of them began following the Seneca prophet Handsome Lake, who helped revitalize Seneca society by providing the basis for the Longhouse religion, which is still an important part of modern-day Seneca life. In 1810, the Ogden Land Company bought the preemptive right to purchase the Seneca lands from New York State; under this prerogative, the company purchased large Seneca tracts on the Genesee River and on the Buffalo Creek, Tonawanda, and Cattaraugus reservations in 1823 and 1826. Not satisfied with these acquisitions, the Ogden Land Company pressed the Senecas to sell more of their land.

The Indian removal policy of the Andrew Jackson administration added to this pressure. The Senecas were successful in resisting such pressures until 1838, when corruption, intimidation, and bribery changed everything.

About half of the Senecas were induced to sign a treaty agreeing to sell their remaining lands and immigrate to Kansas. Some of the chiefs were in favor of the treaty, but most were against it. The treaty became an issue of public debate when the Society of Friends and others undertook the task of having it revoked. The Quaker missionaries and their supporters felt that the Senecas had been defrauded. The public debate that began in 1838 because of the manner in which the chiefs had signed the treaty lasted for more than a decade. Pierce's essay outlines the argument of one side of that debate.

Preface.

The following Address, recently delivered, has been published under the hope that the subject of the wrongs done to the Indian tribes of our country by designing men, may claim more of the public attention. Surrounded as the Seneca Indians are with the conveniences of civilized life, they now are beginning to appreciate the efforts heretofore made by benevolent individuals and associations for their benefit. In order to enable these Indians to retain their lands, and encourage them to withstand the combined efforts of unprincipled men, who are endeavoring to wrest by fraud their property from them, it is hoped the citizens of our common country will join in petitioning the Senate not to ratify the Treaty which the agents of both the Land Company and others, have been endeavouring to make with a part of the Chiefs, during the past year, should they succeed in obtaining it.

In proof of the kind of fraud resorted to, the reader is referred to the case of John Snow's Contract. In order to obtain his signature and influence, not only is a large sum of money to be paid him, but it is also guaranteed that he shall continue to possess his land, and shall not be compelled to remove. Thus, those who are openly and honestly contending for their rights, and entreating for the unmolested possession of their homes, are by the treachery of others, to be forced to relinquish them, whilst those who have thus betrayed them, are to remain in the enjoyment of their lands, and in addition, to receive a large sum of money as the price of their treachery; and this bribe is offered ostensibly for the *Indian's good*, by those professing to be christians. "Therefore all things whatsoever ye would that men should do to you, do ye even so to them."

Philadelphia, 1st mo. 1839.

Address.

The condition and circumstances of the race of people of whom I am by blood *one*, and in the well being of whom I am, by the ties of kindred and the common feelings of humanity, deeply interested, sufficiently apologize, and tell the reason for my seeking this occasion of appearing before this audience, in this city. Not only the eyes and attention of *you*, our neighbors—but also of the councils of this great nation, are turned upon us. We are expected to do, or to refuse to do, what the councils of this nation, and many private men, are now asking of us—what many favour and advocate—yet also what many discountenance and condemn.

My relation to my kindred people being as you are aware it is, I have thought it not improper—rather that it was highly *proper*—that I should appear before you in my own person and character, in behalf of my people and myself, to present some facts, and views, and reasons, which must necessarily have a material bearing upon our decisions and doings at the present juncture of our affairs.

Hitherto our cause has been advocated almost exclusively, though ably and humanely, by the friends of human right and human weal, belonging by *nature* to a different, and by *circumstances* and *education*, to a superior race of men. The ability and humanity of its advocates, however, does not do away the expediency, nor even the *necessity*, of those of us who can, standing forth with our own pen and voices, in behalf of that *same right* and *that same weal* as connected with ourselves, which have been and now are, by a powerful and perhaps *fatal* agency, almost fatally jeopardized.

It has been said and reiterated so frequently as to have obtained the familiarity of household words, that it is the *doom* of the Indian to disappear—to vanish like the morning dew, before the advance of civilization: and melancholy is it to us—those doomed ones—that the history of this country, in respect to *us* and its civilization, has furnished so much ground for the saying, and for giving credence to it.

But *whence* and why are we thus doomed? Why must we be crushed by the arm of civilization, or the requiem of our race be chanted by the waves of the Pacific, which is destined to engulph us?

It has been so long and so often said as to have gained general credence, that our *natural constitution* is such as to render us incapable of apprehending, and incompetent to practice, upon those principles from which result the *characteristic* qualities of christian civilization; and so by a necessary consequence, under the sanction of acknowledged principles of moral law, we must yield ourselves sacrifices, doomed by the constitution which the Almighty has made for us, to that *other race* of human beings, whom the same Almighty has endowed with a more noble and more worthy constitution.

These are the premises; these the arguments; these the conclusions; and if they are *true*, and *just*, and *legitimate*, in the language of the poet, we must say,

"God of the just—thou gavest the bitter cup,
We bow to thy behest, and drink it up."

But are they *true*, and *just*, and *legitimate*? Do we, as a people, lack the capacity of apprehending and appreciating any of the principles which form the basis of christian civilization? Do we lack the competency of practicing upon those principles in any or *all* their varieties of application?

A general reference to facts as they are recorded in the history of the former days of our existence, and as they are now transpiring before the eyes of the whole enlightened world, give an answer which should ever stifle the question, and redeem us from the stigma.

Before citing particular exemplifications of the truth of this, I will allude to one question which is triumphantly asked by those who adopt the doctrine of the untamable nature of the Indian, viz. "Why have not the Indians become civilized and christianized as a consequence of their intercourse with the whites—and of the exertions of the whites to bring about so desirable a result?" Who that believes the susceptibilities and passions of human nature to be in the main uniform throughout the rational species, needs an answer to this question from me?

Recur to the page which records the dealings, both in manner and substance, of the early white settlers and of their successors, down even to the present day, with the unlettered and unwary red man, and then recur to the susceptibilities of your own bosom, and the question is answered.

Say, ye on whom the sun light of civilization and christianity has constantly shone—into whose lap Fortune has poured her brimful horn, so that you are enjoying the *highest* and *best spiritual* and *temporal* blessings of this world,—say, if some beings from fairy land, or some distant planet, should come to you in such a manner as to cause you to deem them children of *greater light* and *superior wisdom* to yourselves, and you should open to them the hospitality of your dwellings and the fruits of your *labor,* and they should, by dint of their *superior wisdom,* dazzle and amaze you, so as for what to them were *toys and rattles,* they should gain freer admission and fuller welcome, till finally they should claim the *right* to your possessions, and of hunting you, like wild beasts, from your long and hitherto undisputed domain, how ready would *you* be to be taught of *them?* How cordially would you open your *minds* to the conviction that they meant not to deceive you *further* and still more fatally in their proffers of pretended kindness? How *much* of the kindliness of friendship for them, and of esteem for their manners and customs would *you feel?* Would not 'the milk of human kindness' in your breasts be turned to the gall of hatred towards them? And have not *we,* the original and undisputed possessors of this country, been treated *worse* than *you* would be, should my supposed case be transformed to reality?

But I will leave the consideration of this point for the present, by saying, what I believe every person who hears me will assent to, that the manner in which the whites have habitually dealt with the Indians, make them *wonder* that their hatred has not burned with tenfold fury against them, rather than that they have not laid aside their own peculiar notions and habits, and adopted those of their civilized neighbors.

Having said thus much as to the question, "Why have not the Indians been civilized and christianized by the intercourse and efforts of the whites?" I would now call your attention to a brief exemplification of the point I was remarking upon before alluding to the above-mentioned question, viz., "That the Indian is capable of apprehending and appreciating, and is competent to practice on those principles which form the basis of christian civilization."

I do not know that it has ever been questioned, and especially by those who have had the best opportunities to learn by *experience* and *observation,* that the Indian possesses as perfect a physical constitution as the whites, or any other race of men, especially in the matter of hardy body, swift foot, sharp and true eye, accompanied by a hand that scarcely ever drew the bow-string amiss, or raised the tomahawk in vain.

I believe also, that it is not denied that he is susceptible of hatred, and equally of friendship,—that he even can love and pity, and feel gratitude,—that he is prone to the adoration of the Great Spirit,—that he possesses an imagination, by which he pictures fields of the blessed in a purer and more glorious world than this,—that he possesses the faculty of memory and judgment, and such a combination of faculties as enable him to invent and imitate,—that he is susceptible of ambition, emulation, pride, vanity,—that he is sensitive to honor and disgrace, and necessarily has the *elements* of a *moral sense* or conscience. All these are granted as entering into his *native spiritual constitution.*

For instances of those *natural endowments,* which, by *cultivation,* give to the children of civilization their great names and far-reaching fame, call to mind Philip of Mount Hope, whose consummate talents and skill made him the white man's terror, by his display of those talents and skill for the white man's destruction.

Call to mind Tecumseh, by an undeserved association with whose name, one of the great men of your nation has obtained more of greatness than he ever merited, either for his *deeds* or his *character.* Call to mind *Red Jacket,* formerly your *neighbor,* with some of you a friend and a familiar, of the same tribe with whom I have the honor to be a *humble member:* to have been a *friend* and a *familiar* with whom none of you feel it a *disgrace.* Call to mind Osceola, the victim of the white man's treachery and cruelty, whom neither his enemy's cunning or arm could conquer on the battle field, and who at last was consumed "in durance vile," by the corroding of his own spirit. "In durance vile," I say—(blot the fact from the records of that *damning baseness,*—of that violation of *all law,* of all humanity,—which that page of your nation's history which contains an account of it, must ever be;—*blot out the fact,* I say, before you rise up to call an Indian treacherous or cruel). Call to mind *these* and a thousand others, whom I have not time to mention, and my point is gained.

Here, then, the fundamental elements of the best estate of human nature are admitted as existing in the natural constitution of the Indian. The question now comes, are these elements susceptible of cultivation and improvement, so as to entitle their possessors to the rank which civilization and christianity bestow?

For an instance of active pity,—of *deep, rational, active pity,* and the attendant intellectual qualities, I ask you to call to mind the *story-surpassing romance* of Pocahontas—she who threw herself between a supposed inimical stranger, and the deadly club which had been raised by the stern edict of her stern father,—she begged for the victim's life,—she obtained his deliverance from the jaws of death by appealing to the affections which existed in the bosom of her father, savage as he was, and which affections overcame the fell intent which had caused him to pronounce the white man's doom. From this time she received the instruction, imbibed the principles and sentiments, adopted the manners and customs of the whites; in her bosom burned *purely* and *rationally* the flame of love, in accordance with the promptings of which, she offered herself at the hymenial altar, to take the nuptial ties with a son of Christian England. The offspring of this marriage have been, *with pride,* claimed as *sons* and citizens of the noble and venerable State of Virginia.

Ye who love prayer, hover in your imagination around the cot of Brown, and listen to the strong supplications as they arise from the fervent heart of Catherine, and then tell me whether

"The poor Indian whose untutor'd mind
Sees God in clouds and hears him in the wind,"

is not capable, by cultivation, of rationally comprehending the *true God,* whose pavilion, though it be the *clouds,* still giveth grace even *to the humble.*

But perhaps I am indulging too much in minuteness. Let me then refer to one more instance which covers the whole ground and sets the point under consideration beyond dispute. The ill-starred Cherokees stand forth in colors of living light, redeeming the Indian character from the foul aspersions that it is not susceptible of civilization and christianization. In most of the arts which characterize civilized life, this nation in the aggregate, have made rapid and long advances. The arts of peace in all their varieties, on which depend the comforts and enjoyments of the enlightened, have been practiced and the results enjoyed by them. The light of revelation has beamed in upon their souls, and caused them to exchange the *blind* worship of the Great Spirit, for the *rational* worship and service of the God of the Bible.—Schools have been established. An alphabet of the language invented by one of their own men; instruction sought and imparted; and letters cultivated in their own as well as the English language.

Hence many individuals have advanced even to the refinements of civilized life, both in respect to their physical and intellectual condition. A John Ross stands before the American People in a character both of intellect and heart which many of the white men in high places may *envy,* yet *never be able to attain.* A scholar, a patriot, an honest and honourable man; standing up before the "powers that be," in the eyes of heaven and men, now demanding, now supplicating of those powers a regard for the rights of humanity, of justice, of law,—is still a scholar, a patriot, an honest and honorable man, though an Indian blood coursing in his veins, and an Indian color giving hue to his complexion, dooms him and his children and his kin to be hunted at the point of the bayonet by those powers, from their homes and possessions and country, to the "terra incognita" beyond the Mississippi.

I now leave this point, on which, perhaps I need not have spoken thus briefly, from the fact that it is granted by all of you as soon as announced; and proceed to make a few remarks confined more exclusively to my own kindred tribe, a part of whom live near this city.

Taking it as clearly true that the Indians are susceptible of cultivation and improvement, even to the degree of physical, intellectual and moral refinement, which confers the title civilized and christianized,—I now proceed to consider whether their condition and feelings are such as to render feasible the undertaking to bring them up to *that degree,*—whether in fact they do not themselves *desire* to come up to it. When I say *they,* I mean those who constitute the body and stamina of the people. As to this point, I take it upon myself to say that such an undertaking *is* feasible, and doubly so from the fact that the object of the undertaking is earnestly desired by themselves.

I know of no way to set this matter in a clearer light than by presenting you with some facts as to the spirit and the advance of improvements amongst them. And this I crave the liberty of doing by a brief detail of items, prefacing the detail by the remark of a highly respectable individual, formerly of Holland, Erie co[unty, New York], but for some eighteen years a resident of Illinois. After an absence of about fifteen years, he returned two or three years ago, and spent the summer in this region, and several days of the time on the Reservation. He frequently remarked that the Indians, during his absence, had improved far more rapidly than their neighbors in the country around them.

In business there is much greater diligence and industry; their teams, in respect to oxen, horses, wagons, sleighs, &c., are greater in number and better in quality than formerly: and in these respects there is a constant improvement. The men labor more, comparatively, and the women less, except in their appropriate sphere, than formerly.

With regard to buildings, they are much more conveniently planned, and of the best materials, both dwelling houses and barns, and new ones constantly going up. Those who have not lands of their own under cultivation, are much more willing to hire out their services to others, either by the year or by shares. This shows that the idea, "to work is thought to be dishonorable," has been done away. There are amongst us, good mowers, and cradlers, and reapers. Blacksmiths, carpenters, shoemakers, and other mechanics, find work enough from their own brethren. There are several wagons in the nation, which are worth more than one hundred dollars in cash; tools of the best quality and of various kinds; manure and other things are sometimes applied, but five years ago almost or quite universally wasted.

With regard to mode of living, tables, chairs, and bedsteads and cooking apparatus have generally been purchased of the whites or manufactured in imitation of them; and they are used to a greater or less extent in almost every family. The habit of taking regular meals is gaining ground, and the provision luxurious. In the care of the sick, they are more attentive and judicious, and rely less on notions and quackery; they employ skillful physicians, and use the medicine with less prejudice, and a great deal more confidence.

Other evidences of improvement we have in the increase of industry, and a consequent advance in dress, furniture, and all the comforts and conveniences of civilized life. The fields of the Indians have never been kept in so good order, and managed with so much industry, as for the few years past. At public meetings and other large assemblies, the Indians appear comfortably and decently, and some of them richly clad. The population is increasing gradually, except when visited with epidemics. The increase of general information is visible: there are many of them, who keep themselves well informed of what is going on in the country; several newspapers have been taken from the cities of Washington, D.C., Philadelphia, New York, and other cities in the Union, and two or three copies of the *Genesee Farmer*. Some young men have a choice selection of books and libraries. All these improvements are advancing at a rapid rate, *except when they are distracted with cares and anxieties.*

In view of these facts, I deem it unnecessary to say any thing further, as to the question, whether or not the undertaking is feasible to bring the Senecas up to the standard which shall entitle them to be called civilized and christianized.

The only question which I shall now consider, included in the subject I am treating, is, *how* can this undertaking be carried into operation most advantageously for securing its ultimate object?

Can it be by remaining where we now are located, or by selling our lands and removing to the afore-mentioned "terra incognita"? The right and possession of our lands is undisputed—so with us it a question appealing directly *to our interest;* and how stands the matter in relation *to that?* Our lands are as fertile and as well situated for agricultural pursuits as any we shall get by a removal. The graves of our fathers and mothers and kin are here, and about them still cling our affections and memories. Here is the theatre on which our tribe has thus far acted its part in the drama of its existence, and about it are wreathed the associations which ever bind the human affections to the soil, whereon one's nation, and kindred, and self, have arisen and acted. We are here situated in the midst of facilities for physical, intellectual and moral improvement; we are in the midst of the enlightened; we see their ways and their works, and can thus profit by their example. We can avail ourselves of their implements, and wares and merchandise, and once having learned the convenience of using them, we shall be led to deem them indispensable. We here are more in the way of instruction from teachers, having greater facilities for getting up and sustaining schools; and as we, in the progress of our improvement, may come to feel the want and the usefulness of books and prints, so we shall be able readily and cheaply to get whatever we may choose. In this view of facts, surely there is no inducement for removing.

But let us look at the other side of the question. In the first place the white man wants our land; in the next place it is said that the offer for it is liberal; in the next place that we shall be better off to remove from the vicinity of the whites, and settle in the neighborhood of our fellow red men, where the woods flock with game, and the streams abound with fishes. These are the reasons offered and urged in favour of our removal.

Let us consider each of these reasons a little in detail. The fact that the whites want our land imposes no obligation on us to sell it; nor does it hold forth an inducement to do so, unless it leads them to offer a price equal to its value. We neither know nor feel any debt of gratitude which we owe to them, in consequence of their "loving kindness or tender mercies" towards us, that should cause us to make a sacrifice of our property or our interest, to their wonted avarice, and which, like the mother of the horse leech, cries, Give, give, and is never sated.

And is the offer liberal? Of that who but ourselves are to be the final judges? If we do not deem one or two dollars an acre liberal for the land, which will to the white man's pocket bring fifteen to fifty, I don't know that we can be held heinously criminal for our opinion. It is well known that those who are anxious to purchase our Reservations, calculate safely on fifteen dollars the acre for the poorest, and by gradation up to fifty and more, for the other qualities. By what mode of calculation or rules of judgment, is one or two dollars a liberal offer to us, when many times that sum would be only fair to the avarice of the land speculator? Since in us is vested a perfect title to the land, I know not why we may not, when we wish, dispose of it at such prices as we may see fit to agree upon.

"But the land company have the right of purchase," it is said—granted; but they have not the right, nor, we trust in God, the power to force us to accept of their offers. And when that company finds that a whistle or a rattle, or one dollar or two, per acre, will not induce us to part with our lands, is it not in the nature of things that they should offer better and more attractive terms? If they could not make forty-nine dollars on an acre of land, I know no reason why they would fail of trying to make forty-five, or thirty, or ten. So I see no obstacle to our selling when and at such reasonable prices as we may wish, in the *fact* that the land company have the right of purchase: nor do I see any thing extortionate in us, in an unwillingness to part with our soil on the terms offered,—nor even in *the desire*, if our lands are sold, of putting into our *own* pockets a due portion of their value.

But the point of chief importance is, shall we be better off? If our object was to return to the manners and pursuits of life which characterized our ancestors, and we could be put in a *safe, unmolested* and *durable* possession of a wilderness of game, whose streams abound in fish, we might be better off; but though that were our object, I deny that we could possess *such a territory* this side of the shores of the Pacific, with *safety, free of molestation,* and in *perpetuity.*

"Westward the Star of Empire takes its way," and whenever that Empire is held by the white man, nothing is safe or unmolested or enduring against his avidity for gain. Population is with rapid strides going beyond the Mississippi, and even casting its eye with longing gaze for the woody peaks of the Rocky Mountains—nay even for the surf-beaten shore of the Western Ocean.—And in process of time, will not our territory there be as subject to the wants of the whites, as that which we now occupy is? Shall we not then be as strongly solicited, and by the same arguments, to remove still farther west? But there is one condition of a removal which must certainly render it hazardous in the extreme to us. The proximity of our then situation to that of other and more warlike tribes, will expose us to constant harassing by them; and not only this, but the character of those worse than Indians, those *white borderers* who infest, yes *infest* the western border of the white population, will annoy us more fatally than even the Indians themselves. Surrounded thus by the natives of the soil, and hunted by such a class of whites, who neither "fear God nor regard man," how shall we be better off there than where we are now?

Having said thus much as to our condition after a removal, under the supposition that we wish to return to and continue in the habits of life which prevailed when the country was first taken possession of by the Europeans, I proceed now to say, that we do not wish so to do, and to repeat, that so far from it, we desire to renounce those habits of mind and body, and adopt in their stead those habits and feelings—those modes of living, and acting and thinking, which result from the cultivation and enlightening of the moral and intellectual faculties of man. And on this point, I need not insult your common sense by endeavoring to show that it is *stupid folly* to suppose that a removal from our present location to the western wilds would improve our condition. What! leave a fertile and somewhat improved soil—a home in the midst of civilization and christianity, where the very breezes are redolent of improvement and exaltation,—where, by induction as it were, we must be pervaded by the spirit of the enterprise,—where books, and preaching, and conversation, and business and conduct, whose influence we need, are all around us, so that we have but to stretch forth our hands, and open our ears, and turn our eyes, to experience in full their improving and enlightening effects,—leave these! and for what? and echo answers *for what?* But methinks I hear the echo followed by the anxious guileful whisper of some government land company agent—for one or two dollars the acre, and a western wilderness beyond the white man's reach, where an Eden lies in all its freshness of beauty for you to possess and enjoy. But ours, I reply, is sufficiently an Eden now, if but the emissaries of the arch fiend, not so much in the form of a serpent as of man, can be kept from its borders.

But I will relieve your patience by closing my remarks; it were perhaps needless, perhaps useless, for me to appear before you with these remarks, feebly and hastily prepared as they were; but as I intimated on the outset, the crisis which has now arrived in the affairs of our people furnish the apology and reason for my so doing. And now I ask, what feature of our condition is there which should induce us to leave our present location and seek another in the western wilds? Does justice, does humanity, does religion, in their relations to us demand it? Does the interest and the well being of the whites require it? The plainest dictates of common sense and common honesty, answer *No!* I ask then, in behalf of the New York Indians and myself, that our white brethren will not urge us to do that which justice or humanity not only do not require, but condemn. I ask then to let us live on, where our fathers have lived; let us enjoy the advantages which our location affords us; that thus we, who have been converted heathen, may be made meet for that inheritance which the *Father* hath promised to give his *Son*, our Saviour; so that the deserts and waste places may be made to blossom like the rose, and the inhabitants thereof utter forth the high praises of our God.

Appendix.

It has been repeatedly said, that "if the Indians had been left to the exercise of their own judgment, they would have consented to have sold their lands in this state; but the interested white man opposed to their removal, have influenced them to reject the 'liberal offer' of the government."

This allegation is without foundation; the Indians know their interest very well; they ask no questions whether it is best for them to sell out and remove; they know that the moment they leave these premises, then will troubles commence; poverty, oppression, destruction, and perhaps war and bloodshed will fall upon them in the western wilderness.

The policy of the general government is well understood by them; and the country assigned them west, has been explored again and again, so that they do not lack knowledge in these respects. With all the light and information on the subject which is necessary to form a correct judgment upon it, they have a hundred times repeated in open council and in the presence of the United States commissioner, that they cannot and will not sell out their lands and remove beyond the Mississippi river. These are the honest judgments of the Indians, and this answer will the commissioner receive from the *honest* chiefs.

But while persuasion and lawful inducements have been held out to them, and they fail to produce the desired effect, the "Ogden Company," through their agents, lose no time in buying over the chief to aid in procuring the treaty. Rewards have been made to promote it, and to induce our nation to consent to it. In the statements which follow, I shall confine myself principally to facts, that the public may be able to judge for themselves as to the correctness of the above remark.

First, the contract of John Snow, a chief; it was made a year ago, and may be known by the date. This is one of the many contracts entered into by the parties; we have them in our hands.

Article of Agreement

Made and concluded this 20th day of July, 1837, between Heman B. Potter, of the city of Buffalo, of the first part, and John Snow, a Seneca Chief of the Buffalo Creek Reservation, in the county of Erie, of the second part.

Whereas, in conformity with the declared policy of the government of the United States, the proprietors of the pre-emptive title of and in the four several tracts of land, reserved by the Seneca tribe of Indians, within the said State of New York, are desirous to induce the above-mentioned tribe of Indians to accept for their future and permanent residence, a tract of country in the territory west of the river Mississippi, appropriated for Indians inhabiting the Atlantic and other neighboring states; and are also desirous, by fair purchase, to extinguish the right of the said Indians in and to the lands in this state, so reserved by them.

And whereas, in furtherance of these objects, and in order to a future treaty by which to effect the same, the said proprietors have authorized negotiations to be opened with the chiefs and other leading men of the said tribe of Indians, and certain offers to be made to them in money as a permanent fund for the nation, and a compensation for their improvements; and have also deemed it advisable and necessary to employ the aid, cooperation and services of certain individuals who are able to influence the said Indians to accept the offers so to be made to them.

And whereas the said Heman B. Potter, the party of the first part, is empowered to act on behalf of the said proprietors, and to contract with any individuals whose co-operation and agency may be necessary and efficient in accomplishing the above-mentioned object; and the said John Snow, the party of the second part, has agreed to contribute his influence and services in the premises; and in case of the extinguishment of the same Indian title to the said reserved lands as aforesaid, to sell to the said proprietors all and singular his improvements of, in and to the same.

Now therefore, it is mutually agreed by and between the parties hereto, as follows:

First. The party of the second part undertakes and agrees to use his best exertions and endeavours to dispose and induce the said Indians to adopt and pursue the advice and recommendations of the government of the United States, in respect to their removal and future location, and on such *said* terms as the party of the first part, and his associates, in the name of the said proprietors, shall propose to sell and release, by treaty, their said reserved lands; and on all occasions to co-operate with and aid the said party of the first part, and his associates, as he may be from time to time advised, in talks and negotiations with the chiefs and other influential men of the said tribe; and in the active application of his whole influence at councils and confidential interviews, for the purpose of effecting a treaty between the said tribe and the said proprietors, for the extinguishment of the Indian title to the said reserved lands.

Second. The second party of the second part hath sold, and hereby doth sell, to the said proprietors, all and singular, his buildings and improvements on the lands so to be released by the treaty, and agrees to accept compensation therefore in the manner hereinafter mentioned; said buildings and improvements in the mean time not to be leased, or in any manner disposed of by said party of the second part.

Third. In consideration of such efforts, co-operation and services on the part of the said John Snow, faithfully bestowed in the premises, and of the sale and release of all and singular his said buildings and improvements upon any of the lands aforesaid, without leasing or otherwise disposing of the same, as herein above stipulated, the said Heman B. Potter, on his part, and that of his associates, agrees to pay, or cause to be paid, to the said John Snow the sum of two thousand dollars, within three months after notice of the ratification, by the Senate of the United States, of a valid treaty between the said tribe and the owners of the said pre-emptive title, or their trustees, by which the right and title of the said Indians shall be effectually released and extinguished in and to the said reserved lands; subject, however, to the following qualification and understanding,—that in case the said treaty shall provide for the payment to individual Indians for their buildings and improvements, then and in that case the said party of the second part shall accept and receive, as part payment of the above-mentioned sum of two thousand dollars, such sum or compensation as he shall or may be entitled to, by and under the provisions of such treaty, for his said buildings and improvements, and the balance of the said two thousand dollars which shall remain, after deducting therefrom such compensation as aforesaid, and that only to be paid by the said party of the first part, as above specified, within the time above-mentioned, or as soon thereafter as the said balance can be ascertained; and in case said party of the second part shall be entitled by and under the provision of said treaty, to the sum of two thousand dollars and upwards, he shall receive the same as may be therein provided, and the said party of the first part shall be discharged from paying any part of the said two thousand dollars.

And the said John Snow shall also be entitled, at a nominal rent, to a lease from the owners of the pre-emptive title, or their trustees, of and for the lot of land actually improved and occupied by him, called the Whipple Farm, near the old council-house, on the Buffalo Reservation, for and during his own natural life, determinable when and as soon as he shall cease to live on and occupy the same; said lease to be executed by the lessors as soon after said treaty as said lands shall have been surveyed and allotted, said lease having reference to said survey.

This agreement on the part of said party of the first part, being expressly dependant upon a treaty to be made and ratified upon terms, conditions, and stipulations to be proposed and offered by said party of the first part and his associates.

H. B. POTTER, [L.S.]
his
JOHN SNOW, [L.S.]
mark
WITNESS—
his
GEORGE JIMESON.
mark.
TRUE COPY.

In addition to the above stipulation, *money* and *brandy* have been used for the same purpose; and finally, intimidation and discouragement are not wanting,—for instance, they will tell us, "Here my friend, you have got to go, there is no earthly doubt—the policy of the government is fixed, and your best course is to get as much money as you can from the pre-emption company, make you a contact," &c. The object of the present council is to give an opportunity for the chiefs to assent to the amendments of the last winter's treaty, or to refuse them. The resolution of the Senate, is in the following words, to wit,—

Provided always, and be it further resolved, That this treaty shall have no force or effect whatever, as it relates to any of the said tribes, nations or bands of New York Indians, nor shall it be understood that the Senate have assented to any of the contracts connected with it, until the same, with the amendments herein proposed, is submitted and fully and fairly explained, by a commissioner of the United States, to each of said tribes or bands, separately assembled in council, and they have given their free and voluntary assent thereto; and if one or more of said tribes or bands when consulted as aforesaid, shall freely assent to said treaty as amended, and to their contract connected therewith, it shall be binding and obligatory upon those so assenting, although other, or others, of said bands or tribes may not give their consent, and thereby cease to be parties thereto: *Provided further,* That if any portion or part of said Indians do not emigrate, the President shall retain a proper portion of said sum of four hundred thousand dollars, and shall deduct from the quantity of land allowed west of the Mississippi, such number of acres as will leave to each emigrant three hundred and twenty acres only.

Source: Pierce, Maris Bryant. *Address on the Present Condition and Prospects of the Aboriginal Inhabitants of North America, with Particular Reference to the Seneca Nation. Delivered at Buffalo, New York, by M. B. Pierce, a Chief of the Seneca Nation, and a Member of Dartmouth College.* Philadelphia: J. Richards, 1839.

24. Appeal to the Christian Community on the Condition and Prospects of the New-York Indians in Answer to a Book, Entitled The Case of the New-York Indians, and Other Publications of the Society of Friends by Nathaniel T. Strong, A Chief of the Seneca Tribe (1841)

After the Revolutionary War, both New York and Massachusetts claimed the Iroquois lands in New York. In 1786, New York was given jurisdiction over the land, but Massachusetts was granted the preemptive right to purchase the land should the Iroquois decide to sell. This right was sold three times over the next few years, during which tracts of land were purchased from the Senecas. The people ended up on several small reservations in western New York. The Senecas soon became demoralized, their social structures decayed, and traditional rituals became less vital due to reservation life.

The Senecas were split into two factions known as the Christian and Pagan parties. The Christian Party welcomed the missionaries and their efforts by adopting the lifestyles and institutions of the white people. The Pagans rejected this missionary influence, and many of them began following the Seneca prophet Handsome Lake, who helped revitalize Seneca society by providing the basis for the Longhouse religion, which is still an important part of modern-day Seneca life. In 1810 the Ogden Land Company bought the preemptive right to purchase the Seneca lands from New York State; under this prerogative, the company purchased large Seneca tracts on the Genesee River and on the Buffalo Creek, Tonawanda, and Cattaraugus reservations in 1823 and 1826. Not satisfied with these acquisitions, the Ogden Land Company pressed the Senecas to sell more of their land.

The Indian removal policy of the Andrew Jackson administration added to this pressure. The Senecas were successful in resisting such pressures until 1838, when corruption, intimidation, and bribery changed everything. About half of the Senecas were induced to sign a treaty agreeing to sell their remaining lands and immigrate to Kansas. Some of the chiefs were in favor of the treaty, but most were against it. The treaty became an issue of public debate when the Society of Friends and others undertook the task of having it revoked. The Quaker missionaries and their supporters felt that the Senecas had been defrauded. The public debate that began in 1838 because of the manner in which the chiefs had signed the treaty lasted for more than a decade. Strong's essay outlines the argument of one side of that debate.

Being a Chief of the Seneca Tribe of Indians, and lately arrived in this city, my attention has been called to a volume composed and widely circulated by the Society of Friends, under the title of "The Case of the Seneca Indians, in the state of New York," the avowed design of which is to defeat the treaty lately concluded between the United States and the New York Indians, and after mature consideration by the president and the senate of the United States, constitutionally ratified. The charges contained in this book, the proofs in support of them, and also the proofs in opposition to them, having all been deliberately investigated and passed on by the appropriate tribunals of your country, our people, after years of suspense and anxiety, considered the question of emigration as settled, and they fondly hoped that their rights under the treaty, being now secure and inviolable, they might commence the preparations necessary for their removal, and with the kind wishes and encouragement of their white brethren, be permitted to enter on the new path which a kind new Providence had opened from their escape from bondage, degradation and misery, with the cheering hope of enjoying, in the asylum provided for them by your government, the blessings of freedom and independence. But alas! as at the outset, so in the progress of our journey, we are met by enemies, powerful in numbers and discipline, but more dangerous in artifice and cunning; disguising their attacks under the false banner of friendship and good will, and seeking to withdraw from us the support even of those who are in reality our friends. Thus we see simultaneous movements in different parts of the country, all organized under the same banner, and all urged on by the same influence. These are but the sequels of continued attempts for two years past to control, through the agency of public opinion and prejudice, the constitutional action on the treaty of the president and senate; and although (now binding both on you and us,) through popular entertainment and excitement to prevent its execution. I will not stop to discuss the propriety of these proceedings, nor their consistency with those principles of peace and order professed by the Society of Friends; but in regard to their last publication, I must be permitted to say, that its gross abuse, garbled statements, and repeated misrepresentations, are in my poor judgment as incompatible with the law of Christian charity, as with the rules of candour and fair discussion: nor can I in adequate terms express my surprise, that on an appeal like this, to an intelligent community upon a question involving the dearest interests of an unfortunate and suffering race of beings, coming from a body of Christian men professing to be the steady friends of that race, and the faithful advocates of their cause, no reasoning should be employed to enlighten the public mind on the merits and effects of the treaty as an instrument to them of good or evil; and that its beneficent provisions in their favour, should be noticed only to condemn and censure them, as too liberal and costly on the part of the government.

In the following remarks, I propose, on behalf of my countrymen, to notice the prominent objections put forth in this volume to the consummation of the treaty, and more seriously, to call your serious and dispassionate attention to the point on which I feel persuaded that, as Christians and philanthropists, you will be most disposed to listen to me—our actual condition, and the bearing of the treaty on our future welfare and happiness.

The subject of emigration is not new to the New York Indians. The advancing settlements of the whites, more than thirty years since admonished them of the necessity of that measure, and long before the existence of what is called the "Ogden Company," led them, as the result of their own calm deliberations, to resolve on securing a seat among their red brethren of the west. Being encouraged in these views by the then president, their attention was first directed to the acquisition of a tract on the White River of Indiana, but the tract being included in a treaty soon afterwards made with the Indian occupants by the government, that attempt of course failed. Subsequently, and as early as 1821, it was removed under the like encouragement, and a purchase was then made from the Menominee and Winnebago tribes, by the Six Nations, the St. Regis, Stockbridge, and Munsee Tribes, (composing all the Indians in this state,) of a tract on the Fox River, emptying into Green Bay; which purchase was confirmed by the government, and was in the following year greatly enlarged. This acquisition soon proved to be so important, that the Menominees, under the influence of the white inhabitants of the territory of which it then formed a part, were induced to deny the validity of the bargain—disputes and bad feeling followed, and before these could be allayed the United States purchased from the Menominees the most valuable part of this tract. The New York tribes remonstrated against this purchase, and the senate after investigating their complaints, in the year 1832 ratified the Menominee treaty, on condition that a tract of 500,000 acres should be set apart for the use of the New York tribes, to be held under the same title by which they held their lands in this state. A portion of the Oneidas and the whole of the Stockbridge and Brothertown Indians removed to, and now reside on that tract—but the arrangement was not satisfactory to others of the New York tribes, who have been since much divided as to the course best for them to pursue, the greater portion of the Christian party among the Seneca tribe and most of the educated and respected chiefs, being decidedly in favour of emigration.

Allow me here to digress for a moment, to show how little you can rely on the facts stated in the volume under consideration. In page 8 you will find the following passage: "A purchase of the Green Bay Lands in 1832 had been made by the government for the future residence of the New York Indians. To the treaty for these lands, made with the Menominees of Wisconsin, *the Senecas were not a party; nor did they desire to be.*" This statement is incorrect in all its parts. The government made no purchase of lands at Green Bay for the future residence of New York Indians in 1832, or at any other time. The purchase in that year was made for the benefit of the United States themselves, and a portion of it (as just mentioned) was given up to the New-York Indians on the ground of a prior claim under their previous purchase of 1821, from the Menominees and the Winnebagos. The Seneca tribe, as one of the six nations, was a party to the last mentioned purchase and paid its full proportion of the purchase money.

For many years past, the condition of the Indians generally and especially that of the feeble remnants of the once powerful nations residing within the old states of the Union, has excited the sympathy of the benevolent, and called forth the talents of the learned, in devising plans by which to rescue them from impending extinction. The subject has by successive presidents been repeatedly urged upon the attention of congress, until at length a well considered system of policy adopted by the national legislature, having for its object the ultimate civilization of the whole body of Indians within the United States. This system embraces all that seems to be necessary to its final success. In a mild and healthful climate, an extensive territory composed of land easy of cultivation, and particularly adapted to the raising of corn, cattle and horses, has been set apart for the exclusive and permanent occupation of the Indians. Sufficient land is to be granted to them in fee, by patent, subject to no pre-emptive right, and by such a tenure as to enable the owners to hold and enjoy in severalty—to transmit to their posterity, and to sell and dispose of among themselves, their respective estates at their own pleasure. Ample protection is guarantied to them in their new home, and the government is pledged to furnish them in the means of elementary education—to provide for their instruction in agriculture and the mechanical trades, and to confer on them the privileges and powers of self government. These benign provisions, together with a just equivalent for the relinquishment of the claims of the New York

tribes on the lands at Green Bay, form the basis of the treaty which the Society of Friends, during its negotiation and ever since its conclusion, have
been seeking to defeat by every means which wealth and combination, talents and sophistry can furnish.

The circumstances that led to this treaty being grossly misrepresented in
the publication under review, it may be proper, briefly, to advert to them.

Within the last twelve years most of the intelligent chiefs of the Seneca
tribe have been again awakened to the great and increasing evils of our condition. We first opened a correspondence with the government of the
United States, imploring its aid and protection in resisting the encroachments of the unprincipled white men who were overrunning and corrupting
us. We were told in answer that it was not in the power of the government to
extend to us the protection required, whilst remaining in the state of New
York, and were advised to remove to the territory provided for us beyond
the Mississippi.

In 1832 an agent of the government proposed to the chiefs in general
council to send a delegation to examine that territory, and select a portion
of it for our future homes. The proposition was well received, but was not
then accepted. The Senecas cautiously determined first to send a delegation
of three chiefs to Washington, headed by Captain Pollard, the father and
pride of our tribe. The delegation proceeded to Washington, had an interview with the president, and became satisfied of his humane intentions.
They asked an appropriation to defray the expenses of a delegation to
explore Indian territory, which was made by Congress in 1834. A delegation
of six chiefs, led by James Stevenson and Seneca White went on the territory,
and returning in the spring of 1835 made a unanimous report in favor of
the new country. Soon afterwards, some individuals among us became dissatisfied with the report, and we resolved on an application for a second
appropriation to defray expenses of another exploring party, and this was
also made. A second delegation headed by Little Johnson and White
Seneca, visited the country in 1837—returned the same year, and by a large
majority reported in its favour. It now became important to act promptly in
order to secure the particular tract that we deemed most desirable, and was
accordingly signified to the government that the New York tribes were ready
to treat with them. A general council was called in the fall of 1837—and
here occasion is again taken for another attack on the pre-emptive owners.—The paragraph last quoted from the case, is followed by this. "The
Green Bay scheme, however artfully planned, turned out a failure. Years
rolled away without its consummation. At length, in the year 1837, under
the management of the agents of that (the Ogden) company, as it is generally understood the United States government was induced to appoint a
commissioner with the *ostensible* object of purchasing from the Indians of
New York, the aforesaid Green Bay lands. The *real* object, however, was to
obtain the *means* and *money* and influence of the government, to assist the
said land speculators, in their efforts to obtain the more valuable lands of
the Indians, lying in the State of New York"!

The manifest object of this and other similar misrepresentations is to show that in every movement looking to the removal of the New York Indians they have been passive, and to draw from each a new pretext for further abuse and invective against the pre-emptive owners. Thus a public treaty, growing out of a series of preliminary preparations between the immediate parties to it, is referred to the *management* of a third party, and the executive department of the government of the United States is held up to its citizens as so far forgetful of its own dignity and independence, as under the guise of an *"ostensible"* object to lend its high powers to a set of land speculators, for a purpose at once base and fraudulent.

It was, both on considerations of propriety and necessity, incumbent on the war department to notify the pre-emptive owners of the intended treaty, and it is to be presumed that this was done; but I am certain that they had no immediate agency in bringing about the council, nor in the selection of the commissioners appointed to hold it.

At this council there was a general attendance of the chiefs. General Gillet of this state, late one of its representatives in congress, represented the United States and opposed the council by a speech explaining the views of the government. Dr. Trowbridge, a most respectable citizen and late mayor of the city of Buffalo, (the superintendent of Massachusetts,) followed in a short address, stating that he was sent there by the governor of that state to see that justice was done to the Indians.

After the question of the removal and the sale of the Seneca lands had been debated for several weeks, the commissioner gave notice that on a certain day he would submit to the council the draft of the treaty, which was presented accordingly with the draft of the conveyance for the Seneca lands; both were read, article by article, to the council and faithfully interpreted in the presence of several persons acquainted with the Indian language; and I here state, of my own knowledge, that both were regularly signed, in general council, by a majority of the Seneca chiefs according to the usage of the Six Nations, each chief signing in his own proper person, except two or three were prevented by sickness from attending and who signed by attorney, as was known to all attending chiefs.

The council was closed by short speeches from the commissioner and superintendent, in which they considered the treaty as a concluded compact, and no dissent was uttered by a single chief on either side.

Up to this period, there was little interference by white men in the deliberations of the council, which were conducted in the usual manner; but when the amended treaty came back, the scene was changed. The opposition had been organized. No particular amendment proposed by the senate was objected to, because as is well known to the authors of the "case" the provisions of the original treaty in reference to the Seneca tribe were left substantially unchanged. The object was to defeat the *whole* treaty. For this purpose the council was overrun by white men—meetings were called and speeches made in opposition to the treaty. The Senecas were exhorted not to sell the lands of their fathers—were told that the government would never redeem their pledges to them—and if they removed they would be destroyed by the wild Indians of the West. In short every argument, which could be addressed to the fears, the passions and the prejudices of an ignorant and suspicious people were made use of. This was done by a combination composed of 1st, the dram-sellers—2d, the lumberers—3rd, the lessees of mill seats—4th, the holders of hydraulic privileges near Buffalo—5th, the holders of licences to live on Indian lands—6th, the missionaries—and 7th, the Society of Friends.

As to the first five of these various classes of Indian advisers and the motives which actuated *them*, it is unnecessary to speak. The ground of opposition assigned by the missionaries (except those of Baptist denomination, who abstained from any interference in the matter,) was, that the treaty made no provision for refunding the money expended by the Board of Missions in making their different establishments on our lands; whilst on the part of the Quakers, it was insisted, as is still done, that the New York Indians possessed in their present positions, all requisite advantages and needed no new system of policy for their improvement. Their soft speech and strong professions of disinterested friendship, blended with insidious suggestions considering the sincerity and good faith of the government— the validity if its title to the tract of country appropriated for the new homes of the Indians—the insalubrity of that country and the fearful dangers to which we should be there exposed, could not fail to produce their intended effect on the more timid of our people.

The seeds of distrust and suspicion, discord and strife, thus plentifully sown, soon yielded an abundant harvest. The anti-emigration party, encouraged by the support of their new allies, assumed a bolder attitude. Violence usurped the place of reason. Before the amended treaty had been submitted to the Indian parties the council house, provided at the public expense for their accommodation, was burnt down, and this flagrant insult to the president and gross violation of the laws, is now noticed in the "case" (p. 11) as one of the "strong marks of disapprobation on the part of the Indians," without one expression of regret of animadiversion. It was indeed a "strong mark of disapprobation," but one little harmonizing with that flattering picture of the present state of our people to be found in the same document (p. 20) where their march of improvement in science and morals, as well as in their physical condition, is represented to be "without a parallel in the history of our species"!

In consequence of this outrage, it became necessary to erect a new council house; and whatever may be your new *indignation*, you cannot be more *surprised* than I have been, to read in the "case" (p. 11) an allegation that the object of the commissioner in this necessary proceeding, was to "give the land speculators an opportunity to perfect their scheme of bribery and corruption"!!

In accordance with such a beginning, our once peaceful council ground was soon converted into an arena for the display of the worst passions of our nature. An organized system of intimidation was employed to deter our weaker brethren from signifying their assent to the amended treaty. Some of them were driven by threats of death to the woods and if, as is alleged in the "case," runners were employed to bring them back to the council house, it was because they were deterred by fear from appearing there, and our friends were therefore obliged to follow them to their retreats and rally them to the independent exercise of their rights.

In confirmation of these statements, I present to you the following extracts from the part of the official report of the U.S. Commissioner. Of the 25th of October, 1838, which relates to the Senecas. (Senate document, No.7)

"Experience having taught me the difficulties resulting from the operations of whites attendant upon any negotiation with this tribe, it was with much reluctance that I made up my mind to undertake the duty of submitting to them the treaty as amended by the senate. But my experience had left me much to learn. It would extend this report to an unreasonable length to give you full account of all the obstacles which presented themselves during the negotiation of the late council. I shall give only a portion from which you can form some idea about the whole. I met this tribe on the 17th of August, in a council house which I had caused to be erected on the reservation, and as very many were absent, at their request I adjourned until the 20th. On returning to the council ground I found my council house had been destroyed by fire, the undoubted work of an incendiary. I soon caused a new one to be erected and I proceeded with the business which I had in charge and fully and fairly explained the treaty and amendments. That I did so, I refer to you a letter from M.[aris]B.[ryant] Pierce, now an opponent to emigration, which is on file in your office. At the first meeting I saw there were very many white men present whose actions and conversations indicated to me that they had purposes of their own to subserve. The Indians as well as white men, all concur to the opinion that the nation must become extinct before many years, unless they emigrate to the West. It seems to be the general expectation that they must ere long remove and all admit that it is best to do so. Still the nation is divided on the question of emigration. There is a large and highly respectable and intelligent portion who are the unwavering friends of emigration, whilst another considerable portion appears to be inflexible opponents. Several of this portion admit that the apprehension at the loss of political power in the tribe, controls their action. There is a third class that appear to not have sufficient independence of mind and character to be described as belonging to and acting with either party; and while the current of their feeling seems to be with the emigration party, they are often restrained from action by the threats and compulsion of the opposite party. This class very naturally received the special attention of those who are really opposed to the treaty, as well as those who had objects of their own in view in pretending to be opposed, or in assuming to have great power and influence in the tribe."

Again—

"John Tall Chief, whose power I witnessed, informed me and the superintendent when he gave the power, that his life was in danger, and he dare not sign in council or be seen by the opposition at my room, that he was in favor of the treaty and amendments, and that I must let him sign by power of attorney. He further stated that he must sign whatever the opposition desired him to, that he dare not refuse, that it was all false to say that threats were not used to prevent chiefs from signing; he and others were threatened. I fully believe this account, and have not one particle of doubt that if left free to act, a very large majority of the nation would freely and voluntarily sign the treaty and assent. If white men had kept away, I believe that this would have been done soon after opening the council."

But as it suits the Society of Friends, and does not interfere with their notions of propriety, to vilify the character and impeach the fidelity of this public functionary, I turn to the testimony of General Dearborn the superintendent of Massachusetts, who was sent from Boston to attend the second council and who appears so to have discharged the duties of his office as to have escaped the censure of the Friends; of his official report to Governor Everett, (Senate document, No. 9) the following is an extract.

"Intimidation has been extensively used by the leaders and *their partisans* in the opposition, for the purpose of defeating the wishes of those who are desirous of removing to the West. The commissioner was informed by the chief of the Tuscaroras, that threats had been sent to them from the Tonawanda Reservation to deter then from ratifying the treaty."

With this brief outline of the means employed by the white advisers of the opposition party to prevent the Seneca Indians from assenting to the amended treaty, I proceed to examine the complaints of the Friends in respect to the number of chiefs who assented to it and the mode in which their assents were obtained.

The whole number of chiefs is variously stated in the affidavits presented to the senate by the opponents of the treaty—that of Big Kettle, the late great leader of the anti-emigration party, declaring it to be 50—(Senate document, No. 5)—others stating it more—others less. To the contradictory affidavits on this subject were all submitted to the senate, but not adverted to in the "case," nor is it deemed convenient to allude in it, to the ignorance to the part of the *chiefs* of the number of those to whom is committed to the government of the nation; a degree of ignorance which furnishes a singular illustration of the rapid improvement and general intelligence of the Seneca tribe alleged by their kind eulogists.

It seems now to be admitted ("case" p. 12) that there were 81 acknowledged chiefs, and that of these, (p. 16) 42 signed the treaty. It is true that in the paragraph which precedes the last of these admissions—the titles of three of the 42, *viz*: John Hutchinson, Charles Greybeard, and Charles F. Pierce to the office of chiefs, are denied; but their titles were fully established, and no proof is offered to disprove them, nor are they questioned even by the opposition chiefs. Israel Jameson, their present and most prominent leader, since charged with the distribution of moneys appropriated by the Seneca nation for the exclusive use of the regular chiefs, having paid to these very individuals, in that character, their full proportions. The money passed through my hands and I vouch for the truth of this statement.

I am reluctant by further details, to add to the unavoidable length of this address, and shall therefore refer, on this point of numbers, to one other document only—the president's message to the senate of 21 January, 1839, stating as an uncontested fact, that 42 out of 81 chiefs had assented to the amended treaty. The message is short, and I have here transcribed it.

"To the senate of the United States—I transmit a treaty negotiated with the New York Indians, which was submitted to your body in June last and amended. The amendments have, in pursuance with the requirements of the senate, been submitted to each of the tribes submitted in council, for their free and voluntary assent or dissent thereto. In respect to all the tribes except the Senecas, the result of this application has been entirely satisfactory. It will be seen by the accompanying papers, that of this tribe, the most important of those concerned, the assent of only forty-two out of eighty-one chiefs has been obtained. I deem it advisable, under these circumstances, to submit the treaty in its modified form, to the senate for advice in regard to the sufficiency of the Senecas to the amendments proposed.

M. VAN BUREN."

It is obvious from this language that the president whilst satisfied that a numerical majority of the chiefs had signed the amended treaty, was still desirous, in a case which had produced so much excitement, to obtain an expression of the opinion of the senate in regard to the sufficiency of an assent depending on a single voice. That circumstance however was not deemed material, and by a resolution of the senate passed 2nd March 1839, the matter was again referred to the president for the exercise of the powers confirmed on him by the original resolution of the 11 June proceeding.

With a view to further information and, as is understood, in compliance with the wishes of the Society of Friends, the secretary of war visited the Senecas in August 1839, and held with them a council. It was an open one and numerously attended by the Indians and their respected friends and partisans, among others, as the case informs us, by three committees of as many distinct branches of the Quaker Society.—The secretary in his address to the council, that "he was sent by the president to confer with them—ascertain their objections to the treaty and listen to everything they had to say on the subject." Talks were delivered by a chief of each party, but these consisted of little more than mutual crimination and tended to throw no new light on the subject. All parties were patiently heard and the council, after sitting two days, was adjourned. The Friends now complain that the secretary lost sight of the object of his mission in not again laying before the council the amended treaty, for its assent or dissent. What would have been the secretary's opinion as to the expediency of such a proceeding, I do not know, but it is somewhat strange that these ever vigilant committees, if assured that a majority of chiefs were indeed opposed to the treaty, did not propose or suggest such a test of relative numbers.

Between the adjournment of this last council and the meeting of congress, new affidavits were procured and further delay asked by the Friends' promulgation of the treaty. The request was granted; additional documents were submitted to the senate by another message on the 13th January, 1840, which message is quoted (p. 10) to prove the president's understanding that the senate resolution of the 11th June, 1838, required the assents to be given in open council. Now whatever may then have been the individual views of the president on that point, it is very clear that the resolution of the senate contained no such requisition. It provided that the amended treaty be submitted and *fully and fairly explained* by a commissioner of the United States to each of the tribes separately assembled in open council, and that it should be freely and voluntarily assented to; but it nowhere directs that it should be *assented* to, in open council. In fact it is distinctly stated in the commissioner's first report, that the signatures of some of the chiefs to the *original* treaty were given out of the council, and that no chief objected to it as irregular. That report was printed—was before the senate when they ratified the original treaty, and by that act, this form of proceeding was virtually recognized and approved.

The circumstances referred to in the speech of Senator Wright, that on the passing of this resolution, an amendment was proposed, requiring in terms *that the assents should be given in open council,* and *its rejection,* sets at rest all question as to the intention of the senate in this resolution.

Again it is alleged (p. 14) that the commissioner took lodgings at a private hotel—that runners were hired to bring in the chiefs—spirituous liquors employed to intoxicate them—false representations to deceive them—threats to intimidate them—and vain hopes to allure them.

As to such of these vague charges as have not been already noticed, I shall merely ask attention to the final reports of the commissioner and superintendent.

On the 30th October, 1838, the following instructions were communicated by the department to the commissioner: (Senate document, No, 5)

"War Department—Office Indian Affairs,

October 30th, 1838.

Sir,

Your report and the treaty with the New-York Indians assented to as amended in the senate of the United States, have been submitted to the Secretary of War. He is of opinion that the consent of a majority of all Seneca chiefs must be obtained, but as you have heretofore met the requirements of the senate by full explanations to them in council, you may proceed to the Seneca Reservation and there obtain the assent of such Indians as have not heretofore given it.

You are accordingly authorized and requested, at your earliest convenience, to proceed to the Seneca Reservation in New-York and carry out the above views. Your service among these people qualifies you fully for the discharge of this duty, and gives assurance of its fair, honest and capable performance.

Very respectfully, &c.
T. Hartley Crawford.
Hon. R.H. Gillet
Now at Washington."

The commissioner, in the official report of his proceedings, under these instructions dated 11th January, 1839, (Senate document, No. 8) thus expresses himself:

"You have heretofore received a full report of all that transpired prior to your instructions of the 30th October last. On the receipt of those instructions I repaired to Buffalo, New-York, for the purpose of carrying them into effect. On my arrival there I was joined by General H.A.S. Dearborn, the superintendent appointed by the Governor of Massachusetts, who continued with me until the close of my visit there. He was present and witnessed every signature to the assent, except on which was taken while he was confined to his room by indisposition. Soon after my arrival at Buffalo I directed the United States sub-agent resident there, to give public notice to the Seneca chiefs that I was present and authorized to receive the signatures of such of their chiefs as desired to give them, and that the superintendent from Massachusetts was also present to discharge the duties assigned him by the authorities of his state."

Again, after stating the number of signatures, he states—

"To these forty-one names may be added that of James Shongo, who signed the assent attached to the printed copy of the treaty now in your possession making all forty-two names, being a majority of three—without the name of James Shongo there is a majority of one.

"In every instance where a signature was received, either General Dearborn or I distinctly inquired of the person offering to sign whether he fully understood the subject and whether he freely and voluntarily signed the assent. In each case a distinct affirmative answer was given."

General Dearborn in his report to Governor Everett dated 2nd January 1839, (Senate document, No. 10) says,

"A list of names of the chiefs who have given their assent is annexed, marked D. They all signed in my presence in person or by attorney, except John Snow who affixed his name on the Buffalo Creek Reservation and I being at the time confined to my bed by sickness, was unable to attend; but it was done in the presence of the commissioner, the Indian agent, James Stevenson, one of the oldest and most respectable chiefs belonging to the christian party and Moses Stevenson, a son of the above named chief.

"The assent of John Buck and Sky Carrier was given by powers of attorney copies which are annexed and marked E., F., and G., and the reasons therein stated why they did not appear in person.

"I invariably asked each of the chiefs, in the presence of all the persons present, whether they were perfectly satisfied with the treaty and the contract for the sale of their right of possession to the lands on which they resided and willingly and freely come forward to sign the treaty, and they all answered the affirmative." On this branch of the case and also on that relating to the manner of receiving the assents, I quote the following remarks from the speech of a very distinguished senator:

"Without discussing the question whether it was the intention of the senate that the assents should be given in council or whether the language of its resolution required that construction, all must admit that but one object was to be accomplished, *viz:* the 'free and voluntary assent' of each separate tribe or band to the amended treaty. Now if the senate pointed out one particular place or manner for expressing those assents, and the Indians chose another place or manner for making the same expression, will it be contended that the treaty should fail rather than the forms required by the senate should not be compiled with, whilst the substance of their requisition has been met by the 'free and voluntary assent' of a majority of chiefs?" And the same senator in another place adds that although "hitherto he had argued the question of the execution of this treaty upon the admission that the assent of a majority of all Seneca chiefs of every grade, was necessary to its validity, this was an admission which he did not make except for the sake of the argument, because it was a position in the soundness of which he did not believe. So far as his acquaintance extended it was a new principle connected with the making of Indian treaties by this or the state governments; and he believed also that it was new to the laws and customs of the Indians themselves."

I now pass to the consideration of the remaining charge, impeaching the validity of the assents to the amended treaty—*viz:* the employment of bribery to obtain them.

I would remark preliminarily that this charge refers to *transactions connected with the negotiation of, and all prior to, the original treaty*—that the charge and all the documents in support of it were spread before the senate—and that this body, by a *unanimous vote,* ratified the treaty as amended, and authorized the president to proclaim it whenever he should be satisfied that, as amended, it has been assented to by the Indian parties. *Assent* was the only act remaining to be complied with in order to give full effect to the amended treaty, all other objections and among them the charge of bribery, being finally disposed of by the concurring voice of a body which white men and Indians have been accustomed to regard as the most august and dignified of your nation—and which the Friends in their letter to Mr. Sivier describe as "the highest tribunal on earth, whether considered in relation to its moral standing or to the intellectual power concentrated in its body."

Let me ask what is the meaning of the term *bribery* as applied to the Indians? If a right to personal gratuities be the *privilege* of chiefs according to the general and well understood usage of Indian communities, then the acceptance of them, being consistent with the official fidelity, involves no violation of duty, and the payment of them is not *bribery.* Now, according to the unbroken custom which has prevailed among the Senecas since the first sale of their extensive possessions in this state, the chiefs have demanded and received personal allowances. This custom was acted on at the treaty of

1797, between Robert Morris and that tribe, held by the late distinguished Colonel Jeremiah Wadsworth as commissioner of the United States, and by a highly respectable superintendent of Massachusetts—annuities for life were then granted to all the principle chiefs of that day and secured by the purchase of public government stocks. Corn-planter, Farmer's Brother, Red Jacket and many others were of the number, and the first of these great men no less than two hundred and fifty dollars per annum was granted for his life and that of his wife and those of his eight children, several of whom are still in the enjoyment of it. At the treaty of 1826, the same usage prevailed. Red Jacket, who opposed the treaty and could claim no allowance, was persuaded, as the opposition chiefs now are, to proceed to Washington and on this same charge to contest the validity of the treaty. Then, as now, the usages of our people were referred to, and there was no interference on the part of the government. At the council held by the secretary in August 1839, the fact of personal allowances to chiefs was referred to by the orator of the opposition party and stigmatized by the epithet of bribery; on which a leading chief on the other side, rose in his place and in the face of the assembled tribes, avowed and justified the practice as one founded on ancient and well-understood usage; and after expressing his surprise that such a complaint should come from such a quarter, pointed with scorn to several chiefs on the opposition benches who were then in the receipt of personal annuities under the treaty of 1826. This usage is not peculiar to any one tribe: it is common, as I understand, to all, and (as is universally understood) the government of the United States in their Indian negotiations are compelled to conform to it. Nor is the usage of modern origin. At the earlier periods of the settlement of this country, *presents*, as they were often called, were freely distributed among the chiefs. At this day, and especially among tribes whose constant intercourse with white men has taught them that money is the surest means of purchasing both luxuries and comforts—when the increased value of their lands enhances their official importance and busy white advisers are ready to stimulate their cupidity, it is not strange that the chiefs should be disposed to make the most of their official perquisites. The difference in practice between the pre-emptive owners of the present time, and those of the time of Penn and other colonists is, that what passed under the name *presents* is now termed *bribery*: that the chiefs were content *then* to receive blankets and cloths, gay calicoes and glittering baubles and trinkets, whereas *now* they demand more substantial allowances in money. In principle there is no difference either as to the giver or receivers of personal gratuities.

With us the chiefs act for the nation in the sale of their land, and if the nation are satisfied with the price, there is no complaint on account of any further benefits that the chiefs can secure for themselves.

I am thus brought to inquire whether or not we have been defrauded in the sale of our lands. In page 2 of the book our authors say that our lands are estimated to be worth from two to three millions of dollars, adding in their accustomed tone of abuse, that this was a "temptation too great to be resisted by the consideration that justice, mercy, truth and fairness must all be trampled under foot before the prize could be obtained!" This enve-nomed arrow shot from the bow of the meek and gentle Quaker, is leveled at a set of gentlemen whose reputation cannot be affected by my praise or censure—as little can it be affected, in the state of New York, by such foul aspersions; nor where they are unknown, can the use of such a weapon fail to suggest to every white man acquainted with the ordinary proprieties of society, that a cause requiring for its support effusions of passion and malev-olence must needs be a weak one. As to the *estimate,* I might say that I know enough of land in the neighborhood of our reservations to justify me in declaring that it is grossly exaggerated; but the question, as concerns our people, relates not to the value of the land as a subject of sale among white men, but to the value of possessory title which we have sold to the pre-emptive owners. Now it is quite certain in addition to what the treaty secures to us from the United States, we are to receive from the pre-emptive owners on this sale of less than 115,000 acres, more than double the amount paid to our nation by Robert Morris upon a sale to him of more than four million of acres! and if I am rightly informed, vastly more than Penn paid to the Pennsylvania Indians for their title to the whole of that fine territory! and I am informed also that the late sales of the Holland Land Company of their large tracts in the Genesee Country were made (as to the unimproved lands) at prices little, if at all, exceeding that which we are to receive, although their sales embraced *both the Indian and the pre-emptive titles.*

As to the general character of the whole bargain, hear what General Dear-born says in his report to Governor Everett.—(Senate document, No. 9)

"Not an objection or complaint has been made by a single Indian during the whole process of the council, as to the price obtained for the right of possession, and I have not seen an individual, other than the persons above named, who does not think the offer of the government, a most generous and favourable one for the Indians.

"The same liberal terms which have been offered, to these Indians, if extended to any county in New-England, would nearly depopulate it in six months."

The opinions of many other intelligent white men to the same effect might be mentioned, but it would be a superfluous tax on your patience, and I shall on this point therefore, refer only to those of the Quakers them-selves, as expressed in their memorial to your house of representatives. The object of this memorial is to induce the house to withhold any appropriation for carrying the treaty into effect, on the ground that although by the consti-tution of the United States the treaty-making power is vested in the president and senate, yet as another part of the same constitution requires the concur-rence of both houses of congress in drawing money from the treasury, it thus enables the house to control and nullify treaties.—Applying this new doc-trine to the present treaty, the memorial proceeds (p. 50) as follows: "There is one feature in the character of this negotiation with the New York Indians, which we think ought to claim the particular attention of your body as the guardians of the public treasure. By that treaty, four hundred thousand dollars of the public money, and one million eight hundred and twenty-four thousand acres of the public lands are to be given to the New York Indians, as an inducement to relinquish their possessions in the state of New York, for the benefit of the Ogden land company. To your memorialists it appears that under this treaty the government gives away a vast amount of property *without any equivalent!* It may well be asked what advantage can accrue to the public from the removal of the New York Indians? As regards to the people of the United States, under whose authority the treaty is said to be made, and from whose resources the means to carry it into effect are to be drawn, it may safely be answered, *none!* In a national point of view, it is a matter of perfect indifference whether the New York Indians remove or do not remove! Why then should our representatives appropriate such a vast amount of money and property to an object in which the community has no interest?" You will recollect that the complaint lately noticed was, that the New York Indians obtained *too little* for relinquishing their possessions in this state, and you perceive that the complaint *now* is, that we obtained *too much*, and that to swell the balance against us, the Green Bay tract containing 435,000 acres, relinquished by the treaty to the United States, (constituting no inconsiderable set-off against their concessions to the Indians,) is entirely omitted in the account!

But I pass over that omission, and call your attention to this memorial, as being a deliberate and recorded avowal of the opinions and feelings of the congregated "committees of the four yearly meetings of Genesee, New York, Philadelphia and Baltimore, in concern of those meetings for the welfare of the natives of our country." Consider these opinions and feelings.—In the exercise of a liberal but tardy act of mercy and justice, the representatives of a rich and powerful nation have been pleased to make a liberal provision to carry out a great and humane system of policy by which to rescue our perishing race from moral and physical ruin—our removal from the corrupting influences of associations with the white population by whom we are surrounded, being an essential part of that system. In their memorial to congress, we find these delegated advocates of the Indian cause censuring the munificence of these provisions—coldly casting up their amount, weighing in a miser's scale the result of their sordid calculations against our temporal and eternal welfare, and seeking in an appeal to the guardians of the public purse, to win their co-operation by an assertion that "in a national point of view, it is a matter of perfect indifference whether the New York Indians remove or do not remove," and that this "is an object in which the community have no interest"!!! If such be *your* views on this momentous subject—if *your* minds are made up to oppose any plans for our salvation, not founded on the dogmas of the Society of Friends, then indeed it is in vain that I address myself to your understandings or your sympathies.

In reviewing a work whose object seems rather to inflame the passions than to call into action the powers of the understanding—to excite prejudice rather than to elicit truth, it is not easy to distinguish between passages too plausible to be entirely overlooked, and others too absurd to need the least notice.

The statements of the "case" respecting the treaties of guaranty between the general government and the New York Indians, and the notable *"census"* taken under the authority of the delegates of the three yearly meetings of Friends, belong to one or the other of these classes.

As to the first—there is no Indian of any pretension to information, who does not understand, that whilst the general government are pledged, as is that of the state, to protect the Indian tribes from lawless violence, neither the general or the state governments can enlarge their rights to property in the land they occupy, nor diminish the rights of the pre-emptive owners. These guaranties therefore, in the relation to the validity of the late treaty, amount to nothing.

As to the last—what does this pretended "census" amount to? The Quakers send emissaries, upon their own representations of the dangers and privations incident to a proposed emigration to the distant regions of the west, to collect the suffrages of men, women and children on that measure—of men too ignorant to appreciate its advantages, and of women and children equally ignorant, but more easily alarmed by well told tales of horror and hardship; and this species of *farce,* devised and got up by the "delegates of three yearly meetings," is dignified by the name of a "*census.*"

The parade of affidavits procured by similar means from people more than "14/13ths" of whom are wholly unacquainted with the nature and solemnities of an oath, would seem to me to deserve no greater attention than the "census," except as evincing the extraordinary means resorted to by a religious society professedly opposed in principle to this form of appeal to the Supreme Being, and generally most uncompromising in maintaining their scruples.

I now turn in the further examination of this angry and most uncandid appeal of the Society of Friends, to the contemplation of the present condition and prospects of the New York Indians, and to a calm consideration to a means by which, under the gracious providence of the common Father of all, we, the most hapless branch of the human family, can be raised to the rank that you, his more favoured children, have so long enjoyed, and made to participate in those rich blessings which have been so bountifully bestowed on you.

The ground has been broken in the book I have been reviewing, but the authors have done no more than to betray their entire ignorance of the subject in all its essential principles.

This is an inquiry worthy, not only of the profound attention of the philanthropist, but demanding an exercise of the highest faculties of the christian; for so far as a sound and operative faith in the great truths of the gospel, may be requisite to bring the heathen within the pale of salvation, this inquiry has reference not only to our temporal, but our eternal destiny.

These considerations whilst stimulating my feeble exertions, will I hope secure for me your dispassionate attention.

In discussing the theory of civilization we are met at the threshold, by the fact, that every attempt which has hitherto been made, whether by legislatures or religionists, to produce a radical and enduring change in manners, habits and pursuits of Indian communities, has proved utterly abortive.

This fact, whilst shewing the inherent difficulties of the problem, points to the propriety of applying for its solution to the master spirits of the age, and of ceasing to rely on the crude systems of conceited visionaries and heated fanatics, who, content with the use of palliatives, never look to the source of the disease. Such master spirits have at length approached the subject, and guided by their lights and the information I have been able to collect in the course of my education and subsequent associations with some of the better classes of white society, I am fully persuaded, as I think must be every intelligent man who dismissing preconceived opinions will devote the powers of his mind to the subject, that the true cause of the failure of past efforts to improve the conditions of Indians, is the disabilities under which they labor in respect to those rights and privileges of person and property, which are the common inheritance of white men.

The aborigines of this continent, from their first intercourse with the nations of Europe, have been the victims of that most unjust principle of colonization upon which the government of each nation first discovering any particular portion of his vast country, assumed over it an unqualified dominion, both as to soil and inhabitants. Upon this principle, the extensive regions claimed to have been discovered by the British subjects were parceled out into colonies and granted to them or to individuals, in fee simple—a title carrying with it the power of alienation to all other subjects, and leaving to the Indian occupants, a mere right of possession which the holders of the government title (hence called the pre-emptive owners) were alone authorized to purchase. Such is the title under which the provinces and colonies forming the older states of the union were settled, and such the title under which William Penn came from England to Pennsylvania, as *proprietary governor,* to reap the benefits of his grant of that whole colony from Charles II. I find from his biography that this distinguished man, whilst in England and before his celebrated treaty with the native Indian occupants, sold portions of his vast territory to his fellow subjects of the British king, and that they accompanied him on his voyage to America, where measures were promptly taken to extinguish the Indian right. Neither Penn or his followers, were stigmatized by the Quakers of that day, as unprincipled "*land speculators,*" nor was it then asserted as is done in the fifth page of the "case," that the pre-emptive title, "vests no right" in the holders of it until the "Indians are disposed to sell," and gives no power over Indian lands "more than that which any citizen of the United States has over the land owned by his neighbor." If this be so, then a very large share of the abuse and opprobrium now lavished on the Ogden company, might have been bestowed on Penn and those who purchased under him, and would have been equally merited by each.

The rights of Great Britain and her colonies which passed by revolution to the states of this union, have since been asserted and exercised by them, in the fullest extent. We Indians thus hold our lands by a title comparatively worthless, and as to personal rights, are placed under restrictions equally severe and humiliating. We are now shut out by all political privileges, and in the country of our birth, are regarded as aliens, being not only deprived of the control of our own lands but incapacitated from acquiring and holding any other, even by purchase from white men! Thus oppressed and degraded, we find ourselves surrounded by white settlements, where a comparison between the condition and privileges of the two populations, would alone be sufficient to check aspirings and subdue the energies of every intelligent member of our community, even were he not compelled further to witness the demoralizing effects of this proximity to the more ignorant and more numerous portion of our people. These, constantly associating with the corresponding classes are always ready to contract with individual Indians for the cultivation of their cleared lands on shares, and to purchase from them a vague license to cut and remove the valuable timber still to be found in our forests; and although cheated and over-reached in all these transactions, the poor Indian (after a fruitful harvest) is enabled to draw from them the means of a scanty subsistence, with such small supplies of money and credit as suffice to gratify his propensity to idleness and his thirst for ardent spirits, but when, as often happens, the corn crop fails, he is thrown a mendicant on the bounty of his white neighbours for the necessaries of life.

Among our young women the baneful effects of the intermixture of the two populations, are still more striking in the general prevalence of that foul disease incident to the indiscriminate intercourse which they maintain with the youths of the neighbouring towns and cities, a scourge which, in the eloquent and touching language of one of the senators in discussing the merits of the treaty, "unknown to the natives until the white man was known—is sweeping over this small remnant of the once proud Seneca nation, sowing the seeds of a slow and miserable and lingering death around the germs of life."

There are many moral, industrious and intelligent men among the New York tribes, but their general condition is much as I have described, one of abject poverty, ignorance and degradation. We are referred in one of the Quaker memorials (p. 29 of "case") to the condition of the people of Great Britain at the time of the Roman invasion. Bear with me whilst I quote and briefly comment on the whole of this paragraph, which appears to me to involve some fundamental principles of great importance to my countrymen.

(P. 29) "Under former administrations it was a favourable policy of the government to promote the civilization of the Indians, and large sums were appropriated for that purpose. But many of our fellow citizens now entertain the sentiment, and we have no doubt sincerely, that the Indian is an untameable savage, made for the wilderness and only capable of subsisting in a state of nature. We think the sentiment is erroneous—that circumstances only make the difference between them and the white men. Our ancestors in the island of Great Britain when the polished Romans invaded their territory, were as savage as the natives of our own country at the planting of the first colony in Virginia; they painted their bodies and clothed themselves in skins. Centuries rolled away; the example of a civilized state with all its advantages was before them, and yet they remained nearly as barbarous as when first visited by a Caesar. Six hundred years after the invasion, they were far less improved in the arts of civilized life, than are our Indians after the lapse of one fourth part of that time. In the Seneca nation, the march in the improvement in science and morals as well as in their physical condition, is perhaps without a parallel in the history of our species. It is true, much is yet to be accomplished—but the lights of experience shine on our path—the faculties of intercourse are astonishingly multiplied—and nothing, we think, is wanting to the consummation of our wishes for the complete civilization of the New York Indians, but a faithful application of the means which a benevolent Providence has put into our hands or placed within our reach."

I am no antiquarian, and shall not question the historical accuracy of the facts here assumed, but let it be admitted, for the sake of the argument, that the inhabitants of Great Britain "were for 600 years far less improved in the arts of civilized life, than are our Indians after the lapse of one fourth part of that time"—what is the practical inference to be deduced from this fact?

In our "march of improvement in science and morals" 150 years have brought to us our present condition: whether, as viewed by the Society of Friends, it be one of hope and encouragement, or, as viewed by others and ourselves, one of utter despair—whether our march *now*, be onward or retrograde, all will agree that it *ought* to be *onward*, and that "much is yet to be accomplished." What then, are the means to be employed for carrying us in on our journey to that point which the Britons and their descendants in this country now occupy, and can they be successfully applied to us, under the circumstances which belong to and are inseparable from, our present position? Opening our eyes to the "lights of experience" which "shine on our path," we shall find that more, much more, than "multiplying the faculties of intercourse" is needed for the desired consummation.

The rights of property are the very basis of the political institutions of Great Britain, and of all the freedom and all the advancement in the arts, which that country now enjoys. In reviewing her history it will be seen, that precisely as the rights of property were secured and respected, in the very same ratio, did the civilization of the nation increase.

When Henry the 7th permitted his nobles to alienate their lands, he said to have added greatly to the respectability of the lower orders by enabling them to become the purchasers of estates. A gradual approximation of the different classes of society followed, whilst the division of land among many proprietors produced the wholesome competition of small interests which, in a commercial and agricultural country, is essential to the general weal.

In tracing the subsequent history of a nation who up to that period, (nearly 1500 years after the birth of Christ and the invasion of Great Britain by the Romans) remained comparatively barbarous, we find that the capacity to acquire and hold *individual* property, and the power to transfer it, at pleasure, and transmit it by will, were essential elements of civilization. These, in fact, are the grand cement of society—without them no man ever achieved any really useful enterprise, or ever steadfastly devoted the active powers of mind or body to the accomplishment of any great and praiseworthy object. Without them, no nation has become, or ever can become, truly civilized.

Now if the condition of our people be such as I have represented—without the capacity to take or hold lands (otherwise than by mere occupation) or to dispose of them—shut out from all civil and political rights—a distinct and degraded and despised class of society, it is impossible to apply to us, whilst thus circumstanced, those means of civilization which were so successfully employed among your ancestors in Great Britain. But what, let me ask, are those *other* means referred to in the paragraph just quoted "which a benevolent Providence has put into your hands or placed within your reach," by the "faithful application" of which, we are to become civilized? Your legislatures may, within another 150 years, admit us into your political family, but they cannot give us an effectual title to land which already belongs to others, nor can they shelter us from the influences which are taking from us the few virtues of the manly savage, and giving us in exchange the lowest vices of the most profligate of your white men, and spreading among our people the seeds of a loathsome disease, are polluting the very fountains of life.

To tell us then what white men *have been,* and what, under the operation of means which are denied to us, they *now are,* is a mockery of our distress, and an insult to your understandings.

If proofs were required as to the practical effects of the disabilities under which we labor, they are to be found in the last 50 years of our history with which many of you must be familiar. Within this period, you have seen that the wild wilderness of the Genesee Country, and the still wider wilderness of the West, have been made "to blossom as the rose." The most needy of your people, planting themselves everywhere among the forests, have been able by their own exertions, to provide a comfortable subsistence for their families, establish schools, erect churches, build up villages and cities and acquire wealth and consideration, whilst the New-York Indians, with the "example of a civilized state with all its advantages" continually before them—possessed of better lands, enjoying the benefit of missionaries and teachers and all the aids of active benevolence, have in the great work of civilization, achieved nothing to justify a hope that, whilst deprived of the incentives and rewards which animate the freeman, they can never be more successful.

The general views here expressed, seem to me to find strong support in those of the senators friendly to the treaty, whose speeches have been given to the public. For this reason, and for the purpose also of making this address in some degree instrumental in rescuing from unmerited opprobrium, the characters of the gentlemen whom I have every reason to esteem, and who have been most wantonly calumniated throughout the publication under consideration, and at the same time of confirming the general accuracy of my own statements on several points in which they conflict with those to be found in that publication, I take leave to present the following extracts, necessarily omitting from their great length, those elaborate and conclusive arguments upon the question agitated in the senate not less than in the "case," as to the validity of the Indian assents to the amended treaty.

Governor Lumpkin—"When I consider the moral degradation of these Indians and reflect that they cannot escape from the destruction attendant on their continuance in their present abodes, I cannot estimate the importance of immortal beings by dollars and cents; I cannot be altogether strict in my inquiry, as to the propriety of the United States incurring some expenditure in an object so essential to the preservation of these people. The president of the United States informs you in his message that this treaty presents the only prospect for the preservation of these people. He says, 'surrounded as they are, by all the influences that work their destruction, by temptations they cannot resist and artifices they cannot counteract, they are rapidly declining,' and 'that where they are, they must soon become extinct.' And sir, this statement of the president is fully sustained by both the senators from New York, as well as by General Dearborn and Mr. Gillett and every other gentleman with whom I have conversed, who is acquainted with the true and present condition of these people. And yet sir, we find persons professing all that is benevolent, pious and good, who are unwilling to let these people go. This treaty is truly recommended by the liberality of its provisions to the Indians. It gives them 1,824,000 acres of land in the Indian territory west, and the sum of $400,000 for their removal and subsistence, for educational and agricultural purposes, the erection of mills and other necessary buildings and the promotion of the mechanic arts, besides some minor but advantageous provisions. In exchange, the government obtains 435,000 acres of the best lands near Green Bay, lying on Fox River and near the best port in Wisconsin. This land is said to be in demand and disconnects the white settlements which are already made in that country. The public interest would be greatly promoted by the early settlement of this 435,000 acres of land with a white population; and if it could be brought into market, no doubt is entertained of its being readily sold and speedily settled by an industrious and enterprising population. At the government price (and it is believed that most of it would sell for more,) it would not only reimburse the treasury for the necessary appropriation to carry out the treaty, but it would exceed it by one hundred and fifty thousand dollars. Indeed it is believed that the demand upon the treasury to carry out the treaty might be supplied from these lands.

—"A territory west of the Mississippi has been procured and sacredly set apart by the government, amply sufficient for the location of all the remnant tribes of Indians which may be found remaining in all the states and territories of this union. It is the settled wish and policy of the government thus to locate those Indians. And sir, if these poor perishing people were entirely destitute of all the necessary means to contribute to their own comfort and settlement in the slightest degree, the duty would become in that case, the more imperative upon the government to provide for them.

"The government has assumed the parental, guardian care of the aboriginal race, and its duty and honor require that it should at all times stand ready and prepared to render a satisfactory account of its stewardship, to a civilized and Christian world. The wise and enlightened policy of collecting, removing and settling these remnant tribes in permanent homes in the West, and thereby relieve the states altogether of this perplexing encumbrance, and at the same time make a last and honest effort to save from extinction a remnant of the native race, has always had my warmest support and approbation.—The plan was first brought to my special notice by observing its recommendation by Mr. Jefferson, and it has since been recommended and sustained, more or less by all its successors. Mr. Monroe most earnestly recommended to congress efficient action to carry out this plan of emigrating the Indians from the states, and settling them permanently in the West. The then secretary of War, Mr. Calhoun, sustained the views of the President in a very able report on the subject.

—"The history of its progress and success is known to the senate and the country. And sir, I consider it now, as I have done from the beginning, one of the most important measures connected with the history and character of our beloved country.

—"Shortly after the close of the revolutionary war the Six Nations of Indians of New York became convinced that the increase of the white settlements around them would make it necessary for them to seek a new home in the West; and in a council held by these people, as early as 1810, they resolved and did send a memorial to the president of the United States inquiring whether the government would consent to their leaving their habitations, and their removing into a neighborhood of the western brethren; and if they could procure a home there by gift or purchase, whether the government would acknowledge their title to the lands so obtained, in the same manner it had acknowledged it in those from whom they might receive it; and further whether the existing treaties would in such a case, remain in full force and there annuities be paid as heretofore. The president answered by saying their request *should be granted;* and under this approbation the treaty of 1821 between the New York and Menominee Indians to which I have before adverted, was made and concluded.

—"It has clearly and obviously become our duty to act in this matter. Does not the interest of New York require that we should act in this matter? The answer is found in the following language from the president of the United States in his message on this subject.

"'The removal of the New York Indians is not only important to the tribe themselves, but to an interesting portion of Western New York, and especially the growing city of Buffalo which is surrounded by lands occupied by the Senecas; and to this portion of the country, the extraordinary spectacle is presented of densely populated and highly improved settlements inhabited by industrious, moral and respectable citizens, divided by a wilderness, on one side of which is a city of more than 20,000 souls, whose advantageous position in every other respect and great commercial prospects, would insure its rapid increase in population and wealth, if not retarded by the circumstance of a naturally fertile district remaining a barren waste in its immediate vicinity.'

"And sir, what does the president say in regard to those persons who are entitled to the revolutionary rights of these lands? His language is

"'Neither does it appear just to those who are entitled to the fee simple of the land and who have paid part of the purchase money, that they should suffer from the waste which is constantly committed upon their reversionary rights, and the great deterioration of the land consequent upon such depredations, without any corresponding advantage to the Indian occupants.'

"In and out of the senate, sir, I have found persons strongly opposed to this treaty because they seem to think it confers special favours on the individuals known as the pre-emptioners. These individuals seem to be viewed in the light of speculators who are endeavoring to defraud the Indians out of their lands. Now sir, nothing, so far as I can discover, can be more unjust toward those injured individuals. The quotations I have given from the president's message, as well as the reports of General Dearborn and Mr. Gillett the United States commissioner, together with all the mass of documentary evidence which we have printed on this subject; yes sir, all go to establish the merit, good character, liberal conduct and fair dealing of these pre-emptioners.

"That the pre-emptive owners of these lands should be desirous to hasten the time of going into possession of their just rights is altogether natural, right and proper. They neither claim or desire any advantage which has not been fairly derived from the state of Massachusetts.

—"Why should I dwell longer on this branch of the subject. For sir, it is obvious, to every one, that if the execution of this treaty be beneficial to all parties concerned, its rejection will consequently be prejudicial to all. Let me then turn to another consideration connected with this treaty, by asking the question—do these Indians wish to be removed? This question is answered in the most satisfactory manner, by an attentive examination and consideration of the actings and doings of these Indians for the last thirty years. Their various efforts, with but little aid and encouragement from any governmental influence, either state or federal, sustain the belief that they are unhappy—very dissatisfied with their present abode, and are truly anxious to emigrate to the west.

"Mr. Gillett and General Dearborn both declare themselves to be perfectly satisfied, that were it not for the unremitted and disingenuous exertions of a certain number of white men, who are actuated by their private interests, to induce the chiefs not to assent to the treaty, it would have immediately been approved by an *immense* majority—an opinion, which we find repeatedly reiterated by these gentlemen.—The president of the United States expresses the opinion, that the same effort that was exerted in opposition to the treaty, if exerted with equal zeal on the other side, would shew a large majority of these Indians in favour of emigration. And from the first commencement of the negotiation, we discover the interference of white men assuming the character of friends to the Indians, strenuously opposing this negotiation and greatly retarding its conclusion.—Indeed it appears that every art was employed to defeat the objects of the government in effecting a treaty. The country beyond the Mississippi was declared to be unproductive and the climate unhealthy. The prospect held out by the government to the Indians was declared to be delusive and deceptive; and in case of removal, they were told they might look forward to wars, privations and sufferings.

—"That an actual majority have assented to the amended treaty, seems no longer to admit of a doubt. The official and personal standing of Mr. Gillett and General Dearborn who have certified the fact, settles this question. I consider the question as heretofore settled by the action of the senate.

"In respect to the mode of assent, I consider it altogether immaterial. The fact of assent I consider a matter of *evidence,* and in the present case that evidence is to my mind entirely satisfactory. That the chiefs who have subscribed to this treaty, did so voluntarily and understandingly, is attested by General Dearborn and Mr. Gillett, whose testimony is unimpeached and I believe unimpeachable.

—"I doubt sir, whether the whole history of our country affords a solitary instance of an Indian treaty which will bear the test of comparison with this much abused treaty, for fairness, liberality, honest execution, and requirements approaching to similar transactions when conducted between equal and civilized nations. But sir, I would emphatically ask, what is the history of the Indian treaties from the first discovery of this continent up to the present day? When and where have we required that more than a majority of chiefs should sign the treaty in open council, to give it validity? When have we required higher evidence than that of General Dearborn and Mr. Gillett, in respect to the number, character and authority of Indian chiefship to a treaty?

"The history and origin of Indian treaty-making in this continent down to the present time, I consider one of the unpleasant if not painful recollections, to the high-minded American citizen. In the early settlement of the country, our ancestors effected by artifice, in the form of Indian treaties, what they were unable to effect by force. This treaty-making system, originating in physical weakness, pretended and appeared to do nothing in acquiring Indian lands, except by obtaining the voluntary assent of the Indians.—Yes sir, *even under the government of that good man William Penn, we find the same estate that made it a crime for any citizen to furnish the Indians with intoxicating drink of any kind, nevertheless allowed the commissioners of the government to administer a prudent portion of intoxicating drink to Indians with whom they wished to form a treaty.* But sir, I forbear to enter further upon the history of Indian treaties. This much I will say: if any gentleman will take the time and labour which I have done to investigate this subject, he will rise from the task fully satisfied that the treaty under consideration, is one among the most fair and honourable transactions of the kind which is to be found on our recorded history as a people.

"I will now ask, Mr. President, how can any senator expect to put the negotiations of an Indian treaty upon the principles and footing of similar transactions with civilized, enlightened foreign nations? Are not these

Indians in a state of dependence and pupilage? Are not we in the place of parents and guardians to them? Shall we then overlook all the facts connected with the subject under consideration? Shall we imagine a state of things which we know has no existence? Has not all the difficulty in regard to this treaty been provided by interested white men? Is not every charge of fraud urged against this treaty, refuted by the fact of the liberal and beneficent terms of this instrument? A charge of fraud cannot be well sustained against a transaction which confers great benefits and no injury whatever.

"Allow me sir once more in conclusion of my remarks, to advert to the bearing of the question now pending before the senate on the destiny and lasting interest of this remnant of the aboriginal race. To me sir, these people are a peculiar and interesting portion of the human family. I consider them human beings. I wish to treat them as such. I cannot in my conscience assign them a place halfway between man and beast. I wish to save them from destruction. Hence I urge their speedy removal from the degraded and demoralizing situation in which we now find them. Their unrestrained intercourse with the licentious portion of the populous cities and villages by which they are surrounded, is prejudicial alike to the Indian and white population. Deprived as these people are, of the right to acquire and hold property in severalty, they are destitute of those incentives to industry and frugality which animate and reward every white man in our happy country. Being debarred all political rights, they naturally consider themselves a proscribed and debased race; and the individual exceptions of intelligence and worth among them, whilst it serve to evince their capability for improvement under more favourable circumstances and to become a civilized people, will not however shield them from becoming a nation of vagabonds and paupers, in their present abodes. During forty years they have made no perceptible advance in the art of civilized life, so that it is impossible longer to resist the conviction, that their preservation from increasing misery and ultimate extinction, can only be found in their separation from the white population, and by conferring on them rights and privileges which, in all countries where they are enjoyed, have been gradually found to lead to civilization and to prepare the way for the introduction of Christianity with all its happy influences."

Senator Wight after expressing his deep conviction of the benefits, present and future, which would be conferred by the treaty on the Indians, and that a just and rational sympathy for this perishing remnant of a once mighty savage confederacy prevailed much more strongly in favour of the treaty than any motives of individual or associated interest; and after premising

—"*That* he should enter upon the discussion with a full and perfect understanding, assented to upon all sides of the senate, that the character and standing and credit of the commissioner who negotiated the treaty on the part of the United States, remained unimpeached and unimpeachable, and that his statements of facts were to be implicitly relied on in all matters touching the execution of the treaty by the Indians." (To which position, as the reporter adds, the *chairman of the committee and all the discussing members assented,*) and after premising also "That the commissioner on the part of the State of Massachusetts, General H.A.S. Dearborn, was present at all the transactions, the validity of which are now in dispute, and is a respectable, credible, and disinterested witness to every fact to which he gives testimony," presents the following summary of the provisions of the treaty:

"Article 1 cedes to the United States the lands of the New York Indians, at Green Bay, not otherwise disposed of, computed at 435,000 acres.

"Article 2 secures to these Indians a country in the Indian territory west of the Mississippi, equal to 320 acres of land for each soul; the whole computed at 1,824,000 acres.

"Article 15 stipulates to pay to the Indians from the treasury of the United States $400,000—'to aid them in removing their new homes, and support themselves the first year after their removal;' to encourage and assist them in education and being taught to cultivate their lands; in erecting mills and other necessary houses; in purchasing domestic animals and farming utensils, and acquiring a knowledge of mechanic arts."

As connected with this branch of the subject he next adverts to the two separate treaties; one between the Seneca band of Indians and the Pre-emptive Company; and the other between the Tuscarora band and the same parties, the first conveying to the company of the ordinary Indian title of possession and occupation in all the remaining lands of the Senecas within the state of New-York, consisting of four reservations, containing together 114,869 acres for the consideration of 202,000 dollars, and then proceed as follows:

"The original treaty which forms the basis of this discussion, was concluded between the New-York Indians and the United States on the 15th of January 1838. About the due execution of that treaty by the Indians, there has not been, and is not, any question. It was presented to all the bands convened in a common council and was assented to by all, to the satisfaction of the senate.

"That treaty thus made on the part of these bands, was subsequently and during the annual session of the senate of 1837–38, transmitted to this body for its ratification by the president of the United States, in the usual form of transacting such business. It was referred to the proper committee of the senate for examination and advisement. The committee found many of its own provisions objectionable to them from being too vague, and presenting too uncertain a responsibility on the part of this government. The removal of the Indians, their subsistence for one year—the erection of mills, school-houses, blacksmith shops, churches and many other expenditures were stipulated, without any amount stated as the maximum of expenditure to which the treasury of the United States might be subjected. The committee as he understood at the time and now believes, referred these matters of ordinary expenditure to the head of the Indian bureau for an estimate of the amount of moneys required to meet them, and framed their 15th article of the amended treaty upon the estimate returned from that officer; thus giving for the objects enumerated in that article, the full amount of that estimate, but limiting the amount which could be called for to the $400,000 therein stipulated to be paid, that being the amount estimated.

"There were other articles in the original treaty stipulated for the payment of gratuities to the individual Indians by name, providing funds for a university and the like, which the committee wholly rejected without proposing any equivalent.

"Thus an amended treaty was formed by the Committee on Indian Affairs of the senate and reported to this body for its acceptance, which met with its unanimous concurrence. It was ratified on the 11th June 1838, and returned to the Indians for their assent with a special resolution, which has laid the foundation for the present controversy.

"It is proper here to remark that the resolutions of the senate of the 11th June 1838, were a complete ratification of the amended treaty on its part—that the instrument in all its parts, was thus made perfect so far as the constitutional action of the this body in the formation of a treaty was concerned, and that the only thing which remained to be done, was the giving the requisite assent by the several bands of Indians according to the resolutions for that purpose which the senate adopted. That resolution was made part of the proceedings of ratification on the part of the senate, was upon its face to be adopted by a vote of two thirds of the senators present, and was therefore, if met by the Indians with the assent required, the final close of our action on the subject of the treaty, in our executive character."

The senator then proceeds to give a detailed history of all the subsequent proceedings, showing that the only question then presented for the consideration of the senate was, whether in point of fact, the Seneca band of Indians had given their assent to the amended treaty in conformity with the spirit and intent of the resolution of ratification of the 11th June 1838; and after discussing this question at great length and with masterly ability, he concludes his speech with the following condensed view of the whole subject:

"Hitherto he had argued the question of the execution of this treaty upon the admission that the assent of a majority of the Seneca chiefs of every grade, was necessary to its validity. This was an admission which he did not make except for the sake of the argument, because it was a position in the soundness of which he did not believe. So far as his acquaintance extended, it was a new principle connected with the making of Indian treaties by this or the state governments; and he believed also that it was new to the laws and customs of the Indians themselves.

"He would call the attention of the senate to two short extracts from the report of General Dearborn of the 2nd January 1839, which would enable him to express his opinion upon this point in an intelligible manner. The first extract is as follows:

"'There are eight clans or families in each of the tribes of the Six Nations, which are designated by the names of Beaver, Turtle, Wolf, Bear, Snipe, Deer, Hawk, and White Crane or Heron. It is expressly prohibited by a law of the tribes for persons of the same clan to intermarry; and it is considered as immoral and irreligious as would a union within the forbidden limits of consanguinity among the Jews and Christians; and I have been assured that an instance of such matrimonial connexion would be considered by the humblest Indian a wicked and monstrous indecency, and has never been known.'

"The second is as follows:

"'There are eight great sachems of the tribe in the Seneca Nation of Indians who are also chiefs. It is the highest title and rank, and the office is hereditary like that of the other chiefs. The present sachems are Little Johnson, Daniel Two Guns, Captain Pollard, James Stevenson, and George Linsley of the Buffalo Creek Band, Captain Strong and Blue Eyes of the Cattaraugus Reservation, and Jeremy John of Tonnawanda, *six of whom have signed the treaty.* Half of them are christians and the others pagans.'

"Now if the agent had been more particular he would undoubtedly have told us, that of these eight sachems or principle chiefs, one belonged to each of the eight families or clans of which he had before spoken, and the symbolical names of each which he had given. He would have learned that they were the great fathers of the nation, the civil chiefs upon whom the transaction of the business of the nation is devolved; and he, Mr. W., did not doubt that had this treaty been negotiated with the state of New York, the signature of a majority of these sachems would have been held sufficient to have constituted it a valid treaty, and that any other signatures of the chiefs of a lower grade, would have been considered a mere matter of personal gratification and not of essential substance. He has theretofore no doubt upon his own mind that the concurrence of six of these sachems in this amended treaty, was of itself, a valid execution of it according to the laws and customs of the Seneca Nation.

"Still he had argued the question upon the other hypothesis, because an examination of the papers had satisfied him that a majority of all the chiefs of all grades, had given an assent which the senate must consider satisfactory.

"He would now consider briefly as he might, the pecuniary interests of various parties to this treaty, and

"*First.* The interest of the state of Massachusetts.

"According to his understanding of the matter, that state had no pecuniary interest whatever in these questions. The charters granted by the crown of Great Britain to the colonies of Massachusetts and New York conflicted as to boundaries, and both colonies claimed the territory west of a meridian line passing through or near the Seneca Lake, and within the present limits of the state of New York. By an amicable adjustment between the two states in the year 1786, Massachusetts released to New York the sovereignty and governmental control over the territory, and New-York surrendered to Massachusetts the right of soil, subject to the Indian title, and the right to extinguish the Indian title in her own way. Not many years after this period Massachusetts sold to private individuals her pre-emptive right to the whole country, reserving the power of guardianship over the Indians which the old states have ever exercised within their limits, and which the United States have exercised without the limits of the states, and within those limits, where the right of pre-emption from the Indians belonged to this government. In this way and for this reason it is, that Massachusetts has been represented in all transactions with the Seneca and Tuscarora Indians in relation to this treaty, the reservations of these lands being within the limits of her original right of pre-emption; but since the sale from her to individuals under whom the present pre-emption company hold, he did not understand that the state had any other interest than the duty remaining upon her as a government, to see that the rights of the Indians were fairly and faithfully protected.

"*Second*. The interests of the pre-emption company.

"The interests of this company would be seen from what had been said in relation to the connection of the state of Massachusetts with this matter. As purchasers from that state, they hold the exclusive right to extinguish the Indian title whenever the Indians shall be induced to surrender the possession and occupancy of the lands. By virtue of that right they have already extinguished the Indian title to an extensive and fertile country, and the present treaty proposes to complete the operation by the extinguishment of that title to all which remains, being about 116,000 acres.

"The interests of this company are direct and palpable.—The purchase from Massachusetts was made in 1796 or 1797, and so far as these lands are concerned, the purchase money paid to that state has been unproductive capital to the company, from that day to the present time. It is abundantly shewn too, that the present reservations are constantly becoming less valuable by being stripped of their timber, which in their natural state, constituted the chief value of two or three of them. This consideration renders it a matter of direct interest to the company to extinguish the Indian title and obtain the actual possession at the earliest practicable day.

"As much has been said of the vast speculation which this company would make by the ratification of this treaty, he had taken some pains to form an opinion upon that point, and had therefore endeavoured to ascertain what had been paid to the state of Massachusetts for the right to extinguish the Indian title. As nearly as he could learn from the documents which had come within his reach, about three hundred thousand pounds New England currency, equal to about $1,200,000, had been paid for the whole purchase, and that somewhere from four to five millions of acres of land were covered by the purchase. He therefore concluded that the price paid to Massachusetts for the right of pre-emption from the Indians, say in 1797, must have been somewhere from the twenty-five to thirty cents per acre. He had not taken the pains to make a calculation to see what, at a fair rate of investment, that price would bring the cost of the land to at this period, but when added to the $212,000 or thereabouts now to be paid, and the gratuities which have been, and are to be given in case the treaty be finally ratified, he had satisfied himself that the speculation of the company would be much less than had been imagined, and that a prudent man who had the money, would pause before he would take property off their hands at principle, interests and costs.

"Still the interests of this company were nothing to him. It was not their advantage which he felt called upon to consult, or which induced him to urge the ratification of the treaty. As constituents of his, as he believed most of them were, and as highly respectable individuals so far as he knew them, he would, as far as lay in his power, do them justice upon this as upon all occasions, but he would not urge this treaty upon the senate to the detriment of the Indians because this company might be benefited by its ratification, as he certainly would not vote for its rejection, to the detriment of the Indians, for fear this company might profit from its operation.

"*Third*. The interests of the state of New York and her citizens.

"The state, as such, had no interest in this question separate from the interests of the citizens to be affected by the continuance or removal of the Indians. The extent of these interests would be best shewn by brief statistical statements.

"The Senecas are scattered through the six counties of Allegany, Cataraugus, Chatauque, Erie, Genesee and Orleans. This band of Indians together with the Onondagas and Cayugas who reside with them upon their reservations number 2,623 souls, and the white population of the counties in which they are, as shewn by the state census of 1835, was 244,144 souls.

"The Onondagas of Onondaga, number 300 souls and are in the county of their name which had at the same period a white population of 60,908 souls.

"The Oneidas at Oneida, are 620 souls, and are in the county of their name with a white population of 77,518 souls.

"The American party of St. Regis number 350 souls, and are in the counties of St. Lawrence and Franklin with a white population of 54,548 souls.

"The Tuscaroroas number 273 souls and are in the county of Niagara which has a white population of 24,490 souls.

"The Stockbridges, Munsees and Brothertowns so far as they remain in New York, are scattered among the other bands and number together 709 souls.

"Thus it will be seen that all these bands and remnants of tribes of nations are scattered through eleven counties of the state; that they number altogether 4,885 souls, and that the white population of the counties in which they are, was in 1835, as shewn by the state census, 461,608 souls, or almost 100 whites to one Indian.

"From this it will be seen that nothing like apprehension from the presence of these Indians can be felt by the whites; that the inconvenience of the reservations to the white settlements; in many cases, the desire to bring into profitable settlement and cultivation the lands they occupy, and the injurious effects upon society, in all cases and with both races, of familiar intercourse between them, are the prominent interests which the citizens of the state of New York have in the ratification of this treaty. To the city and town of Buffalo immediately bordering upon one of the largest and most populous of the Seneca Reservations, and the city and town containing a white population of full 20,000 souls, this question was one of more deep and pervading interest, as it was also, property considered, to the Indians residing upon that Reservation. But he believed he should be justified by the fact if he were to say, that even in the counties where these Indians are, the strong feeling for their preservation, from the accumulated evils which surround them and which is seen are rapidly producing their extinction, creates a deeper interest with the whites for their removal to the Indian country, than any considerations of convenience or property anticipated from the accomplishment of that object.

"*Fourth.* The interests of the United States.

"Much of the debate had turned upon this point, and he was bound to confess that he thought it the strongest ground upon which the treaty could be resisted. Yet he hoped to show that even this ground of resistance was not well taken; and for that purpose he would recur to the facts in the case touching the national treasury.

"He had before remarked that the small sums to be paid to the various bands amounted to about twenty thousand dollars, and that the general payment stipulated to be made to all bands in proportion, *per capita,* as they should remove west, was four hundred thousand dollars. These payments together, would be about four hundred and twenty thousand dollars, but of the whole sum he did not believe an amount exceeding ten thousand dollars would be called for during the present year. Such was the condition of all these Indians, that he did not suppose it possible that any considerable proportion of them, if even a single Indian, could remove after this advanced period in the spring, and after the appropriations under the treaty could be made.—Of the sums payable to the various bands, he recollected but one sum of one thousand dollars to the St. Regis, which was payable before removal, and that sum was not required to be paid until the expiration of one year from the final ratification of the treaty. The immediate demand upon the treasury therefore, was not to alarm anyone; but the ultimate payment was considerable: and how was the treasury to be compensated for it? This was the essential inquiry and if it could be satisfactorily answered, he hoped this objection to the treaty would be considered obviated.

"The answer then was, that the first article of the treaty cedes to the United States the tract of land owned by these bands of Indians at Green Bay in the territory of Wisconsin, being 435,000 acres. At the present minimum price of the Government for the public domain, this land will bring into the treasury $543,750; while its location upon the Fox river and its quality are said to give it peculiar prominence and insure its instant sale for immediate settlement. He thought it therefore fair to anticipate in case of a prompt survey and sale, that this land would bring into the treasury all the money required to carry the treaty into effect, as soon and as rapidly as it would be wanted, and would afford a surplus more than equal to the expenses of the survey and sale.

"To this extent therefore no argument against the treaty could be drawn from the demands it would create upon the public treasury. Another argument had been used however having the same tendency, which required examination. It was the country stipulated to be given to these Indians west, was more than equivalent for their Green Bay lands, inasmuch as three hundred and twenty acres for each soul, was given in lieu of one hundred.

"The answer to this was, that the country west was a part of that great country west of the States, which the United States, in the prosecution of a wise and humane policy towards the remaining Indian tribes, have set apart for their permanent and peaceful and undisturbed homes; and for the appropriation of which forever to that object, the faith of the nation has been most solemnly pledged. It was wholly immaterial therefore in a pecuniary sense, what Indians should occupy any particular portion of the territory. The whole was set apart for Indian occupancy; and in no treaty heretofore made with any Indians in the Union with a view to their removal to the Indian country west of the Mississippi, had value of that portion of the country to be assigned to them, been taken into the account or made a matter of estimate in the purchase from them of their possessions within the States. This country had been set apart from the extensive domain of the Union as a home for the red men, whom the cupidity of the whites had driven from the homes and hunting grounds of their fathers, and many of whom had not for this cause like many of these remnants of bands yet lingering in New York, any country to exchange for that quiet home thus offered to them. The policy therefore had been to purchase their possessions and pay the estimated value of them, independently of the new country to be assigned to them; and he believed, if the treaties were carefully examined, it would further appear that the expenses of their removal, and their subsistence for one year at their new homes, had been paid from the public treasury, over and above the value of the lands purchased from them. Not so in this case. The value of the lands purchased was not problematical. They were already in the middle of a settled and rapidly settling country. Their quality was well known, and their location of the most desirable character, and yet at the minimum price of the Government lands, they would bring more than a hundred thousand dollars beyond every sum to be paid under the treaty and the cost to the United States of the country given to the Indians, west, besides.

"Was this treaty to be rejected on account of its unfavourable influence upon the pecuniary interests of the United States? He trusted not.

"There was another view of this point which would place the interests of the United States in a different light. It was admitted on all hands, that the treaty had been assented to, and was perfect and binding as to all bands except the Senecas. It had been before seen that the Green Bay lands were the property of the New York Indians generally and equally. A portion of those lands, equal to sixty-five thousand acres, had been by a late treaty, granted in severalty to that portion of the Oneidas now at Green Bay; and they had ceased to be any longer parties to this treaty. The quantity of land remaining was four hundred and thirty-five thousand acres, the common property of all the bands, this portion of the Oneidas only excepted. The population of all the bands as given in the schedule annexed to the treaty and forming a part of it, was five thousand four hundred and eighty-five souls. Deduct the Oneidas at Green Bay, six hundred souls, and there would remain a population of four thousand eight hundred and eighty-five, owning the four hundred and thirty-five thousand acres of land. Of this population, the Senecas and the Onondagas and the Cayugas residing upon their reservations, numbered two thousand two hundred and thirty three. These taken from the four thousand eight hundred and eighty-five would leave two thousand two hundred and fifty-two, as to whom the treaty was admitted to be ratified and perfect. Now the right of all these Indians in the Green Bay lands, is a common, undivided right; and if therefore the treaty be not confirmed as to the Senecas, the United States will be the owner of the two thousand two hundred and fifty-two shares in common with the Senecas, who will remain the owners of the two thousand six hundred and thirty-three shares, the whole being in common and undivided; and the common interests of all the proprietors being in and to every part. The United States therefore will be unable to realize anything for their interest, because they can neither convey nor give title to a single separate foot of the land.

"Still by the last article of the treaty, the United States must pay that proportion of the four hundred thousand dollars which two thousand two hundred and fifty-eight bears to two thousand six hundred and thirty-three, because as to the two thousand two hundred fifty-two Indians, the treaty is perfect. In other words, the United States must advance the gratuities to the small bands, amounting to twenty thousand dollars, and must pay about half of the four hundred thousand dollars, and will have as a compensation for these payments, a common and undivided right with the Senecas, to about one half of the Green Bay lands, a right of which it cannot avail itself for any useful purpose whatever, while thus held in common with the Indians. On the contrary—confirm the treaty as to the Senecas, as it is confirmed to the other bands, and the right to the Green Bay lands becomes perfect, and the treasury will be fully indemnified for all the payments required to be made under the treaty.

"Could anything more be required to show the true pecuniary interests of the United States to be favourable to the confirmation of the treaty? It was due to the territory of Wisconsin too, if within the fair exercise of the powers of the senate, that these Green Bay lands within the immediate neighbourhood of one of its most important trading towns, should be disencumbered and opened for a market and for a settlement. This was an interest of the United States which could not be disregarded, whether it was looked at in reference to the sale of our other lands there, or to our duty towards the present inhabitants of that territory.

"*Last and most important.* The interest of the Indians, parties to the treaty.

"In a pecuniary sense their interests are clear, strong and decided. They are altogether 4,885 souls and they are to receive from the pre-emption company about $212,000 in money and from the United States about $420,000 more, and at their new homes, secure from the encroachments of the whites 320 acres of land to each soul, man, woman and child of all the bands. All this they are to have in addition to the annuities which they annually receive from the United States and from the state of New-York, and which are to be regularly paid to them by an express stipulation of the treaty. These annuities together cannot fall short of the sum of $20,000 and are believed to exceed that amount. Then all, or nearly all the bands, except the Senecas and Tuscaroras, have land to sell to the state of New York, and for which by the long established practice of the state, they will receive the full appraised value in money, or in permanent annuities as they shall choose.

"Was ever an entire community so rich as these Indians will be in lands and money? Well as General Dearborn said, the same liberal terms which have been offered to these Indians if extended to any county in New England, would nearly depopulate it in six months.

"If such are clear and strong advantages to the Indians, pecuniarily, from this treaty, what are they to expect from the change proposed in their physical and moral condition? It was only necessary to look back to the days of the American revolution to answer this inquiry. Then the New York Indians were the mighty Iroquois, an enemy almost as terrible as our revolutionary fathers, as the civilized enemy with whom they were contending. Even in a divided state and with one of their strongest bands, the Oneidas, arrayed upon the side of the patriots in that glorious contest, the five remaining allied bands held our arms at bay for years, and rather advanced upon, than were driven from the settlements, though opposed by some of our most brave and skillful generals. Some sixty or seventy years have passed, and now the New York Indians are the miserable scattered remnants of these powerful nations, and also of the St. Regis, the Stockbridge, the Brothertown and the Munsee tribes, and numbering in all less than five thousand souls. Some of the bands of the Six Nations have entirely disappeared, and others are reduced to a few families, and have no home but as such as they enjoy from the generosity of their allied neighbours. The same generous attachment to their race, has given a home among the Six Nations to the Stockbridges from Massachusetts, the Brothertowns from Rhode Island and Connecticut, and the Munsees from Pennsylvania, from the Wyoming country, all the remnants of once powerful Indian nations driven from their lands and their homes by the (to them) desolating march of civilization, and having no where to rest their feet, until our faithful allies, the Oneidas, tendered them a resting place and a home on their country.

"What has produced this startling change in these hardy children of nature within the short space allotted to the life of a single man? The answer stares us in the face. Not war, nor pestilence, nor famine, but the friendly touch of the white man. The progress not of arms against them, but of settlements and civilization around them. Look at the Senecas. They constitute a moiety of all the Indians now in New York. In the war of 1812–15, they numbered their thousand warriors and sent them to the field led by the gallant Frasier to strengthen our army upon the frontiers and with territory of the enemy. Where now are those thousand warriors of the Senecas? Did that war reduce their numbers? No sir, peace and friendly intercourse with us has done it; and already that thousand has become reduced to four hundred if not within that number."

"He spoke from a statement given to him by to intelligent chiefs of the nation. The statement was too long to trouble the senate with, but it gave a history of the perishing condition of that people which could not fail to move all to their relief. They were perishing from their contact with the whites; while so far from improving from the civilization around and among them, they are seen as people, worse fed, worse clad, and worse provided than they were when they had never seen a white man. The labours of philanthropists have been sedulously performed among portions of this tribe for a series of years, without being able to arrest their downward and rapid march towards complete extinction. While some are made wiser and better by their white associates, a vastly larger number are made more idle and more vicious.

"The paper before him gives a description of the state of society upon the Buffalo Creek reservation, produces by the proximity of the large and populous town of Buffalo, which cannot be read without pain and loathing. Superadded to all the other vices which have never failed to be imparted to the Indian from association with our cities, seduction and prostitution of the Indian females are said to have become frightfully common; and that the most dreadful of all the consequences of pollution of this sort, has reached the tribe and is rapidly spreading itself among this portion of it. Thus a scourge more deadly and fatal than any other which has ever afflicted the Indian—a scourge unknown to the Indians until the white man was known, is sweeping over this small remnant of the once proud Seneca nation; sowing the seeds of a slow and miserable and lingering death around the germs of life. The statement before him expressed the confident belief that a majority of the children born alive in the nation, die within the age of twelve months, many from exposure, from want of proper nourishment and ordinary comforts, from the carelessness of parents, and not a few from disease inherited from the mother.

"He would not, he could not dwell upon this picture; and yet there are those whose mistaken sympathy would hold these people where they are, to perish under the load of vice which surrounds them, pervades their society in every form, and is sweeping them into the grave with unexampled rapidity. Not so with him. He would change their condition. He would remove them from the contamination which surrounds and is overwhelming them. He would place them where they could again be Indians—where they may again have before them the motives of ambition, of enterprise, of pleasure, of profit which stimulate the Indian; and where secure from the encroachments of the whites, they may again become independent, and free, and virtuous.

"But Mr. President, (said Mr. W.,) reject this treaty—combine, as you will then combine, the cupidity of the pre-emption company with that of the white settlers who now surround them and from interest resist the company and the execution of this treaty, for the common object of both, is gain from the Indians and from their lands, and when they find that a division of interests defeats either, a combination may be easily formed which will favour both. I say accomplish this, and then what will be the condition of the New York Indians? How long will they be able to withstand a combination of interests so strong and so strongly wielded? They cannot withstand it sir; and a few years will shew you their history in that of the Stockbridges, the Brothertowns, and the Munsees. They will be found miserable wanderers among their red brethren in some remote parts of the country, without a home, or the means to procure one; without the comforts of life or provision for their future support; their members but a fraction of the present population; and their last hope buried with the last council fire which burned upon those reservations they have been compelled to abandon to their white neighbours to avoid perfect extinction.

"May I not hope I have succeeded in proving that it is within the power of the senate to declare the assents of the Senecas to this treaty, satisfactory; and thus to save them from a fate so certain and so sad?"

I regret that I have not been able to obtain any report of the speech of Senator Talmadge, another able advocate of the treaty.

The following talk of Capt.Pollard to the U.S. commissioner is among the senate documents, and when it is known that this venerable sage of more than fourscore years and the head chief of our nation, is as conspicuous in wisdom and virtue as in years, I feel confident that his views of the great interests of our people cannot be unacceptable.

"Substance of a talk delivered to the United States commissioner, by Captain Pollard head chief of the Seneca Nation, 26 December, 1838.

"My friend:

"Knowing that you are about to leave our people and return to your family, I sent for you to speak a few words before you go. You are young and full of vigour and health, but I am old and helpless. Time and disease have deprived me of activity and health, and left me a feeble tottering wreck. You now see me on a sick bed from which I am unable to rise, and you will probably see me no more. From this couch I expect to pass to the cold lifeless house of death.—For a long time I have performed the duties of a fearless warrior and an honest man. My whole thoughts are upon my people and their future destiny. My last prayer is for their happiness and perpetuity as a nation. I could not rest without seeing you and through you speaking to my great father concerning them. He is good and loves them, and will listen to what I say.

"At the time of the first war between your people and the King of England, I was a young warrior and followed the council of our chiefs. They were guided by bad men and the consequences are to be lamented. All the Six Nations except the Oneidas and the Tuscaroras were on the side of the British King who lived beyond the salt water. They raised the tomahawk upon the colonies when they were feeble, and destroyed many of your people. I remember well being at Wyoming when we followed the advice by those who were governed by vile passions. I was in the battles opposing General Sullivan when he entered New York from Pennsylvania and marched to Genesee. In the valley of the Mohawk and at Cherry Valley and other places, our people inflicted severe blows on your people. For these causes our villages and fields were laid waste and destroyed, and we lost our country by the fortune of war. We were then at the mercy of your people and had no homes but such as you would give us. Captain Brant went to England after the close of the war, and on his return I learned that he had secured a country for himself and the Mohawks in Canada. The other nations who had taken up arms with the king, were left to seek clemency and homes at the hands of their conquerors. Corn Planter and Farmer's Brother were sent to negotiate with the United States. They made a treaty which you will understand. Although we were permitted to reside on a certain tract mentioned in the treaty, we were told that the right of the soil belonged to others. This I have always believed. Our wise men have always believed it. We have long known Massachusetts and those claiming under her, had rights to our land. This made me uneasy and unhappy. We have repeatedly admitted this Massachusetts right, and sold parts of our reservations to those setting it up. Last winter when Dr. Trowbridge was superintendent on the part of Massachusetts; we parted with our right of possession to the residue of our reservations, and unless the government approves of the amended treaty as assented to by us, our children will be without homes. If the purchasers should not hold the lands, still we shall be restless and unhappy, knowing that our rights are not as perfect as those of white men. While others are claiming our lands, we shall not improve and cultivate them with a light and cheerful heart. If our lands are not sold, we have no guarantee that our chiefs may not sell them at any day. This uncertainty in our condition depresses us and destroys our industry. We shall never be contented and happy until we have permanent homes and separate property like the white man. To this effect our great father President Monroe advised us. Experience proved that his advice was good. We need homes that our chiefs cannot sell; such homes as are provided in the treaty.

"We listened to the advice of our father, the president, when he advised us we would better our condition and perpetuate our nation by removing to the West. We have resolved to go west and settle where our homes will be our own, and where we shall go beyond the example and advice of bad men, who advise us for their own interests. They love their own interests better than they love us, and they have tried to prevent our agreeing to the amendments to the treaty. A majority of the Seneca chiefs have now signed the assent. That is sufficient. All has been done consistent with our Indian customs, which we understand better than white men. Those who obey bad advisers will try to mislead the president by objections which are not good. We who have followed the advice of the government, might raise many objections against them and their conduct. We could raise many good objections against them. Our proceedings will bear scrutiny better than theirs. The question is, will the government now do what is promised in the treaty? What will become of us if no new homes are given us? Whether it gives them or not, does not affect our arrangement with the pre-emption purchasers. That stands by itself. The other New-York Indians have secured new homes, and shall we not have them also? If the president rejects our doings, what will be our fate? We shall suffer for having listened to his advice. Those who have scorned to adopt his council will place their feet upon our necks, and grind us unto the earth. We shall suffer for taking his advice, and those who spurned it, will be our oppressors, because we were in favour of emigration. Those who have refused to listen to his admonitions have done so, not because they were good, but because they were deceived by falsehearted white men. All admit we must remove soon or become extinct as a nation. No one says our treaty is not a good one. The sooner we go to our new homes, the sooner we shall be happy. If we remain where we are, we shall soon disappear like those who once resided east of the Hudson river. As the treaty now stands, those who wish to stay behind, can do so, and live on the lands they occupy, so long as they live. This is what those who opposed emigration last year desired. I have heard they stated so in their papers at Washington. As it now stands they cannot be oppressed under the treaty. I am old and do not expect to see the new country set apart for my nation, but those who succeed me will go there and be happy. There they can raise horses and cattle almost without labour, and the ground is easily cultivated and produces abundantly. Here our people are poor, our valuable timber is mostly gone, and we have but few fields; they are small and yield us but little; we must emigrate or we shall never be prosperous and happy. It would be too great a penalty upon us if we have committed any error in our proceedings, to destroy them all and ruin us forever. Let our great father guide us as we do our children, and we shall pursue the right path which leads to happiness.

"I wish you to tell the president what I have said, and none but bad men and those who are misled, disobey his wishes. Deceptions and threats deter many from doing and saying what their hearts dictate. I have nearly done. I could not rest in my bed until I had said so much. I could say many things more on this subject, but cannot now. My limbs refuse to support me, my body is weak, and my eyes are dim with age. I shall soon account to the Great Spirit for what I do and say. He knows whether I speak truth. He penetrates the motives of us all.

"You are going to your home and I do not expect to see you again. My sun is almost set and darkness will soon be upon me. But your sun is at its meridian. May it long shine and lead you on in happiness and prosperity.

"Such is the prayer of Pollard. Farewell."

With these accumulated evidences of the yet deplorable condition of the New York Indians, no man whose eyes are not blinded to the truth, can fail to see the urgent necessity of some more efficient system of measures for its melioration. No man whose heart is not insensible to human misery, can wish to withhold from them its benefits. And yet when under such a system, devised by the collected wisdom, and based on the ample resources of your government, the portals of civilization are thrown open to us, we are met at the threshold, by an organized body of christians professing to be friends, yet acting as enemies. The New York Indians although exposed on all sides to extraneous influences chiefly exerted to subserve private views, have nevertheless succeeded in securing to themselves the advantages of the government system, and the Seneca tribe have at the same time effected a sale of their remaining lands, on terms incomparably more just and liberal than any previous sale. The dearest interests of all demand a speedy consumation of these arrangements; yet the Society of Friends, are still obstinately trying to defeat them.

The employment of donations to ensure the co-operation of chiefs, although a necessary means of negotiating purchases of Indian lands, is seized on as the principle ground of their opposition. Now, however contrary to your notions of morality may be this practice, you have seen that it is sanctioned by Indian usage, long prevailing and openly asserted, without contradiction, in the presence of one of the highest functionaries of your government and of the assembled tribes. Upon what principle then of expedience, or of mercy, or even of sound morality, can this objection be applied to a transaction with Indians, which, in the language of Governor Lumpkin, "confers great benefits, and no injury whatever?" and on which hang all their hopes of salvation?

I have had occasion in the course of my remarks to advert to several circumstances, exhibiting on the part of this society, the most striking inconsistencies.

I call on you to reflect whether their appeal to the house of representatives from the decision of a body whom they themselves declare to be "the highest tribunal on earth," can be reconciled with the sincerity of that declaration? Whether their attempt to induce the interference of that branch of your national legislature, in order to control the treaty-making power belonging to the president and the senate, be consistent with patriotic regard to the great principles of your constitution? Whether their efforts to influence legislation on their present memorial by means of popular excitement and prejudice, be delicate or decorous? So their lavish praises of the great pre-emptioner, Penn, whilst at the same time they denounce as odious "land speculators," the pre-emptioners of the present day, who sustain towards the government from which they derived the pre-emptive title, and towards the Indians in possession, the very same relation as he did—their unmeasured abuse of the present pre-emptioners for having purchased the lands at an unfair price, when they well know that we are to receive for these lands, more than Penn paid for the whole province of Pennsylvania, or Morris for the whole Genesee country—the opprobrious epithets which they apply to the "Ogden Company," for employing presents in order to propitiate the influence of Indian chiefs, when it is an undisputed fact that similar means (except the cheap persuasive of *a moderate portion of intoxicating drink,* peculiar, perhaps, to Pennsylvania,) were employed by their same great exemplar and from his time down to the present day, have been employed by all individual pre-emptioners and also by the government itself—that their grave quotations from legal authorities to show that the use of such means vitiates all purchases from Indians, whilst they complacently enjoy their own estates acquired in the same manner, (the recollection of which, as to Morris' treaty, must still be fresh in the minds of the Genesee friends) without offering to restore these *ill gotten* possessions to those who, on the principle they assume, are still the rightful owners—and their wanton impeachment of the fidelity of the United States commissioner, whose official conduct has met approbation of the executive, whose character, standing and credit, "are vouched by the *unanimous* voice of the senate, to be 'unimpeached and unimpeachable,' and whose 'statement of facts in all matters touching the execution of the treaty by the Indians,' is by the common assent of that body, declared to be worthy of implicit reliance—all appear to me to be alike inconsistent with that pure morality, that truth, candour, forbearance, and universal good will, which the Society of Friends claim to be its peculiar characteristics."

There is yet another instance of inconsistency in their conduct. The public are constantly edified by yearly discourses from this society on the subject of negro slavery, setting forth its sinfulness and urging emancipation as an act of christian obligation. Yet how different is their conduct in regard to the Indian tribes in this state, of whom they profess to be special protectors and who, although free in name, are more effectually shut out from all privileges which render freedom a blessing, than are the negroes! The negro slave it is true, owes obedience to, and labours for the benefit of his master, but he and his children are bountifully fed and clothed, kindly nursed in sickness and provided for in old age. *We* are not compelled indeed to labour; but when overtaken by want, visited by sickness or enfeebled by old age, have no right to ask of white men to feed, clothe, nurse or support us. The *negro,* by a long course of voluntary exertion, may perhaps purchase his freedom—buy lands and dispose of them—and many also (in this State at least,) acquire the right of suffrage and other civil rights. To *us,* all these privileges are forever denied by your laws. *Negro slavery* can only be abolished by subverting private rights, whilst national policy sustained by public opinion, encourages and facilitates efforts for *Indian emancipation.* Yet the friends plead without ceasing, the cause of the negro whilst they labour indefatigably to perpetuate the bondage of the Indian.

Whence all these strange inconsistencies? Can it be that this Society having (as stated in one of their memorials to the president,) assumed the character of "Friends and counsellors to the Indians—sent agents to reside among them to instruct them in the arts of civilized life, and at great expense of time and money laboured for their civilization and improvement"—still, honestly believe in the superior efficiency of their own system, and so believing cannot conscientiously surrender us to the care of our legitimate guardians and protectors? If this be so, (and I am unwilling to impute to them any worse motive) we may forgive their error, but cannot too deeply lament, nor too severely reprove, that pride of opinion—that arrogance of pretension—that inexcusable conceit, which setting at naught the testimony of experience and history, the concurring opinions of successive presidents and heads of the Indian department, and the collective wisdom of congress, would lead them, on the issue of their own speculative theory already falsified by their own vain experiments, to suspend the momentous question of our civilization—and presumptuously to incur the awful responsibility of endangering our everlasting destiny.

To conclude—the Society of Friends may succeed in wresting from us the charter of our freedom and leave us in hopeless dependence on the worthless charities of short-sighted enthusiasts, but what, let me ask, will be to us, the consequences of their triumph? I put this inquiry with solemn earnestness, and again use the words of that venerated chief, whose impressive appeal is already before you. "The question is, will the government now do what is promised in the treaty? What will become of us if no new homes are given? Whether it gives them or not, does not affect our arrangement with the pre-emptive purchasers. That stands by itself. The other New York Indians have secured their new homes, and shall we not have them also? If the president rejects our doings what will be our fate? We shall suffer for having listened to his advice. Those who have scorned to adopt his council, will place their feet upon our necks, and grind us into the earth."

Source: Strong, Nathaniel T. *Appeal to the Christian Community on the Condition and Prospects of the New-York Indians, in Answer to a Book, Entitled The Case of the New-York Indians, and Other Publications of the Society of Friends.* New York: E. B. Clayton, 1841.

Part III: Removals

25. Escaped Slave Advertisements (1830–1837)

The large tribes occupying the Southeast were slaveholding societies at the time of removal. Many contingents of Choctaws, Muscogees (Creeks), Seminoles, and Cherokees included numbers of African-descended people, both slave and free. As the sampling of runaway slave advertisements reprinted below indicates, the slaves of white owners found the large groups of Indians moving west an opportunity to escape their bonds. Others with apparent attachment to the tribes sought to follow them to the West. Still others, because of their apparent attachment to those left behind, sought to escape from their tribal owners in the Indian Territory and return to the South.

Runaway Negro in Jail

Was recently committed to the custody of the undersigned, a Negro man, who says his name is PLEASANT, that he belongs to a Mr. Stokes, a Negro trader, who bought him in North Carolina, and that he ran off from his master, when passing through the Choctaw nation of Indians towards Natchez, a short time before Christmas last. He is a stout made fellow, five feet and five inches high, about twenty-six years of age, and has a small scar over his right eye. The clothing he wore when committed to jail was a pair of striped cotton pantaloons, and a coarse cotton shirt, and carrying a bundle consisting of two pair of blue cotton jeans pantaloons, one striped cotton vest, two cotton and one fine linen shirts.

The owner of said Negro is requested to come forward, prove his property, pay charges, and take him away, otherwise he will be disposed of as the law directs.

J. W. Boone, Sheriff of Chicot county, A.T.
April 15, 1830

Ran Away

From Newberry, living in the Chickasaw Nation, on the Reynoldsburgh road, four Negroes, viz: BILL, a black man about twenty years of age, common size, scar on his face and neck, and a blemish in one eye, (not recollected which,) speaks the Chickasaw tongue very well.

Also a black woman about the same age, of common size, speaks Chickasaw; also two small children, a boy and girl. The girl about three or four years of age, speaks Chickasaw only—the boy one year old.

They carried away with them a black stud horse, common size, blind; also a small gray mare, branded thus [upside down U] as he believes, not recollected where, also an old rifle gun.

There is good reason for believing that the above Negroes have been run from the Nation by white men. A liberal reward will be given for securing the slaves in any jail and information given to this Agency, to Col. Joseph McKane of Bolivar, or Carr, Wood & Co. of Memphis Tenn. All good citizens will feel an interest in lodging in jail the thief or thieves and giving information as above, that justice may be done.

Benj. Reynolds, Agent
Sept. 21, 1830

$200 Reward

Ran away from the subscriber, living near the falls of Coosa river, Autauga county, Ala., about the 1st of January last, two Negroes, named Willis and Stephen. Stephen is about 22 years of age, full face, black smooth skin, thick short feet, and is I suppose, five feet 4 or 5 inches high. Willis is a yellow lad, 17 years of age, no particular marks recollected. He had an iron ring round one of his legs when he left me.

These Negroes carried off with them a large yellow dog with the end of his tail cut off. The last certain account I have of them they were making for the Cherokee Nation. I have good reason to believe that they have been run from there to the Creeks or Cherokees west of the Mississippi, by some white villain or Indian.

I will give the above reward for the apprehension of the villain and the Negroes, with sufficient proof to convict him—or fifty dollars will be given for the delivery of the Negroes to me, at my residence as above mentioned, or twenty dollars for securing them in some safe jail, so that I get them, and all reasonable expenses paid. Any information of them will be thankfully received.

Howell Ross
April 19, 1832

$300 Reward

In December, 1831, Two Negro Men, were stolen, from the subscriber, living 8 miles east of Huntsville, Alabama. One named Shadrack, between 30 and 40 years of age, tolerably stout, but not very tall, complexion a little inclined to be yellow, and has a very daring or brazen look. The other named Isham, about 30 years old, is a stout black fellow, has very perceivable scars about his head—agreeably to my recollection, one over his left eye, and one over the left ear; of the precise place however I may be mistaken—has, I believe, one or more fore teeth out, and a down look, particularly when spoken to.

I have every reason to believe that said Negroes were stolen by some white villain or villains, and taken to the Indian nation in the Mississippi, and in all profanity sold to the Choctaws, or others, or traded for cattle; and possibly may be taken to the Arkansas, with the Emigrating Indians. Persons living with the Indians, or in the Indian county, will do me a favor by making inquiry after these Negroes, and should they be apprehended and delivered to me, near Huntsville, as above state, I will pay the above reward of Three Hundred Dollars—or if secured in any jail in Arkansas, and information given to me so that I get them again, I will give One Hundred and Fifty Dollars—and Two Hundred Dollars if secured in jail in Mississippi, or any other State, and information given me thereof. Said Negroes have no doubt changed their names.

Richard Haughton
Madison County, Ala
January 25, 1833

25 Dollars Reward

Ran away from Ne-ta-ki-jah, a Choctaw Chief, residing in the Choctaw Nation on Red river, about the last of January, a Negro Man named Eaf or Ephraim, who formerly belonged to Mr. Stephen Harris, of Conway county, and more recently to Dr. M. Cunningham, at Little Rock, who sold him last winter to Ne-ta-ki-jah, from whom the subscriber bought him. Said Negro is about five feet six or seven inches high, well made, countenance rather pleasant than otherwise, between 25 and 30 years of age, very talkative, fond of drinking and gambling, has a strong propensity to be roguish, and is a pretty shrewd fellow. He has been seen prowling about Little Rock since he ran away, and, I understand, was subsequently apprehended near the Saline, in Pulaski county, but broke custody, and made his escape.

I will pay the above reward to any person who will apprehend said Negro, and secure him in jail, so that I get him again, and all reasonable charges in addition, if delivered to me at Doaksville, near Fort Towson.

Josiah Doak
Doaksville
February 7, 1833

$100 Reward

Ran away from Ne-ta-ki-jah, a Choctaw Chief, residing in the Choctaw Nation on Red river, about the last of January, a Negro man named Eaf or Ephraim, who formerly belonged to Mr. Stephen Harris of Conway county, and more recently to Dr. M. Cunningham, at Little rock, who sold him last winter to Ne-ta-ki-jah, since when, he was sold to Mr. Josiah Doak, from whom the subscriber bought him. Said Negro is about five feet six or seven inches high, well made, countenance rather pleasant than otherwise, between 25 and 30 years of age, very talkative, fond of drinking and gambling, has a strong propensity to be roguish, and is a pretty shrewd fellow.

I will pay the above reward of One Hundred Dollars for the apprehension and delivery of said Negro to me, near Little Rock; or fifty dollars for securing him in any jail, so that I get him again.

Sam'l L. Rutherford
Little Rock
May 15, 1833

ON the sixth of November, A.D. 1833, two Negro men were committed to my custody, as Jailer of the county of St. Francis, who say that they belong to Charles Wilson, living near Doke's Stand, in the county of Madison, State of Mississippi. One of said slaves is about twenty eight years of age, five feet eight inches high, and is afflicted with a disease said to be venereal, of a dark complexion; he says that his name is Peter. The other slave is about thirty years of age, five feet ten inches high. They were taken up on the road leading from Memphis to Little Rock, A.T., in company with the emigrating Choctaw Indians. The one last described speaks lively, calls his name Ben, and says that he has a wife belonging to an individual who has resided and is now emigrating with the Choctaw Indians. He states that he is his master's wagoner. The owner of said slaves is requested to come forward, prove his property, and pay charges, or they will be dealt with according to law.

Tho's J. Curl, Sheriff and Jailer, St. Francis county, A.T.
Nov. 9, 1833

A Runaway Negro in Jail

A runaway slave was committed to my custody, as Jailer of the county of St. Francis, on the 7th of November, A.D. 1833, who states that he belongs to Richard Anderson, living near Hardinsville, Madison county, Mississippi. Said slave is about five feet six inches high, supposed to be about eighteen or nineteen years of age, and has a remarkable scar on the left side of his head, near the ear. He speaks quickly, and has a down look. He was taken up on the road leading from Memphis to Little Rock, A.T., in company with the emigrating Choctaw Indians. The owner of said slave is requested to come forward, prove his property, and pay charges, or he will be dealt with according to law.

Tho's J. Curl, Sheriff and Jailer St. Francis county, A.T.
Nov. 9, 1833

$30 Reward

The undersigned hereby offers a reward of Thirty Dollars for the apprehension of the following descried three runaway Negroes, who broke Jail in St. Francis county, Arkansas Territory, on the night of the 27th November, 1833, viz: Peter, Ben, and another whose name is unknown, but supposed to be Irwin.

Peter is about 28 years of age, five feet eight inches high, dark complexion, and is afflicted with a disease supposed to be venereal.

Ben is about 30 years of age, five feet ten inches high, speaks lively, and says his wife belongs to an individual who has resided in the Choctaw nation, and has emigrated with the Choctaw Indians.

The other Negro, whose name is supposed to be Irwin, says he belongs to Richard Anderson, living near Hardinsville, Madison county, Mississippi. He is five feet six inches high, supposed to be about 18 years of age, speaks quickly, and has a down look.

I will give the above reward for the apprehension of the above described Negroes, on their delivery to me, at the Jail of St. Francis county, Arkansas Territory, or ten dollars for either of them.

Tho's J. Curl, Sheriff and Jailer of St. Francis county, A.T.
Dec. 12, 1833

250 Dollars reward

Ran away from the subscriber living near Tuscumbia, in the State of Alabama, two large and very likely Mulatto Negro, men, named Colin and David.

Colin is 28 years old, rather thin face, about 6 feet 1 or 2 inches high, and weighs about 175 pounds.

David is 25 years old, full face, 6 feet 2 or 3 inches high, weighs about 190 pounds, very likely and very stout.

They are brothers, and favor each other very much; pleasant spoken, very intelligent, and artful. I think they both had small whiskers. About the 15th December last, they were seen going down the Tennessee river in a canoe, dressed as Indians, and passing themselves as such. They can both speak some words of the Chickasaw language, and I am told that their disguise is so complete that it will be difficult to detect them, unless their hair is examined, and their hands, which are harder than those of Indians. They may perhaps throw off their disguise when they get far from home. They each took with them blue broad-cloth round jackets, and pantaloons of gray twilled woolen goods. They had several blankets, one of which had yellow stripes at each end.

The above reward will be given for their apprehension, and delivery to me, or to C. Bishop, Postmaster at Tuscumbia, or Two Hundred Dollars, if secured in any Jail so that I get them again, or one half that sum for either, and all necessary expenses paid.

If taken, they must be well secured, and whoever takes them must have plenty of help and be well armed.

Wyatt Bishop
Tuscumbia, Al.
Jan. 24, 1834

A Negro in custody.

There was this day committed to my custody, as Deputy Sheriff and Jailor of Miller county, Arkansas Territory, a Negro Boy, who says his name is Cammel, and that he belongs to Benjamin Hawkins. He says he ran away from his master when he was about to move away from the old Creek nation to the Spanish country. He is about twenty years of age, black and likely.

There being no Jail in this county, I have placed him in the hands of John Robbins, and taken his bond for the delivery of said boy when called for. The owner of said boy is requested to prove his property, pay charges, and take him away, otherwise he will be dealt with as the law directs.

Joseph Savage, Dep. Sh'ff and Jailor, Miller county A.T.
March 15, 1834

Stop the Runaway!

Ran away from old Spouk-oke Har-yo, one of the Chiefs of the Creek nation west of the Mississippi, a Negro man named Harry, about 40 or 50 years of age. He is deaf, and stutters, and appears to talk with considerable difficulty, making signs and a kind of stuttering noise when trying to talk. Has a hole or slit in his left ear, a little piece of it hanging down. When he ran off, he took with him one rifle gun, ten beaver traps, one falling axe, and a canoe. Any person hearing any thing of, or personally knowing where said Negro is, will confer a favor on a helpless old man, by giving information where he is to be found, so that he may be recovered. Information respecting said Negro, communicated by letter to the subscriber, directed to Western Creek Agency, via Fort Gibson, will reach the owner.

Joseph Blair
April 21, 1834

$50 Reward

Ran away from the subscriber, on the 5th inst., a Negro man named Mitch, aged about 40 years, of yellow complexion, about six feet high, stout and robust in his appearance. Said Negro was purchased by me, a short time since, of Peter Fletcher, Esq., of Crittenden county, A.T.; and I think is likely to be lurking about there, unless he may have attempted to reach the Chickasaw Nation, where he is acquainted. He performs well on the violin, and carried off with him a rifle-gun and hunting apparatus. I will give the above reward for his apprehension and delivery to me in Memphis, or his confinement in any jail, so that I recover him again.

LAWSON H. BEDORD
Memphis,
March 24, 1835

$300 Reward

Ran away, in February last, from the farm of the subscriber, in Chicot county, Arkansas Territory, two negro men viz:

George, a small active fellow about 4 feet 7 or 8 inches high, about 21 years of age; his mouth large, and his color black.

Tom, a large fellow, a little upwards of 6 feet high, black complexion, and wears a gloomy countenance; about 28 years old.

Ran away, at the same time, from the farm of A. H. Sevier, a Negro man named Ton, about 6 feet high, 30 or 32 years old, of black complexion, his jaws appear to be swelled from tooth ache.

These Negroes were purchased in the Creek Nation of Indians, west of Arkansas, and are supposed to be together, and will probably go to the Creeks, either on the east, or west of the Mississippi river.

I will give the above reward for the above described three Negro men, or ONE HUNDRED DOLLARS for either of them that shall be delivered to me, or my agent, either on my farm, in Chicot county, Arkansas Territory, or at Little Rock.

Benjamin Johnson
Little Rock,
April 11, 1836

A runaway negro in jail

Committed to the Jail of Union county, Arkansas Territory, on the 21st of March, 1836, by Thomas Franklin, an acting Justice of the Peace in and for said county, one Negro man slave, who calls himself William, and says he belongs to a Mr. Johnson, living in Little Rock, A.T. Said Negro is about 28 years of age, about 5 feet 10 or 11 inches high, dark complexion, spare made; says he was purchased in the Creek Nation by his master, and speaks that language fluently. Had on, when committed, a coarse frock coat, coarse woolen pantaloons, a black fur hat somewhat worn.

The owner of said Negro is requested to come forward, prove property, pay charges, and take him away, or he will be dealt by as the law directs.

John H Cornish, Sheriff Union county, Arkansas Terr.
March 30, 1836

$100 Reward

Ran away, from the subscriber, on the night of the 2d June, from the steamer Arkansaw, a Negro man named Toney, about 6 feet high, 30 or 32 years of age, black complexion, and jaws swelled a little, as if from tooth ache.

He is the same Negro that ran away from the farm of Col. A. H. Sevier, a month or two since, and was taken up, in the Creek nation, and brought down on the steamer Arkansaw, from which he has again made his escape. I will give the above reward for his delivery to me at Little Rock, or in Chicot county, or will pay any reasonable compensation for his apprehension in any jail, that I can get him.

Benj. Johnson
June 3, 1836

One hundred dollars reward

Will be given, for apprehending my Negro man Simon, and delivering him to me, at Fort Gibson, or securing him in any Jail in the State of Arkansas, so that I get him again, or forty dollars, if taken in the Indian nation, and returned to me. He is very black, about 31 years of age, 5 feet 5 or 6 inches high, and well made. Had on when he absconded, on the 7th inst., a fur cap and a drab surtout, and rode away a light cream-colored mate. He was raised in Chalmers county, Alabama, afterwards sold to Winey, a Creek Indian woman, with whom he immigrated to the Creek nation west. He was last seen on the road to Little Rock, and it is supposed he will attempt to make his way to Alabama or Georgia, by the route the immigrants came.

B. L. E. Bonneville
Fort Coffee,
Nov. 18, 1837

Source: Arkansas Gazette, May 4, 1830; October 12, 1831; May 16, 1832; January 25, February 7, February 27, March 6, March 22, November 13, and November 18, 1833; April 21, April 29, March 15, and May 6, 1834; and April 5, 1836. Transcription of slave advertisements by Amanda L. Paige.

26. Letters of Henry C. Brish about Removal of the Senecas of Ohio (1832)

In a treaty of February 28, 1831, the Senecas of Ohio agreed to remove to the West. They left Sandusky that fall, traveled by canal boat from Dayton to Cincinnati, and there boarded a steamboat that took them to St. Louis. There, Henry C. Brish, who was conducting the party, procured wagons and horses for an overland journey to the northeast corner of Indian Territory, but they were halted in December by cold weather and an outbreak of the measles, which forced them to camp for the winter near Troy, Missouri. Brish went to Muncie, Indiana, where he met a group of Senecas who had traveled overland from Ohio, and he led that party to Troy, where they joined the others in May 1832. Brish's letters to William Clark, superintendent of Indian affairs at St. Louis, are reprinted below. They chronicle the story of the combined party's difficult overland journey to Indian Territory.

Troy [Missouri], May 8, 1832.

Dear Sir: I have experienced much difficulty and delay in reaching the encampment of the Senecas, who remained here during the winter on account of the high water of Quiver [Cuivre] river. We crossed it by swimming the teams with the empty wagons, and after loading, proceeded with the Indians and their baggage about five miles up the river, when we had the good fortune to employ a boat, which, although small, has accomplished the object of crossing us.

The [overland] party which came on last have now joined their friends, and on tomorrow we shall start the whole upon their journey. I have been obliged to leave six of the party which encamped here during the winter in their wigwams, being too ill to be moved, and will no doubt die in a short time. Sixteen others are very sick, but I have made the most comfortable arrangement to carry them on, and have employed additional teams for that purpose. The roads are almost impassable, and I apprehend a tardy trip. The small spring branches in this neighborhood were yesterday deep enough to swim a horse.

Camp, 15 miles east from Jefferson, May 16, 1832

Sir: The Senecas under my charge have been overtaken by two young men of their tribe, belonging to a party (42 in number) which has for some years past resided near St. Genevieve. The chief of my party, at their request, solicit their removal to the lands assigned them; for which I refer them to you. Their expenses in coming here have been paid by themselves; they will also have to pay hire for the horses which they are now riding, and they request, as "they are poor," that the whole amount expended by them may be refunded to them; for their services in performing this errand for their friends they request some "little presents." We are getting along well, considering the excessive badness of the roads and the great number of the sick. The measles have broken out among the Indian children, and I fear that many of them will die in consequence of the exposure to which they are unavoidably subjected.

Camp, at Marais des Signes, near Harmony Mission, June 12, 1832

Sir: We have been here waiting two days for the river to fall sufficiently for us to cross. I was under the impression on my arrival at this place and until this morning, that we should be compelled to take the route by way of "White Hair's village," it being the only wagon road; but very fortunately I met with a man this morning who is perfectly acquainted with the whole country, in a direct line, between this and the Seneca lands; he is recommended by the gentlemen of the missionary establishment as worthy of confidence, and I have employed him as a guide. By this route we shall reach our destination four or five days sooner than by "White Hair," and our new guide assures us we shall have a better road. We have found the road to this place deep and muddy, and expect difficulty throughout the journey, as the mud stiffens, particularly at the water courses, which have been very high. We leave here in the morning; the river will be low enough for our wagons to cross empty; our baggage will be carried over on horseback. We are now preparing to bury an Indian woman; several others (children) are at the point of death. We have been delayed much by sickness; it was unavoidable.

I have been informed by the person whom Mr. [Isaac] McCoy employed to survey the Seneca lands, that there is not more than 50 or 100 acres of good land in the whole tract; that the rest is a bed of flinty rocks, Mr. McCoy's report to the contrary notwithstanding. If this is the fact, God help the poor Senecas; they expect to become agriculturists at their new home.

Encampment, Grand River, June 6, 1832.

Sir: Our journey to this place has been very slow, in consequence of the almost continual hard rain, and the excessive deep state of the roads. The smallest streams and drains upon the prairies have several times delayed us by being swimming deep. We have had much trouble and some delay on account of sickness, which has gone the round of the whole Tribe. We have been encamped at this place since Saturday last, waiting for the river to fall sufficiently for fording. Until yesterday it has been ten feet above that point; it is now falling rapidly, and I am in hopes we shall soon cross. The rivers in advance of us are almost out of their banks, and we shall perhaps have some difficulty on account of them.

I am sorry to inform you that Col. [David] Bailey must lose considerably by his contract to furnish rations for my Indians, in consequence of those failing to comply who had contracted to furnish him with the necessary provisions; compelling him therefore to pay high prices for his supplies, and to procure them from more remote points. He has notwithstanding procured the quantity contracted for, with me, for provisioning the Indians during the next six months, without a murmur at his loss. Provisions of every kind are high and scarce in this country.

Much difficulty exists between the Seneca and Cayuga parties of my Indians; they are constantly quarrelling, and at times I am fearful they will break out into open hostility. They give me much trouble.

July 16, 1832

Sir: I have the honor to inform you that on the 4th day of July (inst.) I succeeded in reaching and placing the Seneca tribe of Indians from Sandusky upon the lands assigned them under the treaty of 28th February, 1831. This, sir, was a laborious duty; and in the discharge of it I have encountered many difficulties which were unlooked for and unexpected. On reaching the encampment of the party which remained in the neighborhood of Troy during the winter, I found upwards of 100 Indians sick of different kinds of disease, principally however with the measles; most of whom were too ill either to walk or ride on horseback, and I was compelled, being the only alternative, to increase the number of wagons for that party to twenty four; which, together with those employed with the party which arrived this spring past, made thirty. With this number I performed the journey throughout, notwithstanding the increase of sickness, and the frequent solicitations of the Indians to employ others; although I was obliged to admit, at the same time, that more were absolutely necessary for the comfort of the sick. But, sir, the number already in service being so much above what was supposed necessary upon the estimate, and consequently the expense incurred so much greater, obliged me to resist all their importunities to employ more, and proceed with the number stated as well as possible. The immense quantity of baggage taken by these people left but little room for the sick in the wagons; and there were several instances in this journey, where the sick, the dying, and the dead were crowded together in the same wagon, and it was unavoidable. I regret to inform you that nine of the tribe (4 adults and 5 children) died between the Osage Mission, at Harmony, and the Seneca lands. Such as were Christians required time to perform the burial rites as they understood them; and such as were pagans solicited the privilege of performing theirs. Neither could be interfered with, and of course much time was spent in this way. For a statement of the extreme distress suffered by these poor creatures, I would respectfully refer you to Doct. John T. Fulton, special agent for the removal and subsistence of Choctaw Indians, who was the bearer of letters to me from the War Department, and subsistence office, Arkansas, and met me previous to my arrival upon the Seneca lands, and who visited the sick at my request, and afforded relief to many of the sufferers.

In the outset of our journey we had to contend with high water; in some cases we could cross streams by raising our loading in the wagons to a pitch above the water, in others we had to make entire bridges; and in others, where the streams were too large for either, and no mean of ferrying offered, we were obliged to wait for the water to fall, which was the case at Grant river (Mo.) and at Marais des Signes, Osage Mission. At both these places, after the water had abated sufficiently to be crossed, there were still difficulties to overcome, for such is the nature of the soil along these streams, that immediately, and for some time after a high stage of water, the bank will mire either horses or oxen in ascending or descending them. All such places required bridging the banks, which not only took up much of our time, but imposed much labor upon the wagoners and others in the service. The difficulty in crossing wet bottom prairies can scarcely be imagined, and we could only cross them by disengaging the oxen and horses from half the wagons and adding them to the other half, and then the whole to those left; this had to be done repeatedly in the course of almost every day, which of course was calculated to retard our progress very greatly.

In the last part of our journey the flies attacked our horses and oxen in such immense swarms that we could only travel before daylight or after dark. This severe duty rendered a noble set of horses and oxen almost unfit for service, and I have no doubt most of them will be lost to the owners.

These, sir, are the plain causes of the protracted journey of the Senecas to their lands. I assure you there has been no unnecessary delay. I charge myself with cruelty in forcing those unfortunate people on at a time when a few days' delay might have prevented some deaths, and rendered the sickness of others more light, and have to regret this part of my duty, which, together with the extreme exposure to which I have been subjected, and the sickness consequent upon it, has made the task of removing the Senecas excessively unpleasant to me.

It affords me pleasure to inform you that the lands given by Government to the Senecas are of the best quality, as it respects water, soil, and timber; the streams particularly are the most beautiful I have ever seen; pure and healthy, and stored with fish. Their present location, or encampment, is upon Cow Skin, or Elk river, at present called Seneca river, and they manifest a determination to support themselves hereafter by agricultural industry; and I believe if the Government will furnish them with all the necessary means to begin that pursuit, they may be preserved, and become a happy and prosperous people.

Henry C. Brish, Agent for Senecas

P. S. I forgot to mention that we were detained five days in crossing the Missouri at Jefferson City, there being but one boat, which was so small that a wagon could only be taken without the team at a trip, and then the team, making in that way two trips for each wagon and team.

Source: U.S. Congress. Senate. *Correspondence on the Emigration of Indians, 1831–1833.* 23rd Cong., 1st sess., 1834. S. Doc. 512. 4:116–119.

27. Journal of a Party of Choctaws Proceeding with Horses in Charge of Lieut. J. Van Horne, United States Disbursing Agent for the Removal of Indians from Vicksburgh Mi. to Join the Main Party of Choctaws Emigrating West of the Mississippi River on the Road Leading to Fort Towson. Also Journal of a party of Upwards of Six Hundred emigrating Choctaws on their Way from Little Rock, Ar. Ter. to their New Country Near Fort Towson (1832)

The largest number of Choctaws to remove to the West made their journey during the removal season of late 1832 and early 1833. Choctaw removal parties were organized according to the name of the district chiefs or other leaders with whom the people identified. In November 1832, Lieutenant Jefferson Van Horne of the Third Infantry received orders to act as disbursing agent and conductor for a small group of Choctaws who were driving a herd of horses belonging to a large party of Choctaws from Greenwood LeFlore's district. The main body boarded steamboats at Vicksburg, Mississippi, while Van Horne and his party crossed the river and traveled overland to a point near Little Rock, Arkansas, where they rejoined the main group on its way from Little Rock to the Western Choctaw Nation. Van Horne was immediately reassigned to act as disbursing agent for over 600 Choctaws who were traveling overland from Rock Roe, Arkansas, where they had left the steamboats. Van Horne met them east of Little Rock and traveled with them during the remainder of their journey. The two journals he kept during the trip are reprinted below.

Journal 1st

Nov. 2nd On 2nd November 1832 about 9 o'clock A.M. I started agreeably to my instructions with all the horses & cattle belonging to Greenwood Laflore's party from Walnut Hills near Vicksburgh, Mi and proceeded eight miles up the Mississippi River to Thompson's ferry, where the United States snag boat Heliopolis commenced crossing them about 2 o'clock. 8 [miles]

3rd It was half past 8 o'clock on the 3rd before all the horses, 244, were crossed but as I was anxious to make a start, I with some difficulty packed the horses with provisions which the party had received on separating from the main body and then proceeded six miles. We stopped early for the party to encamp on an elevated spot convenient to wood and water. Turned the horses out into a spacious cane brake contained on all side by the river and the fence of an adjacent plantation. My party consisting of Indians, negroes & squaws numbering 47. Rained moderately during the evening. 6 [miles]

4th It continued to rain most of the day but as the roads were good, I thought it best to take advantage of them. We started at about one half past 7 o'clock and encamped at about 4 o'clock P.M. The horses were contained at night in a dense cane brake between the river and the ditch of the levee. The pack horses were supplied with corn. 21 [miles]

5th It continued to rain powerfully until about half past 11o'clock A.M. The steam boats with the main body stopped near our encampment to get wood. I put an Indian of my party (who had become lame and unfit to travel) on board. Two Indians, (as I afterwards discovered,) left the boats here & joined my party. At half past 10 o'clock, we started and traveled over a good road, through a slight rain, until a short time before sunset; when we encamped on the edge of the swamp two miles beyond Lake Providence. In the afternoon we crossed Tensas River. The baggage, provisions, two pack horses, and six old men & women crossed in the boat (ferriage 621/2 ct.). The remainder forded. I swam the horses. 21 [miles]

6th Started at 8 o'clock, on a cold morning. Made twelve miles, over very deep and bad swamp where many of the ponies (weak and exhausted when we started,) were mired; and we had to pull them out. One or two that were unable to get along were knocked in the head by their owners. When we arrived at the Bayou Mason, I called for some time for the ferryman. At length, a drunken old hag bellowed from the cabin on the opposite side, that there was no man about; and I must wait until he should come. Upon this, I commenced crossing the horses. We drove in about twenty. They swam over, and every one mired on the opposite shore. I induced an Indian to swim over, and bring the raft. About a dozen of us crossed, and with some difficulty pulled all the horses out. I now crossed all the people & baggage on the raft, and drove the remainder of the horses in lower down, where they crossed without difficulty. Mrs. Fields (a squaw who herself owned 5 horses & who on the whole trip was giving us trouble every day by falling to the rear with her party,) had not yet come up. I passed on with the main party, and encamped 15 minutes past 4 o'clock, where cane, wood & water were abundant, leaving Mr. Byrn to assist her party over. As we received no assistance in crossing, as the old woman would not sell me any corn, and not only refused to accommodate us in any way, but was boisterous & abusive, I went off without paying her for the use of the raft. Mean time the ferryman arrived and assisted in crossing Mrs. Field's party. He urged and prevailed on Mr. Byrn to pay $2 for the use of the raft & canoe and the assistance afforded in crossing. 12 [miles]

7th The weather very cold with rain & sleet. About twenty horses strayed off last night. We were detained until eleven o'clock searching for them. Found it difficult to keep the horses together. Some could not yet be found. Encamped at 4 o'clock, and turned the horses into a cane brake surrounded by the waters of Bayou Mason. As the horses were much exhausted by crossing the swamp, I issued corn to them. 12 [miles]

8th Waited for the party and the horses that were not yet found. Started about half past 10 o'clock, and proceeded 10 miles to Morris's (the last house in the settlement). Encamped at 4 o'clock. As we now had a wilderness, where for 25 miles, the trail was very dim, swampy and impossible for a stranger to follow, I hired Morris to guide us. Ever since August last, when I had a severe attack of bilious fever, my health had been bad, and my bowels in a disordered state. For the last day or two I had the dysentery very severely. I had become prostrated. In the evening one of my party called me aside, told me his systems, and desired the prescription for cholera. I gave it. As it was very cold, this man and myself slept before the fire, at Morris' house. The symptoms increased on me until near midnight, when the constant purging & vomiting and terrible cramps and pain in my stomach & bowels, induced me to take 20 grains calomel & a large pill of opium. These I threw up. While vomiting through the floor, (from which Morris had torn up a plank,) and bent double with pain, I was repeating the dose; I was ordered to leave the house. Morris said he had a large family, that their lives and his own were at stake, that I had imposed on him in coming there in that situation & that I must quit the house. The ground was already covered with frost & was freezing severely. I rolled myself in my blanket, after begging in vain to remain, and walked three fourths of a mile to my tent. Fortunately the last dose remained on my stomach, and in the morning I felt relieved, except that I was debilitated and dizzy from the effects of the opium. 10 [miles]

9th This morning Morris refused to go as our guide. I mounted my horse before sunrise to endeavor to get another guide. I was unable to get one, who could be of service. A young man attempted to guide us, but on reaching Bayou Mason, I discharged him, as he could not find the way. Owing to my exposure and exertions, I threw up the castor oil I had taken in the morning, and my suffering for two or 3 days, exceeded any thing I ever experienced. I could with difficulty keep upon my horse, and was often compelled to lie on the ground. My patient recovered. These were the only cases of sickness on the journey. We swam Bayou Mason and encamped where there was abundance of cane, wood & water, at 15 minutes past 4 o'clock. The road this day was very bad & the weather disagreeable. 10 [miles]

10th Started at 8 o'clock. Our route continued very bad. We passed Lakeport where I purchased some provisions, and crossed the difficult Bayou (outlet of Old river lake). Encamped about 4 o'clock, in good range. Three Indians who had been left on shore by the steam boat, joined us. 12 [miles]

11th Started at half past 8 o'clock, through cane brakes and thick undergrowth for about five miles without any road or trail, and eight miles through the swamp between the Mississippi & Bayou Bartholomew. As there is much cane on this part of the route, I could nearly always encamp where it is abundant. Stopped at 4 o'clock. 13 [miles]

12th Started at 8 o'clock. Traveled all day through a bad swamp, crossing many bayous, over some of which we had to swim our horses, and cross ourselves on trees. We encamped at half past 4 o'clock on dry ground. Water, wood, & young cane abundant & convenient. 13 [miles]

13th Proceeded at 8 o'clock through excessively bad swamp. Crossed Bayou Bartholomew, swimming the horses over. As the weather was cold, the Indians & baggage were crossed in the boat. As the horses were much exhausted corn was issued to them at this place where we stopped 15 minutes before 4 o'clock. 10 [miles]

14th Issued corn to the horses for the day and one bundle of fodder for each horse for tomorrow; as I was informed neither corn nor good range could be found on our route. Set off at half past 7 o'clock. For fifteen miles the road was muddy. After that the road is good. A good horse was killed this day, by a tree falling on its neck as we were passing along the road. Another was so badly foundered that we were obliged to leave him. Encamped 4 o'clock. 20 [miles]

15th Started at half past seven and encamped at 4 o'clock. 20 [miles]

16th Detained until ten o'clock, collecting the horses. Encamped at half past three o'clock. Cane, water, & wood convenient. 10 [miles]

17th Started at 8 o'clock and encamped about 4 o'clock. Issued five days rations to the people and one day's ration of corn to the horses. 15 [miles]

18th Excessive and constant rain all day. Very cold. Started at ten o'clock and encamped at 3 o'clock P.M. 10 [miles]

19th Very cold. Started at 9 o'clock. Road very muddy and bad. Crossed many difficult bayous, some of which we had to swim. Encamped at 4 o'clock. 15 [miles]

20th Issued two days rations to the people and corn to the horses. Started at half past 8 o'clock. The roads still bad and covered with water. Encamped at half past four o'clock. 26 [miles]

21st Started at eight o'clock. Traveled over a small path, filled with bushes & logs, and encamped at four o'clock. [22 miles]

22nd Started at half past seven o'clock. Path very dim, and obstructed with bushes. Reached Brummet's on the old Towson road, eight miles west of Little Rock about 2 o'clock P.M. Made issues to the people and the horses. I was told here that Laflore's party (to which my horses belonged) had not yet reached Little Rock. I rode to the latter place in the evening to ascertain satisfactorily. I there learned that this party had passed by near Brummet's the morning of the day we arrived there. 21 [miles]

23rd I returned to Brummet's and proceeded with the party to overtake Laflore's people. On my way, the road was crowded with emigrating Choctaws. Some of my party anxious to join their wives & relatives hastened on and united with them in the evening. Others joined next day. As Capt. J[acob] Brown Principal Disbg. Agt. informed me that from a recent occurrence, my services were required with the party of 1800 then coming on between Rock Roe & Little Rock. I directed Mr. Byrn to go on with and unite Field's party, (and a few others who were in the rear) with the main body, which he did, (as he informed me,) at the Washita [Ouachita] river. 22 [miles]

24th I proceeded on the 24th to Little Rock, (30 miles.) On the next day 25th I crossed the Arkansas river and reported to Maj. F. W. Armstrong Spec. Agt. 22 miles east of Little Rock. Maj. Armstrong told me that as soon as the party could be divided, either that evening or on arriving at Little Rock, I would be placed in charge of a party of upwards of 600. That until then, I would remain with and assist in the transportation of the whole detachment. Arrived at Little Rock, the division was made. Lieut. Montgomery crossed the Arkansas on the 28th with a party of about 600. Mr. Byrn was appointed assistant conductor to my party by Maj. Armstrong.

Journal 2d

29th At sunrise on the morning of the 29th November, I commenced crossing the party of Six Towns assigned to me; consisting of 629 people, with 14 hired teams and 9 native teams. I counted the people as they crossed the Arkansas. We encamped about 4 miles from Little Rock, convenient to water and wood. 4 [miles]

30th Proceeded at half past seven o'clock over a good road to the stand on Hurricane Creek where the party arrived at half past four o'clock. Issued two days provisions and forage in the evening. The whole party was comfortably encamped and cooking their suppers early in the evening. 15 [miles]

Dec. 1st Started at eight o'clock, and proceeded leisurely over a good road until about half past two o'clock. We could easily have gone much further; but Lieut. Montgomery's party was not far ahead, and I deemed it best to keep a day's journey in rear of them. The party traveled with great cheerfulness and harmony; and were fast improving in health. When I joined the main body east of Little Rock, great numbers were sick, and considerable numbers dying. 11 [miles]

2nd It rained powerfully last night. Started at eight o'clock. Issued two days supplies for the 3rd & 4th. Six people and twenty-four horses joined from the horse party. I rejected a quantity of beef presented at this stand. It had been slaughtered too long and was spoiled. Other beef was furnished in its place. Encamped at half past three o'clock, convenient to wood and water. 12 [miles]

3rd Started at eight o'clock. I gave a certificate for crossing 584 of my people, (small children not counted) at the ferry over the Washita river. Sixty-five of David Fulsom's people, who had fallen back from Lieut. [J. A.] Phillips' party, being unable to get over, requested me to cross them. I did so. All the teams and horses of my party forded but the river was too deep & swift for the people to do so. A man in the employ of Davis, the ferryman, made several of my party drunk, notwithstanding I went into his shop before my party came up and obtained his pledge that they should not have any liquor. Some of Lieut. Phillips party whom I found here had been beastly drunk for many days. We encamped about 4 o'clock on the banks of a beautiful creek. 12 [miles]

4th Started about 8 o'clock. One birth since last issue. Issued to 634 people. Encamped about 4 o'clock on a fine stream. 12 [miles]

5th All the captains [family or clan leaders] called on me in a body and desired me to wait until the cart of their head man Etotahoma (which broke down last evening, and was unable to get to camp,) should be brought up. I had sent back more than once, and had much trouble to get this old man and his cart along. His oxen were poor and worn out, and his cart badly constructed. But he was looked to and beloved by the whole party. He would not part with his cart, and although it might have been policy to go on and leave the wretched old establishment, I found it impossible to get his people along without him. He was old, lame, and captious, and gave us more trouble than all the rest of the party. Proceeded at half past 9 o'clock, and crossed the Cadeau [Caddo]. As the weather was cold and the water deep and swift, the teams, horses and young men forded, and the women, children and old men were crossed in the boat. Etotahoma's cart was brought up & repaired. Encamped about 4 o'clock. 9 1/2 [miles]

6th Started at eight o'clock. Encamped at the stand at Hignight at half past three o'clock and issued two days supply. 13 [miles]

7th Rained all last night, and the whole day severely. Found it difficult to start the party at nine o'clock. Etotahoma's cart fell to the rear again. I sent back Mr. Bryn and the interpreter with a yoke of oxen and a driver to bring it up. Encamped about four o'clock. The rain continued in the night. 12 [miles]

8th Started at 8 o'clock. The Little Missouri river had risen considerably but I managed to get the teams and horses through it. I crossed the people in the boat counting only grown persons. I gave a certificate for the passage of 340. The road was quite muddy this day. We encamped at the stand at half past three o'clock & two days provisions & forage were issued. 13 [miles]

9th Notwithstanding I had hired a yoke of oxen and driver to bring Etotahoma's cart up with the party, he failed to bring it further than Little Missouri river. Many of Etotahoma's people had stopped behind, and this morning all the captains called on me and requested that the party might lay by this day (Sunday,) to allow all to get up with the party, and that they might wash, mend their moccasins and rest. They said Etotahoma was their chief, that they all love him, that he was old & lame, and that they were all unwilling to go on and leave him behind. I remained, made a new axeltree for his cart, brought it up with a fresh yoke of oxen, and to prevent any more trouble hauled his cart with this yoke of oxen all the remainder of the journey. Five people with five horses came to me here, stating that they had quit Lieut. Phillips' party to hunt their horses which had strayed. As they were known to my interpreter, I took them on with my party.

10th Started at 8 o'clock. Road much cut up and muddy. Reached Washington, Ark. at two o'clock. As there was no water on the road short of eight miles, we encamped here. I here paid off and discharged Mr. Byrn Ast. Conductor, Maj. Campbell Ast. Agent having joined and reported for duty. 12 [miles]

11th Started at eight o'clock. Road heavy and muddy. Encamped at the stand at half past three o'clock and issued. 10 [miles]

12th Started about eight o'clock. Road muddy as far as Mine Creek, then good. Encamped at half past 4 o'clock. 14 [miles]

13th Started at half past seven o'clock. Issued provisions and forage at nine o'clock A.M. and proceeded through a heavy rain. Encamped at half past four o'clock. 16 [miles]

14th Proceeded at half past seven, over three miles of bad & 13 miles of good road. Reached the stand at Little River at 4 o'clock. Provisions & forage issued in the evening. 16 [miles]

15th Commenced crossing the river at day-break. I counted the people by companies as they crossed. I remained to cross the whole party and directed Mr. Campbell to go forward six miles and a half, and show them where to camp. Some teams arrived at the camp in the day, and one or two did not get up until dark. 6 1/2 [miles]

16th Started at eight o'clock, and encamped at sunset. 16 [miles]

17th Started at half past 7 o'clock, and made two miles to the stand at D[avid] Fulsom's. Here I obtained two days supplies for the 18th & 19th and left the 5 people & five ponies of Lieut. Phillips' party, who came on with me. We then proceeded twelve miles further, and encamped on a beautiful spot convenient to excellent water and wood. 14 [miles]

18th Started at eight o'clock. For the last few days we had been met by many of the Choctaw emigrants of proceeding years coming to meet their friends and relatives. My party had dressed themselves neatly for the occasion, and seemed in fine health and spirits. Agreeably to the wishes of the party, and of Col. [Joel] Nail, their chief. I made a final encampment at half past one o'clock, four miles east of Clear Creek, where I forthwith discharged all the teamsters, and mustered the people, who were enrolled by the issuing officer, numbering 648 persons.

J. Van Horne Lieut. 3rd Infy.
Disbursing Agt. Choctaw removal.

Source: National Archives Record Group 75, Records Relating to Indian Removal, Records of the Commissary General of Subsistence, Letters Received, Box 6, Choctaw 1833 File. Journal transcription by Carolyn Yancy Kent.

28. Journal of Occurrences Kept by the Conductors of the Lewistown Detachment of Emigrating Ohio Indians, Senecas and Shawnees; Commencing on the 20th of August, 1832, and Ending on the 13th of December, 1832 (1832)

The Senecas and Shawnees of Lewistown, Ohio, removed under a treaty of July 29, 1831. They departed on August 20, 1832, and arrived in the northeastern corner of Indian Territory (now Ottawa County, Oklahoma) on December 13. Leaving Ohio in late August 1832, the party experienced frequent delays because of weather and the logistics required in coordinating the removal of the Wapakoneta and Hog Creek Shawnees and the Ottawas of Maumee, who were removing at the same time and following the same route as far as middle Illinois. Shawnees themselves to a large degree dictated their movements. They had been determined to travel by horseback instead of by water as the government had wanted them to do, and they at times prevailed upon the conductor to remain in camp to rest or to dry their tents and blankets. Upon their arrival in the West, they found their assigned lands west of the Neosho unsuitable. The next month, they negotiated a treaty with the Stokes Commission for land north of the recently arrived Senecas of Sandusky River, with whom they formed the United Nation of Senecas and Shawnees. The journal of their removal is reprinted below.

August 20th, 1832. Agreeably to previous notice given them, the Senecas and Shawnee Indians this day assembled at Lewistown, Logan county, Ohio, to receive rations. At their request, provisions for four days were issued to them. The proper officers of this detachment were present, and inspected the provisions and the issues, both of which were satisfactory. The utmost harmony prevailed throughout the day; and in the evening, the Indians returned to their homes, well satisfied with the manner of drawing, and with the quantity and quality of their food. Each family drew separately.

Since there was no definite time set for the commencement of their journey, and their houses thought the most proper places for them to remain, while rendered unwell from the effects of vaccination, it was considered most expedient for them to continue their former manner of living, until they should recover their health after being vaccinated, and a time fixed for their departure.

Tuesday, August 21st. Civil John, the head chief of the tribe, and some of the principal men were called together, by the request of Lieutenant [Jeremiah F.] Lane, to ascertain whether there was a possibility of prevailing on them to go by water. James McPherson was the interpreter. They say what they have said before, that "they depended on Colonel [James] Gardiner to carry their understanding of the treaty into effect. They are ready, willing, and anxious to go, and always have been; but it is useless to try to persuade them to go by steamboats." They say, that some of their old and infirm women say, "we will not go in steamboats, nor will we go in wagons; but we will go on horseback; it is the most agreeable manner for us; and if we are not allowed to go so, we can, and will, remain here and die, and be buried with our relatives; it will be but a short time before we leave this world, at any rate, and let us avert from our heads as much unnecessary pain and sorrow as possible."

In the evening they departed, expressing a desire to hear the final conclusion of their great father, the President, and the Secretary of War, with respect to the route which it is wished they should pursue. They ardently hope that they will be permitted to go by land, on horseback.

Wednesday, 22d. The Indians remained at home to-day, and in the evening sent word to their conductor, James McPherson, that they would meet at his house to-morrow, for some purpose which they did not explain.

Thursday 23d. The Indians met this morning, agreeably to their appointment of yesterday, and made known the business for which they assembled. It was this, namely: a young man, (one of their friends, and a member of their band,) had just arrived from the Big Spring reservation, to inform them, that the Indians of the Grand reservation were drawing up writings in a secret manner, to establish a claim to a part of the avails arising from the Big Spring reservation, which were affirmed to be unjust by the Indians of the Big Spring reservation, and by the Lewistown Indians, their friends and relatives.

They (the Lewistown Indians) wished the interference of their friends, J. McPherson, and Major [G. W.] Pool, the assistant agent, in their favor, and their cooperation with Colonel Gardiner to protect their rights. They requested that Mr. Gardiner should be informed immediately of their claim, and exert himself to avert its deleterious effects on them and their property.

They were assured that they might rely on the interposition of these officers in their favor, to protect their rights. They then departed for their homes in peace and confidence.

Friday, 24th. The Indians this day collected at a grove, near the house of James McPherson, and received rations for four days. Civil John said that the tribe should be assembled at his house, on Monday next to be vaccinated.

Saturday, 25th. The Indians all remained at home to-day.

Sunday, 26. To-day, also, the tribe remained at home.

Monday, 27th. This day Dr. [Abiel Hovey] Lord, with an assistant, proceeded to Lewistown, and vaccinated about one hundred and twenty of them; they were well pleased with his operation.

Tuesday, 28th. Dr. Lord vaccinated the remaining part of the Indians to-day. Provisions were issued for three days.

Wednesday, 29th. The Indians remained at their homes to-day.

Thursday, 30th. To-day also they remained at home.

Friday, 31st. Several of them took their horses to be shod to-day, to have them in readiness to start. Colonel Gardiner directed this to be done.

Saturday, September 1st. Several more of the Indians took their horses to be shod.

Sunday, 2d. The Indians remained at home to-day. At night they made a feast, which is termed by them the "death feast," or *feast of death.* They celebrate, in feasts of this kind, the good and worthy qualities and actions of some deceased person of the tribe, and mutually and undisguisedly lament their death by tears and lamentation. They adopt some person in his place for the purpose of perpetuating his name, and the memory of his actions.

Monday, 3d. The Indians assembled to-day, by order of Colonel Gardiner, to receive their blankets, tenting, and rifles, which were given to them. They appeared well pleased with them.

They were told by Mr. Gardiner to make every possible endeavor to be prepared to start in ten days. They said they would do so. They expressed great pleasure at hearing they were permitted to go by land, and that no delay in preparing was allowed. They said, that it was their desire to get to their destination as soon as possible. They fear that cannot be done before winter sets in; but they will endeavor to get there this season.

Tuesday, 4th. The Indians remained at their homes.

Wednesday, 5th. Several of them took their horses to get shod to-day.

Thursday, 6th. They continued making preparations to start.

Friday, 7th. To-day they continued preparing.

Saturday, 8th. The Indians commenced delivering their chattel property to General J. McLane, the appraiser, for sale.

Sunday, 9th. They remained at home.

Monday, 10th. They continued delivering their property.

Tuesday, 11th. They commence assembling at Lewistown, in conformity with directions to that effect from James McPherson.

Wednesday, 12th. They continued assembling at Lewistown. Some of them were engaged in taking more property to sell.

Friday, 14th. They were reminded of the necessity of being prepared by the appointed day to set off. Monday was appointed as that day.

Saturday, 15th. The Indians assembled to-day, and received the mount of money due them for their improvements, from Colonel John McElvain.

Sunday, 16th. They remained principally at Lewistown.

Monday, 17th. They received the proceeds of the sale of their property.

Tuesday, 18th. A part of them attended the funeral of Mrs. McPherson, who deceased yesterday, and whom the Indians had esteemed as a relative more than a friend.

They say they will start to-morrow; they were reminded of the necessity of being ready, and promised to finish their arrangements to-day.

They have settled nearly all they owe in the neighborhood. Sixteen horses were distributed among them to-day.

Wednesday, 19th. Nearly all of them left Lewistown to-day, and encamped at the distance of ten miles.

Thursday, 20th. Those Indians who started yesterday proceeded to Hardin, a village nineteen miles from where they were encamped. The remainder traveled ten miles.

Friday, 21st. To-day those who arrived here first remained; and the balance of the tribe came up at night.

Saturday, 22d. By order of Colonel Gardiner, the Indians remained at their encampment to-day—order reigned.

Sunday, 23d. The detachment was ordered to march this morning. We encamped late in the evening at the distance of eighteen miles from Hardin.

Monday, 24th. We struck our tents at 8 o'clock, and marched to Greenville, fourteen miles; we could have gone farther, but a severe storm arose to prevent us.

Tuesday 25th. Upon a solicitation of the principal chief and others, the Indians were permitted to remain in camp long enough to dry their tents and blankets, which were wet in the rain yesterday.

At 11 o'clock we marched on, and at sunset, encamped at a distance of thirteen miles from Greenville, on the road towards Richmond, Indiana.

Wednesday, 26th. We struck our tents at 10 o'clock, and marched ten miles, being within four miles of Richmond; near which place we were ordered to remain by the superintendent, until further orders should arrive from him.

Thursday, 27th. The Indians remained at camp to-day.

Friday, 28th. Nearly all of the Indians went into town to-day; some to see the place, some to trade, and some to get intoxicated.

Saturday, 29th. A severe rain prevented them from leaving their encampment to-day.

Sunday, 30th. We are ordered, at 12 o'clock, by the superintendent, to march on immediately. By night, we succeeded in passing through Richmond, and two miles farther; making six miles.

Monday, October 1st. To-day, some difficulty arose among the teamsters, which detained us until 11 o'clock; at which time we left the camp and proceeded through Centerville. Our start was so late, and the road being so muddy, that we travelled only seven miles.

Tuesday, 2d. Struck our tents at 9 o'clock, and marched thirteen miles and a half, where we halted for the night.

Wednesday, 3d. At 10 o'clock we commenced travelling, and at five gained the distance of fifteen miles.

Thursday, 4th. We commenced marching at 9 o'clock, and at 5, encamped at the distance of sixteen miles from our last encampment.

Friday, 5th. We started at 9, and passed Indianapolis two miles, making to-day, eighteen miles.

Saturday, 6th. We remained in camp to-day. Our orders from the superintendent were, to remain near this place until he should direct us to proceed. In the evening, the superintendent arrived at Indianapolis.

Sunday, 7th. We received orders this morning to march a few miles. The Ottawa detachment is but a few miles in our rear. At two o'clock, we left the encampment, and marched eight miles.

Monday, 8th. We struck our tents at 9, and at 5, encamped at the distance of nineteen miles.

Tuesday, 9th. We travelled thirteen miles to-day, over a very bad road.

Wednesday, 10th. The Indians express an anxious solicitude to remain to-day to rest themselves and their horses, and to dry their tents and blankets, which were wet in a storm last night, &c., &c. Their wishes appeared so reasonable that they were granted the privilege of remaining.

Thursday, 11th. The detachment marched sixteen miles—no impediment.

Friday, 12th. We marched nineteen miles to the Wabash river.

Saturday 13th. We were detained late in crossing the river. For the sake of economy, the horses were made to ford the river, while the most of the women and children were taken across in boats. The river was not low enough for it to be considered safe fording for any but men, or those who were good riders.

The detachment marched seven miles from the ferry, (Clinton).

Sunday, 14th. We marched into Illinois to-day, and to the distance of eleven miles from our last encampment.

Monday, 15th. We started this morning about 7 o'clock, and marched until dark, at a pretty rapid gait, which took us at the distance of twenty-seven miles. There was no water to be had between these two encampments, and the Indians were apprized the previous evening of this fact, and ordered to be prepared to start very early, that we might reach the Ambroise river.

Tuesday, 16th. At the request of the chiefs, and by permission of Col. Gardiner, the superintendent, the detachment remained on the encampment to-day for the purpose of refreshing themselves.

Wednesday, 17th. We started about 11 o'clock and marched 7 miles to where we encamped. There is no water for twelve miles farther.

Thursday, 18th. One of the chiefs lost some of his horses, which detained us until 11 o'clock, when we left the encampment. In the evening, we encamped at the distance of twelve miles.

Friday, 19th. We marched twenty-one miles, having travelled late.

Saturday, 20th. This day, early, it commenced raining, and continued until noon, at which time all the tents were wet, and the horses were in the woods. We remained at the camp.

Sunday, 21st. We struck our tents at 11, and marched fourteen miles.

Monday, 22d. We started at 9 o'clock, and travelled late; we made the distance of twenty miles.

Tuesday, 23d. We travelled seventeen miles to-day; the roads were good, and the day fair. We encamped six miles west of Vandalia, Illinois.

Wednesday, 24th. We travelled nineteen miles; we had an excellent road.

Thursday, 25th. By order of the superintendent, the detachment remained stationary. An express was sent by him to St. Louis for information respecting the prevalence of cholera—the best place and manner of crossing the Mississippi river. He addressed these inquiries to Governor [William] Clark.

Friday, 26th. Removed from the road, that travellers from St. Louis might not come among the Indians, for it is now understood that cholera is prevailing there to a considerable extent.

Saturday, 27th. The detachment remained in camp.

Sunday, 28th. The Indians remained in camp; quietness was exhibited from every tent; good feeling abundantly prevailed throughout the day. The Indians have not for several days had an opportunity of procuring liquor; they consequently remain sober.

Monday, 29th. We this day received orders to march by Col. [J. J.] Abert, who assumed the future direction of the emigration on the 27th.

We started about 10 o'clock, and marched to the distance of fifteen miles on the road to Kaskaskia, where General Clark advised the superintendent to have this detachment of Indians taken across.

Tuesday, 30th. In consequence of some of the principal men of the tribe being behind, the Indians refused to go until they should come up. It was not till past noon that they arrived, and it was then too late to get to the next stream of water; so we were compelled to remain.

Wednesday, 31st. We marched fourteen miles.

Thursday, November 1st. A chief and his son were left behind yesterday to hunt for their horses, and have not yet come up. The chiefs here refuse to leave him any farther behind. They say that they are afraid that they are lost. We were constantly compelled to remain for those behind.

Friday, 2d. We struck our tents at 9 o'clock, and encamped at 5, having travelled seventeen miles.

Saturday, 3d. We marched fourteen miles.

Sunday, 4th. We travelled twenty miles, which brought us within four miles of the ferry, at the Mississippi, where we were to cross.

The conductor rode to Kaskaskia to see Colonel P[ierre] Menard, to whom he was directed by Colonel Abert for information respecting the route, and assistance in crossing the river. In the evening, the conductor returned to camp.

Tuesday, 6th. This morning the Indians proceeded to the ferry; the wind blew so severely that the ferrymen refused to cross. It continued so all day.

Wednesday, 7th. To-day about two-thirds of them were taken over, which occupied their time until dark.

Thursday, 8th. The remaining part of the Indians were taken over to-day.

Friday, 9th. The Indians remained at camp, for the purpose of getting their horses shod.

Saturday, 10th. The Indians had considerable difficulty in finding their horses. We started late, and only travelled eight miles.

Sunday, 11th. We travelled eighteen miles.

Monday, 12th. We travelled seventeen miles.

Tuesday, 13th. We travelled four miles, one west of the mine of Burton, where we encamped for the purpose of having the remaining part of the horses shod.

Wednesday, 14th. We remained to-day for the purpose of getting horses shod, and giving the squaws an opportunity of washing their clothes and blankets.

Thursday, 15th. It was late this morning before the Indians could collect their horses; we travelled only eight miles.

Friday, 16th. We travelled sixteen miles to the Merimack river.

Saturday, 17th. A family was left behind a day or two ago, which the Indians say they intend waiting for at this place.

Sunday, 18th. It rained all day, so much that the Indians would not start.

Monday, 19th. It was so cold that the Indians refused to travel. It snowed and blowed terribly.

Tuesday, 10th. A child died this morning, (the only death which has occurred in this tribe,) which detained us until late. Some horses strayed away, which added to the delay. We traveled seven miles.

Wednesday, 21st. We travelled eighteen miles.

Thursday 22d. It rained and snowed so much that the Indians could not travel.

Friday, 23d. We marched fifteen miles.

Saturday, 24th. We struck or tents at 8 o'clock, and marched until about 5. We made the distance of sixteen miles. The horses of two of the teamsters ran away, and their wagons were consequently left behind.

Sunday, 25th. A part of the detachment travelled ten miles, and the remainder continued stationary. The wagons which were left behind yesterday arrived in the evening.

Monday, 26th. The Indians who remained behind yesterday, waiting for the teams, joined those in front.

Tuesday, 27th. We marched ten miles.

Wednesday, 28th. We struck our tents at 8 o'clock, continued travelling until late in the evening, by which means we made the distance of eighteen miles.

Thursday, 29th. We travelled thirteen miles to the Gasconade.

Friday, 30th. The Indians remained to-day for the purpose of waiting for some of their brethren who are behind.

Saturday, 1st December. It commenced raining in the night, and continued all day, so that the detachment could not travel.

Sunday, 2d. We were compelled to cross a stream several times to day which nearly swam the horses; so that we were detained along the road so much that we travelled but eight miles.

Monday, 3d. We travelled 14 miles. One keg of powder and one hundred pounds of lead were given to the Indians to-day, by Lieutenant Lane, upon the condition that they should pay for it in game, which should be divided among all as other supplies of provisions.

Tuesday, 4th. We travelled twenty miles to-day. We started early, and had a good road, and travelled late.

Wednesday, 5th. We travelled thirteen miles to-day, which brought us to the White river.

Thursday, 6th. We remained at the encampment for the purpose of refreshing the detachment.

Friday, 7th. About 11 o'clock we left the encampment and crossed White river, and marched nine miles beyond it, making ten miles to-day.

Saturday, 8th. We travelled twelve miles, to Gibson's fork of the Neosho.

Sunday, 9th. We travelled fifteen miles.

Monday, 10th. We travelled seven miles today. We could have gone farther, but it was necessary to halt to get corn and meat.

Tuesday, 11th. We travelled thirteen miles.

Wednesday, 12th. We travelled twelve miles to the Seneca agency.

I delivered the Indians into the care of Major [Augustin] Kennerly, the agent for the Senecas, agreeable to instruction. They will remain upon the land of their brethren, the Senecas, until an exchange of their tract of land is made, at which time they will remove to the piece given them.

I and my assistant [Daniel R. Dunihue], with the chiefs and others of our detachment, went to examine their tract which is situated west of the Neosho, and does not extend within less than five or six miles of it; but, in consequence of its being too high to ford, we were compelled to remain on the east side. There was no boat in which we could cross.

The resident Senecas say it cannot be cultivated; that there is scarcely any timber upon it, and but little good soil, and withal, entirely unadapted to their purposes.

Upon this representation, they refused going to see it, but they have since been over to make an examination of its advantages and disadvantages, but what their conclusion is I have not yet learned.

Daniel M. Workman, Conductor of Lewistown Emigrating Indians,

By Daniel R. Dunihue.

The following is a copy of the column of Remarks added to the muster roll of the Seneca and Shawnee Ohio Indians, who have lately emigrated west of the State of Missouri, furnished the agent to whom they were consigned at their new homes.

Dated December 18, 1832.

Two men, while on the route, left the family of Civil John and Joined the Shawnees.

Two also left the family Totola and joined them.

One birth on the route, in Baptiste's family.

Louis Dougherty and family and John Dougherty and family joined the Shawnees, while on the route, with the exception of one woman, who is now with John Smith's family.

One of the men mentioned in the family of Coloshete did not emigrate.

One birth, on the route, in Setting Bear's family

Joe White and family joined the Shawnees, while on the route.

One birth, while on the route, in the family of Peter Knox's son.

Powlas Brant left his family, while on the route.

Silversmith's son and wife were numbered in the family of the widow Turtle, but on the route separated from them.

One child died while on the route, belonging to the family of the Tall Man's widow.

By the various changes made during the route, it will be perceived that there are now but 220 persons.

Daniel R. Dunihue, Enrolling Agent.

Source: U.S. Congress. Senate. *Correspondence on the Emigration of Indians, 1831–1833.* 23rd Cong., 1st sess., 1834. S. Doc. 512. 4:77–84.

29. Excerpt of a Letter from J. J. Abert to Lewis Cass (1833)

The Wapokoneta and Hog Creek Shawnees of Ohio removed under a treaty of August 8, 1831, and the Ottawas on the Maumee River agreed to remove under a treaty of August 30. Both groups removed west of Missouri in 1832. Adding to the rigors of their journey west, the tribes found the land in what became Kansas inhospitable and stark in comparison to the woodlands they had left. Special Commissioner for Removal Lt. Col. J. J. Abert attempted to mollify the leaders and quiet their outspoken dissatisfaction with the West. On January 5, 1833, in a letter to Secretary of War Lewis Cass, reprinted in part below, Abert told how he gave the government horses used in the removal to the tribes and how he paid the Ottawas an advance on the money due them. Despite Abert's efforts, a number of the Ottawas returned to Ohio and warned the remaining Ottawas that the western lands were uninhabitable.

Being fully aware that disquietudes, and many of them well grounded, existed with the main body which were conducted to the vicinity of the Kansas, I determined, before leaving them, if possible, by any reasonable arrangements, to appease these disquietudes, and to leave the Indians as satisfied with the treatment extended towards them, as they evidently were with the appearance of their new lands. For this purpose, I had first all the Shawnee chiefs called together, and in the presence of the agents resident with them, as well as of those who had been employed in conducting them to their new homes, I expressed to them the great pleasure I felt at the fortunate and early termination of the emigration. Then alluding to the losses which they had sustained during the route, and the desire I felt, from the known paternal feelings of their great father, the President, towards them, to fulfill in the most liberal spirit of the treaty, in relation to their emigration, I offered in lieu of and in full compensation of all those losses, to give to them the public horses yet remaining, and which had been used in the emigration of their tribe, and also the several sets of wagon gears and the public saddles which had been similarly used; these to be received by them in lieu of their losses during the march, and not as any part of the articles stipulated in the treaty.

I also stated to them that the feeding under the treaty would commence on the 1st of January, 1833, but, in the meantime, they would be fed as usual at the expense of the United States.

To prevent any misunderstanding on these subjects, I had the proposal twice explained and interpreted by that able interpreter, Mr. Shane, and as many of the chiefs spoke English well, there can be no doubt that the whole matter was correctly understood.

The chiefs, after a consultation with each other, expressed their satisfaction at the proposals I had made, and accepted them freely upon the conditions stated. A statement of the agreement was afterwards reduced to writing, having no means of writing at hand at that time, and herewith accompanies this report.

The chiefs then desired me to state to you, their great anxiety to have the special tract of 100,000 acres, intended for their use, surveyed as early as possible, and also that the farming utensils and the various tools provided for in the treaty might be delivered as early as possible. They wished to accompany the commissioners in this survey, and were particularly anxious that the mill sites should be selected, as their desire is to establish their permanent residences as conveniently accessible to these as possible.

The chief, Perry, of the Shawnee village, and of the tribe removed thither some years since, desired me to assure you that he had rigidly followed the advice of his great father, in cultivating peace and harmony with all the adjacent tribes, between whom the Shawnees, there existed the most cordial and friendly intercourse. That his people were generally separated upon distinct tract, cultivating the soil, and were contented and comfortable.

On the next day, I had a council for similar purposes with the small band of Ottawas, which formed a part of the emigration. This band is connected by intermarriages with the Shawnees of Waupaughkonetta, look up to them as an "elder brother," and accompanied them in the emigration.

Their particular selection of lands was selected about forty miles from the Shawnee village, and amid strangers to them. The Shawnees had invited them to remain in the vicinity of the village until the spring, which they were extremely desirous of doing, contemplating the course of sending an exploring party upon their lands during the winter to select the spot upon which they were ultimately to settle. This was stated to me by the chiefs in council, with an expression of their strong desire to be indulged. So reasonable a desire was not opposed by me, and particularly as I was assured by the agent, Mr. [Richard W.] Cummins, that they could be fed with much more certainty near the village, and could be much more carefully watched over, no special agent being yet appointed to attend to them, and they, on that account, being placed under his care.

I then, also, proposed to these chiefs the same remuneration for their losses which had been proposed to the Shawnees, adding, however, that, in consideration of permitting them to remain near the Shawnee village, they were to remove themselves to their new lands, about forty miles distant, at their own expense, as soon as the weather would admit.

The chiefs then complained of the disappointment in not yet receiving the $2,000 stipulated to be paid in the treaty, urged me to make some arrangements by which they should be paid at least a part of this sum, as it was absolutely necessary to meet their present wants. Fully aware of this and of the poverty of this tribe, I obtained three hundred dollars from the agent, and paid it to them as a part of the $2,000 stipulated for the treaty.

The whole arrangement was then reduced to writing, and signed by the chiefs and myself; and I am happy to add, that it gave them great satisfaction.

Having now completed all of the arrangements, which appeared to me necessary, in order to heal the disquietudes which had existed with these Indians—having seen them contented and preparing their lodges for winter, and the contractor on the ground and furnishing them with provisions, I considered myself as having fulfilled the duty which had been committed to me, and I took my departure from them, leaving them under the care of Major Cummins, the resident agent, and Major [John] Campbell, his assistant, gentlemen whose intelligence, knowledge of their duties, and efficiency and benevolence of character could leave no doubt that the Government would be faithfully served, and the Indians kindly and correctly attended to.

On my return, I stopped at St. Louis, and duly informed General Clark, the superintendent of Indian affairs, of all the arrangements herein spoken of, and furnishing him with duplicates of such as had been reduced to writing, and then set out for this place, where I arrived on the 30th of December, and, on the 1st of January, 1833, again resumed the duties of my office.

Source: U.S. Congress. Senate. *Correspondence on the Emigration of Indians, 1831–1833.* 23rd Cong., 1st sess., 1834. 4:7–8.

30. Journal of a Party of Seminole Indians Conducted by Lieut. J. Van Horne U.S. Army Disbursing Agent Indian Removal from McLain's Bottom Arkansas, to the Seminole Country West, on the Canadian (1836)

Holata Emathla's band was the first group of Seminoles to remove, choosing not to engage in the armed resistance to removal known as the Second

Seminole War. The group of nearly 400 left Tampa Bay by schooner on April 11, 1836, bound for New Orleans. From New Orleans they traveled by steamboat and keelboat in tow up the Mississippi and the Arkansas. However, low water in the Arkansas made it impossible for them to get farther than McLean's Bottom, a small boat landing east of Fort Smith. Lieutenant Jefferson Van Horne of the Third Infantry received orders to escort the Seminoles from McLean's Bottom to the Seminole country in Indian Territory. As Van Horne's journal of the experience, reprinted below, reveals, he had little sympathy for the Seminoles, who were beset by illness during their difficult overland journey. Among the number of casualties was Holata Emathla himself, who died in the Choctaw Nation just a few miles from his destination.

I was proceeding from Little Rock, Arkansas, towards the Seminole Country, with directions from Capt. [Jacob] Brown that "should the Seminoles not have reached their location, to proceed to their camp, ascertain the cause of detention, as well as take upon myself such direction of the movement as shall be deemed best calculated to facilitate the arrival of the party in their new Country." Learning that, the party had landed from the Steam Boat at McLain's [McLean's] Bottom on the 9th May, repaired to the Camp at that place, where I arrived on the 13th May, and commenced enrolling the party, which we did not finish until next morning.

May 14th 1836. I understood that about Twenty were sick when the party debarked; the Doctor now reported Seventy eight sick, whom it would be necessary to transport. In this state of things, guided by the Doctor's opinion that the party were unable to travel, Lieut. Meade who had charge, was delaying. As the Teams, Agents &c. were waiting at a heavy expense, and as it was the Doctor's opinion that the measles would run through the whole party, and the sickness was likely to continue on the increase for some time rather than to diminish, the more especially as it was understood they would not submit to the Doctor's prescriptions, and their proximity to the river enabled them to bathe the sick constantly in cold water, which was sending them rapidly to the grave; As their Camp was very filthy, and the people in the neighbourhood were complaining of their destroying their timber, and as it appeared to me they would be as likely to improve in health by travelling slowly, as by laying in a polluted camp, I thought it best to urge an immediate departure. Besides the Indians, there were two Waggon Loads of Indian Goods to transport. Lieut. [George] Meade had directed the employment of Twelve Waggons. Eleven only were procured. I issued Four days rations of Corn, and started the party four miles in the evening. On account of the great number of sick and the great quantity of surplus Corn and meat, these Indians had accumulated, their stubbornness and obstinacy, and unwillingness to move, I was obliged to leave four wagon loads behind, and return for them, taking up two loads in the evening, and two the nest morning.

May 15th. It rained heavily. After getting up the sick, we started about Eleven o-clock, though with great difficulty on account of the great number of sick and dying, among whom was the son of the Principal Chief very low. We placed the sick in the Waggons ourselves, and in spite of every effort were obliged to leave a load behind. We made six miles. It rained all day. Roads bad, two of the party died.

May 16th. It continued raining heavily. The Indians begged for the sake of the sick, of whom there are from one hundred and thirty to one hundred and fifty, many very low, that I would not move to-day. We had every difficulty to contend with, in the way of rains, bad roads, sickness, unwillingness to move, and the degree to which these people seem to have been humoured, petted and pampered. Teams loaded with corn, meat and flour, great quantities of which they wasted or left on the way. They desired not to travel until the sick were recovered. We were every day using efforts to get additional Teams, but thus far without success.

May 17th. It continued raining. At length we obtained an additional Waggon, and brought up the sick from Camp. They begged not to be moved in the rain. A principal Man very low, they begged me to let them stay till he died and was buried. He died and was buried.

May 18th. Started at nine o'clock. Made Ten miles to the commencement of a prairie, where we were obliged to encamp at three o'clock, as we would find no encamping place for Ten miles farther. Issued Beef.

Before my arrival Lieut. Meade had purchased Twenty Beeves at $3. Per cwt [hundredweight] to supply the party on the route, and employed two men at $2 each per diem (going and returning) to drive them. From this through, this would have cost about $84. Eighteen of these Steers he turned over to me. The drivers were not responsible for the Cattle. One steer had already escaped from the drivers, and they called on me for more aid. I should not have made this purchase, as Beef is about $2 per cwt the greater part of the way. There would likewise be a considerable surplus or deficiency. The Contractor would not admit our right to issue the surplus, which would then be thrown on our hands, and in case of a deficiency, it would be at the point most difficult to supply. I therefore discharged these drivers to day and gave $60 to the Seminole Contractor to drive them and supply us whenever we needed, he being responsible for the Cattle. In case of a surplus the United States to have the right to issue said surplus, as part of the year's supply of the party. In case of a deficiency the Contractor was to be allowed to furnish said deficiency and to receive contract price. (There was a surplus of 4770 pounds, which supplied the party after their arrival for fifteen days.)

May 19th. It rained powerfully. An Indian Doctor (Hotulge Yohola) a principal man, dying. All the chiefs were very urgent to remain until he should die and be buried. All joined in the request and evinced such unwillingness to go, that I thought nothing but force would start them. I wished to leave that as the last resort.

May 20th. Started at nine o'clock. Made nineteen miles to the Vache grasse. Continued raining. Part of the road very bad. Many of the Teams mired down constantly, and we were compelled to haul the Waggons through deep mire for long distances with ten yoke of oxen to each. We continued at this with five Teams in rear, until late at night trying in vain to get them out of the swamp. They remained two miles in rear until early on the morning of

May 21st. When we hauled them out by main force. It rained every day powerfully, the Streams very full, roads miry. We passed on to camp; and as our Oxen and drivers were wore out and exhausted, we stopped at Bailises', five miles at four o'clock at a good encamping place convenient to good water and wood. Issued Beef.

May 22nd Started at nine o'clock. Made ten miles to Poteau river. Road boggy in places. Poteau not fordable, obliged to travel without a road two and a half miles through the woods and ferry over it. I rode forward and made an advantageous agreement for crossing our party at the ferry at a reduced rate. An axle tree gave way one mile short of the Poteau, Waggon detained. It joined our party at the Agency. Occupied until dark crossing Waggons over Poteau; broke the Boat, and unable to cross four Teams until morning. The party encamped early in the afternoon. After dark a Choctaw introduced a Gallon of whiskey into Camp, which I took from him. He had escorted two Seminoles to a store at Fort Smith, each of the three had brought a Gallon of whiskey. In the morning I found the same Choctaw with two Bottles of whiskey in our Camp. I took them from him and poured the whiskey on the ground. This was the only occasion on which whiskey found its way among the party while under my charge.

When I took charge of the party two white men were under pay at $2.50 per diem. Hagan as Interpreter and Ayers as Issuing Agent. They were represented to me as inefficient, and so I found them, especially the latter, who was a decided encumbrance. I was informed that they received $1.00 per diem until the party left the Steam Boat from whence they had been promised $2.50 per diem. As there was only one Indian in the party who could interpret at all, and he very indifferently, I found it necessary to retain Hagan, at least until I should learn something of the Indians. I designed not to employ Ayers, but Hagan would not continue with the party unless Ayers should also be allowed to accompany it. I was thus obliged to retain both, until yesterday finding their births no sinecures, as I obliged them to do duty, Ayers under plea of sickness applied for his discharge, as did Hagan to day. I have experienced great inconvenience all the way for the want of a faithful and efficient interpreter.

May 23d. Making Axle tree and repairing the Boat detained us. Started about ten o'clock, reached the Choctaw Agency, nine miles, about three o'clock; except three wagons, (including the one which had broken its Axle tree,) which arrived at dark. I intended going three miles further, but the Superintendent said he had been delaying his journey to Red River two or three days, to have an interview with the Seminoles; and recommended me to encamp at his Agency for the purpose. Issued Corn in the evening.

May 24th. It rained heavily last night. Three died in the morning, Black Dirt's wife and daughter and Tustenue [Tustenuggee] Harjo's principal warrior, others very low. Having heard they were to have a talk, they dressed themselves in the morning, and nothing could induce them to omit it. They urged on the Superintendent the great number of Sick, the dead and unburied, others near their end; that their effects were soaked with rain, the sick suffering from exposure to it. The Superintendent thought the circumstances rendered it necessary to lay by for the day and asked if I did not think so also. I told him it was not for me to dissent from his opinion, but that this had been the language used and the posture of affairs each day since I took charge. That each day, I had equal, nay, superior difficulties to combat with, and that at no time on our journey, had the morning opened with so fine a prospect of a good day's journey, and conjured him to give his influence in urging them forward so soon as he was done talking with them. I then retired, until his talk was closed; when finding that they were pitching their Camp with the fixt purpose of remaining at least for the day; I very reluctantly yielded. It rained very powerfully during the after part of the day and the night. Some one ready to breed trouble had put Black Dirt up to require of me Coffins and burial for his wife and daughter; this had been done for them on the water; myself and Mr. Chase were obliged to expose ourselves to a soaking rain to effect this.

May 25th Wet morning. Found it difficult as usual to start them. We made about five miles through the rain, which fell in a constant torrent. The earth covered with water, thus becomes so soft that our Waggons mired at every step. We were obliged to drag them in succession with ten or twelve yoke of oxen which we did until we got them all together at a small Creek at dusk. Every soul soaked with rain, some of the Teamsters shivering with ague, the poor Indians suffering intensely. Some of our Waggons broke down, the oxen were exhausted by floundering in the mud. The whole Country one Quagmire.

May 26th Found it impossible to proceed. To attempt it is to exhaust ourselves and endanger the safety of the Indians, drivers and oxen. Before us, within a few miles are several impassable streams. Behind us the Poteau has cut off our supply of Beef, the contractor having toiled several days in fruitless efforts to cross our Beef Cattle. He drowned three today in the attempt. We are to day making repairs to the Waggons. The Indians drying their effects. Myself and Mr. Chase broken down and exhausted by toil and exposure of preceding day and night, being soaked with rain.

May 27th Numbers very low and dying, several died. They again besought me to remain. I was obliged to return to the Agency and purchase Beeves at an exorbitant price, as our own could not cross over the Poteau &c. Indians were in want of Beef. Found Indians obstinately bent on remaining and that only force could remove them. Issued Beef in the evening.

May 28th After much difficulty in getting our Sick in the Waggons, being obliged to carry and lift them in ourselves, we started about Ten o'clock. In crossing the Cassia [?] one Waggon upset. Roads boggy in places. Banks of streams very steep and difficult to ascend. Made fifteen miles to a good encamping ground near the Sans Bois, which we had hoped by this time to find fordable, having had no rain for the last day or two. Found it out of its Banks, rapid, and entirely impassable. During the night it fell about seven feet. Contractor not come up with the Beef Cattle. On account of the continual heavy rains and exposure the sickness and mortality has increased ever since we started. From one, two, to three deaths per diem, we have now four. The effluvia and pestilential atmosphere in the Waggons, where some twenty sick or dying lay in their own filth, and even the tainted air of their camps is almost insupportable, and affects more or less those exposed to it.

May 29th Obliged to wait the subsiding of the water.

May 30th Sans Bois still deep and rapid, so much so that the Indians with their usual perverseness were unwilling to cross, and we were obliged to take a Team one mile, and let them see it cross over and return in safety before they would venture.

According to the Contract made before my taking charge, the Teamsters were to subsist themselves and their Oxen. In consequence the Oxen being turned loose to graze, were frequently astray in the morning. Such was the case this morning. As we were starting, a woman died, and her relatives desired to wait and bury her. These things delayed us, and we were late in starting. The roads were deep in places, so that we had frequently to double our Teams, and the crossing of the Great and Little Sans Bois so bad, that notwithstanding all my cautions to the drivers to be careful, two of the Waggons overturned, one at each of these streams. We encamped on the Bank of the Little Sans Bois, about half an hour before sun set, having made five miles. Issued Beef.

May 31st I was obliged to hire a driver in place of one whose oxen were strayed off and who had gone in pursuit of them. I had frequent and importunate applications from the Chief to buy Horses for them. Holata Emathla and Tustenue Harjo, Principal Chiefs were very urgent this morning. My private means would not admit of this and I was ignorant of their public resources. Holata Emathla was hauled in a Waggon to day. Started about Ten o'clock. One of the teamsters sick. We had much difficulty to get his Team along. Teamsters and all attached to the party seem more or less affected by the prevailing sickness. In the post oak woods the roads are very deep, so that we had to double Teams, and were often obliged to raise the Waggon wheels from the mire with levers and other means, to get along. A Waggon was turned at the steep and difficult crossing of a Creek. While I was exerting myself to extricate the Sick, the Indians by concert quickly threw out the Sick and baggage from the other Waggons, before they could cross the Creek. We were thus obliged to stop short of our intended goal. We made eight miles. I rode on two miles to get information of the route.

June 1st The Doctor who had given Holata Emathla repeated portions of Calomel, pronounced him very sick. He said he expected to die in a few hours, and begged that I would detain the party until he was buried, or at least until morning. I told him that if he could not go with the party, that he had better remain with his family at a Choctaw house near by and let the party proceed. All were unwilling to leave their Chief, and represented the piteous condition of the sick. We remained and issued Corn and Beef.

June 2nd Holata still low, and the whole renewed their request to wait another day for Holata to die pledging themselves to take him with them in the morning if he lived. I found that force only would move them, as on yesterday, and they were so well provided with arms and ammunition and seem so intractable and stubborn, that such a resort might have been hazardous. They have all along thrown every difficulty in the way; and on my urging them, they said I might abandon them. This I did not wish to do, except in the last resort. Their suffering Condition and the number of sick and dying was such, that I deemed it best to yield to this delay rather than desert them. Since we left the Choctaw Agency, they seem willful, and to consider themselves beyond the reach of restraint.

June 3d Started at ten o'clock; made Eleven miles. Had several bad Creeks with steep Banks to cross. Had some difficulty in finding the correct route. In some places roads almost impassable. Obliged to Bridge and cut trees out of the way, and to select the best ground for our route. Road miry in many places. In the evening we came to a deep and boggy Creek whose course we had to search for some miles to find a practicable crossing place. We were obliged finally to unload and haul the Waggons over empty. This detained us until morning. Holata Emathla principal Chief died during the night. He was buried in the morning by his people on a handsome eminence overlooking the stream, one & a half miles from the Canadian. His body and his effects were encased in a strongly built wooden pile, built to the height of Five feet above the surface of the Earth. The neighbouring ground was carefully cleared of grass and leaves, and a fire left burning near his head. He declared from his first attack that he could not survive. He was of pleasing manner, and good person; cool, crafty, and politic; he was wanting in decision, and could not be depended upon.

June 4th Started about nine o'clock. The frequent reoccurrence of deep Creeks and ravines with abrupt banks, obliged us to pursue a circuitous route. For the last few days we are obliged to hunt out open woods, or make our own roads, as the Waggons can not follow the little Horse trail which we follow with the assistance of a guide, that I found it necessary this morning to employ as we once missed our way. The tongue of a Waggon broke to day, which detained it until early next morning. We had two high, steep and very rocky hills to ascend to day. Flies bad in the prairie. Some of the Waggons stuck fast repeatedly which detained them until near dark. Made Ten miles.

June 5th Started at Eight o'clock. We had much difficulty in ascending a very high steep and Rocky mountain. I rode on to the Canadian about Ten miles and endeavoured to find a ford. My guide could not find the way around a deep Creek putting it between us and the fording place. We could not understand the Indians living here until our Interpreter came up with the Waggons, when a Creek Indian told me he could show me the way over. As I was very anxious to get the party over on to their own Lands as soon as possible after so much delay, I mounted my house and the Waggons followed us. The route soon became very bad; impassable; and while we were endeavouring to find a better one, the Indians apprehensive of danger in crossing this boggy river, and persevering to the last in their disposition to retard our progress and prolong the journey, were clamorous to have me encamp for the night, and commenced unloading and encamping. Finding on examination that it was entirely impossible to cross our Waggons, I caused them to be drawn up close on the bank, where was a spring of excellent water and a handsome encamping place. I immediately obtained two canoes with which the party commenced crossing the river. I discharged the Teams, Issued Beef, and the articles guaranteed by Treaty. The party continues very sick. Three or four die daily. They continue in spite of all that can be said to them to bathe those in Cold water who have the measles; and to press unmercifully the stomachs of all the sick whatever the disease be. I was desired by them to name the successor to Holata as principal Chief. I told them that Eneah Thlocko, (son of Holata,) had been very sick ever since I had joined, and I could not therefore judge so well of his fitness or indeed of the fitness of others, as themselves from my short acquaintance with them, and urged them to make the selection themselves agreeably to their usages. Eneah Thlocko was appointed principal Chief. Fuckalusti Harjo or Black Dirt is the most able and influential Chief. Although we were told at McLains's Bottom that the distance to the Seminole Lands was but one hundred miles, we thus found the whole distance travelled by land 127 Miles through a Country unfrequented except by Hunters.

Respectfully submitted,
J. Van Horne, Lieutenant.
Seminole Lands, 6 June 1836

Source: National Archives Record Group 75, Preliminary Inventory 163, Entry 201, Records of the Commissary General of Subsistence, Letters Received, 1831–36, Box 15, St. Louis, Seminole File.

31. Journal of My Journey with Two Thousand Creek Indians Emigrating to Arkansas, Tuck-e-batch-e hadjo Principal Chief (1836)

Muscogee (Creek) removal was not only one of the most costly in human life but also one of the most remarkable for the suffering of the people. A noted example was the experience of a contingent of more than 2,000 Cussetas and Cowetas who were sent west in September 1836. They traveled from eastern Alabama to Memphis, where some were put aboard steamboats and others began a journey overland through the Mississippi Swamp to Indian Territory by way of Little Rock, Arkansas. Before Memphis, they had been subjected to forced marches, which left stragglers along the way without assistance. Despite appeals from Tuckabatche Hadjo, the leader of the group, for days of rest and for assistance for the stragglers, the Alabama Emigrating Company agents, contractors for the removal, cared less about the Creeks than about profit. Fortunately, Marine Lt. John T. Sprague had been assigned as the military observer, whose job it was to see that the contractors fulfilled their obligations. At Memphis, Sprague threatened to assume control of the removal if the agents did not give better treatment to the Creeks. As Sprague's journal reprinted here reveals, he exerted a good deal of control over the contractors beyond Memphis; however, the Creeks' journey remained difficult and beset by logistical problems.

On the 3d of August I reported to General at Head Quarters, Tuskegee, Al. agreeable to his [Gen. Thomas S. Jesup's] order, remained there 4th 5th 6th 7th 8th or rather made that my Head Quarters and from there visited such places as directed by the General. 9th recd orders to prepare Jim Islands and Tuck e-batch-e hadjo for removal and repaired immediately to their camps; remained with them until prepared, on the 23d recd orders to start them on the 24th, 28th recd order prolonging the time five days to the 3d of September, 3d of September turned over to the Alabama Emigrating Co. 1943 Indians as in camp-enrolled and prepared for removal in presence of a large crowd, Capt. Seals and Dr. Hill I took as witnesses, Sunday the 4th sent them the rolls completed by Lt. Crabbe, U.S. M. Corps, 27th August Dr. Hill the Surgeon ordered by General Jessup to accompany me reported for duty; ordered him to join the train as soon as it moved, sent an express to General Jessup the 4th reporting the progress.

September 5th Monday. Went to Casiter [Cusseta], saw Tuck-e-batch-e hadjo. Camp stirred, early in the morning saw Jim Islands' people preparing, they started in the afternoon.

September 6th Tuesday. Went to Columbus to start Ben Marshall's Camp, they having delayed coming into camp much longer than necessary: started them the next day, 8th. Ben Marshall's Indians all gone, remained in Camp

[No entry for the 7th.]

8th Thursday. Arrived at West Point

9th Friday. Left West Point, camped at La Fayette

10th. Left La Fayette camped 12 miles

11th 12th. Still in confusion, camped 10 miles

13th. All came up with the train 12 M. East of the Coosa River

14th. On the March—travelled 12 Miles, roads bad

15th. On the March—travelled 10 Miles, roads good

16th. On the March, travelled 12 Miles; within 10 miles of Elyton, Indians intoxicated, weather pleasant

17th Passed through Elyton and camped three mile west of it; roads very good, country poor, Indians intoxicated, camped 10 miles

18th Sunday. Travelled 14 miles—roads bad—through a very mountainous country, country very poor, 12 Miles

19th Monday—Camped west of the Black Warrior River, Country mountainous and poor, no houses, roads very bad, Indians sober, 10 Miles

20 Tuesday. Country more mountainous than any portion we have passed and much less cultivated, distance traveled fifteen miles, this distance was accomplished with much fatigue to the party but the scarcity of water compelled it—The regular time of starting the day also mentioned was 7 o'clock A.M., but the party seldom got all in motion til 8—Camped usually about 4 P.M.

(Henry Marshall with his family of twelve including himself joined the emigrating train on the night of the 13th inst.—at the Coosa River 80 miles from La Fayette

Sunday the 18th inst. Mr. Mc Millian an express sent to me by Genl Jessup & Capt. Page returned I sent Capt. Page the rolls of the Party—also wrote him & Genl Jessup with the promise that I would send him the rolls of the Indians which were not enrolled through the Post Office as soon as they could be finished.)

21st Wednesday Camped at Plum Creek, Morgan Co.—distance traveled to day sixteen miles, we were compelled to go this distance from the scarcity of water, arrived at the Creek at 4 P.M., Indians all came up before sun down. Col. [Felix G.] Gibson came to see soon after dark, Tuck-e-batch-e hadjo, had been to his tent with his principal chiefs and expressed his determination to go no further until he and all his people had rested one day; and that in the morning his sick, aged and children would remain behind agreeable to his order, the rations which had been issued to them two hours previous he declined accepting and had advised his people not to take them. He evinced much anger and left the tent saying the "word is out." This morning early, I found him [Tuck-e-batch-e hadjo] in Conversation with the Contractors, (Gibson & [Charles] Abercrombie) and found that he had been urging upon them the necessity of resting one day, they declined and give him reasons. I told him that I was convinced of the propriety and of the advantages all would derive from it, but I did not think this was the proper time; we were in a very poor country, provisions were scarce, corn and fodder was dear, and that in three or four days we should be in a country better able to supply their wants and at a much cheaper rate. We left without coming to any conclusion. I sent for the Interpreter, Jesse, at 10 A.M. sent word to him that I should see him early in the morning, and cautioned him about letting his young men go out in the morning to hunt, as he had directed them, that the people here were hostile to them and were all strangers.

22d. Saw Tuck-e-batch-e hadjo this morning, we concluded to go on to the stream 14 miles where he said he should remain one day and if his people were inclined to obey his talk they would remain also. Arrived at the Stream at 4 P.M. Camped distance 14 miles; roads bad most of the way leading through deep swamps, the country much more abundant; farms large and well cultivated.

23d Friday—Most of the Indians prepared for a start, Tuck-e-batch-e hadjo expressed his determination to remain to day and advised all the Cuseters to remain with him, nearly all were intended to do so, and commenced throwing out their baggage from the wagons; this I remonstrated against and obliged many of them to put them in again. The train started at 8 o'clock A.M. Tuck-e-batch-e remained behind and about two hundred followed his example in spite of all my efforts to prevent it. Camped at McCrary's—12 Miles.

Saturday 24th Started at 7 A.M. roads good, county much better; farms large and highly cultivated, passed through a small town called Courtland. This is a village of about one thousand inhabitants, houses principally brick and has the appearance of being a place of some considerable business. Every effort was made to prevent the sale of Whiskey to the Indians, but they got it and the larger portion of them were intoxicated before night. Camped at Town Creek—distance traveled today 16 miles.

Sunday 25th At Town Creek The Indians resting and taking a general wash, had a talk with them, told them Tuck-e-batch-e hadjo was not the person for them to listen to about stopping and that what he said to them was not good unless it came first from me. Mr. Gibson & Odum gone to Tuscumbia to enquire about the route. Tuck-e-batch-e came up with his Indians about ten A.M.

On the night of the 23d at Mc Crarys I waited upon the contractors by the advice of the Doctor and by what I knew to be the state of the whole party and requested them to halt one day. They objected to it. I laid before them the fatigued state of the Indians, their sickness, the weakness of the ponies, and that in a faithful discharge of my duties I felt myself to require a day for the comfort and convenience of the Indians, and that if they would not I should find myself justified in acting in compliance with the [number not given] Article of the Contract. They with great confidence denied my authority to halt the party and the 25th was determined upon for me to halt. I gave the order.

Monday 26th The party left camp at 7 A.M. arrived at Tuscumbia at 2 P.M. camped 1/2 mile from town: distance 15 miles; road good.

Tuesday 27th Left Tuscumbia at 1/2 past 7 A.M. Camped at Caney Creek, road hilly, water scarce, distance 9 miles.

Wednesday 28th Left Camp at 7 A.M. roads good, provisions scarce. The road to day was through the Chickasaw Nation, but few settlers, camped at Bear Creek: distance 15 miles.

Thursday 29th Still in the Chickasaw Nation, roads good, corn very scarce, but few houses upon the road. Camped at Indian Creek: distance 12 miles. Wrote a letter to the contractors, ordering provisions required by the contract to be issued.

Friday 30th Left Camp at 7 A.M. roads very hilly and rough, provisions and settlers scarce, country very poor, still in the Chickasaw Nation. Camped at Owens at 5 P.M. Distance 17 miles. This distance was accomplished with great difficulty and with much fatigue to the Indians: but the scarcity of water compelled the party to go much farther than was proper for the comfort and convenience of the Indians, and a large number of them arrived in camp very late, a few as late as 9 P.M. The great scarcity of water, is the great objection to this route. Indians and horses almost suffered for water. We found the party of Indians (3000) in charge of Dr. Sevier camped here which makes our situation still more unpleasant and O-poth-le-olo's party having camped here a few days previous has been the means of draining the country of its resources. I am going to see Dr. S. and to make some arrangements to separate our parties.

October 1st Saturday: Saw Dr. S. last night agreed that my party should take to the right hand forks of the roads seven miles distant, Dr. S. the left. These roads come together within twenty miles of Memphis: the left hand fork is fifteen or twenty miles the farthest. Dr. S moved off early, my party at 8 A.M. Knowing that our yesterday's march was a very arduous one, I concluded to make a close examination into the state of the party. I knew that from the roughness of the roads, the scarcity of water and the distance, many would be unable to proceed to day on foot, and that many would be found sick. At $\frac{1}{2}$ past 9 A.M. I found in the camp about one fourth of the party, and all the wagons belonging to the party gone; they were two miles on the road, one wagon that had been broken down the day before came up, I requested the driver to stop and take in a lame man which I had seated by the side of the road; he declined doing it and drove off, in the camp I collected the blind, lame and the sick and who were totally unable to go on, and I also found families whose baggage had been thrown out by the waggoners without any means whatsoever of getting on, I endevoured to find one of the agents or some of their assistants and found they, all of them, were four miles upon the road, relying with confidence upon the paragraph of the contract which says, "any pecuniary expenditure for the comfort and convenience of the Indians may be made &c." and I succeeded in finding a wagon sufficiently large to transport those who had no horses or any means of conveyance. This wagon was not as large as I wished and I endeavoured to find another but could not. The Indians agreed to pack themselves & horses if I would have their children put in with the sick and lame. I did so, and they left their camp at one P.M. I remained with them until they arrived in camp at 8 P.M. On the road I found one blind man and one in the most perfect state of decrepitude. I could not get any means of conveyance for them, the wagon having more than could be hauled, but assured them that tomorrow they should ride, and if the wagons would not allow them to get in, to report it to me immediately and I would apply the remedy. I learnt from Mr. Hill that the party camped at 5 P.M.—distance 16 miles, roads good but water very scarce. This distance is more than should be travelled, but it could not be avoided there being not a sufficient quantity of water for the party upon the road. We left the Chickasaw Nation—the line six miles behind. Some of my party were talking of remaining in the Nation. I had a long talk with them and told them that should they remain I should send soldiers for them immediately.

I hired wagons for the purpose of bring[ing] up the lame and blind and sick which had been left through the negligence of the Agents, brought on to Camp two who were taken sick on the road, the wagons refused to attend to them. One blind one and one feeble from old age, brought them into Camp. The agents refused to pay for the wagon. I remonstrated with them upon the course they were pursuing, and told them that the disregard to the comfortable conveyance of the Indians I could not endure any longer.

Sunday 2d. Left Camp at 8 A.M. Those that had come up were got of[f] with some degree of comfort. I returned five miles from the Encampment and on the way counted one hundred & ninety Indians who from the distance and fatigue the day before were unable to get up. Among these were many sick, feeble and the poorer class of Indians. I urged them to come up but they declined it to be impossible. The roads to day were very good the weather very pleasant, the country well settled and cultivated. Passed through a small town called Purdy, camped at McCullocks—distance travelled to day 15 miles the Indians much fatigued. To day when remonstrating with Mr. Gibson, one of the Agents, upon the course they were pursuing, I assured that I should consider it to be my duty to see that no Indians were left behind. He said I might, they should not. I told him that I should confine the march to twelve miles a day, hereafter, and that I should order it. He said I might, he should not obey it. Great dissatisfaction in camp arising from the fatigue of the party and the disregard paid to their comfort. Wrote a letter to night to the Agents expressing my wish that some remedy should be provided for the difficulties which existed, and remonstrated strongly against their conduct and ordered them to confine the march to twelve miles a day.

Monday 3d. Sent my letter to the Agents. Mr. Gibson called to see me and said my letter was a reiteration of our conversation yesterday. I asked him if I was to understand them as disregarding the contents of my letter. He replied that they had not had time to reflect upon it. I requested him to give me an answer in writing. The roads very good to day. Country settled, corn scarce, with difficulty enough could be procured for the party. Tuck-e-batch-e hadjo, with many of his chiefs stopped me to day and held a long talk. The amount of it was precisely what I had expressed in my letter this morning. He expressed his determination to halt his Indians unless something was done. I listened to him and we agreed that this evening we should wait upon the Agents and he to them should express his opinions and wishes. Camped at 4 P.M. at Webbs,—distance 12 1/4 miles. I endeavored to find the Chief but found him intoxicated.

Tuesday 4th. Left camp at Webbs at 1/2 past 7 A.M. roads very good. Country well settled, passed through a small town called Bolivar, Tenn., a place of some business—took active measures to prevent the sale of Whiskey. Succeeded in a measure, Camped at Hardiman's Mills distance traveled to [day] 13 miles. More attention paid to the sick & others than usual, but not enough. More men are required to attend to it. Neglect and indifference still the same. Many Indians came into Camp tonight intoxicated. Tuck-e-batch-e hadjo very much so. Jesse, my interpreter, refused to act as such any longer, his life he said was in danger. Four Indians attacked him yesterday with the determination to kill him as they s[ai]d but for the timely interference of some friends who got him off. They said he was engaged with the white men in driving them on like dogs, he was against them, so was all the white men of the party, and they would kill him and the whites. The Chief came to see me this morning, very much dissatisfied at the treatment he had received from the Agents, and assured me that he would go with me to them to day on our arrival in Camp. He came to Camp very much intoxicated, which obliges me to postpone it. Wrote to the Contractors to move the train of Waggons at 8 [o']clock A.M. to commence on the morning of the 6th.

Wednesday 5th Waggons left Camp at 8 o'clock. What men there were endeavoured to have things arranged but it is impossible that so few men can do so important a duty in the short time in which it must be done. Many indians refused to go on to day, saying they were fatigued and sick. I induced many to go on, and many determined to stay. Tuck-e-batch-e hadjo with his family remained behind. I returned to Boliver, saw Col. Danlap Member of Congress, who urged the necessity of all these indians going west of the Mississippi with the best feelings toward the government. I obtained from him letters of credit at Memphis. While in Boliver saw Mr. Campbell Agent of the Taledaga Party. I told him all I had encountered and expressed my determination that this party should not cross the Mississippi in charge of the present Agents. I left Boliver at 3 P.M. On my way I found many that were sick, many lame, and many children. I wrote a note back to Mr. Campbell who was coming on the same road, requesting him to pick up all he should find on the way. I endevoured to find waggons, but could get none. I urged them to come on, they said they would go as far as they could. I arrived in Camp at Evans Creek at 5 o'clock, distance traveled to day, by the party, 15 miles. On my arrival in Camp, I determined to halt the Party tomorrow the 6th and allow those belonging to the party to come up. Being so near Memphis (45 miles), I thought it necessary that the whole party should be together. I accordingly ordered the Agents to halt the Party.

Thursday 6th I was up this morning before daylight. Orders had been given by the Agents to gear up the Waggons for a start. I went through the Camp and directed the Indians to take all in the Waggons out of them, that the waggons were going off. They done so. In about an hour after the order which had been given was ordered to be suspended. We have not moved today and Indians are all sober. I wrote a letter to the Agents expressing my determination that the Party should not go to Arkansas in their charge. Sent an order to the Military Agent of the Taledaga Party not to pass us on the road unless by general consensus of all concerned. Recd for answer that they were astonished at receiving such an order. The Indians remained sober all day and conducted remarkably well. I requested them not to go into the potato & corn fields adjoining the Camp. They complied strictly with my request. In this Evening Mr. Abercrombie called to consult me upon tomorrow's march. He said there was no water for twenty miles. I told him that if this was the Case we should be obliged to go it, but it was too far. Went into Camp, consulted with the Chief who expressed his willingness and promised to give his people a talk that evening upon the necessity of it. I went all through the Camp and urged them to get up early. Mr. A. consultation with me was the first during the journey.

Friday 7th I went into Camp at day-light, urged the Indians to an early start. The indians were all prepared at 1/2 past 6 A.M. The train started at 20 m[inutes] past 7. Past through Sommerville 3 m. from Camp, a very pretty and business like looking place of about one thousand inhabitants. Roads to day were remarkably good. Country well cultivated. The first Waggon arrived at Camp at 4 P.M. The waggons and Indians were strewn for twelve or fifteen miles. Camped at Cypress Creek, distance traveled 20 Miles. No water upon the road, not enough to water the horses. All the Indians could produce was from wells, and that with difficulty. The Indians came up better than expected at night.

Saturday 8th The train of waggons left Camp at 8 A.M. All moved off together. The indians kept up with the waggons all day. Great scarcity of water upon the road. Creeks all dry, obliged to go 17 Miles. The road was unusually good and level. The Country well settled and cultivated, fine extensive cotton plantations extending for miles. Camped at 4 P.M. at Wolf River in the vicinity of a small town called Raleigh 9 miles from Memphis. Many indians did not come up till morning. I ordered the party to halt but afterwards concluded to move two miles to a more suitable camp ground.

Sunday 9th Moved Camp two miles to give the Taledega Party of Indians an opportunity to Camp in our rear. The train moved at 10 A.M. I started to Memphis seven miles to see Members of the A. E. Company, took with me Tuck-e-batch-e hadjo. I saw Mr. Ingersoll and Mr. Campbell two of the contractors. I expressed to them my determination that Mr. Gibson & Abercrombie should not cross the Mississippi in their charge and that their attention to the Indians had been of such a character that they had violated both the letter and spirit of the contract. Go they should not, and new agents must be appointed. They said that tomorrow there should be some decisive measures taken. I remained in town in hopes of seeing all of the Agents, and getting a decisive answer. The agents were all very much engaged in getting boats to cross the Mississippi. No boats are here but small ferry boats and steam Boats are required. O-pothe-le-ola's party in charge of Capt. Bateman I found two miles from Memphis. The Party in charge of Lt. Scriven was twelve miles from Memphis.

I represented to Capt. Bateman the state of my party, that unless new agents were appointed I could not discharge my duty to the Government and that either they (the agents) must be removed or I must be relieved from the duty.

Monday 10th In Memphis, arrangements making to go by land, through the Swamp. Still in Memphis. The Agents were not prepared to give me an answer. Saw Mr. Lawrence, President of the Memphis Bank, gave him Mr. Danlap's letter. He said he thought there would be but little difficulty in my getting what money I should want if these Indians came upon my hands. O-poth-le-o-lo's party began to cross the river to day in the ferry boat. Steam Boats were expected at night. I left town at 4 P.M. Came out to Camp.

Tuesday 11th In Memphis. Steam Boat arrived at night. O-poth-le-olo objects to go by water to Rock Roe, round the swamp. No answer from the Agents.

Wednesday 12. Opoth-le-olo has concluded to go by water. All busy loading. Recd a letter from Capt. [John] Page, which completely destroyed all grounds I had taken against the conduct of the Company (see letter on file). Tuck-e-batch-e hadjo came to see me, said he must go by land and requested me to go the swamp and ascertain correctly its state. I told him I would.

Thursday 13th Opoth-le-olo's party left in the Steam Boat this afternoon at 5.

Had an amicable arrangement [with] the members of the Company. The assurances they have given me are sufficient. Mr. Abercrombie has quit the party. Mr. Gilman goes in his place.

Friday 14th Still in Memphis. O-poth-le-olo's party gone. Lt. Scriven's party commenced crossing the river to day. I was to have gone to the Swamp to day. The Indians came in for that purpose, but we could not get a wagon. Concluded to start tomorrow morning, five Indians going. The Party is two miles from town.

Saturday 15th Still in Memphis. Lt. Scriven's party crossing the river. I started with four Indians to look at the Swamp. We went fifteen miles, stopped at Mrs. Williams' on the U. S. Road. This road for this distance is very good.

Sunday 16th Left Mrs. W. at 1/2 past 6 A.M. The road for four miles was good. We soon after came into the swamp. The Indians soon after concluded that it was impossible to pass through with loaded wagons. We continued on five miles and found it almost impossible on horse back. The Indians wished to return. We dined at Mrs. W. and got back to Memphis at 7 P.M., distance 30 miles.

Monday 17th Lt. S. party not crossed the river, still crossing, I was in Camp. Tuck-e-batche hadjo and Chiefs, I held a long talk with [them]. He said he would take my advice. Talk was good; he would tell his people so. The whole party concluded to go by water.

18th Tuesday Lt. Scriven's party have all crossed the river. All waiting anxious to be moving, the Indians very impatient. The weather very pleasant. The Boat which took Capt. Bateman's party is expected to night.

19th Still in Memphis. The Boat expected last night arrived this afternoon.

20th Thursday Lt. Scriven's Party and the remainder of O-poth-le-olo's party preparing to get off.

21st Friday. The Cowetas belonging to my Party commenced crossing the river.

22d Saturday My Party still crossing. Lt. Scriven's party started this afternoon. I proposed to the Agents to purchase a Boat and take my party to Little Rock if the Chiefs would consent to it. I saw the Chiefs, they consented, the Boat was bought, and tomorrow the Boat is to be in readiness to load.

23d Sunday The Boat is not quite ready. Moved the Cuseter [Cusseta] Camp within one mile of town. Tomorrow morning I fixed for them to come and load the Boat. The horses are to go through the swamp, accompanied by as many men as are disposed to go. The wagons go in the Boat. The weather is still very fine. I have been constantly engaged the last Eight days in going with a body of Waggoners to get Ponies belonging to the Indians that have been stolen by other Indians and sold, and have succeeded in getting fourteen.

Monday 24th Still in Memphis. Commenced raining this morning; the whole day was very unpleasant. The Coweta Indians all crossed to day.

Tuesday 25th Rained all day. Tuck-e-batch-e hadjo declined letting his Indians move from Camp. He said they should remain and cross the Mississippi tomorrow. A few however crossed the river.

Wednesday 26 Weather still unpleasant; roads very muddy. All the Cusseters crossed to day. After ascertaining correctly that [no?] more were behind I crossed in the last boat: about 5 P.M. We are making every arrangement to get off early tomorrow morning. The accommodations for the Indians is a good sized Steam Boat called the John Nelson, and two large flat boats. All of which I have ascertained from the best authority to be good, comfortable and substantial boats. A large body of Indians go through the swamp with all the Horses. All wagons are taken to pieces and put in the boat. As near as can be ascertained there will be about fifteen hundred men, women and children going in the boat, and five or six hundred go through by land. Every provision I am assured has been made on the road and I have given Mr. Freeman my assistant, under whose charge the party goes, to see to it strictly.

Thursday 27th The weather still rainy and cold. The Party to go through the Swamp left at 9 A.M. in charge of Mr. Freeman.

The Party in the Steam Boat under my immediate charge left the Arkansas side at 10 A.M. We were obliged to touch on the Memphis side to take in a few of Jim Island's Indians who had come up with him the night before. Here I had a long conversation with Islands. He said it was impossible for his Indians to get ready to go with us and would prefer remaining a day or two. I immediately saw Mr. Gibson, Mr. Hendricks, Mr. Campbell, and Mr. Beattie. They were convinced that from the great sale of Whiskey it would be improvident for our boats to remain a moment longer than possible. They all assured me the best provision should be made for all the Indians left behind. I took Islands to them and told him what arrangements had been made and that Mr. Beattie and Hendricks were the Agents to whom he must make all his applications. This was perfectly understood, and I left with the most perfect confidence in their assurances.

At $1/2$ past 12 M. we again started. The boats were very comfortable, not much crowded. At $1/2$ past four the Boat landed for the night. Corn and Bacon was issued as usual computing the number on board at fifteen hundred. The distance to day was estimated at 16 or 18 miles.

The weather has cleared up, bright star light, fine moon, and tomorrow bids fair to be very pleasant.

Friday 28th Up early this morning, surrounded by a dense bank of fog. The fog came up a little about 7 A.M. Got the Indians on board, but soon found it too thick to run. At 10 A.M. the fog cleared up got started day clear. Camped four miles below Helena on the Arkansas side. Distance to day 70 miles.

Saturday 29th Got under way at day-light, weather very unpleasant and cold and cloudy. Camped at Montgomery's Point on the Arkansas side: distance to-day called 75 miles, but by the channel of the River I have but little doubt but that its nearer one hundred. Weather very unpleasant, raining hard.

Sunday 30th Left Montgomery's Point at $^1/_2$ past 7 A.M. Entered the mouth of White River at 9 A.M. Came up this river six miles and there concluded to take the principal outlet of the Arkansas, after ascertaining there was a sufficiency of water and if this should be the case, we could be confident in finding enough to ascend the Arkansas to Little Rock. The distance through this outlet is six miles. At $^1/_2$ past 11 A.M. came to the mouth of the River and found water enough through the outlet. The water of the Arkansas has a most singular appearance resembling the colour of a half burnt brick. Here is its proper termination. It then forms two arms, one of them at low water empties its self into the Mississippi, and at high water the other, or the most northerly arm, empties the greater portion of the waters of the Arkansas into White River and from thence into the Mississippi. This arm is the one principally navigated by Steam Boats most of the year.

This morning early, the Steam Boat Farmer with Mr. Campbell's Party on board passed us on its way to Rock Rowe: up the White River. Camped on the south side of the Arkansas about 5 P.M. five miles below the Post of Arkansas. Distance come to day 40 miles. Weather still bad.

Monday 30th Left Camp at 7 A.M. Current very strong, river rising rapidly; it came up two feet last night. Found great difficulty in stemming the river with the two flat boats in tow. We averaged to day about one and a half miles an hour. Camped at 5 P.M. three miles above the Post of Arkansas. Distance to day 13 miles. Done raining, weather clear but cold.

Tuesday November 1st Left Camp at $^1/_4$ past 6 A.M. Came up the river two miles where we concluded to leave the flat boats and equally divide the party taking on board the Steam Boat one half and leaving the other until the boat could go to Little Rock and return. Left this place at 8 A.M. Boat very much crowded, river still rising. Camped at 5 A.M., distance to day 50 miles. Placed markers upon the bank of the river to ascertain correctly the stage of the water. Weather very pleasant.

Wednesday 2d At 2 o'clock A.M. found the river had fallen two feet, and there was no time to be lost. Started the Indians in Camp at 1/2 past 2 A.M., got them all on board at 3, and at 1/2 past 3 A.M. the boat got under weigh. The day remarkably fine, every thing indicating very strongly a rapid fall of the river. Camped at 1/4 past 5 P.M.; the day pleasant and warm, distance to day 75 miles.

Thursday 3d Left Camp at 4 A.M., river still falling. Morning very pleasant but cold. The Indians came on board with great reluctance. The Boat for the last three days very ditry and exceeding offensive. On the 31st Octr. I requested Mr. Gibson, the Agent to adopt some method to have it partially cleaned. [Gibson's response has been marked out and is unreadable.] Arrived at Little Rock at 1/2 past 4 P.M., distance 78. Weather very fine.

Friday 4th Remained at Little Rock; the Arkansas still falling, fell sixteen inches last night. Undetermined whether to venture farther up by water or not. A part of the Ponies and Indians which came through the swamp joined us last evening.

Saturday 5th. Concluded to send the S. Boat back immediately to bring up the remainder of the party from Post of Arkansas. The boat left at 8 A.M. I proposed to Tuck-e-batch-e hadjo to start all that came up in the boat and get across a bad swamp forty five miles up the country, where there would be an abundance of game and provisions, and where we would wait until the whole party could get together. This he positively declined doing. Here, there is no provisions and the quantity of whiskey sold to the Indians jeopardizes the lives and property of all the Citizens. I directed all the Indians that were willing to go with me to put their baggage in the waggons and start immediately. All consented but the Chief and about one hundred indians. The party started about 3 P.M. Camped at 5. Distance 5 miles. Weather very pleasant.

Sunday 6th Left Camp at 8 A.M., road very rough, weather pleasant. Camped at 5 P.M., distance 15 miles, at [Emzy] Wilson's.

Monday 7th Left Camp at 9 A.M., roads very rough and in many places very muddy. Camped at 5 P.M., distance 18 miles; ten waggons remained owing to the bad state of the roads.

Tuesday 8th Left Camp at 8 A.M. Crossed the Cadron Creek and camped, distance 3 1/2 miles. There we expected to meet the Party that came through the swamp. Little Rock was the place agreed upon, but unbeknown to me the Agents directed their Agent to go forty miles further up to the Cadron as all the Indians were going up by water. There we could hear nothing of our Party. Concluded to go on and go through the Point Remove bottom. As everything indicated rain, about noon Mr. Gilman, the Agent, came up with the waggons that were behind last night.

Wednesday 9th Left Camp at 8 A.M., weather very unpleasant, raining hard, roads exceedingly bad. Came to [William] Plummer's. Camped at 4 P.M., distance 7 miles.

Thursday 10th Left Camp at 8 A.M., roads very bad. Weather cold, rained most of the day very hard. Came to Mrs Slinkard's. Camped at 1 P.M., distance 9 miles.

Friday 11th Left Camp at 9 A.M. Came through the Point Remove Bottom, which was almost impassable, much worse than it has been for a year past. Camped at 1 P.M., distance 5 miles, at Blount's.

Saturday 12th Started at 1/2 past 8 A.M. Weather cleared up last night and the day is very clear but cold. The indians suffer greatly from being in their bear [sic] feet and thinly clad. Came to [Kirkbride] Pott's. Camped at 4 P.M., distance 12 miles, roads much better, country quite hilly. Here, I have ordered the Party to halt until the whole party can get together. The Dardanelles on the Arkansas is eight miles from here. There we expect to meet the John Nelson, with the remainder of the Party. Sent a man there yesterday to look out for her. The Indians and Ponies that came through the Swamp are expected here tomorrow.

Sunday 13th Still in camp, weather very pleasant. Ponies from the swamp not arrived. They are constantly coming in in small parties. Complaints are made to me by citizens against the Indians who are left behind; that they kill their stock. Sent back Mr. Freeman to urge them to come up and to collect them and keep them under his immediate charge. The Agents also have gone back.

Monday 14th Last night an express came reporting the arrival of the John Nelson at the Dardanelles. I got all the lame, sick and blind together with those who were disposed to go, into waggons and took them to the Boat. Tuck-e-batch-e hadjo who came up in the Boat was opposed to going on board again, which deterred many who came with him from going. He said a large portion of his Indians were behind with many of his family and until he could meet these he would not go on. I however succeeded in getting on board about three hundred and placed them in charge of Doctor Will, with instructions not to keep the Party in his charge until I should arrive at Fort Gibson. The Boat left at 5 P.M. Gibson the principal Chief in Camp of the Cowetas came to me this morning and requested that we might remain here until his indians could get up, that now families were separated, and those who had horses were obliged to walk, and that many children were here, and many were behind without their parents. I told him we should wait.

Tuesday 15th The Boat came back this morning in the expectation of getting those on board who declined going yesterday but could not succeed. When the boat landed those on board commenced bringing off their baggage, and said they would not go as they had been told that they were to be taken into a distant country where they were to be placed under soldiers and their men placed in irons. I assured them that it was false and urged them to take their baggage back, if they would do so, I would be up with them in four or five days and do as I had always done for them. To this they assented, their baggage was again taken on board and the boat started at 11 o'clock A.M. The distance from this place to Fort Gibson by water is near four hundred miles, by land one hundred and seventy. The weather the last two days has been very pleasant, the water in the Arkansas still rising. At 12 M. Waggons were procured and Tuck-e-batch-e hadjo and those with him were brought to camp. He complained of being very sick. I returned to Camp this afternoon. Ponies and indians behind not arrived. Mr. Odum & Mr. Love (?), two Agents were sent back to day to bring up all behind. I told the Agents yesterday, that their entreaties, threats or representatives could not drive me from what I had promised the Indians and from what I conceive now to be my duty: the Indians should be got together and should be kept together, and that not an Indian should go from this place until I was convinced that none were behind.

Wednesday 16th Still in Camp, weather pleasant. Waggons and Ponies not arrived. The Indians have been coming in in small parties of six, eight and ten every day.

Thursday 17th Ten Waggons, a large number of ponies & Indians arrived to day in charge of Mr. Freeman. Mr. Hudspeth, one of the sub Agents of the Company arrived also. He says that Narticker, brother of Tuck-e-batch-e hadjo, was in the Mississippi Swamp with about one hundred Indians and that they were determined to take their own time in coming. I advised Mr. Gilman, the Agent, to start tomorrow, that nearly all the Indians were up excepting those in the swamp and as they were not disposed to come up I did not think those here ought to wait for them. Every preparation is making to start tomorrow. The weather to day is very unpleasant indicating snow or rain.

Friday 18th Rations were issued this morning for two days. Rained hard all day. With difficulty I could get the Indians to go for their rations. Finding it impossible to start to day from the violent rain, we shall endeavor to start tomorrow.

Saturday 19th This morning there was every indication of a pleasant day. We started from Camp (Pott's) at 1/2 past 9 A.M. A cold rain commenced this afternoon. The roads were very muddy and the creeks very high. Four, five and six waggons were down in the mud at once. Camped at Dwight on the Illinois B[ayou] at 5 P.M. But two waggons got to camp to night. The rest were strung upon the road for ten miles: distance to day 13 miles. Cloudy and cold, has the appearance of snow.

Sunday 20th Rained all day, very unpleasant and cold; remained to day at Dwight. Four of the waggons came to camp to day. Every thing indicates fair weather.

Monday 21st Left Camp at 8 A.M. Came one mile over a very bad road to a small creek, which we found very high with a bank upon the opposite side which required two hours to get our waggons up. Came on to Piney Creek, which we were obliged to cross by ferry. Arrived there at 3 P.M. Camped at Mays: distance 12 miles. Weather clear but cold. Six of our waggons behind.

Tuesday 22d Remained to day at Mays for the purpose of getting all up in the rear. All the waggons and Indians came up to night and tomorrow we intend to make a fair start. The road we are told is much better than that we have passed over. Weather very pleasant but extremely cold.

Wednesday 23d Left Camp at 8 A.M. Indians and waggons all started together, road good, weather very cold but pleasant. Arrived at Spadra River at 1 P.M., distance 9 miles. Here, we found Mr. Gibson from the Steam Boat John Nelson which was at the mouth of the river. I directed all the waggons to go to the mouth of the river and the indians to follow. Arrived there at 5 P.M., 2 miles. In the evening I assembled all the Chiefs and urged upon them the necessity of all the women and children going up in the boat. They very readily consented and said all would be prepared to go in the morning.

The Arkansas river is at a stand, with about six feet rise of water.

Thursday 24th This morning all the Indians were prepared to go in the boat, most of them were on board. At 11 A.M. the boat was ready so far as the indians were concerned; all of them that were going were on board. A difficulty occurred, however, between Mr. Gibson who had been acting as Captain of the boat and all the crew, from the Pilot down. They had concluded to leave the boat to a man if he continued on board of her. They would not, they said, submit longer to his conduct towards them. Two Hours elapsed. Mr. Gibson was determined to remain. The indians were all on board waiting anxiously for the boat to start. I was determined that the indians should not remain in suspense any longer, and I told Mr. Gibson & Gilman (the Agent) that unless some course was determined upon and pursued within one hour I should direct all the indians to come ashore, camp them, and take decisive measures to take them to Fort Gibson myself. To this they replied, "there shall be no longer delay." At 1 P.M. Mr. Gilman reported to me that Mr. G. would go by land and he should take charge of the boat. The crew consented to this. The boat left at 1/2 past 1 P.M. with about as near as could be estimated, one thousand indians. All the Indians that go by land camped at Ward's on the Spadra, 2 miles from the river.

Friday 25th Left Camp at 1/2 past 8 A.M., roads good, weather very pleasant, country well settled. Camped at Pace's; distance 12 miles.

Saturday 26th Started from Camp 1/4 8 A.M. road very good, level, weather pleasant. Camped at Blount's: distance 23 miles. This distance was much longer than we had ever travelled before, but the Indians being mostly mounted they were anxious to get to Fort Gibson as soon as after the Steam Boat as possible. I told the Agent that if he would have a waggon expressly to carry all on foot I had no objection to the party proceeding as fast as possible. They did so, and they [moved?] on without difficulty.

Sunday 27th This morning I placed the party in charge of Mr. Freeman, my assistant. Those on board the Steam Boat, being more there than on shore, I was anxious to get to their place of destination as soon as the Boat did. I according left this morning with the determination of being at Fort Gibson as soon as possible: distance 75 or 80 miles. Came to Van Buren: distance 30 miles.

Monday 28th Left Van Buren at 8 A.M., road good but hilly, weather pleasant. Came to Mrs. McCoy's, 30 miles. At Van Buren I heard that the Steam Boat got aground opposite Fort Smith & remained there one day but had got off.

Tuesday 29th Arrived at Fort Gibson at sun down. Left Mrs. McCoy's at 8 A.M., weather pleasant, roads very rough, passing over very high mountains and through quite an unsettled country. Distance to day 32 miles. I could hear nothing of the Boat, the river being from twelve to fifteen miles from the road.

Wednesday 30th Sent a man down the river to enquire for the Boat.

Thursday December 1st The man sent down the river not returned. A rumor was about that the Boat had gone back to Fort Smith.

Friday 2d The man returned. Ascertained that the Boat had gone back to Fort Smith, and that the Party of Indians with the horses were camped thirty miles from this, and that waggons had gone back to bring up those (Indians) at Fort Smith. Making preparations to start for that place in the morning. Weather very pleasant, water in the Arkansas low.

Saturday 3d Left Fort Gibson at 9 A.M. Stayed at McCoy's.

Sunday 4th Left McCoy's in search of the party, found them part at Winters, 10 miles from McCoy's.

Monday 5th Camped with the Party at Mc[Coy's], weather pleasant.

Tuesday 6th Camped at McKay's, distance to day 15 miles, weather pleasant.

Wednesday 7th Remained at McKay's to day for the rear of the party to get up.

Thursday 8th Still at McKay's, weather pleasant.

Friday 9th Left Camp at 1/2 past 8 A.M. Came to Drew's. Camped, distance 15 miles.

Saturday 10th Left Drew's at 9 A.M. Came to Fort Gibson, distance 4 miles. Here General [Matthew] Arbuckle ordered the Party to halt and camp within one mile of the Fort. I camped the Party in the immediate vicinity of O-poth-le-o-hola's, and by order of the General informed the Agents of the Company that tomorrow the Government would take charge of the Indians. I had the Indians counted. They amounted to 1605. This number together with 395 that arrived here in the Steam Boat on the 20th ult. makes two thousand. A small party are yet behind in charge of an Agent. This party were those who expressed a determination to remain in the swamp. I heard from this morning, they are coming on and will be here in two or three days.

Sunday 11th Waiting for the Party behind.

Monday 12th Still waiting the arrival of party.

Tuesday 13th Preparing the rolls. Party behind not arrived.

Wednesday 14th Not arrived.

Thursday 15th Mr. Odum arrived with the Party in his charge amounting to two hundred and fifty. Mr. O. reports Tuck-e-batch-e hadjo behind waiting for his brother.

Friday 16th Capt. [J. R.] Stephenson received them and camped them with the rest of the party.

Saturday 17th Capt. Stephenson is preparing the roll to be delivered to the Company as soon as the few behind are brought up. The number of Indians which the roll calls for have arrived.

Sunday 18th Capt. Stephenson acknowledges the recpt [receipt] of the complete roll. He gave the roll up to me for my disposal. I signed it and turned it over to the Agent Mr. Gibson.

Monday 19th Engaged in settling up my accounts, and giving the Indians blankets according to the treaty.

Tuesday 20th Still engaged in settling my accounts and in giving to the Indians of my party blankets, by the request of the General. Made my report to Mr. Harris. Put it in the office this night to go in the mail tomorrow morning, reporting the arrival of my party. The whole number after deducting deaths and adding births amounted to 2087.

From one hundred & fifty to two hundred Indians have been counted here more than the roll. A remark respecting it made upon the muster roll.

I hope no apology is necessary for the appearance of this journal. The inconveniences attending a journey like this, and, more particularly, the great want of any convenience of writing is the cause of its appearance.

I was obliged to cut it down both in matter and material sufficient to get it into my saddle bags. It was my intention to have copied it and written it out more fully, but the want of time has prevented it.

J. T. Sprague
April 6th 1837.

Source: National Archives Record Group 217, Records of the Department of the Treasury, Second Auditors Records, Entry 525, Indian Affairs, Settled Accounts and Claims, Box 238, File 1687 John C. Reynolds.

32. Journal of Occurrences on the Route of a Party of Emigrating Creek Indians Kept by Lieutenant Edward Deas, U.S. Army Disbursing Agent in the Creek Emigration, in Charge of the Party (1837)

As part of the forced removal of the Muscogees (Creeks), militias were used to gather those Creeks who had fled the Creek lands and taken refuge among the Cherokees. In the spring of 1837, Creeks were rounded up as far away as North Carolina and gathered into holding camps near Gunter's Landing, Alabama. Directed by Lt. Edward Deas, a party of Creeks left Gunter's Landing in May 1837 and descended the Tennessee, Ohio, and Mississippi rivers to the Arkansas, which they ascended to the Indian Territory. By the time they arrived in the West in June, 80 Creeks had died or escaped. Deas's journal of occurrences during the trip west is reprinted below.

16th May 1837. Today the Party of Creek Indians; the collection of which for Emigration I have been charged with, was turned over by me to an Agent of the "Alabama Emigrating Company" at a point four miles South of Gunters Landing N. Alabama.

The Party numbers 543 as shown by the muster rolls. After due consideration of all the circumstances I find that the Route by water to the new Indian country West of this Mississippi River at the present time, is preferable to that by land. I have therefore indicated this mode of transportation for the present party.

These Indians are a part of those Creeks, that fled from their own country in Alabama after the treaty with that tribe of 1832; hoping probably by taking refuge among the Cherokees to be placed upon the same footing, with the latter people in reference to the necessity of Emigrating to the West.

They have been apprehended at various points in the Cherokee Nation, scattered over an extensive tract of thinly settled or barren country. For this reason and owing to the inaccessible retreats in which they were found by the troops, and the difficulty in procuring subsistence and transportation in such places, and also the necessity of employing agents of intelligence to take charge of the Indians when apprehended, it has required a good deal of experience to prepare the present party for emigration. Nine flat-boats have been purchased by the Contractor to be used until steam conveyance can be procured below the Muscle Shoal Falls, in the Tennessee River. Four of these Flats are of the largest class about 80 feet long, the others 50 & 40 feet in length, This allowance is sufficient to ensure health and comfort to the people. I turned the party over this morning at the encampment of Tennessee volunteers about 4 miles south of Gunter's Landing, where the Indians have been grounded for the last week. They were moved to the water's edge by noon, and about sun-set the whole embarked on the Flat-boats & are at this time (10 o'clock PM) progressing slowly by the force of the current.

There are but very few cases of sickness at present and the weather is very favorable in this respect.

17th May. The boats continued to float all last-night and until to-day at noon, when they reached Ditto's Landing 30 miles from point of starting. They were then obliged to stop until 5 PM on account of wind, when they again set out and are still floating (10 o'clock PM).

18th May. About 4 o'clock this morning a heavy wind suddenly arose, by which the boats were compelled to land in the dark and we were so unfortunate as to lose Fifteen of the Indians who took this opportunity of making their escape. Owing to the continuation of the wind the boats could not re-embark until near sun-set, and are still floating (10 o'clock P.M.).

19th May. The Flat-Boats with the Party on board continued to float all last night, and to-day until 3 o'clock P.M, when they were landed on account of wind, a few miles above Decatur; which place is 60 miles from Gunter's Landing. The Party re-embarked about sun-set, and is still now progressing slowly. (10 o'clock P.M.)

20th May. Early this morning the weather became stormy and the Boats were obliged to land before day light, and in consequence we have lost more of the Indians by desertion. The boats were separated when they were landed, and immediately after some of the smaller ones touched the shore, the people on board of them took advantage of the Darkness, and rain, to make their escape.

As soon as the other boats landed, every exertion was made to overtake and bring them back. By offering a reward of one dollar for each that should be returned, I recovered 15. The remainder 56 in number, could not be overtaken in time, and succeeded in making their escape to the mountains, 5 miles distant.

The weather has continued rainy thro' the day. No progress has been made, but we shall probably start to night. We are at present at Brown's Ferry, 12 miles below Decatur.

21st May. About Midnight the boats set-out & came thro' the Elk River Shoals to Lambs Ferry, 16 miles. We there stopped long enough to procure

Pilots & hands to pass the Muscle Shoals, which are some what difficult of navigation. The Boats entered the Rapids at 10 o'clock A.M. and reached the foot of the Shoals at 4 P.M. without any accident.

The length of the shoals is 15 miles and at some places the rim is 2 or three miles wide, and is filled with small islands. Many of the passes are very rapid, and experienced Pilots are necessary to carry a Boat thro' necessity, though in case of accident, then is no other danger than the loads of the boat & cargo. The Party is at present landed on the north bank of the River, about 6 miles above Florence.

22nd May. The Boats started this morning at 4 o'clock floated 16 miles, and again landed the Party 6 miles below Tuscumbia. An arrangement was made at that place today, for a S-Boat at Waterloo, 30 miles below, at the foot of the Rapid water. Nothing of consequence has occurred, the Indians continue healthy, generally, and apparently well satisfied. No further desertions have taken place.

For the last week has been uncommonly cool for this country, at this season. Yesterday and today the weather has been very fine. I should have mentioned on the 20th at Decatur I engaged a Dr. Morrow to accompany the Party at $85 per month, & expenses in place of the physician who started from Gunter's Landing at which place one could not be hired for less than $5 per day.

23rd May. Early this morning the Party again started, and reached Waterloo at 10 o'clock A.M. The Steam Boat Black Hawk was then got in readiness for the reception of the Indians. One large Keel and two of the large Flats were taken in tow, and at 4 o'clock P.M. the whole Party re-embarked, and we have since come 40 miles & landed for the night, at the foot of an Island in order to prevent desertions, should any of the Indians be so disposed. The Black Hawk is of about the middle size of Steam Boats, & her guards have been covered, and every thing done to accommodate the Indians to the best advantage on board of her.

24th May. The Boats got under way this morning early, and reached Savannah Tenn^e an hour afterwards. One of the flats was left at that place, as it impeded very much our progress, and was not at all necessary, to the comfort of the people. The other Boats have been rendered as convenient for them as possible by constructing temporary sheds & cooking-hearths, in the Flat Boats, & on the Deck of the Keel. All appear well pleased with the rapid progress we are making, about 8 miles an hour. A child that has been sick for some time back, died today & was buried in the afternoon at a wood landing.

Nothing of importance has occurred thro' the day.

25th May. The boats continued to run thro' last-night, passed Paducah today at one o'clock, and stopped for the night about sun-set, near the mouth of the Ohio, on the Illinois Shore. Another child died to-day owing probably to the folly of its mother, in putting it in cold water. Since leaving Gunter's Landing, the weather has been uncommonly cool, for the season. Since yesterday afternoon, there has been an almost constant drizzling rain. Up to the present time the rations have been issued without any failure. I had 17 bushels (all that could be had) of dried Peas issued at Tuscumbia in place of part of the meat-ration, which is too great for the present inactive situation of the people.

26th May. This morning about day-light the boats started, the weather fine and still cool. In the forenoon we reached New Madrid, where a short stop was made, to procure Corn. Since that time no interruption has occurred, & the boats will continue to run thro' the night.

27th May. The Boats passed Memphis this morning early, but we have made no stops, as intimation had been given, that some of the Indians wanted to visit the Chickasaw country, & would attempt to leave the party for that purpose.

28th May. The boats continued to run thro' last night, & reached Montgomery's Point, this morning about day light. We entered the mouth of White River at 8 o'clock having stopped a short time at the Point, and passed thro' the cut-off into Arkansas R., about $1/2$ past nine. We have since come about 50 miles, up the latter stream, and stopped for the night at 8 o'clock P.M.

The Arkansas is not a very good stage at present, for small boats, and is on the rise, which will probably continue for some time.

The Spring Fresh has just begun. Had we arrived 2 or 3 days sooner we should have been delayed, as small boats are fast on the Bank above, until yesterday. The rise of this river at this season, is said to be owing to the melting of Snows in the Rocky Mountains, and consequently depends upon its time of occurrence, which of course varies with the season. As last winter was a severe one, & the warm weather having set in late this spring, it is reasonable to expect a heavy rise this summer.

Nothing of importance has taken place to-day, the weather continues fine tho' warm. The boats stopped for the night at dark, having come about 50 miles.

29th May. An Indian man & a very old woman both of whom have been sick since starting, died to-day. As it is necessary at present to stop at night, an account of navigation, and as the people can therefore go on shore to sleep & cook, if they choose, we left the Flat Boat this morning, the steam boat & Keel being sufficient to transport the Party, under such circumstances.

The boats got under way early this morning, and stopped at sunset having come about 75 miles.

30th May. The people came on board & the boats started at 6 o'clock A.M. and passed Pine Bluffs in the forenoon. As we shall be able to reach Lt. Rock early to-morrow by running tonight, and the Indians willing to do so, I have consented to its being done. The River has risen so suddenly within the last few days, that the Pilots think there is no longer danger from snags, or other obstructions at night.

31st May. We reached Little Rock this morning at 7 o'clock, stopped there about an hour, and then continued to run until 7 P.M. having come about 50 miles.

When the Boats landed a very few of the people went on shore, and as they appeared sincerely desirous of continuing to run thro' the night, we accordingly started again at 11 P.M. It rained last night but cleared up this morning before reaching Lt. Rock, and the weather is at present fine tho' warm in the daytime.

A female child died this afternoon, but nothing else of importance has occurred thro' the day.

The River is now said to be 12 or 14 feet above low water marks.

1st June 1837. We continued to run thro' last night, and to-day; the weather very fine tho' warm. An old woman who has been ill with the consumption more than a year died this afternoon. We are still running (10 o'clock P.M.) and are about 200 miles above Little Rock by water.

2nd June. We continued to travel through last-night & to-day and reached Fort Smith this evening at dark, and are still progressing at the rate of between 3 & 4 miles an hour (10 o'clock P.M). It should have been mentioned that every day a considerable stop has been made in day time, at wood landings, giving the Indians an opportunity of leaving the Boats, and Bathing, and also of taking exercise, the want of which to people of their habits is the greatest objection to transporting them by water. I do not think that the present Party has suffered on this account.

3rd June. We reached Fort Coffee this morning about 2 o'clock, stopped there a half an hour; and then continued to run until 11 A.M. when the boats were obliged to stop 2 or 3 hours to procure wood, which was gathered and cut, by the hands and Indians, who were hired to do so, so little navigation takes place on this part of the River, that wood landings are very few in number. After laying in a sufficient supply, the Boat again started and will continue to run thro' the night.

We passed the mouth of Canadian River about sun-set and are now between 50–60 miles above Fort Coffee and about 30 from Fort Gibson (10 o'clock P.M.)

Another death occurred this morning at Fort Coffee (an infant). For 5 or 6 days after we entered the Arkansas, we traveled at an average of some three or 4 miles per hour, but since then, the current has become so much more rapid, that we have been gradually running slower, and at present the speed of the Boats does not exceed 3 miles.

4th June 1837. We continued to travel through last night, and this forenoon at 7 o'clock passed the mouth of Grand River. The Indians had said to me, that they wished to be landed on the west bank of the Verdigris, near the Creek Agency. When we reached the mouth of Grand River, I sent an Indian Runner to inform the Disburs. Agent of the bank (West), that the Party was in the vicinity, in order that arrangements might be made for its immediate reception, at the point of debarkation. The boats reached the creek Agency at 8 o'clock, and the Indians were immediately mustered, with as much accuracy, as it was possible for the operation to be performed with. The Party was received immediately after it arrived, and the number after deducting desertions and death upon the boats, amounted to Four hundred and sixty three.

Fort Gibson Arkansas Territory

June 5th 1837. Today the muster roll of the Party of Indians that was yesterday delivered over by me, at the Creek Agency on the Verdigris River certified by the Disbursing Agent, of the Creeks (West.) I have no fault to find with the emigrating Company in regard to the removal of this party. I believe the Indians have received every allowance they were entitled to, and with one trifling exception, were treated in company with the requirements of the letter and spirit of the Emigrating Contract. This exception was the failure to have constructed some necessary fixtures which were essential to cleanliness on the boats and which I was promised should be put up, before starting. Their construction were delayed several days and never were finished as I wished them to be. Had not their necessity been superseded in a few days, by the frequent stopping of the Boats, I should have employed carpenters to make them & have charged the expense to the Contractors.

When the miserable and impoverished condition of many of these people, some months previous to starting is considered, and the imperious effects that such circumstances, was calculated to produce upon the health & constitutions of many of them; and when it is also remembered that they were in a party closely confined under guard, for several weeks previous to setting out; and when the unhealthy season of the year is also taken into account; I do not think that the amount of sickness & number of deaths upon the route has been by any means great.

The foregoing remarks embrace every occurrence of any importance that has taken place to my knowledge, from the time the party started from Gunter's Landing, until its arrival and delivery, in the new country next of the Mississippi River

Edw Deas

1st Lt. U.S. Army & Disburs^{g} agent with Creek Emigration

Source: Journal of Occurrences of Lt. Edward Deas 1837, National Archives Record Group 75, Records of the Bureau of Indian Affairs, Letters Received, Creek Agency Emigration, Microcopy 234, Roll 238, Document D 97.

33. George H. Proffit's Removal Journal (1837)

George H. Proffit was the assistant agent for Potawatomi removal in 1837. His journal was sent as a report to C. A. Harris, commissioner of Indian affairs, by Proffit's supervisor, Superintendent A. C. Pepper. Although the journal tells us little about the daily lives of removing Indian people, it does give us some idea of the violent behavior of the unsavory characters who embarked with the Potawatomis, who were traveling peacefully, highlighting the lack of planning and sensitivity of the removal contractors. Also, the journal mentions the whiskey traders who preyed on this and other groups.

Camp on Crooked Creek

Sunday, Aug. 13. Officers at Camp employed in issuing rations & enrolling such Indians [as] may arrive for emigration.

Monday, Aug. 14. Officers employed as yesterday.

Tuesday Aug. 15. Officers employed as yesterday.

Wednesday, Aug. 16. Officers employed as yesterday.

Thursday Aug. 17. Officers employed as yesterday.

Friday 18 Aug. Officers employed in forming new muster roll and in making preparations for starting West of the Mississippi.

Saturday 19 Aug. Officers employed as yesterday.

Sunday 20th Aug. 1837. Officers employed at camp in preparing to emigrate since Indians may revolt.

Monday 21 Aug. Officers employed as yesterday.

Tuesday 22 Aug. Officers employed as yesterday.

Wednesday 23 Aug. Officers employed in superintending the loading of waggons. 5 o'clock P.M. The emigrating party left camp at Crooked Creek. George H. Proffit, Conductor. Joseph Barron Assistant conductor and interpreter. Doctr. Jerolaman, Attending Physician. This day travelled about six miles and issued provisions for three days.

Thursday 24th August. This day travelled over an even country about fifteen miles passing through Monticello, the county seat of White County. When about three miles from Monticello our party was detained for some time by the arresting of Baptiste Dutroit, a quarter blood Pottawattomie at the tent of George W. Ewing of Logansport. In consequence of the arrest of this man, his Wife a pottawattomi and two children left the emigrating party.

Friday 25 Aug. Early this morning we were joined by Dutroit, his Wife and two children, he having been released. Travelled this day about 17 miles passing by the Tippecanoe battle ground. The last doz. miles of the march found the country very broken. Issued provisions for Autumn.

Saturday 26th Aug. Travelled about three miles when the party is obliged to camp for the day. A heavy rain continuing in excess. This day issued rations for 27, 28, 29 Aug.

Sunday Aug. 27, 1837. left the encampment at 1/2 past 8 o'clock A.M. and travelled until 5 P.M. resting about one hour at noon. This day traveled about 16 miles over a tolerable even country.

Monday Aug. 28. Left the encampment at 1/2 past seven and travelled until 1/2 past 5, resting about 1 1/2 hours in the course of the day. Progressed about 14 miles over a very broken country with small prairies.

Tuesday Aug. 29. Left the encampment about 8 o'clock A.M. and travelled until about 1/2 past 5 P.M. The excessive heat obliged the party to halt about 2 hours in the middle of the day. Travelled about 14 miles through a broken country. Camped 10 miles from Danville in Illinois. Issue rations for 3 days.

Wednesday Aug 30. Early this morning Nas-wa-kay the principal chief of the p. was taken very ill, having a severe attack of Cholorea Morbus. Owing to the illness of this chief and his dangerous situation the party remained in camp all this day.

Thursday Aug. 31. The attending Physician reported the Chief Nas-wa-kay as unable to travel and that it would be dangerous to remove him. The party therefore remained in camp this day.

Friday 1st September. Nas-wa-kay having measurably recovered the party left the encampment at 8 o'clock A.M. and travelled with an hour's intermission until about 5 P.M. fifteen miles through a level country. The roads very heavy. Passed through Danville in Illinois. Issued rations for the 2nd.

Saturday. Left the encampment at 1/2 past 8 o'clock A.M. and travelled until 1/2 past 5 P.M. resting about one hour and a half. Travelled about 15 miles through the Grand prairie passing through Georgetown. Issued rations for 3. 4. 5th Sept.

Sunday Sept. 3. Left the encampment at 1/2 past 7 A.M. and travelled until 1/2 past 5 P.M. resting about 1 hour. Travelled about 19 miles over a level country.

Monday Sept. 4. Left the encampment at 1/2 past 7 A.M. and progressed until 6 P.M. resting about 1 hour, passing over a level country about 20 miles.

Tuesday Sept. 5. A heavy rain detained the party in camp until 10 o'clock A.M. Travelled until 4 P.M. 11 miles. Rain obliging the party to halt for the night. Issued rations Bacon & Wheat.

Wednesday Sept 6. Left the encampment about 10 A.M. the party detained by rain. Travelled about 12 miles. Roads very bad. Issued rations of Beef and Flour for 7. 8. 9th.

thursday Sept.7. Left the encampment at 1/2 past 8 A.M. Travelled until 5 P.M. about 14 miles over a level country. Weather excessively warm, roads very heavy. Rested 2 hours.

Friday Sept. 8. Left the encampment at 8 A.M. and travelled until 1/2 past 5 P.M. resting about 1 hour. Progressed 17 miles, the country broken and bad roads.

Saturday 9. Sept. Left the encampment at 1/2 past 7 and travelled until 5 P.M. a rain forcing the party to halt about 5 miles from Vandalia in Illinois. Travelled 18 miles. Country somewhat broken. Issued ration of fat pork, and flour for 10th.

Alton Illinois 17. Sept. 1837

Sir,

I have the honor to transmit herewith the Journal to this date. On my arrival at this place I found the regular ferry boat sunk and nothing but a small flat to ferry us across the river. The waggoners considering it unsafe the owners of the ferry have at my request procured a larger one, but the wind has this day been so high as to render the ferrage of the river dangerous. As soon as possible I shall proceed on my Journey. You will perceive by the Journal that Jackson has stabbed Dutroit. He is quite dangerous, but expressed a willingness to risk a passage in a waggon. The numerous groceries [places where whiskey was sold] on the rout[e] through this state have almost rendered it impossible to keep the Indians together.

Sunday Sept. 10th 1837. This day the party was detained in camp by a very heavy rain which rendered it impossible to progress on the rout[e]. Issued rations of beef and flour for 11th. 12th. 13th. Sept.

Monday Sept. 11. Remained in camp until 10 o'clock A.M. Indians employed in drying tents, baggage. We travelled about 9 miles. Roads very bad. Passed through Vandalia.

Tuesday Sept. 12. Lef[t] the camp at 8 A.M. and travelled until 5 P.M. resting about 2 hours, progressed about 16 miles over a level country. Issued rations for 14. 15. 16. Sept. beef & flour.

Wednesday Sept. 13. Left the camp at 8 A.M. and travelled until 5 P.M. resting about 1 hour. Travelled 18 miles over a level country. Issue rations for 14. 15. 15. Sept. beef & flour.

Thursday Sept. 13. Left the camp at 8 A.M. and proceeded until about 5 P.M. resting about 1 hour. Travelled 19 miles over a level country.

Friday Sept. 15. Started at 8 P.M. and travelled until 1/2 past 4 P.M. resting one hour, proceeding 18 miles over a level country. Encamped 1/2 miles from Alton. About 8 o'clock P.M. Andrew Jackson one of the party stabbed J. B. Dutroit a quarter blood. The wound being considered quite dangerous a consulting physician was called.

Saturday Sept. 16. Rained all day. About 4 P.M. the sheriff of the country with a civil process demanded the body of Andrew Jackson for trial. The request was complied with and said Jackson ordered to post bail for his appearance at court. He made his escape from the officer and has not been [h]eard from. Issued rations of Beef and flour for 17. 18. 19.

Sunday Sept. 17. Remained in camp all day a high wi[n]d rendering the ferrage of the river dangerous, there being not[h]ing but a small flat boat at the ferry, the regular ferry boat being sunk. Dutroit considered quite dangerous.

Monday Sept. 18. Dutroit somewhat better. The party left the camp at 8 A.M. and proceeded to the ferry intending to cross. On our arrival found the ferry boat rendered unfit for use, a waggon having injured the bottom of the boat. Seeing no prospect of a safe ferrage and wind being high started for St. Louis and progressed 13 miles. Encamped at 1/2 past 5 P.M.

Tuesday Sept 19. Left the camp at 8 A.M. and travelled until 6 P.M. crossing the Mississippi, progressed this day 14 miles. Issued rations for beef and flour for 20. 21. 22. 23.

Wednesday Sept 20. Left the camp at 8 A.M. and travelled until 1/2 past 5 P.M. 14 miles over a very broken country. Crossed the Mississippi at St. Charles.

Thursday. Sept. 21. Remained in camp all day, a woman being delivered of a child and consequently unable to travel.

Friday Sept 22nd. Left the camp at 8 A.M. and travelled until 5 P.M. 17 miles. Roads generally good. Being apprehensive of further difficulty with Jackson and considering his life in danger, sent him to W. Davis the Agent for the Pottawattomies. Issued rations for 24. 25. 26. Sept. Beef and cornmeal.

Sunday Sept. 24. Left the camp at 1/2 past 7 A.M. and travelled until about 5 P.M. 18 miles passing through Warrenton. Roads good.

Monday Sept. 25. Left camp at 8 A.M. and travelled until 6 P.M. over a level country. 21 miles. Passed through Danville.

tuesday Sept. 26. Remained in camp all day detained by a very heavy rain. Issued rations of Bacon, flour and corn for 27. 28.29. Sept.

Wednesday Sept. 27. Remained in camp until 10 A.M. drying baggage. We travelled 12 miles over a level country. Roads rendered very heavy by the rain. Encamped at 5 P.M.

thursday Sept. 28. Left the camp at 7 A.M. and travelled until about 5 P.M. 18 miles passing through Fulton. Country broken.

Friday Sept. 29. Remained in camp until 10 A.M. detained by rain, travelled this day miles over a very broken country. Encamped at 5 P.M. a very heavy rain preventing the party from reaching the river. Issued pork & flour for 3 days.

Saturday Sept. 30. Rain continued until 11 A.M. Remained in camp this day.
Harmont, Missouri
Oct. 27, 1837
Sir:

I have the honor to inform you that the Emigrating party under my charge arrived at their destination on the 23 inst., and were received by the Agent Mr. Davis. I much regret that the movements of the party have been less speedy than was anticipated. The almost continued rains caused the rivers and creeks of the country through which we travelled, for a long time impassable. We were obliged to encamp on the bank of Grand River nine days, there being neither a bridge or ferry across the stream.

Other water courses presented obstructions of the same nature. In the requisitions made upon the disbursing officer, I have had an eye single to strict economy & hoping that the management of the party since it has been under my charge, will meet your approbation.

I have the honor to be subservient myself your Obt. Servt.
George H. Proffit, Cond. Pott. Emgr.
Indian Agency, In.
Nov. 18, 1837.
Sir.

Yesterday evening Doctr Jerolaman who accompanied the Pottawattomie emigration as Physician returned to this place; and reports that the emigrants arrived at Col. Davis's Agency on the 23rd Oct. without any loss by death, and with an increase of one by birth on the rout[e].

Mr. Proffit and Leut. Searight were both detained by illness on the road in Missouri. This accounts for my not having received any reports from the conductor since the 30th of Sept.

When Mr. Proffit recovers his health he will no doubt make his report, which I will transmit to you.
A. C. Pepper
Superintendent

Source: HowNiKan 9 (August 1987): 6–8, 20.

34. A Journal of occurrences in conformity with the Revised Regulations No 5. Paragraph 8. Kept by B. B. Cannon, Conductor of a Party of Emigrating Cherokee Indians, put in his charge, at the Cherokee Agency East, by Genl. N. Smith, Superintendent of Cherokee removals, on the 13th day of October 1837

A party of over 300 Cherokees led by B. B. Cannon left the Cherokee Agency at Calhoun, Tennessee, in October 1837, traveling overland to the Cherokee lands west of Arkansas. Their route took them through Tennessee, western Kentucky, and southern Illinois, where they crossed the Mississippi River into Missouri near Cape Girardeau. From there, their journey took them southwest across Missouri, through the northwestern corner of Arkansas, and into the Cherokee Nation. Cannon's journal, reprinted here, provides insights into the illnesses, cold temperatures, road conditions, and deaths experienced by the Cherokee people during their journey. Cannon's journal is also significant because it details the route that the Cherokee overland parties, except two, took under the forced removal of 1838 that gave rise to their Trail of Tears.

Oct. 13th, 1837.

Sent the wagons to the Indian encampment and commenced loading, in the evening.

Oct. 14th, 1837.

Completed loading the wagons and crossed the Highwassee river at Calhoun, encamped, at 5 o'c. P.M.

Oct. 15th, 1837.

Marched the Party at 8 o'c. A.M. halted and encamped at Spring Creek, at 11 o'c A.M. where Genl. Smith mustered the Party, which consumed the remainder of the day, 5 miles to day.

Oct. 16th, 1837.

Marched at 8 o'c. A.M., halted and encamped at Kelly's ferry on Tennessee river, at 4 o'c. P.M. Issued corn & fodder, Corn meal & bacon, 14 miles to day.

Oct. 17th, 1837.

Commenced ferrying the Tennessee river at 8 o'c. A.M., having been detained until the sun dispelled the fog, every thing being in readiness to commence at day light, completed ferrying at 4 o'c. P.M. and reached little Richland creek at 8 o'c. P.M., where the Party had been directed to halt and encamp, Issued corn & fodder, 7 miles to day.

Oct. 18th, 1837.

Marched at 7 ½ o'c. A.M., one of the provision wagons oversat, detained a half hour, no damage done, ascended Wallens ridge, (the ascent 2 miles) halted at Ragsdale's at 1 ½ o'c. P.M., encamped and issued corn & fodder, corn-meal & bacon, 10 miles further to water, all wearied getting up the mountain, 5 miles today.

Oct. 19th, 1837.

Marched at 7 ½ o'c. A.M. descended the mountain, halted at 2 o'c. P.M., at Sequachee river near Mr. Springs, Issued corn & fodder, 11 ½ miles to day.

Oct. 20th, 1837.

Marched at 6 ½ o'c. A.M., ascended the Cumberland mountain, halted at Mr. Flemings, ³/₄ past 3 o'c. P.M., encamped and issued corn & fodder, corn meal & Bacon, 14 ½ miles to day.

Oct. 21st, 1837.

Marched at 7 ½ o'c. A.M., descended the mountain, halted at Collins river, 4 ¼ o'c. P.M., encamped and issued corn & fodder, the Indians appear fatigued this evening. 13 miles today—road extremely rough.

Oct. 22nd, 1837.

Marched at 8 o'c. A.M. passed through McMinnville, halted at Mr. Britts ½ past 12 o'c. M., encamped and issued corn & fodder, corn meal & Bacon, Sugar and coffee to the waggoners & Interpreters, no water for 12 miles ahead, procured a quantity of corn meal and bacon to day. ## 7 ½ miles to day.

Oct. 23rd, 1837.

Marched at 6 ½ o'c. A.M., Capt. Prigmore badly hurt by a wagon horse attempting to run away, halted at Stone river near Woodbury, Te. ½ past 4 o'c. P.M., encamped and issued corn & fodder, 20 miles to day.

Oct. 24th, 1837.

Marched at 7 ½ o'c. A.M., halted at Mr. Yearwoods, 4 o'c. P.M., rained last night and to day, Issued corn & fodder, corn meal and bacon, 15 miles to day.

Oct. 25th, 1837.

Marched at 8 o'c. A.M., buried Andrew's child at ½ past 9 o'c. A.M., passed through Murfreesborough, halted at Overall's creek, 4 o'c. P.M., encamped and issued corn and fodder, 14 miles to day.

Oct. 26th, 1837.

Marched at 8 o'c. A.M., passed through three turnpike Gates, halted at Mr. Harris, 3 o'c. P.M., encamped and issued corn & fodder, corn meal & bacon, 16 $\frac{1}{2}$ miles to day.

Oct. 27th, 1837.

Marched at 7 $\frac{1}{2}$ o'c. A.M., passed through two Turnpike gates, and crossed the Cumberland river on the Nashville toll bridge, at Nashville, halted at Mr. Putnams $\frac{1}{2}$ past 3 o'c. P.M., encamped and issued corn & fodder, Isaac Walker and [sic] emigrant belonging to the Party, overtook us. Mr. L. A. Kincannon, contracting agent, left us, and returned home, having, on the way, near McMinnville signified his intention, verbally, to do so, assigning as the reason the delicate situation of his health, 13 miles to day.

Oct. 28th, 1837.

Rested for the purpose of washing clothes, repairing wagons, and shoeing horses. Reese, Starr and others of the emigrants visited Genl. Jackson who was at Nashville, Issued corn & fodder, corn-meal and bacon, Assigned Mr. E. S. Curry to supply the place of Mr. Kincannon.

Oct. 29th, 1837.

Marched at 8 $\frac{1}{2}$ o'c. A.M., halted at Long creek $\frac{1}{2}$ past 2 o'c. P.M., encamped and issued corn & fodder, 13 $\frac{1}{2}$ miles to day.

Oct. 30th, 1837.

Marched at 7 $\frac{1}{2}$ o'c A.M., halted at Little red river $\frac{1}{2}$ past 5 o'c. P.M., encamped and issued corn & fodder, corn-meal & Bacon, 18 $\frac{1}{2}$ miles to day.

Oct. 31st, 1837.

Marched at 8 o'c. A.M., halted at Graves, Ken. 3 o'c. P.M., Issued corn & fodder, 16 miles to day.

Nov. 1st, 1837.

Marched at 8 o'c., A.M., buried Ducks child, passed throug [sic] Hopkinsville, Ken, halted at Mr. Northerns $\frac{1}{2}$ past 5 o'c. P.M. Encamped & issued corn & fodder, Flour and bacon, 19 miles to day.

Nov. 2nd, 1837.

Marched at 8 o'c. A.M. and halted one mile in advance of Mr. Mitchersons, 3 o'c. P.M., encamped and issued corn and fodder.

Nov. 3rd, 1837.

David Timpson and Pheasant, emigrants belonging to the party, came up last night in the stage, having been heretofore enrolled, and mustered, marched at 8 o'c. A.M., passed thro' Princeton, Ken., halted and encamped near Mr. Barnetts, at $1/2$ past 4 o'c. P.M. Issued corn & fodder, Flour & bacon, 17 miles to day.

Nov. 4th, 1837.

Marched at 8 o'c. A.M., halted and encamped at Threlkelds branch, 4 o'c, P.M., Issued corn & fodder, 15 miles to day.

Nov. 5th, 1837.

Marched at 8 o'c. A.M., passed thro' Salem, Ken., halted and encamped at another Mr. Threlkelds branch at 4 o'c. P.M., Issued corn & fodder, corn meal, a small quantity of flour, and bacon, 13 $1/2$ miles to day.

Nov. 6th, 1837.

Marched at 7 o'c. A.M., arrived at Berry's ferry (Golconda opposite on the Ohio river) 9 o'c. A.M., every thing in readiness to commence ferrying, but prevented on account of the extreme high winds and consequent roughness of the river, which continued the remainder of the day, encamped in the evening, Issued corn & fodder, 5 $1/2$ miles to day.

Nov. 7th, 1837.

Commenced ferrying at $1/2$ past 5 o'c. A.M., moved the Party as it crossed one mile out and encamped. Completed crossing 4 o'c. P.M., all safely, Issued corn & fodder, corn meal & bacon, 1 mile to day.

Nov. 8th, 1837.

Marched at 8 o'c. A.M., Mr. Reese & myself remained behind, and buried a child of Seabolts, overtook the Party, halted and encamped at Big Bay creek, 4 o'c. P.M., Issued corn & fodder, (James Starr & wife, left this morning with two carry-alls to take care of, and bring on three of their children, who were too sick to travel—with instructions to overtake the Party as soon as possible without endangering the lives of their children.)—15 miles to day.

Nov. 9th, 1837.

Marched at 8 o'c., A.M., halted and encamped at Cash creek, $1/2$ past 4 o'c. P.M., Issued corn & fodder, corn meal & Bacon, 15 miles to day.

Nov. 10th, 1837.

Marched at 8 o'c. A.M., were detained 2 hours on the way making a bridge across a small creek, halted at Cypress creek, 4 o'c., P.M., encamped and issued corn & fodder, & salt, 14 miles to day.

Nov. 11th, 1837.

Marched at 8 o'c, A.M., passed thro' Jonesboro' Ill., halted and encamped at Clear creek, in the Mississippi river bottom, $1/2$ past 3 o'c. P.M., Issued corn &

fodder, corn meal & bacon—13 miles to day, issued sugar & coffee to the wagoners, & interpreters.

Nov. 12th, 1837.

Marched at 8 o'c. A.M., arrived at Mississippi river, 10 o'c. A.M., Commenced ferrying, at 11 o'c. A.M., directed the party to move a short distance as they crossed the river, and encamp, Issued corn & fodder, Starr came up, the health of his children but little better, Richard Timberlake and George Ross, overtook us and enrolled, attached themselves to Starrs family.

Nov. 13th, 1837.

Continued ferrying from 7 o'c. until 10 o'c. A.M., when the wind arose and checked our progress, 3 o'c. P.M., resumed and made our trip, suspended at 5 o'c. P.M., Issued corn & fodder, corn meal & bacon, buried another of Duck's children to day.

Nov. 14th, 1837.

Crossed the residue of the Party, Marched at 10 o'c. A.M., halted and encamped at Mr. William's, Issued corn & fodder, sickness prevailing, 5 miles to day.

Nov. 15th, 1837.

Rested for the purpose of washing &c., Issued corn and fodder, corn meal and bacon.

Nov. 16th, 1837.

Marched at 8 o'c. A.M., left Reese, Starr and families on account of sickness in their families, also James Taylor (Reese's son in law) and family, Taylor himself being very sick, with instructions to overtake the Party, passed thro' Jackson, Mo., halted & encamped at widow Roberts on the road via Farmington &c., Issued corn only, no fodder to be had, 17 miles to day.

Nov. 17th, 1837.

Marched at 8 o'c. A.M., halted at White Water creek 4 o'c. P.M., Issued corn & fodder, corn meal and beef, 13 miles to day.

Nov. 18th, 1837.

Marched at 8 o'c. A.M., halted and encamped at Mr. Morand's 5 o'c. P.M., Issued corn & fodder, Flour & bacon, 16 miles to day.

Nov. 19th, 1837.

Marched at 8 o'c. A.M., halted and encamped $1/2$ past 4 o'c. P.M., at Wolf creek, Issued corn & fodder, 14 miles to day.

Nov. 20th, 1837.

Marched at 8 o'c. A.M., passed thro' Farmington, Mo., halted at St. Francis river, 4 o'c. P.M., encamped and issued corn & fodder, Flour & beef, 15 miles to day.

Nov. 21st, 1837.

A considerable number drunk last night obtained the liquor at Farmington yesterday, had to get out of bed about midnight to quell the disorder, a refusal by several to march this morning, alledging [sic] that they would wait for Starr & Reese to come up at that place, Marched at 8 o'c., A.M. in defiance of threats and attempts to intimidate, none remained behind, passed through Caledonia, halted at Mr. Jacksons, encamped and issued corn & fodder, beef and Bacon, mostly bacon, 14 miles to day.

Nov. 22nd 1837.

Marched 8 ½ o'c. A.M., pass through the lead mines (or Courtois diggings), halted at Scotts, 4 o'c. P.M., issued corn, fodder, and corn meal, 13 miles to day.

Nov. 23rd, 1837.

Rested for the purpose of repairing wagons, shoeing horses, washing &c., Starr, Reese, and Taylor came up, the health of their families in some degree improved, Issued corn & fodder, and beef, weather very cold.

Nov. 24th, 1837.

Marched at 8 ½ o'c. A.M., Considerable sickness prevailing, halted at Huzza creek, 4 o'c. P.M., encamped and issued corn & fodder, 12 miles to day.

Nov. 25th, 1837.

Doct. Townsend, officially advised a suspension of our march, in consequence of the severe indisposition of several families, for a time sufficient for the employment of such remedial agents as their respective cases might require. I accordingly directed the Party to remain in camp and make the best possible arrangement for the sick, In the evening issued corn & fodder, flour and beef.

Nov. 26th, 1837.

Remained in camp, sickness continuing and increasing, Issued corn & fodder, beef & corn meal.

Nov. 27th, 1837.

Remained in camp, sickness continuing to increase, Issued corn & fodder, Bacon & corn meal.

Nov. 28th, 1837.

Moved the Detachment two miles further to a Spring and School-house, obtained permission for as many of the sick to occupy the school-house as could do so, a much better situation for an encampment than on the creek, sickness increasing, Issued corn & fodder.

Nov. 29th, 1837.

Remained in camp, sickness still increasing, buried Corn Tassels child to day, Issued corn & fodder.

Nov. 30th, 1837.

Remained in camp, sickness continuing, Issued corn and fodder.

December 1st, 1837.

Remained in camp, sickness abating, Issued corn and fodder, Bacon & corn meal, Buried Oolanheta's child to day.

Decr. 2nd, 1837.

Remained in camp, sickness abating, Issued corn & fodder, Beef & corn meal.

Decr. 3rd, 1837.

Remained in camp, sickness abating, Issued corn & fodder.

Decr. 4th, 1837.

Marched at 9 o'c. A.M., Buried George Killian, and left Mr. Wells to bury a waggoner, (black boy) who died this morning, scarcely room in the wagons for the sick, halted at Mr. Davis, 12 past 4 o.c. P.M., had to move down the creek a mile off the road, to get wood, Issued corn & fodder and corn meal, 11 miles to day.

Decr. 5th, 1837.

Marched 9 o'c. A.M., left two waggoners (black boys) at Mr. Davis sick, this morning, halted at the Merrimack river, $1/2$ past 3 o'c. P.M., Encamped and issued corn and fodder, corn meal and beef, 10 miles to day.

Decr. 6th, 1837.

Marched at 9 o'c. A.M., passed Masseys Iron works, halted at Mr. Jones' $1/2$ past 3 o'c. P.M., encamped and issued corn and fodder, 12 miles to day.

Decr. 7th, 1837.

Marched at 8 $1/2$ o'c., A.M., Reese's team ran away, broke his wagon and Starrs carry-all, left him and family to get his wagon mended, at 17 miles, and to overtake if possible, halted at Mr. Bates son, 5 o'c., P.M., encamped and issued corn and fodder, corn-meal & bacon, 20 miles to day.

Decr. 8th, 1837.

Buried Nancy Bigbears Grand Child, marched at 9 o'c. A.M., halted at Piney a small river, $1/2$ past 3 o'c. P.M., rained all day, encamped and issued corn only, no fodder to be had, several drunk, 11 miles to day.

December the 9th, 1837.

Marched at 9 o'c. A.M., Mayfields wagon broke down at about a mile left him to get it mended and overtake, halted at Waynesville, Mo. 4 o'c. P.M., encamped and issued corn & fodder, beef & corn meal, weather extremely cold, 12 $1/2$ miles to day.

Decr. 10th, 1837.

Marched at 8 o'c. A.M., halted at the Gasconade river 4 o'c. P.M., Issued corn & fodder. 14 miles to day.

Decr. 11th, 1837.

Marched at $1/2$ past 8 o'c. A.M., halted at Sumner's 4 o'c. P.M., encamped and issued corn & fodder. 15 miles to day.

Decr. 12th, 1837.

Marched at 9 o'c. A.M., halted one mile in advance of Mr. Parkes at a branch, 4 o'c. P.M., encamped and issued corn & fodder, corn meal, beef and a small quantity of bacon. 14 miles to day.

Decr. 13th, 1837.

Marched at 8 $1/2$ o'c. A.M., halted at a branch near Mr. Eddington's, 4 o'c. P.M., encamped and issued corn & fodder, Reese & Mayfield came up, 13 $1/2$ miles today.

Decr. 14th, 1837.

Marched at 8 o'c. A.M., halted at James fork of White river, near the road but which does not cross the road, 3 o'c. P.M., Mr. Wells taken sick, Issued corn meal, corn & fodder, 15 $1/2$ miles to day.

Decr. 15th, 1837.

Joseph Starrs wife had a child last night. Marched at 8 $1/2$ o'c. A.M., halted at Mr. Danforths, 1 $1/2$ P.M., waggoners having horses shod until late at night, encamped & issued corn & fodder & beef. 10 $1/2$ miles to day.

Decr. 16th, 1837.

Issued sugar & coffee to the waggoners & Interpreters this morning, Marched at 9 o'c. A.M., passed through Springfield Mo., halted at Mr. Clicks,

4 o'c. P.M., encamped and issued corn & fodder and corn-meal. 12 miles to day. (left Mr. Wells)

Decr. 17th, 1837.

Snowed last night, Buried Eleges wife and Chas. Timberlakes son (Smoker), Marched at 9 o'c. A.M., halted at Mr. Dyes 3 o'c P.M., extremely cold weather, sickness prevailing to a considerable extent, all very much fatigued, encamped and issued corn & fodder, & beef. 10 miles to day.

Decr. 18th, 1837.

Detained on account of sickness, Doct. Townsend sent back to Springfield for medicines, buried Dreadful Waters this evening, Issued corn and fodder & corn meal.

Decr. 19th, 1837.

Detained to day also on account of sickness, cold intense, Issued corn & fodder and beef.

Decr. 20th, 1837.

Marched at 8 $\frac{1}{2}$ o'c. A.M., halted at Mr. Allens $\frac{1}{2}$ past 3 o'c. P.M., encamped, and issued corn & fodder & corn meal. 15 miles to day.

Decr. 21st, 1837.

Marched at 8 o'c. A.M., halted at Lockes on Flat creek, 12 past 3 o'c. P.M., encamped and issued corn & fodder, & beef. 15 miles to day.

Decr. 22nd, 1837.

Buried Goddards Grand child, Marched at 8 o'c. A.M., halted at McMurtrees, 3 o'c. P.M., encamped and issued corn & fodder and corn-meal. 15 miles to day.

Decr. 23rd, 1837.

Buried Rainfrogs daughter (Lucy Redstick's child). Marched at 8 o'c. A.M. halted at Reddix, 3 o'c. P.M., encamped and issued corn & fodder & beef. 16 miles to day.

Decr. 24th, 1837.

Marched at 8 o'c. A.M., halted at the X hollows, had to leave the road $\frac{3}{4}$ of a mile to get water, 3 o'c. P.M., Issued corn & fodder, Pork and corn meal. 15 miles to day.

Decr. 25th, 1837.

Marched at 8 o'c. A.M., took the right hand road to Cane hill, at Fitzgeralds, halted a half mile in advance of Mr. Cunninghams at a branch, 3 o'c. P.M., Issued corn & fodder and salt Pork. 15 $\frac{1}{2}$ miles to day.

Decr. 26th, 1837.

Marched at 8 o'c. A.M., halted at James Coulters on Cane hill, Ark. $\frac{1}{2}$ past 3 o'c P.M., encamped and issued corn meal, corn & fodder, 16 $\frac{1}{2}$ miles to day.

Decr. 27th, 1837.

Buried Alsey Timberlake, Daughter of Chas Timberlake, Marched at 8 o'c. A.M., halted at Mr. Beans, in the Cherokee nation west, at $\frac{1}{2}$ past 2 o'c. P.M., encamped and issued corn & fodder, Fresh pork & some beef. 12 miles to day.

Decr. 28th, 1837.

The Party refused to go further, but at the same time pledged themselves to remain together until the remuster was made by the proper officer, for whom I immediately sent an express to Fort Gibson, they alleged at the same time that the refusal was in consequence of the sickness now prevailing and that only.

Doct. Reynolds Disbursing agent for the Party dismissed the wagons from further service, Buried another child of Chas Timberlakes, and one which was born (untimely) yesterday of which no other account than this is taken, Jesse Half Breeds wife had a child last night, issued Pork, corn meal and flour, corn & fodder for to day.

Lieut. Van Horne arrived late this evening, having missed the express on the way.

Decr. 29th, 1837.

Remustered the Party, Issued a small quantity of corn meal & Pork yet on hand.

Decr. 30th, 1837.

Completed the Rolls of Remuster, turned over the Party to Lieut. Van Horne, and dismissed my assistants.

Respectfully submitted B. B. Cannon. I would remark here that all supplies, both of forage and subsistence, were purchased, and Pikages, toll and ferriages contracted for on the way west by a contracting agent, and paid for on my request by Doct. Reynolds, the Disbursing Agent for the Party.

Source: National Archives Record Group 75, Records of the Bureau of Indian Affairs, Letters Received, Cherokee Emigration, 1837, Document C-553, filed in Special Case 249.

35. Journal of Occurrences in the Route of Emigration of a Party of Cherokee Indians, Kept by Lieut. Edward Deas, U.S. Army, Conductor of the Party, from Waterloo, Alabama, to the New Country West of the Mississippi River (1838)

As the deadline for Cherokee removal, set by the Treaty of New Echota in 1835, drew near, the United States began to remove those who had voluntarily assembled for removal. A party of 250, in addition to a number of perhaps 100 more Cherokees who had chosen to remove on their own resources, left Waterloo, Alabama, in early April 1838 with Lt. Edward Deas acting as their disbursing agent. The government's plan was to remove the Cherokees by water, but as Deas's journal, reprinted below, indicates, the low level of water in the Arkansas River as a result of a deepening drought created great obstacles to removal. Such events resulted in the government's decision in the early summer of 1838 to delay Cherokee removal until the fall.

6th April 1838

Yesterday a Party of Cherokee Indians, in number Two hundred & fifty, together with some other emigrants of the same tribe who are removing on their own resources, arrived near Waterloo, Ala. by water, under the charge of the Superintendent of the Cherokee Emigration. The S. Boat Smelter, provided under the contract for Transportation, had been waiting the arrival of the Party, and to day the Indians were established on board of this boat, and one large Keel with double cabins, made & furnished in the manner mentioned in the above named contract. The Present Party, having been previously Enrolled, were to-day turned over to me as Conductor, and immediately afterwards (about 10 o'clock A.M.) the boats were got under weigh and continued to run until after sunset, having come more than 100 miles and laid by on account of the darkening of the night. The weather is remarkably fine at present, and the Party healthy.

The Smelter appears to be a very good boat, over 150 Tons Burthen, a fast runner, and well adapted to the business of the removal of Indians. The Keel in tow is commodious and appears convenient for the Indians. Temporary cooking-hearths are constructed on the top of it, and there is also a cooking-stove in the after part of the Steam Boat.

7th April

The Boats got under weigh this morning at eight and continued to run without any occurrences of importance until near sun-set, when we reached Paducah at the mouth of the Tennessee River, and anchored a short time near the Town, not willing to land on account of the Indians having access to the Whiskey shops. On attempting to set out again about dark, some water was washed into the Keel, (owing to waves in the Ohio) and the Indians in it were seized with a panic consequence of supposing the Keel to be sinking, and rushed out of it into the Steam Boat.

There was no danger, but I found it would be impossible to convince them of that fact, and therefore determined to proceed without the Keel, the S. Boat being large enough to transport the party, by giving them the main cabin and lower and forward decks, and having cooking hearths constructed on the latter.

The Party having been removed to the S. Boat, we set out from the mouth of Tennessee River about 10 P.M. and are now progressing speedily towards the mouth of the Ohio (12 o'clock P.M.).

8th April

The Boat stopped to wood early this morning and passed the mouth of the Ohio about 6 A.M. and has continued to run this day without any accident or occurrence of importance, and is now a short distance above Memphis, (about midnight).

9th April

We reached Memphis last night about 12 P.M. and stopped a short time to procure some Fresh Beef and other supplies. The Boat then continued to run (stopping once to wood) until about 3 o'clock this afternoon, when we reached Montgomery's Point and there stopped in the stream a short time to take in a Pilot for the Arkansas River. We find the Arkansas not very high, but shall probably be able to reach Little Rock and may perhaps go still higher. The present party has been subsisting since starting on Bacon, Pork, Flour, & Meal, and a small quantity of Fresh Beef.

10th April

We continued to run last night until about 11 o'clock when a slight accident happening to the machinery, the Boat was obliged to lie by 3 or 4 hours, and then set out again and continued to run (stopping once to wood) from that time until this evening about 7, and then stopped for the night, it being too dark, and the water too shallow to proceed until the morning. We are now 40 or 50 miles below Little Rock.

11th April

The Boat got under weigh this morning early and reached Lt. Rock about $1/2$ past 11 A.M. I had her anchored in the stream to prevent access to Whiskey and went on shore for the purpose of consulting the Principal Disbursing Agent as to the probability of being able to proceed further up the river on the Smelter.

I found it would be useless to attempt to proceed further in a Boat of her size, and therefore made an arrangement forthwith with the S. Boat Little Rock which is, I found, on the point of setting out for the upper Posts with two Keels in tow.

The Captain agreed to take the present Party as far up as possible for $5 each for the whole distance and proportionately for a less [amount], which I ascertained to be a reasonable term, and the best arrangement I could possibly make at present. The Party is to have the entire use of one Keel, the Top of the other, & all parts of the S. Boat except the cabins. After landing some provisions from the Smelter I proceeded with the Party on board of her, about 5 miles above the town and landed for the night. The Little Rock is to come up in the night, and take the Party from the Smelter in the morning.

I purchased to day under authority from the Superintendent of the Cherokee Emigration, Eighty Barrels of mess Pork, and Eighty barrels of Flour, and turned them over to the Principal Mil[itary] Disb[ursing] Agent at Little Rock, for the use of the Cherokee Emigration in the ensuing summer & fall. I obtained this provision by paying only its cost and carriage.

12th April

The Little Rock and Keels are heavily loaded the other nearly empty and fitted up for the Indians arrived last night at the point at which I stopped the Party, and early this morning the people and their Baggage were trans-ferred on board of them, from the Smelter. We then immediately got under weigh and proceeded 5 or 6 miles, when the heavy Keel sprung a leak from running on a Bar or Snag, whereupon the Captain found it necessary to run ashore to prevent her sinking. The whole day has been consumed in getting out the Freight from this Keel and stopping the leak. Intelligence has also reached us from above, from which it is probable that the Boats cannot take up the present Party & also the freight, without much delay. As this would endanger the health of the people (which I deem a paramount considera-tion) I have determined, if possible, to induce the Captain of the Little Rock to leave his heavy Keel and all his freight, and take up the Party on the S. Boat and other Keel, empty or nearly so. It is desirable to proceed with all possible dispatch, as besides other reasons the Small-Pox is in this section of country, a disease, apparently, of all others the most fatal to Indians.

13th April

This morning I made a contract with Captain [Philip] Pennywit (a copy of which I shall forward to the Department and which therefore need not be here given) to proceed up the Arkansas with the Present Party, with the Little Rock and one Keel in tow, both empty. The Freight was landed as soon as possible and about 4 o'clock P.M. we got under weigh and have come about 10 miles and stopped for the night.

14th April

The Indians were got on board this morning at light and the boats have continued to run thro' the day, only stopping a short time to Wood, and by 3 o'clock P.M. had come 50 miles and reached White's or Lewisburgh Bar 4 miles below that place. The Keel was then landed and every means used to get the S. Boat over the Bar, but without effect. The party is now encamped on shore for the night.

Provisions have been issued since starting for 4 days at a time. Yesterday Pork and Flour were issued in that quantity.

15 April

This morning after the people had had their breakfasts, they walked about 5 miles up the south bank of the Arkansas for the purpose of lightening the Boat. A different channel was then tried by the Captain with success, and by noon we reached a second Bar about 2 miles above Lewisburgh. This it was found impossible to get over and at night the Keel Boat was sent ashore with the Indian Baggage & the Party is encamped on the south bank of the river, the S. Boat being on the Sand Bar. The Party remains healthy and the weather continues remarkably fine, as it has been since setting out upon the present journey.

16 April

The forenoon was spent in trying to force the S. Boat over the Bar without effect, and the afternoon was consumed in getting her ashore on the north bank of the river.

The Party remains encamped on the south bank. The river is rising very little and the weather now looks stormy.

17th April

Much rain fell last night and the people not having Tents, I found it necessary to hire a small house to protect them from the weather. This morning another trial was made to get over the Bar which was successful, and about 11 A.M. the S. Boat reached the point at which the Indians were encamped and after taking the Party on board continued to run until a short time after dark, and stopped for the night at the foot of Five Islands, having come between 30 & 40 miles. Rations of Prime Pork, Fresh Beef & Flour were issued to day for 4 days as usual.

18th April

The Boats started this morning at day light and continued to run until the afternoon with little interruption, but on reaching Bohlinger's Bar opposite to Scotia it was found impossible to proceed, partly owing to a strong head wind. The Boats were therefore landed on the south bank of the river, having run to-day 30 or 40 miles.

19th April

The Boats were separated this morning in order to get over Bohlinger's Bar which was done about 10 A.M. After this they were again lashed, and continued to run until about dark, and stopped between the mouths of Horse-Head and Spadra Creeks after running between 20 & 30 miles.

20th April

The Boats started at light and continued to run until about 11 A.M. with slight interruption from S. Bars when we reached Titsworth's at McLean's Bottom, having come 25 or 30 miles. I determined to land the Party at this place for the reason, that there would be but little probability of the Steam Boat getting the whole distance to the Cherokee Country, and as the end of the journey would therefore have to be performed by land, under any arrangement, it is better to stop at a point where wagons can be procured.

21st April

The Party is now encamped on the south bank of the Arkansas at Tits-worth's in McLean's Bottom. This is a tract of country extending about 10 miles along the south bank of the river and from one to three miles wide and is fertile and well settled. I am now making preparations to proceed by land with as little delay as possible. Rations of Prime Pork and Flour were issued to-day for 4 days.

23rd April

On arriving at the present place of encampment, I employed a person acquainted with the surrounding country, to ride through the neighborhood for the purpose of Employing wagons. To day a sufficient number has come in as engaged and I have entered into the necessary contracts with their respective owners, and to-morrow the Party will set out.

24th

This morning the different Families were assigned to their respective wagons. On weighing the Baggage yesterday it was found to amount to much more than the allowance mentioned in the Regulations, but as the Indians were allowed to bring it with them this far, it appeared just, and I consider it my duty, to transport to the end of the journey the Baggage that was their possession when the party was turned over to me as Conductor, at Waterloo.

16 large Wagons and one small one were found necessary and the loading up being finished about noon, the Party was started, and has come about 6 miles and stopped for the night at McLean's Prairie. The wagons are all hauled by oxen, except one of four horses.

25th April

It rained very hard last night, but cleared up before day. The Party was started this morning about 8 o'clock and has come to-day 11 miles to the edge of Grand Prairie. Nothing of importance has taken place. We encamped about 3 o'clock P.M.

26th April

The Party set out this morning about 8 o'clock, crossed the Grand Prairie which is 10 miles wide, and came on 5 miles further and encamped about 4 o'clock P.M. Two small children (one a slave) that were sick before setting out on the journey, died this evening. Nothing else of importance occurred thro' the day.

27th April

The Party started this morning about the usual hour, and encamped this afternoon at 3 P.M. after traveling about 11 miles. The roads from McLean's Bottom have been level & in good order but the country is not very well watered. The weather has been rather too warm for expeditious travelling. We are now about 5 miles from Fort Smith.

28th April

The Party reached Fort Smith to-day about 10 A.M. and the crossing of the river was immediately commenced and continued without interruption until dark, when more than half of the Wagons and nearly all of the people were got over and encamped on the Cherokee side of the River.

The ferry is not a very good [one] the Boats being too small.

29th April

The Ferriage of the Party was finished about 2 P.M. when we again set out and came about 5 miles this afternoon and encamped for the night at 5 P.M.

Most of the people wish to stop at Salisaw Creek, about 30 miles west of Fort Smith & on the road to Fort Gibson, to which point therefore I propose to transport them.

30th April

It rained very hard last night and to-day, and still continues to do so. The Party however set out in the forenoon about 9 o'clock and after travelling 13 miles encamped at 4 P.M. The roads to-day were tolerably good, though rather hilly for several miles after starting. Nothing of importance took place.

1st May

The weather cleared up last night and the Party started at 7 A.M. and after travelling about 12 miles reached Salisaw Creek in the middle of the day and encamped near McCoy's.

The roads to-day were generally level passing mostly thro' prairies, but were muddy owing to the recent rain.

The Indians were to-day received at the present place of encampment by the Disbursing Agent for the Cherokees (West); they having been previously mustered, and the Party found to number Two hundred and forty-eight, as shown by the Muster-Roll; two deaths only having occurred and they, as has been stated, being small children that were sick before the Party set out upon the journey. After the Party arrived to-day at its place of destination, I paid off, & discharged the Wagoners and also the agents of the Government by whom it was accomplished.

The only source of annoyance upon the journey has resulted from the people obtaining liquor, the use of which with Indians as far as I have observed invariably results in rioting, fighting or disorder of some kind. The infamous traffic of Whiskey with Indians is carried on to a greater extent at Fort Smith than at any place I have seen, and could any means be devised to check, or put a stop to it, much good must be the result to the neighboring Tribes, or emigrating Parties that may be obliged to pass in that vicinity.

As far as I have observed there is never any difficulty in managing Indians, when sober, provided they are properly treated; but when under the effects of liquor (in the use of which they have no moderation), they are unmanageable, and in many instances Evince such feelings of hostility, as to endanger the lives of the Agents in charge of them while in the performance of their duty.

When we landed at McLean's Bottom, I found the people unprovided with Tents, or any protection from the weather, and as the Physician was of the opinion that their health would suffer from exposure, I considered it my duty to purchase for their use, as much cotton domestic as was sufficient to shelter them from the rain.

The foregoing remarks embrace all matters of interest that came under my observation respecting the Party, from the time I took charge of it, until its arrival at its place of destination in the new country.

Edwd. Deas, Lieut. U.S. Army, Conductor

Source: Journal of Occurrences of Lt. Edward Deas April 1838, Special Case Files of the Office of Indian Affairs, 1807–1994, National Archives Microfilm Publications, Microcopy M574, Roll 69, Document D217.

36. Excerpt from the Journal of Rev. Daniel S. Butrick, May 19, 1838–April 1, 1839: Cherokee Removal (1838)

A native of Massachusetts, Daniel Sabin Butrick was ordained as a minister in 1817 and left for the Cherokee Nation shortly thereafter. He remained with the Cherokees as a missionary and teacher in the eastern Nation, during their removal, and in Indian Territory. His is one of the few eyewitness accounts of the removal and of the hardships suffered as the roundup of people for removal commenced. He also provides a history of the removal debate within the tribe, although from an anti-removal point of view. Butrick's diary is important, if only for the chronicle of human suffering it provides, often with poignant attention to detail.

Brainerd. May 26. 1838 [Saturday]

The daily words in the United Brethren textbook were, "I am thine. Save me." (p.s. 119:9) This day a number of Georgia citizens near New Echota took sixteen Cherokees and drove them to the fort and then requested permission of General Scott to take them out and whip them, though in this they were not gratified. This was done probably to remind General Scott that no farther delay would be made with regard to collecting the Indians. The soldiers at the various posts now commenced that work which will doubtless long eclipse the glory of the United States. General Scott gave orders that no improper language should be used towards the Indians, and that in case any of them attempted to escape by flight, no gun should be discharged at them. But these orders were, in general obeyed or not, according to the disposition of the under officers, and soldiers.

In Georgia were supposed to be about 8,000 Cherokees. These, in general were taken just as they were found by the soldiers, without permission to stop either for friends or property.

As the soldiers advanced towards a [unreadable] house, two little children fled in fright to the woods. The woman pleaded for permission to seek them, or wait till they came in, giving positive assurances that she would then follow on, and join the company. But all entreaties were vain; and it was not till a day or two after that she would get permission for one of her friends to go back after the lost children.

A man deaf and dumb, being surprised at the approach of armed men, attempted to make his escape, and because he did not hear and obey the command of his pursuers, was shot dead on the spot.

One man, it is said, had shot a deer, and was taking it home to meet the joyful salutations of his family, when at once he was surprised & taken prisoner to a fort.

Women absent from their families on visits, or for other purposes, were seized, and men far from their wives and children, were not allowed to return, and also children being forced from home, were dragged off among strangers. Cattle, horses, hogs, household furniture, clothing and money not with them when taken were left. And it is said that the white inhabitants around, stood with open arms to seize whatever property they could put their hands on. Some few who had friends to speak for them, were assisted afterwards in getting some part of their lost goods.

Thus in two or three days about 8,000 people, many of whom were in good circumstances, and some rich, were rendered homeless, houseless and penniless, and exposed to all the ills of captivity.

In driving them a platoon of soldiers walked before and behind, and a file of soldiers on each side, armed with all the common appalling instruments of death; while the soldiers, it is said would often use the same language as if driving hogs, and goad them forward with their bayonets.

One man, on being pricked thus, and seeing his children thus goaded on, picked up a stone and struck a soldier; but for this he was handcuffed, and on arriving at the fort, was punished and on starting again was whipped a hundred lashes.

Those taken to the fort at New Echota, were confined day and night in the open air, with but little clothing to cover them, when lying on the naked ground.

Thursday May 31.

Just before night a young lieutenant called and requested accommodation for two or three officers, and permission for a company of Cherokees to camp near. Though we are not in the habit of entertaining any white men, yet for the sake of the poor Cherokees we worked to accommodate the above officers.

Astoundingly a little before sunset a company of about two hundred Cherokees were driven into our lane. The day had been rainy, and of course all men, women and children were dripping wet, with no change of clothing, and scarcely a blanket fit to cover them. As some of the women when taken from their houses, had on their poorest dress, this of course was the amount of their clothing for a journey of about eight hundred miles. As soon as permission was obtained from the officers, we opened every door to these poor sufferers. Mothers brought their dear little babes to our fire, and stripped off their only covering to dry.

O how heart rending was the sight of those little sufferers, their little lips blue and trembling with cold, seemed yet to form a smile of gratitude for this kind reception. We wept and wept again, and still wept at the thought of that affecting scene. Our prayer is that these dear children, who must doubtless be soon ushered into eternity, may be taken into the arms of their dear Redeemer.

In the company were one or two blind men, and several persons unwell. One poor old creek, being sick and wet was nourished by our fire.

A little before dark, the Capt. took an interest and went to those at the meeting house and told them he had the power to destroy them, and was ordered to do so if they did not behave well. He then told them that after the drum should beat, no one must be seen out doors till morning. His interpreter told him that some might be obliged to go out, having the dysentery. The Capt. replied that in that case they must call, and ask permission or they would be in danger of being shot.

Sabbath June 3.

Most of our neighbors are now with us, going this evening or tomorrow to the camps, choosing to go in by themselves, rather than be driven in by soldiers; and though we held public worship, yet we were considerably interrupted.

Last week a young officer told the public in this neighborhood, that they had better go to the agency, as they would fare better there than at the camps near this place. Accordingly most of the people started on Saturday. But when the commander had knowledge of this, he sent the same officer to order them back this morning; therefore they returned wet and weary, and some of them almost exhausted, especially one old lady, near a hundred years old, who had travelled nearly all the night and day before.

During this week I visited the camps in company with br. Vail, and found our dear br. Epenetus Aehaia, and his wife and children among the prisoners. They had been at Brainerd to attend a sacramental meeting on the third Sabbath of May; and as they had a son with us at school, they spent one week with him; and on the 28th of May, left to return home about one hundred miles. On that day they proceeded to Dogwood flat, where they spent the night.

In the morning, on hearing that the soldiers were taking all the people prisoners in Georgia, they set out to return back to us. The wife and children were riding one horse and Epenetus was walking. They had not proceeded far, however, before they were taken by a company of soldiers and driven to a fort near Lafayette courthouse.

There they were kept with about five hundred others for ten days and then driven in the usual manner to the camps. His wife had been so overcome by the scenes as to be now unable to do anything.

Br. Epenetus has long been a member of the Presbyterian church, and is now a ruling elder in the church at Brainerd. His wife is also a member of the same church.

While at the fort the whole company of five hundred had resolved to have nothing to do with the treaty money, and chose Epenetus to be the speaker, and make their purpose known to the commissioners, who were waiting with the money to pay them. Epenetus, therefore, when occasion called for it, told the commissioners that they did not come to that place voluntarily, but as prisoners, that the treaty was not made by the authorities of the nation, and they should have nothing to do with it. As prisoners they must receive their food, but they would take no money nor clothes offered on account of the treaty. Epenetus being put forward in this drew upon him doubtless the opposition of the commissioners and other officers.

On account of his son being with us and the sickness of his wife, Mrs. Butrick petitioned the agent to suffer the family to live with us, at least till called to go to the West. The commissioners replied that they were ready to grant the family any favor in their power, only she must advise him to receive his valuation money and bring his children to receive clothes. But as she did not feel prepared to advise in this matter all further entreaties were in vain.

It is said that the Cherokees told the commissioners that they did not wish any of their clothing, since they had clothing enough of their own which they had not been allowed to take.

Sabbath. [June 10th]

Brs. Mills, Jesse, and many others came from the camps, and we commenced meeting about ten O'clock. In the forenoon, Moses interpreted for me, and in the afternoon preached himself in Cherokee.

After meeting I brought forward all the arguments I could think of to dissuade the young men from playing cards, and on returning to the mission house I endeavored to get br. Mills to engage to be instant in season and out of season in leaving the young men at the camps from so injurious a practice.

He said the young men would be angry with him if he should attempt to talk to them on the subject; and that judge Hooks told him to let the gamblers alone. I told him judge Hooks was doubtless fearful he might get into some difficulty with them, but he need not fear, if he reproved in love.

Thursday. [June 28th]

Mr. Nave, who has a Cherokee family, says that as a company of prisoners were about to cross the creek at his house, he heard a horseman say, as he rode up, that a certain old Creek woman had given out, and some waggons must stop and take her in. Soon after a soldier on foot, came up and all the waggons and the company started on. He supposes the old woman had been killed by the soldier, and hid away, as he and several others hunted afterwards, but could find nothing of her.

Last night a company of about twenty Cherokees returned, who had escaped from the late company of 1,100 who had been started off to the West by land. They say that the whole company almost famished—that for two days together they had nothing to eat, and the rest of the time but very little. They say that as the company were about to cross the river, on starting one woman was very sick unable to sit up, and lay on the ground, that a soldier came along, and kicked her in the side and drove her into the boat, and that after landing, she was just seen, and then in a short time was missing. They suppose she died. Six individuals had died before they left the company.

It is said that many old women, driven in this company, cried like children when they started, saying they never could live to walk that journey in this hot season. But their cries could not be heard. They were driven on.

Sabbath July 1.

Soon in the morning a large company of United States troops came up and stopped in the lane. Then a number of volunteers from the camps made their appearance about the saw mill. Every thought and every view was painful. Nothing of the Holy Sabbath. Br. Vail concluded not to leave home as so many were about, and therefore I rode alone to the camps.

On the way I met crowds of people, some with dishes as if going after berries, and many I feared were going to the creek.

On arriving at the camps, I spoke from 2 Tim 4:8. Before closing my meeting I told our dear friends that I had before come to the conclusion not to visit the camps on the Sabbath, lest I should see them playing cards, though I had been persuaded to come today. I told them however, that if they continued to profane the Lord's day by playing cards, they might depend upon it, that the wrath of God would pursue them to death.

Their almost universal Saturday night frolics, carried through the Holy Sabbath, had already drawn down Divine wrath upon them. True, they might say their enemies were cruel, but suppose they were, how did they get this power over them; unless the Lord was angry with them, why should He thus give them up.

On returning home I met the soldiers and Cherokees, who had been to Brainerd; and on arriving found that the women had been in the creek, swimming while the soldiers stood by them on the bank and other young men were in the creek, naked but just below. We held a prayer meeting.

Soon after on going to the creek for water, found a company of young men and boys in the creek, close by the road. I talked at length persuaded them to put on their clothes. But almost immediately another company was there. I talked again, and told the young men we could not endure such conduct any longer. Some also were fishing. We were pained to the heart at the profanation of the Holy Sabbath.

But the few Cherokees of whom I speak above are evidently exceptions, the women who infested the place by going into the creek while the soldiers were standing by, might be some who had been seduced by the soldiers.

Br. Vail, the other day, on going to the landing, saw six soldiers about two Cherokee women. The women stood by a tree, and the soldiers with a bottle of liquor were endeavoring to entice them to drink though the women, as yet were resisting them. Br. Vail made this known to the Commanding officer, yet we perceive no notice was taken of it, because it was reported afterwards that those soldiers had the two women out with them all night.

A young married woman, a member of the Methodist society, was at the camps with her friends, though her husband was not there, I believe, at the time. The soldiers, it is said, caught her, dragged her about, and at length either through fear or other causes was induced to drink and yield to their seduction, so that she is now an outcast, even in the view of her own relatives. How many of the poor captive women are thus debauched, that eye which never sleeps alone can tell.

The United States have now ascended about to the top of the climax. For about ten years, it would seem, that the power, the wisdom and the funds of the whole union have been employed for the temporal and eternal ruin of this little handful of Indians.

In the first place, they were rendered lawless, and it was made a penitentiary crime for any of their rulers to execute or attempt to execute their laws. Thus all the laws which the council had wisely enacted respecting liquor and gambling, were at once annulled, and every one left to follow his own inclination.

The country was soon filled with liquor to overflowing; and stores of liquor and cards were set up to induce gambling, while white gamblers were strolling through the country, seeking whom they could destroy. Many of the white men who established little stores to induce drinking and gambling go in with some Cherokees, who thus became engaged with them in carrying the plans of government into effect, thus gambling spread like wild fire through the country with none to check it.

The young people were not only almost compelled to disregard their own chiefs, but also taught to despise their parents and teachers, except such as would countenance all their wicked ways.

Thus the young men have been taught to treat the Bible, the Holy Sabbath, the ministers of the gospel, and all the duties and ordinances of religion, not as unenlightened heathen, but with all that contempt and acrimony peculiar to the Voltaires of the present age.

The young women who have been educated at mission schools, and by great expense and labour, taught to read and understand the Holy Bible, are the first victims of these emissaries of darkness. Because they understand English, the dark rhetoric of hell has an immediate and distinct effect on their minds, and they are pressed into the service of darkness, and become the ringleaders of wickedness. On this account most of the labour and expense of the mission have been wrested into the service of Satan.

I have often been led to regret that any Cherokee had the least knowledge of the English language. They have not only been engaged in drinking and gambling, but also in profaning the Holy Sabbath, and the sainted Name of God. And with regard to the Holy Sabbath many professors of religion in the surrounding states, are among the first to exert an unholy influence by travelling on business, visiting and talking entirely on worldly subjects.

But notwithstanding all the warning and sacrifice and example of men in high standing, the distraction of the poor Cherokees was not effected but by the direct power of the United States. An army containing as many soldiers probably, as there are adult Indians in the nation, was thrust into the country. These soldiers were armed with guns, bayonets, swords, pistols and all the horrid artillery of death. The few guns the Indians had were taken from them, and in the heat of summer they were crowded into camps, or driven in most distressing manner to the West.

The fever and dysentery are now desolating the camps, yet thus far the mortality is not greater than might be expected.

Wednesday July 12. [Actually July 11]

Soon in the morning a young man with a measure to make a coffin for the little child of sister jenny. This was an only son, and the father and most of the children being absent, rendered the situation of the mother particularly distressing.

We understand that two Cherokees were playing cards the other day, when one, getting angry, shot the other, who fell dead instantly.

Soon after breakfast, our dear br. Mills and family came from the camps. These being out the house with many others, prevented my attending meeting at the camps, therefore Moses went alone.

Soon the bereaved mother with the company of mourners arrived. The corpse was swung under a pole, by means of a shirt, and carried by two men. It was layed out in a shade, near the graveyard, till preparations were made for burying it. Then the corpse was put into the coffin and deposited in the silent grave. Br. Mills made a short address to his people, and prayed, the whole scene was affecting.

The recollection of the father, with five or six children, mostly small, driven from their mother, as prisoners of war, in time of peace, and especially, torn from this only son, the embrace of this only brother, never to see him again till time shall be no more, rendered the scene affecting. Their eldest daughter, having now separated also from her husband, we here see two women in effect widows, in a strange land, among strangers, though in the land which gave them birth.

Many of these dear people might almost take the word from the mouth of the weeping prophet, and say, "Was ever sorrow like unto my sorrow?"

Evening prayer meeting.

Wednesday July 19. [Actually July 18]

Devoted to writing letters.

In one I gave a brief sketch of affairs in the country for a few years past.

Many years ago, the government of the United States, by their agents, advised the Cherokees to scatter from their towns, and make individual improvements for the purpose of raising cattle, horses, hogs, etc. and also in order to cultivate more land in raising grain, cotton, etc. than they could while crowded up in towns.

They also advised them to get looms, spin, weave, make cloth and household furniture, in order to live more comfortably.

They advised them again to improve their government, establish courts of justice, and make laws for the better regulation of their national affairs; and also urged their attention to schools and the education of their children.

The United States, in order to encourage the Indians in improving their condition, and for other reasons, guaranteed their country to them forever, and pledged the faith of the U. States that they should be protected on it, as long as they wished to remain here.

The Cherokees, on their part, endeavored to follow the advice given them by the president, who termed himself their father. They dispersed from their towns, erected convenient houses for their families, and many of them cleared and formed large farms, and soon possessed numerous flocks and herds; while their women made rapid advances in the manufacture of cloth, and the arts of domestic life.

The council also encouraged schools, and granted to missionaries every advantage they could desire. They allowed them to clear and cultivate what land they wished, to erect such building and machinery as they pleased, to enjoy the benefits of ferries, and pass turnpikes free of expense; and also in all their journeys, to share gratuitously all the luxury and hospitality of the country.

They also improved their government, forming it, as far as possible after the model of that of the U. States, and established regular courts of justice. They enacted laws to prevent gambling, drinking, and other immoral conduct. They established houses of entertainment on the large roads, & exerted themselves to the utmost to accommodate their guests with the best the country would afford. They also treated all white people with kindness, and payed the strictest regard to all their treaties with the U. States. Thus they engaged in good earnest to become an enlightened people.

But their rising prosperity soon excited the envy and malice of their white neighbors. They were slandered, and their motives were impeached, and they were condemned for following the advice of the highest officer in the U. States.

It was said that they separated from each other, and settled on farms, because they had no friendship for each other, and were afraid to live together, that they had no word for love, and that the worst white man made a kinder husband than the best Indian. They said that learning made the Indians swindlers, and insinuated the idea that missionaries taught them to be such. And the improvement of their government was considered high treason against the United States, a government within a government.

Horrid! All seemed to stand aghast at this awful monster; and nothing would do but the chiefs and national council must be crushed at once.

It was made a capital crime by the legislature of Georgia for the council to convene at the national council house, or for any officer to attempt to execute the laws of the nation. A number of the officers, for violating the above law, in obedience to their own rules, were arrested, and driven from place to place, and harassed about as if real criminals.

And in the meantime, swindlers of every description were crowding the country with cards, liquor, and fanciful goods, seducing all classes and orders of Cherokees into arts of iniquity and disorder. Neither the intercourse law, nor the laws of the nation could be executed with regard to the sale or introduction of liquor, gambling, etc. and the laws of the states were not observed. So that in one sense the doors of morality and good order, were closed, and the doors of immorality, and every species of iniquity were set wide open by state authority, and the most daring wickedness committed with impunity. Some bought liquor & squandered much of it away in hiring Cherokee women, of the basest kind, to prostitute themselves to their lust. Others brought it to seduce the Indians to drunkenness, in order to cheat and abuse them.

At Cassville, it is said, some poor Cherokees were enticed to drink, and when drunk, one of the women was taken out into the public street, and her clothes pulled up, and tied over her head, and thus she was left to the gaze of the multitudes passing by.

Again, an aged Cherokee woman went to that vile town on business with her grand daughter, and grand son. On leaving the village, it is said, they were followed by two young men and after they had proceeded some distance, the men overtook them, seized the young woman, pulled her from the horse, as she sat behind her brother, drawing their knives at the same time to keep the brother and grandmother from them.

They drew the young woman some distance from the road, and while one was abusing her in the most shameful manner, the other was fighting away her almost frantic grandmother & brother.

After abusing her in this manner as long as they wished, they took her to a vacant house near by and frightened her friends away, and it was not, I believe, till the next day, that she was permitted to wander, in shame, to her home.

Almost all means were resorted to, to seduce the virtuous, and to render the virtuous more vile; while the Indians, being considered savages, were denied the oath, and of course must submit to whatever abuse was heaped upon them.

The desire of the Cherokees to become farmers, in accordance with the advice of the U. States and live here, at least, till they would make some advances in husbandry, was deemed stubbornness, and an insufferable affront to those who wanted their land. On this account every exertion was made to get the whole nation away.

As early as 1818, the governor of Tennessee adopted a method by which he probably supposed the limits of that state would be cleared. He encouraged the citizens of the state to come into that part of the nation, and buy improvements of such Cherokees as were willing to go to the West.

Thus when one Indian was found willing to emigrate the place he lived on was purchased as the individual property of the white man. He was then asked if he had no other improvements. The idea of fraud and deception being thus suggested, he would, perhaps take the purchaser off a mile or two, and show him where, a few years ago, he commenced an improvement. This place, of course, became also the property of the whites. In a short time, nearly the whole Tennessee line, on the Cherokee side, became settled with whites.

The nation was alarmed at this unlawful and wicked procedure—sent a delegation to Washington City, obtained redress, and had the whites driven again to their own side of the line; though the delegations were obliged to have the line altered, and cede to the state of Tennessee, or to the U. States, for that state a very large tract of land, having their bounds then established forever, unless they might choose to alter them.

Then the nation was greatly encouraged, and made rapid advances in almost every kind of improvement, and in their prosperity more than ever, encouraged missions, schools, and good order.

But this was only the opening of the clouds in a stormy day, portentous of increasing blackness, and an overwhelming tempest.

Soon the state of Georgia, that evil,—that unfeeling—unmerciful,—conscience seared—heart hardened state, commenced her operations; and governor Clark it is said, saw that he would set his foot on the whole Cherokee country.

Two commissioners were appointed by the President, and two by the state of Georgia, met the national council at New Echota to negotiate a treaty. The chiefs, however, were united in rejecting all their overtures on the subject. General McIntosh, a chief of the Creek nation was present. He was also the Creek King in the Cherokee council as Maj. Ridge was the Cherokee King in the councils of the creek nation.

These Kings represented their respective nations in the councils of the other. The commissioners engaged general McIntosh to make certain propositions to the Cherokee chiefs, which he did by means of Alexander McKay. He told Mr. M. that if the council would sell a certain part of their country, the commissioners would give the chiefs individually, so many thousand dollars, and then would give them collectively so many thousand more to divide among their friends. Mr. M. replied that the amount offered was great, and they would pay particular attention to his proposition, but thought it had better be made in writing, and addressed to the chiefs. This was agreed to and Mr. M. was the bearer of the letter.

The council was convened early the next morning, and general McIntosh was present and took his seat. The Principal chief, J. Ross, arose, saying that he had never before had such indignity offered to his character. The letter he held in his hand, offering bribes to seduce him, and his fellows to sell the interests of their people, and betray their trust for money, was the greatest possible insult. He said he had rather be as poor as the worm that crawls on the earth than act the part of a traitor. He then read the letter.

This being done, Maj. Ridge, the speaker of the council, arose, and made a most pathetic and eloquent address, and at the close, set general McIntosh aside, from ever attending a Cherokee council again, forbidding him a seat in any of their conventions. He immediately retired, took his horse, and returned to his own nation, and was never again in this country, but soon after fell a victim to bribes, and was killed by his own people.

Georgia began to despair of either bribing the chiefs, or of purchasing the land by fair treaty. The course of a carnivorous, unfeeling animal was now resorted to as an example for legislatures to follow. It was said that the owl seated himself on the limb, beside the fowl he wished to devour. He then pushed the fowl farther and farther towards the end of the limb, till it fell to the ground, and then seized it as his prey. Thus, it was said, the whites must do with the Indians.

Georgia, therefore, commenced her grinding oppressive measures, taking for her guide this principle, "Power gives right." They also annulled the laws of the nation, stripped the chiefs of all authority, robbed the nation of civil liberty, and usurped entire control over it, i.e. that part included in the chartered limits of Georgia. Alabama did nearly the same.

These measures were supported by what was called the Georgia guard, a band of soldiers armed for war, and constantly riding through the country. The character of this guard has been seen in the history of missionaries whom they dragged to prison.

The Legislature ordered a survey of the country in direct violation of the intercourse law, and treaties with the Cherokees. The land was then disposed of by lot, and though the Cherokees were not to be driven away at that time, yet they were limited to their present improvements, and forbid clearing or occupying any new land.

They were also forbidden employing any white man to assist them, and by doing so, must forfeit the whole of their improvements.

Now as the Cherokees had long been in the habit of showing kindness to white people, especially to strangers, they could not at once overcome the current of their own feelings, so that when a white man came along with his family, and pleaded necessity and wished to labour only a few days, to get something to carry them on their journey, the Cherokees could not readily turn him away. And after being employed in this manner, this stranger would sometimes, it is said, take the advantage of the law and rob his benefactor of the farm he had been hired to work.

In this way we understand br. D. Steiner lost a part of his improvements.

Br. George Hicks also, a very industrious honest Indian, who had long been a worthy member of the United Brethren's church, had had for some time a white man in his family whom he had obliged with a home as he had none of his own. This man he did not immediately drive from his house, on the passage of the above law, and on that account was himself driven with his family into the woods. The weather was wet and cold, and the ground covered with snow, when a white man came to his house, and ordered him to take away all his furniture, etc. as he wanted the house. Mr. Hicks told him that rather than take his family out doors during such weather, he would give him two dollars per day, if his family could remain in the house till he could find some place to put them.

But this could not be granted; and the man commenced fetching his own furniture into the house. The house was built of hewn logs, and had a good roof, good floors etc. There was also some valuable furniture in it. One cupboard especially which cost $25, chairs, table etc. These Mr. Hicks had to remove, and eventually most were lost.

The man also ordered him to take away his creatures, and clear his corn cribs, as he wanted them. Mr. Hicks was therefore obliged to take his family into the woods, when he found an old sugar camp, into which he crowded his beds etc., till he could obtain assistance to move to Mr. Clauders on Connessauga.

But to attempt to tell the distress occasioned by the above law would be vain. I will therefore state but one case more.

A man by the name of Big cabin, who had been many years a chief or councellor was sick with the consumption, & ready to die. But in some way a white man got the advantage of him by means of the law above stated, (I think) and ordered him directly to leave his house. His friends entreated that he might remain till he died; but in vain. His children were obliged to make a litter and carry him about 12 miles, where he lived but a short time. He was a member of the Presbyterian church.

The Cherokees were not allowed to punish, nor attempt to punish any crime whatever. Therefore some most notorious murderers were suffered to pass with impunity, & gambling spread like fire through the country.

Gold mines were found on Cherokee land worth millions of Dollars. These were taken by the sovereignty of Georgia, and any Indian found digging gold was condemned to severe punishments.

The Cherokees at length became willing to dispose of some part of their country, but nothing would satisfy the avarice of the white man but the whole. Agents were scattered through the country, to hire, flatter, persuade, or frighten the Cherokees individually to sell their improvements to the whites and go to the west.

Thus general Jackson adopted the same method to get the Indians away which had been declared illegal by the Executive in a.d. 1819. These agents were called enrolling agents, and the persons who sold their possessions, were styled Arkansaw Emigrants, and the possessions thus sold were declared to be the property of the U. States, to be rented to any white man who might wish to intrude into the country.

Thus the United States, by its agents, encouraged and persuaded individual Cherokees all over the country to act contrary to the known will of their chiefs, and the few of their council, by disposing of their improvements to white men, not citizens of the nation, and by introducing white men into the country.

This was also a violation of the intercourse law. But although extravagant prices were offered, but few could be found willing to sacrifice the confidence and affection of their countrymen for money.

But as if every expedient to get the Indians away must be a virtue, and be supported by law, it was made a high misdemeanor for any one even to speak against enrolling, or say a word to discourage any Cherokee from doing so.

Every method was honorable which bid fair to succeed in getting an Indian, male or female, old or young to enroll, the card table, and the intoxicating bowl, became sacred things, and numbers were enrolled while in a state of intoxication.

And let the offense of the criminal be what it might, he was readily pardoned on advocating a removal to the West. Some were taken for alleged debts or offenses, and dragged about from the expectation that a fright might make them yield. And as drunkards who have wasted their property and become insolvent are generally ready to enter into any measures which promise a reward, so it was with some persons now.

This was the case especially with Mr—[Major Ridge]. He had wasted a good property, and involved himself in debt. On this account, as I have been informed, he enrolled for the west and became himself an enrolling agent. And when the national council appointed a delegation to go to Washington, and endeavor to secure their rights, this man gathered a party called the Arkansaw party, consisting of a few individuals, mostly like himself, and this party sent also a delegation to Washington, to act in conformity with the wishes of enrolling agents.

On arriving at Washington, this party delegation, secretly entered into arrangements with the President, general Jackson, to make some negotiations relative to a treaty, though with no more authority than any other individuals.

Mr.—, [Major Ridge even though Butrick won't identify him] the leader of this delegation, doubtless knew the evil that might justly overtake him when his conduct should be known by his own people, and therefore it is said, refused to sign the propositions which were to be the basis of a treaty till the President had assured him that if he would do it, those propositions should be the basis of the treaty, and that he and his fellows should receive the protection of the United States.

The propositions were then signed, and the national delegation were obliged to return, without effecting anything for the benefit of the nation, while the enrolling business still went on with increasing strength.

The character of Mr.—, being notoriously profligate could not stand long at the head of a party. Therefore, on his return he consulted Messrs. John

Ridge and Elias Boudinot, and it would seem rather gave the business into their hands.

These dear young men had become discouraged about keeping the country from the grasp of the whites, and seemed ready to adopt measures for present relief which in other circumstances they would have abhorred.

In the autumn of this year they gave notice of a council to be held at or near Mr. Ridge's at which about fifty persons assembled, to talk about measures of a national character, independently of the national council.

These persons chose their officers, adopted certain resolutions, and appointed a delegation to Washington City. This delegation therefore again stood in opposition to that of the national council, and as the President seemed predisposed to favor them, the national delegation could effect nothing. This party delegation headed by Messrs. Ridge and Boudinot, taking the ground of Mr.—the year before, entered still farther into arrangements for a treaty, and not only made propositions, but had them printed, and sent through the nation.

This excited great indignation against them. The Arkansaw party now assumed the name of the Ridge party. Mr.—again returned; and an agent was sent to this country to negotiate a treaty on the spot. His orders were to treat with the head men and warriors of the Cherokee nation. He arrived, and unfortunately for the honour of religion, he sustained the name of a minister of Christ.

Now the Ridge party seemed to unite with the national council, and all were to act in unison. By previous arrangements the Ridge Party met the national council, now convened at Red Clay, and after much deliberation agreed to relinquish their separate existence, as a party, and desist from all individual acts separate from, or independent of the national council, and unite with that body as their council, and the council of the nation.

Accordingly when the council chose delegates to Washington, they chose several who had been attached to that party, among whom were Messrs. Ridge, E. Boudinot and Charles Vann. Mr. Boudinot, however, declined going on account of his business at home, and his brother Stand Watie went in his stead.

The council being convened, the agent Rev. J. F. Schermerhorn, made his appearance. His object, however, was soon discovered, viz., to impose a treaty on the nation according to his own mind, and in order to effect this, to put down the principal chief if possible.

In the early stage of the business, therefore, he accused Mr. J. Ross of falsehood. His address to the council was so entirely unbecoming a man of his profession, that the council absolutely declined hearing him. But the non-agent, instead of being ashamed of his impoliteness, to say the least, was it is said, intoxicated with anger, & mad because the reputation of Mr. Ross for honesty stood on a foundation not to be shaken by the breath of slander.

Mr. Schermerhorn then without consulting the council, appointed a meeting at New Echota for the purpose of treating with the Cherokees, and declared that all Cherokees who did not attend that meeting, should be considered as coinciding with whatever might be done by them who did attend.

But as the council knew he had no right to make laws for them, and as he had rendered himself unworthy [of] their attention, they directed their delegation to proceed to Washington, and lay the subject of their grievances before the heads of department.

When the time arrived for Mr. Schermerhorn's council, about three hundred men, women and children were assembled, but among them were, we understood, but seventy nine men who would do anything respecting a treaty.

Br. Elias Boudinot, who had just before agreed to unite with the nation, and do nothing individually, as I have been informed, was now induced to stand at the head of a party in acting in direct opposition to the authorities of the nation.

He and Mr. Schermerhorn, and a few others, between seventy and eighty, it is said, made the treaty. These, with a few exceptions were among the common people. But few men of influence, or character were among them.

A gentleman, part Cherokee, present, it is said told Mr. Boudinot that they would be surely killed if they made that treaty. Mr. Ross, from this time I believe was spoken of as being at the head of a party, yet it must be known to all that the nation is not a party, nor the principal chief, placed in that office, and kept there by the almost unanimous voice of the people, the leader of a party.

The council above mentioned, having concluded the articles of the treaty, chose a delegation to go with it to Washington city. It has been said, however, that Mr. Schermerhorn was not to present this treaty for ratification, without the concurrence of the national delegation.

Soon after this party, or treaty, delegation started a protest, signed by 12,000 Cherokees, was sent to Washington, declaring that the treaty was not the act of the nation, but made in direct opposition to the national authorities.

This protest was presented to the senate, and the information it contained, was in substance confirmed by the United States officers, in the service of the U. States. But all was unavailing. The Senate of the United States, with their eyes open, ratified the treaty, and thus made it the supreme law of the land. Mr. Ross was slandered and vilified without the privilege of defending his own character, Mr. J. Ridge and S. Watie now deserted the national standard, and joined their own party in supporting the treaty.

Mr. Ross, however, from the politeness of Mr. Van Buren, flattered himself with some expectations of relief, when he should come into office. But although the unofficial discourse of Mr. Van Buren seemed favourable, yet when he spoke as he meant, he told Mr. Ross that the treaty had been ratified, and must be enforced.

Mr. Ross returned, a national council was again called. The people solemnly declared they would never acknowledge the force of that treaty which they knew to be a mere fraud. They therefore again appointed a delegation to plead for redress, but this was also vain.

Again the nation was convened, and met by an agent from Washington City, Col. Mason. From the private conversation by this gentleman, the Cherokees began to suppose he was favorable to their wishes, and would do all in his power for them. But when he delivered his public address, it was of the same character as the official reply of the President.

The council again appointed a delegation to represent their case in Washington. They also sent a memorial with 15,000 signatures, protesting against that fraudulent treaty.

At Washington City, Col. Mason was appointed to confer with this delegation, and seemed still to favour their wishes. Their hopes were greatly revived. Thus, they were pleased and drawn along with hopes of success, while the nation was filling up with United States troops.

At length Mr. Ross wrote home, that if they could not effect a new treaty they would be at the Agency on the 23rd of May, in time to suffer with the nation.

But then new expectations were excited, and the subject of their grievances laid before Congress, and this while the Delegation were in hopes of saving the people, the order was given to general Scott to proceed without delay to take the poor Indians prisoners, and hurry them off according to the treaty. Having thus detained Mr. Ross from these scenes of distress, it was then thrown up to him as a stigma that he left his people to suffer alone without returning to share their afflictions.

But why pursue this woeful subject.

Thursday July 20. [Actually July 19]

Went to the camps on the side of the hill just this side of the camps, lay a very old man, near the point of death. He had been sick some time with the dysentery. He had a small piece of an old blanket under him, and nothing over his body except a handkerchief drawn about his middle, and no shelter, but a few bushes and a piece of bark three of four feet long.

I inquired if he had any medicine, or any one to take care of him. He replies that a certain person came to him sometimes, but not often, and that he could get no medicine. I inquired if he would take medicine from a white doctor? He said he would.

While we were talking a young Cherokee interpreter came with some medicine in papers for him to take. I told him it would do no good to leave it unless there were some one to administer it. He replied that he could not stay.

At length a certain woman agreed to give him the medicine, though doubtless ignorant of its nature; I went on determined to see the physician, and endeavor to have some care taken of the unhappy sufferer.

On the way to the physicians shop, I had to pass a company of white men playing cards. I stopped and remonstrated against the practice, as being unlawful and wicked, tending to almost all evil, and a most pernicious example before the Cherokees. But they were steel hardened.

I proceeded, but found the physicians were absent, and therefore I called on judge Hooks, an officer in the camps. I stated the case of the old man, and urged the necessity of the most punctual attention to the sick Cherokees in order to secure their confidence, and lead them to take medicine willingly, referring at the same time to an idea prevailing among the Indians, that one of the physicians at the camps, was killing the people. Judge Hooks replied that he was sorry to say it, that one of the physicians, Dr. Grant, had told him that he make no pretensions to the knowledge of medicine, but was merely a dentist. Judge Hooks remarked farther that a man who favored the administration could obtain any employment, qualified or not, or to that effect.

The above Dentist, who is now trifling with the lives of the poor Cherokees, is a Methodist preacher.

Source: The Journal of Rev. Daniel S. Butrick. Monograph One. Park Hill: The Trail of Tears Association, Oklahoma Chapter, 1998.

37. The Drane Contingent of Cherokees (1838)

The last major Cherokee removal party conducted by the U.S. government was directed by Superintendent for Cherokee Removal Nathaniel Smith and Captain G. S. Drane of the U.S. Army. The party traveled from east Tennessee overland through northern Alabama to Waterloo, where they boarded a steamboat for the West. The party had left before John Ross and other Cherokee leaders had persuaded federal officials to allow the Cherokees to delay the forced removal until the fall of 1838 and to conduct the removal themselves. Word of the agreement reached Drane's party at Bellefonte, Alabama, before the new policy was announced by Gen. Winfield Scott, causing a revolt among the Cherokees in Drane's party. The editor of the *South Western Christian Advocate* reprinted articles from the Bellefonte *Jacksonian*, Huntsville *Democrat*, and *Florence Gazette* following the Cherokees' trek across northern Alabama. Although the writer of the article below indicates that most of the Cherokees were recaptured, Drane claimed to have lost 193 escapees before he reached Waterloo. In addition, 141 Cherokees died on the trip.

Bellefonte, Ala. June 28.

On Monday evening a body of 1070 Cherokees, under the guidance of Gen. N[athaniel]. Smith, principal agent, arrived at this place—some hours after Capt. [G. S.] Drane, U. S. Army, came in when the command was transferred to him.

The Indians formed their camp with regularity, refreshed cheerfully, and behaved with the utmost decorum,—when they had finished supper, they made seats and by the sound of a trumpet summoned their people to prayers. They sang hymns in the Cherokee language to old familiar tunes; exhortations were delivered by two preachers full blooded Indians, named Wolf and Lewis Downing—never have we witnessed a religious congregation of any sect better conducted, or more reverence to a sacred subject displayed.

So far they were reconciled and consistent. Mark the event and contrast in consequence of the arrivals of a letter.

On the morning of Tuesday they breakfasted in the same temper, struck their tents, and prepared for the march. An Indian courier arrived from the agency with a packet to Dr. Willoughby, (Medical agent,) and stated to the Cherokees that the letter contained matter authorizing the detachment in the name of John Ross, to return to their homes, there to remain until September; this caused much excitement and some confusion. The Indians rushed to the wagons and seized their baggage. It was forcibly recovered by the officers of the detachment, whose strenuous exertions in personally resisting the attempt of the Indians to possess themselves of the baggage is much to be applauded; more so, as they were not supported by any military force.

About three hundred unreflecting Indians took this in dungeon and in small groups ran to the woods leaving their property.

The Bellefonte infantry company, commanded by Capt. McReynolds, and some prudent Cherokees pursued them and brought them back, with the exception of fourteen or fifteen stragglers.

The detachment is now encamped at Roseberry Creek. It is the intention of Captain Drane to wait for the company forming at this place, which will be immediately completed, to guard it as far as Waterloo. The medical gentleman pronounced it to be a healthy condition.

The letter in question is from a person named McFarlane, residing near Calhoun; strange! that it is dated previous to the departure of the officers of the detachment; and that it should contain matter of which they are entirely ignorant. Capt. Drane conversed with General [Winfield] Scott in person, and such an order was not mentioned.

It is needless to say that the statement of the Indian courier was premature.—Inconsiderate communications in these cases are of mischievous tendency; they produce disorder and excite the feeling without any beneficial result, with this trifling exception credit is due to the emigrants for their general good conduct. It is to be hoped that in future they will not give confidence to any information unless conveyed officially.—[Bellefonte] *Jacksonian*.

The Indians referred to above passed though this place [Huntsville, Alabama] on Monday last. Some deaths had taken place since they left Bellefonte, but we understand that there was less sickness among them than when they departed Georgia. Capt. Drane is indefatigable in administering to their wishes and general comfort.—Ed. *Democrat*.

The detachment of Cherokee Emigrants under Capt. Drane, (seven or eight hundred) passed here [Florence, Alabama] on Monday going to their destination West. They are to take boats at Waterloo, from whence to their new country, they will be carried in seven or eight days.—*Florence Gazette*.

Source: South Western Christian Advocate 2, no. 38 (July 19, 1838): 256.

38. Journal of an Emigrating Party of Pottawattomie Indians, From Twin Lakes, in Marshall County, Ia., to Their Homes on the Osage River in the W(ester)n Territory. Conducted by Wm. Polke, Esq. (1838)

The removal of more than 800 Potawatomis from Twin Lakes, Indiana, in the summer and fall of 1838 resulted in what the descendants of survivors on the trek call the Trail of Death. The event has received much public attention in recent decades because of the efforts of the Fulton County Historical Society in Indiana and others. The people were forcibly rounded up by the Indiana militia after their chiefs has been taken hostage by U.S. officials. The journal, reprinted below, was kept by Jesse C. Douglass, enrolling agent, on behalf of William Polke, the conductor of the party. Douglass reports the deaths of 39 people, mostly children, and his entries mute the ruthlessness of the militia's roundup of the people, the contention for leadership among the Potawatomis, the Potawatomis' revolt against the attending physician, the white whiskey sellers and other hangers-on about the camps, and the chiefs' biting statement to U.S. officials after their arrival in the West. On the other hand, he plays up the parade-like atmosphere generated by the Potawatomis' passing through Springfield, Illinois, and other towns.

Thursday 30th. August, 1838—Commenced collecting the Indians at Twin Lakes Encampment, Marshall County, Indiana, and succeeded in gathering by night time, about one hundred and seventy.

Friday, 31st. Aug.—Received considerable accessions to the numbers of yesterday. The day was employed in bringing in the Indians and their baggage.

Saturday, 1st Sept.—Succeeded after much difficulty in enrolling the Indians, and found the number in camp to be seven hundred and fourteen.

Sunday, 2nd Sept.—Loaded thirteen wagons with the baggage belonging to the Indians and prepared for a march.

Monday, 3d Sept.—A party of 42 Indians were brought into camp, and the business of emigration so arranged as to expedite our departure on tomorrow.

Tuesday, 4th Sept.—Left Encampment at Twin Lakes at half past 9 o'clk A.M. leaving behind on account of sickness of the chief San-ga-na, with his family consisting of 13 persons, three of whom are very sick, and proceeded on our march. Messrs. Wheeler & Hopkins agree to furnish provisions during the sickness of the family, and until such time as San-ga-na may be able to report himself at the agency at Logansport, preparatory to his emigration west. The day was exceedingly sultry, and the roads choked up with dust. Travelling was attended with much distress on account of the scarcity of water. Reached Chippeway at sunset having travelled a distance of twenty-one miles, five miles further than it was the intention of the Conductor to have gone, but for the want of water. The number of horses belonging to the Indians is estimated at 286, the number of wagons engaged in the transportation twenty-six. Provisions and forage rather scarce and not of the best quality.

Wednesday, 5th Sept.—Fifty-one persons were found unable to continue the journey, the means of transportation not being at hand they were therefore left, the most of them sick, the remainder to wait upon them. Proceeded on our route, and reached at half past 12, at noon, the point determined as the location of our second encampment, a distance of nine miles from the encampment of the day before. The scarcity of water in the country again retarded the progress of the emigration, the distance being either too great or too short between the watering places. A child died on the evening of this day, and was buried on the morning of the 7th. A child was also born during our encampment. A party of three Indians joined us today shortly after coming into camp. Subsistence generally consisting of beef and flour, and that very difficult to acquire, having in most cases to transport it from Logansport, a distance from the furthest point of 46 miles. (During the night of the 4th instant at the encampment at Chippeway, twenty persons affected their escape, stealing two horses from the Indians remaining behind, and have not since been heart of.)

Thursday, 6th Sept.—Left the Encampment at Una Creek at 9 in the morning, and travelled encountering fewer difficulties on our route, than on either of the previous days, to the encampment settled upon in the immediate vicinity of Logansport, having accomplished on our third day's march, a distance of seventeen miles. During the evening of our arrival, nine of those left at Chippeway came up.

Friday, 7th Sept.—Two wagons with the thirteen persons left at Chippeway arrived in camp today. Kock-Koch-kee, with his party consisting of fifteen persons, as also Co-co-ta, Che-shaw-gen, Way-wa-he-as-shuk and Pawk-shuk, with their families, making in all eighteen persons, came into camp today. A child died this morning.

Saturday, 8th Sept.—A child three years old died and was buried. The chief We-wiss-sa came in with his family consisting of six persons, to join the emigration, himself sick. Two wagons that had been sent to Chippeway returned bringing with them twenty-two persons, the whole number of those left behind, save the few who had effected their escape, and nine others who wished to remain until they are better able to travel. C. Martin has agreed to furnish them while sick at that place.

Sunday, 9th Sept.—Physicians came into camp today, and reported three hundred cases of sickness, generally of a temporary character, and which they are of opinion, may be removed by a two-day course of medicine. A kind of Medical hospital has been erected to-day, which is likely to facilitate the course of medical regime proposed by the physicians. A child died to-day. The priest formerly attached to the Catholics among the Pottawatamies, asked and obtained leave to say mass to-day and perform the ceremonies of his church in camp. The rites are now being performed. This Evening Sidney Williams and Wm. T. Polke, who had been dispatched in pursuit of the Indians, who escaped from Chippeway, returned, having reconnoitered the villages and cornfields on the Reserve without receiving any intelligence on the fugitives. They brought into camp three Indian horses which they had found on the road. A child died since dark.

Monday, 10th Sept.—The morning was early employed in preparations for a removal. Nothing of any note occurred during the morning. At 10 o'clk. we got under way and proceeded on our journey, leaving behind us of sick and attendant twenty-one. The day was hot—we had the advantage ever of being in the vicinity of water, our route lying on the northern bank of the Wabash the whole distance. We reached our encampment at Winnemac's old village, at about 5 o'clk. a distance of perhaps ten miles from the camp at Logan. Provisions of the same character of those of yesterday and the day previous. Bacon is not to be had—beef and flour constitutes generally our provisions. A child died since we came into camp. A man also died tonight after several days sickness.

Tuesday, 11th Sept.—Left Winnemac Encampment at 10 A.M. and journed westward. Our route lay through an open, champaign, country, which circumstance rendered the travelling more pleasant than that of any previous day. The sick along with us appear to be recruiting and everything bids fair for a comfortable and prosperous emigration. If we may be allowed to judge from the gayety of our encampments—the bright smiles that gild the sunny faces of our unhappy wards, and the contentment which seems to mark the sufferance of imposed restrictions, we may safely calculate upon the pleasantest and happiest of the emigrations west. We reached our present encampment (Pleasant Run) at 5 o'clk—having accomplished a distance of seventeen miles. Provisions beef and flour, bacon difficult to be procured. A source of considerable expense is the foraging of Indian horses. We generally, however, manage to pasture them during our encampment, as cheaply as possible.

Wednesday, 12th Sept.—At half past 8 o'clk. we struck our tents and started on the march. At 11 we reached and forded the Tippecanoe river. A little after 12 we passed the Battle Ground and at 1 arrived at our present encampment (Battle Ground). Distance from the Encampment of yesterday fifteen miles. Immediately after our arrival the Indians were collected, and Dry Goods consisting of Cloths, Blankets, Calicoes, etc., to the amount of $5469.81 were distributed among. Nothing of importance occurred during the remainder of the day. The Indians appeared to be well satisfied with the distribution of the Goods. A very old woman—the mother of the chief We-wiss-sa—said to be upwards of an hundred years old, died since coming into camp.

Thursday, 13th Sept.—We commenced our journey this morning about 9 o'clock, and after traveling until 4 this afternoon, reached the encampment near Lagrange—some eighteen miles from the camp of yesterday. With the exception of the sultry heat of noon-day and the excessive dust of the roads, our marches are very pleasant. This Evening two neighboring physicians, Drs. Ritchie & Son were called into the camp (the situation of the sick demanding it) and have visited and prescribed for most of those indisposed. They report 106 cases of sickness.

Friday, 14th Sept.—Left Lagrange encampment at an early hour and proceeded at a quick pace on our journey, passing over a dry and seemingly unhealthy portion of the country. Our party continues to mend in health. Occasionally however, and indeed not unfrequently, persons thro-weariness and fatigue take sick along the route. This occupies much of our time. We place them in the wagons which are every day becoming more crowded and proceed. Reached our camp ground near Wiliamsport at 4 P.M. As we advance farther into the country of the prairies water becomes more scarce—the streams are literally dried up, and we have reason to fear that unless soon refreshed with rain, our future marches will be attended with much pain, and suffering. To-day we made 18 miles. Two deaths took place this evening.

Saturday, 15th Sept.—Early on this morning we were on our way, and travelled without interruption until 12 o'clk. M. When we arrived at an unhealthy and filthy looking stream, at which, from the reports of the citizens of the country, we were forded to encamp. The young men among the Indians during the afternoon, to the number of twenty-five were permitted to go on a hunting excursion—a permission which they have for some time seemed to covet. We travelled to-day about 10 miles. Two small children died along the road.

Sunday, 16th Sept.—At 8 o'clock we were loaded in our saddles. Seven persons were left sick in camp, among the number a woman who was about to be confined. A few minutes travel brought us to the Grand Prairie, a portion of which we passed over, arriving at our present Encampment at Danville, Ill., at about 3 o'clk. P.M. The heat along with the dust is daily rendering our marches more distressing. The horses are jaded the Indians sickly and many of the persons engaged in the emigration more or less sick. The whole country through which we pass appears to be affected—every town, village, and hamlet has its invalids. We travelled to-day, fifteen miles, passing the dividing line between the two states at about 11 1/2 o'clock. We find provisions and forage, the further we advance, demanding most enormous prices. It is worthy of remark, perhaps, that such a season for sickness in this country is almost unparalleled. In the little town, adjoining which we are now encamped, containing a population of from eight hundred to a thousand four persons died yesterday.

Monday, Sept. 17th—Left the Encampment at Danville at 9 in the morning, and proceeded to Sandusky's point, a distance of six miles, where we encamped for the remainder of the day and night. Soon after our arrival in Camp, Joseph Moreland, who was left as Interpreter for the sick remaining at the Camp of Saturday last, came up with his party, it having received an accession by the birth of a child. Provisions and forage we find scarce. Subsistence generally beef and flour. A young child died directly after coming into camp.

Tuesday, 18—The accumulation of business, together with the discharge of a number of the volunteers in service, rendered it necessary that we should remain in camp a day or two—beside which the weak condition of many of the emigrants demanded rest. During the evening to-day a woman and a child died. A child was also born. The health of the emigrants continues very bad. Scarcely a day but new cases are reported. In the main however, a daily improvement may be calculated upon. Dr. Jerolaman, the physician to the emigration, arrived in camp to-day, and commenced the discharge of his duties. He is assisted for the time by Dr. James H. Buell of Williamsport, Indiana, whose services were enlisted during the absence of Dr. Jerolaman. In their report of to-day they say, "there are at this time sixty-seven sick—of that number there are forty-seven cases of intermittent fever—thirteen of continued, and three of diarrhoea, and two of scrofula. Of the whole number eight may be considered dangerously ill." Provisions and forage still continue to be scarce.

Wednesday, 19th.—The business for which we remained yesterday in camp is but half concluded. The sick require active treatment, such as they cannot receive while on the march. To-morrow morning most of the volunteers will be discharged when we expect to proceed on our way. The report of the physicians varies but little from that of yesterday. They report six or eight cases as very dangerous. A child of six or eight years old died this morning. Also, late at night an adult person.

Thursday, 20th.—At three o'clock we were up and busily preparing the discharge of the volunteers. At sun rise they were mustered and marched to Head Quarters, where, after being addressed for a few moments by the General in command, they were discharged and paid off. Sixteen of the mounted volunteers, upon a requisition of the Conductor were retained in service, and are now under the immediate charge of Ensign Smith. At 9 o'clock a few hours before which an elderly woman died, we prepared for our march. We left the camp at half past 9, and reached our present encampment at about 2 P.M. During the march of the party, Gen. Tipton who has heretofore been in command of the volunteers, and superintended the present emigration, took his leave and left us in charge of the Conductor, Wm. Polke, Esq. While on the march a child died on horseback. A death has also occurred since we came into camp this evening. We are now encamped at Davis' Point, a distance of ten miles from the camp ground of yesterday. To-morrow we expect to reach Sidney, which is reported to be a good watering place.

Friday, 21st.—Left Davis's encampment at half past 9. At a little before two we reached Sidney, near the spot selected for Encampment. The health of the Indians is the same—scarcely a change—the worst cases generally prove fatal. Physician reports for yesterday, "their condition somewhat better. There are yet fifty sick in camp—three have died since my last report."

The farther we get into the prairie the scarcer becomes water. Our present encampment is very poorly watered, and we are yet in the vicinity of timber. A child died since we came into damp. This morning, before left the encampment of last night, a chief, Muck-Kose, a man remarkable for his honesty and integrity, died after a few days' sickness. Distance travelled to-day twelve miles. Forage not so scarce as a few days ago. Bacon we occasionally procure—beef and flour, however, constitute our principal subsistence.

Saturday, 22nd—At 8 o'clock we left our Encampment, and entered the prairie at Sidney. The day was exceedingly cold. The night previous had brought us quite a heavy rain, and the morning came in cold and blustery. Our journey was immediately across the prairie, which at this point is entirely divested of timber for sixteen miles. The emigrants suffered a good deal, but still appeared to be cheerful. The health of the camp continues to improve—not a death has occurred to-day, and the cool bracing weather will go far towards recruiting the health of the invalids. A wagoner was discharged to-day for drunkenness. Dissipation is almost entirely unknown in the camp. To-night, however, two Indians were found to have possessed themselves of liquor, and became intoxicated. They were arrested and put under guard. Some six or eight persons were left at Davis's Point this morning, for want of the means of transportation. They came in this evening. We are at present encamped at Sadner's [?] Grove, 16 miles distant from Sidney. Water scarce.

Sunday, 23rd.—Left our encampment at 8 o'clock, having been detained for an hour at the request of the Rev. Mr. Petit, who desired to perform service. The day was clear and cold. Our way lay across another portion of Grande Prairie, which, as was the case yesterday, we found without timber for fifteen miles. Physician reports the health of the camp still improving. "The number of sick" the report says "is forty.—There have been two deaths since my last report, and four or five may be considered dangerous." A child died early this morning. One also died on the way to our present encampment. Distance travelled to-day fifteen miles. We are at present encamped at Pyatt's point on the Sangamon river, along the banks of which our route to-morrow lies. Subsistence, beef and flour—better, however, than usual.

Monday, 24th.—At 9 this morning we left Pyatt's Point (the encampment of yesterday) and proceeded down the Sangamon river, fifteen miles, to the place of our present Encampment, Sangamon Crossing. Physician reports "there have been two deaths since my last, and the situation of several of the sick is much worse. I would recommend that twenty-nine be left until tomorrow." At the suggestion of Dr. Jerolaman twenty-nine persons were accordingly left behind with efficient nurses. They will join us to-morrow. We find a good deal of difficulty in procuring wagons for transportation—so many of the emigrants are ill that the teams now employed are constantly complaining of the great burthens imposed upon them in the transportation of so many sick. Subsistence and forage the same as yesterday. A child died during the evening.

Tuesday, 25th.—To allow the sick left at Pyatt's Point yesterday time to join us—to give the emigrants generally a respite, and to bring up the business of the emigration, it was determined to remain in camp to-day. The baggage wagons were weighed and reloaded during the day, and the matters of the emigrants made more comfortable. Some time in the afternoon the sick left at the encampment of yesterday arrived. Directly after their arrival a woman among the number died. The rest were but little if any improved. A child also died this evening. The farther we advance the more sickly seems the character of the country. It is sometimes very difficult to procure provisions and forage, owing to the general prostration of the husbandry. Most of the Indian men were permitted to go on a hunting excursion to-day. They brought in a considerable quantity of game.

Wednesday, 26th.—Left our Encampment at the Crossing at 8 o'clk in the morning and proceeded on our route. The sick appear somewhat recruited. Owing to the indisposition of our physician no report has been made since Monday. The weather still continues delightful—the roads, however, are again becoming dusty. Provisions and forage seem not so scarce as farther back—the country through which we are now passing is more thickly settled. Distance traveled to-day fourteen miles.—We are now encamped near Decatur, Ill. forty miles from Springfield. A child died after dark.

Thurs, 27th.—At 8 this morning we were loaded and on our horses. We travelled until 2 and arrived our present encampment, Long Point, about fourteen miles distant from the camp of last night. During the march, and indeed for the last three days, a considerable number of the Indian men were scouring the prairies in search of game. Their success has been such as to supercede entirely the necessity of issuing rations. The camp is now full of venison. Mr. Shields, one of the assistant conductors, left us this morning on account of indisposition. A substitute, it is thought, will not be necessary as the emigration is already far advanced on its route. We find no difficulty in procuring water, and have every reason to believe that the greater portion of our route will be found to furnish a sufficiency for the party. Physician still indisposed. Forage and subsistence the same, with the difference that we have less difficulty in its purchase.

Friday, 28th.—Left Long Point at a little before 8 and crossed the prairies bordering the Sangamon river, which we crossed at Dingman's ferry, and pitched our tents on its banks. We are now within a few miles of Springfield, which place we shall pass through to-morrow. Judge Polke, the Conductor, on the occasion of passing through a village of the character of Springfield, requested I-o-weh, one of the principal chiefs, to arrange and accoutre the Indians as to insure good their appearance. The chief was delighted with the proposition, and no doubt the emigration to-morrow will present quite a gaudy appearance. As an inducement they were promised some tobacco, which they have been much in want of for several days. The day has been very warm, which added to the length of our march, fatigued much the emigrants. The illness of the camp is disappearing gradually, and we may safely calculate upon a great diminution in the number of sick at the next report of the Physician. Forage and provisions becoming plenty, as we nearer approach the settled portions of the state. Distance travelled to-day eighteen miles. Two children died during the night.

Saturday, 29th.—In order to pass Springfield at as early an hour as possible, we rose before light, and at 8 were on our way. The Indians amongst whom a degree of pride was excited, arranged themselves into line, and with an unusual display of finery and gaudy trumpery marched through the streets of Springfield, which were so much crowded as to render difficult the progress of the Emigration. We passed clearly through, however, and that too, without the detention of a single Indian. At 3 we reached our present encampment, McCoy's Mills, distant from last night's camp seventeen miles. This morning, Dr. Jerolaman on account of his continued indisposition, requested leave to remain in Springfield a few days to recruit. Permission was granted. Our march to-day was through an exceedingly dry region of Country. We are now encamped on a stream affording very little water.

Sunday, 30th.—We left McCoy's Mills at about 9 o'clock and at 12 reached Island Grove—the place of our encampment six miles from the Camp of last night. Our march was made necessarily short on account of the scarcity of water—this being the only watering place nearer than 10 or 15 miles. The death of a child occurred a few hours after our encampment. Health of the sick still improving. Provisions and subsistence good and healthy. The Indians still continue to bring in large quantities of game—sufficient for their subsistence—and they greatly prefer such provisions as they acquire by the chase. One of the Dragoons was dismissed last night for intoxication—Nothing of the kind is permitted.

Monday, Oct. 1st—Early in the morning we left Island Grove, and after travelling over prairie country seventeen miles reached our present encampment, near Jacksonville, at 3 in the afternoon. Nothing occurred during our march save that a child fell from a wagon, and was very much crushed by the wheels running over it. It is thought the child will die. To-night some of the chiefs reported two runaways, who left this morning. During the Evening we were much perplexed with the curiosity of visitors, to many of whom the sight of an Indian emigration is as great a rarity as a travelling Caravan of wild animals. Late at night the camp was complimented by a serenade from the Jacksonville Band.

Tuesday, Oct. 2d—We struck our tents at 8 this morning, and prepared for a march. Owing to the very great curiosity manifested by the citizens generally, Judge Polke, after being solicited, marched the Emigration into the square of Jacksonville, where we remained for fifteen or twenty minutes. Presents of pipes and tobacco in abundance were made by the citizens to the Indians, who appeared quite as much delighted with the favor shown them as with the excellent music of the band which escorted us around the square. We continued our journey, and at 3 o'clock reached our present encampment, about sixteen miles from Jacksonville. The day was excessively warm, and the dust very afflicting—added to which water was scarcely to be found on the route. Provisions and forage we find considerable quantities without difficulty.

Wednesday, Oct. 3d.—Left Exeter encampment at a little before 8 o'clock, and without any occurrence of note reached the Illinois river about 11—9 miles distant from last night's camp. We immediately commended the ferriage of the river (preparations for which had been made the day before) and by 9 o'clock at night we succeeded in crossing with the last team. We are now encamped on the opposite shore from Naples, where we shall perhaps remain to-morrow. A child died directly after our arrival at the river.

Thursday, Octr. 4th—Although the business of crossing the river was completed last night, it was thought advisable by the Conductor to remain in Camp to-day. The Indians made use of the opportunity thus afforded them, to furnish themselves with moccasins, wash their blankets and clothes, and do many other things necessary to their comfort and cleanliness during the journey. The health of the Indians, is now almost as good as before we commenced our march from Twin Lakes—a few days more will entirely recruit them. A young child died in this evening.

Friday, Oct. 5th—Left Encampment opposite Naples at 8 o'clock, and reached a little after 12, our present camp, at McKee's creek, twelve miles from the Illinois river. We were forced to-day to leave the road and travel a considerable distance to find water, even such as it is—usually in standing ponds. The smaller streams are nearly all dry. Subsistence beef and flour. Forage good and healthy.

Saturday, 6—At a little before 8 in the morning we left the encampment of last night. During last evening, we were visited by a fall of rain which rendered the traveling to-day unusually pleasant—the dust has been completely laid, and the air much cooled. Water on the route was only to be found in stagnant ponds. At 3 o'clock we reached our present encampment, which from the barrenness of the spot in everything save grass, brush and weeds, we have appropriately named Hobson's Choice. Beef and potatoes were issued to the Indians this evening. Forage, corn and hay. A child died since we came to camp. Distance travelled to-day eighteen miles. Every day but adds to the improvement of the afflicted.

Sunday, Oct. 7th—We were on the march this morning at half past 7 o'clock. The journey was pleasant, and the road better than usual supplied with water. The distance to Quincy, of which we are now within six or seven miles, was too great for one day's journey. We therefore encamped at Mill creek, but twelve miles distance from Hobson's Choice camp. To-morrow we shall reach Quincy at an early hour, and as soon as possible cross the river on the opposite bank of which we expect to remain two or three days, to allow the teamsters and others engaged in the service, time to repair their wagons, &c. A child died shortly after we arrived in camp.

Monday, Octr. 8th—In order to reach Quincy and forward the ferriage of the river as much as possible, parties of the emigration were detached and sent a-head at 7 o'clock. At 10 a great portion of the emigrants had reached the river, seven miles from the camp of last night. A steam ferry-boat which had been previously employed, was in waiting, and the Indians were immediately put on board. By night we succeeded in crossing all the Indians, horses, and several wagons. The remainder will be brought over as early as convenient, to-morrow. It is with the utmost difficulty that many of the Indians are restrained from intoxication. A guard has to be kept under arms in every town through which we pass. Tomorrow will be employed in the payment of the officers and troops. Three children died since morning.

Tuesday, Octr. 9—The wagons belonging to the emigration were early engaged in ferrying the river, and by night time all were over. During the day, the officers were busily employed in making out the accounts of the officers, laborers and wagoners of the emigration, most of whom will be paid and settled with up to the 30th ult. Two Dragoons Messrs. Kelley & Smith declined going further with the emigration. They were accordingly discharged. Dr. Jerolaman came into camp to-day—his health is still very delicate. Several of the chiefs assembled to-day, and requested of the Conductor liberty to remain in Camp every Sabbath for devotional exercises. Leave was granted. The health of the Indians is still improving. Mr. H. Barnett, a dragoon, was also discharged to-day.

Wednesday, Oct. 10th—The settlements of yesterday were concluded to-day, and every person engaged in the service save the Officers of the emigration, was paid up to the 30th ult. In order to allow the wagoners an opportunity of repairing their wagons, shoeing their horses and making other repairs necessary for the safe prosecution of the journey, much extra ferriage was done during the two days of our encampment at the river. This might have been avoided by remaining on the Quincy shore, but the dissolute habits of the Indians, and their great desire for intoxicating drinks, forbid such a step on the part of the agents of the government. At sunset all the wagons undergoing repairs, were in camp, and we were prepared for next day's journey.

Thursday, Octr. 11th—At 9 o'clk the emigration moved from the encampment of the last two days. The rest of yesterday and the day before had much recruited the health and spirits of the Indians—the march was pleasant and without the occurrence of any difficulties. We are now encamped at Pleasant Spring, near Palmyra, Mo. Capt. J[oseph] Holman, of Peru, Ia. arrived in Camp to-day. He serves the capacity of Assistant Superintendent, having received his appointment at the suggestion of reports of the unfavorable health of the officers of the emigration. A woman died shortly after our encampment to-day. An ox wagon engaged in the transportation of Indians, having lost its cattle was forced to remain behind with its load. The wagon along with those left to hunt the oxen will be up to-morrow. Distance travelled to-day 13 miles.

Friday, Oct. 12th—Early this morning we prepared for marching, and at 8 1/2 o'clock were under way. We passed thro' Palmyra at about 10, and had little difficulty in preventing the excesses of the Indians. After we arrived in camp, however, two or three were found to have procured liquor and become much intoxicated. They were immediately arrested and put under guard. We are now encamped on See's [?] creek, thirteen miles from Pleasant Spring, the camp of last night. The health of the Indians is considered so good that medicine has not for some time been administered to them. Subsistence beef and flour. Forage corn and corn fodder. The Indians' horses are suffered to graze through the woods. The wagon left behind yesterday came up to-day. Gen. A. Morgan, who has heretofore been acting in capacity of Assistant Superintendent in the emigration gave notice that he should offer his resignation in the morning.

Saturday, Oct. 13th—This morning as we were on the eve of leaving our encampment, a number of the Indians headed by the chief Ash-kum came up to Head Quarters, and requested an interview with the Conductor and Gen. Morgan. Ash-kum arose and in a short talk informed the Conductor that the Indians were unwilling that Gen. Morgan, whom they had been taught to recognize as principal in the emigration, should leave them. They felt, he continued, that Gen. M. was near to them as a protector—he had made them pledges upon which they depended, and the fulfillment of which induced them in part to consent to their emigration. The Indians also requested through Ash-kum liberty to travel less and remain longer in camp. Judge Polke answered. He informed them that Gen. Morgan had voluntarily offered his resignation—that he had been appointed to conduct the emigration &c, &c. Gen. Morgan also responded and returned his thanks for the interest of his red children. The chief I-o-weh dissented in strong terms from the sentiments expressed by Ash-kum. He stated that these men (alluding to Ash-kum and his friends) were not chiefs—that they were not entitled to respect as such. He wished that Judge Polke should conduct the emigration, and that Gen. Morgan should return home. He felt contented along with the officers left with the emigration. The emigration left at 9 o'clock, Gen. Morgan having taken his departure before. The emigrants suffered much from the wind and dust during the march. At 3 o'clock we arrived in camp at Clinton, a distance of seventeen miles from See's creek encampment.

Sunday, Octr. 14th—To-day according to a promise made the chiefs a few days ago, we remained in camp. The Indians attended church during the day, and seemed quite happy.

Monday, Oct. 15th—At 8 o'clk. This morning we were on the march. The day was very windy, which rendered our passage across the prairie very disagreeable. Many of the Indians suffered a good deal. At noon we reached our present encampment, near Paris, twelve miles distant from the camp of last night. During the night the chiefs, according to an arrangement of last night, along with a large number of the Indians, came up to Head Quarters, and repeated their request of last night. The Speaker said that he did not demand it for himself or for his associates alone, but for every man, woman and child in the camp—they all united in soliciting the discharge of Dr. Jerolaman. The Conductor briefly informed them that Dr. J. had received his appointment from government—that he felt a delicacy in discontinuing an officer of government—that the Indians were not compelled to receive the services of Dr. J. they were free to choose for themselves—that he thought it his duty to retain his services as physician for the officers of the emigration, and that viewing their request in the light he did, he could not consistent with his duty, grant their request. He hoped they would forget their prejudices, and still continue friendly with Dr. J. and that his decision might not affect the feelings of amity which had so far subsisted between the officers and their red brethren. In conclusion, he informed them that he had purchased, in the hope of allaying their discontent, a keg of Tobacco, which he wished them to smoke in token of friendship. The Indians then retired, not without, however, first requesting leave to review the subject again. Subsistence, beef, corn & potatoes. Forage corn and hay.

Tuesday, Oct. 16th—Left Encampment at Paris this morning at 8. Our march was unusually long—water being scarce throughout the country. At 3 o'clk. We arrived at Burkhart's encampment, eighteen miles from Paris. The day was quite cold—the ground being frozen a good deal last night. Health still improving—complaints of sickness are scarcely ever heard.

Wednesday, Oct. 17th—Altho' the appearances of the weather were unfavorable, it was early determined to move. At 8 the snow commenced falling very fast, and continued during the greater part of the day. Travelling was difficult, the road being exceedingly slippery, and the snow falling so fast as to completely clog the horses' feet. At 3 oclock we reached our encampment near Huntsville, about 13 miles from Burkhart's. The Indians travel without complaint, and seem quietly to approve of the exertions of government to place them at their new homes. Subsistence flour and beef. Forage corn and hay. The snow at night changed to rain, which almost inundated the encampment. A quantity of straw was procured, which generally distributed throughout the camp rendered the Indians tolerably comfortable for the night.

Thursday, Oct. 18th—To-day owing to the continued rain we were forced to remain in camp. Added to which the state of the roads forbid our travel. Nothing occurred during the day, save the drunkenness of a few of the Indians who had procured liquor at Huntsville. To-morrow we expect to move. Provisions and forage the same as yesterday.

Friday, Oct. 19th—Early this morning the Indians were busily engaged in making preparations for a march. At 8 o'clock we were on the way—at 12 we reached encampment on Middle Chariton, eleven miles from the camp of last night. The day was cold and clear—the journey, however, was accomplished without the distress of Wednesday. The Indians still seem to be anxious to reach their destination.

Saturday, Oct. 20th—Left Chariton Encampment at 8 o'clock this morning. The road was quite muddy, and the air very cold. At 12 we reached our present Encampment on Grand Chariton, two miles from Keatsville [Keytesville]. To-morrow being the Sabbath, we shall remain in camp. The health of the Indians is almost completely restored. There are perhaps scarcely a dozen cases in camp. Subsistence beef and flour, of which the Indians are becoming very tired. Bacon and pork cannot be procured. Forage hay and corn. Distance travelled to-day eleven miles.

Sunday, Oct. 21st—To-day we remained in camp to allow the Indians, according to a request made by them, an opportunity to worship. During the day a considerable quantity of apples and cider was purchased and given to the Indians. The health continues good. One or two of the Officers have within the last few days been much indisposed.

To-morrow we expect to reach and partially ferry Grand river.

Monday, Octr. 22nd At an early hour this morning, we left our encampment, and passing through Keatsville, journeyed towards the Missouri River. At 2 o'clk. P.M. we reached Grand River, preparations for ferriage of which had before been made, and immediately commenced its crossing. By dark all the Indians and many of the wagons were over. The remainder will cross in the morning early and by 12 we hope to be able to continue our journey. Distance travelled today fifteen miles.

Tuesday, Octr. 23—The morning was early employed in ferrying the remainder of the wagons. By 12 o'clock, all the wagons were across, and we prepared for the continuation of our journey. The bottom lands of the Missouri being too flat and wet to remain upon an hour longer than was essentially necessary, at 10 o'clock. we left Grand River encampment, and passing over prairies (the cold being severe) arrived at Thomas's Encampment at a little after 4. A distance of ten miles. Subsistence Beef, flour and corn. Forage corn and corn fodder.

Wednesday, Oct. 24th This morning before leaving Camp a quantity of Shoes were distributed among the indigent and barefooted Indians, the weather being too severe for marching without a covering for the feet. At 8 we left Thomas's Encampment, & at 12 o'clock reached Carrolton, near which place we are now encamped. Distance twelve miles. Nothing occurred on the way. The cold was intense on the prairies. The country through which we passed today is very much excited. Nothing is heard—nothing is talked of but the Mormons and the difficulties between them and the citizens of Upper Missouri. Carrolton is nightly guarded by its citizens.

Thursday, Octr. 25—Having an unusually long journey before us across a prairie, we moved from Carrolton encampment at half past 7 o'clock and without meeting with any difficulties or obstructions, but somewhat fatigued, we arrived at Snowden's near whose farm we encamped. The journey was made unnecessarily long because of the scarcity of water and timber and the absence of provisions and forage. Sometime after our encampment the Conductor was waited upon by a gentleman, who it appeared had been delegated by the Citizens of Richmond (a village near us) to request assistance as they really anticipated an attack from the Mormons tonight. Judge Polke informed the gentleman that such a step on his part would be entirely without the line of his duty. His duties were particularly delegated to him by the government, to which he was responsible for the faithful performance of the same. He hoped that the excitement would abate and the aid, which he required be rendered unnecessary. Provisions and forage as usual.

Friday, Oct. 26 At 8 o'clock we left our Encampment and at 10 reached the Missouri River, opposite Lexington. We immediately commenced ferryin and shall perhaps be able to get the wagons all over before night. We found the ferry engaged in crossing females who were flying from their houses. Great excitement prevails. Reports are rife throughout the Country of bloodshed, house burnings, &c. The people seem completely crazed. By sunset all the wagons save a few were on the opposite bank of the River. Early in the morning we shall proceed to cross the Indians.

Saturday, Oct. 27 At sunrise the ferry boats were busily plying from shore to shore. As fast as the Emigrants reached the southern bank they were hurried on their journey. At 2 o'clock. the party were all over the River, and hastened to join the front of the Emigration. At 10 o'clock the front of the Emigration reached our Encampment at Little Schuy creek, 8 miles from last night's camp.

Sunday, Oct.28 To-day we remained in Camp—having during the week, marched a considerable distance, besides ferrying two rivers on the route. Health of the camp as good as it has been. This morning the Indians with Ash-kum at their head, came to Head Quarters and informed the Conductor of some difficulties which they were fearful might occur in the exercise of the unrestricted power claimed by I-o-weh, whom they did not choose to acknowledge as a chief of the blood. They also requested information in regard to annuities, &c, &c. Judge Polke hoped that they would cease to speak of a subject which could not be of benefit to them, but on the other hand might affect the progress of the emigration. When the journey was completed they were at liberty to speak and decide among themselves. He had yet some tobacco, which he should offer them in hopes that they would still continue in peace and harmony. He also informed them what he knew of their annuities, &c. The Indians then retired apparently contented. A child died during the night.

Monday, Oct. 29th—At 8 o'clock we resumed our journey, the morning being delightful and fine for travelling. At 12 we reached Prairie creek ten miles from Schuy creek. Subsistence flour, corn-meal, beef and pork and game of every kind. Forage, corn, hay and fodder. At 5 o'clock Capt. [Jacob] Hull arrived in camp with the Indians left at Logansport and Tippecanoe, numbering in all some twenty-three. They were in tolerably good health and spirits and will perhaps accomplish the remainder of the journey in the company of our party.

Tuesday, Oct. 30th—We marched from Prairie Creek this morning at a little before 8, and at 1 P.M. reached our present encampment at Little Blue River, fourteen miles from this morning's camp. The journey was unusually pleasant—the day warm, and the emigrants in the company of their friends, who came up yesterday evening, very gay and cheerful. Some time after our encampment Capt. Hull reported himself to the conductor and the number and condition of the emigrants under his charge. They number in all twenty-three, having five horses and three transporting wagons in company. They will be attached to the emigration under the charge of Judge Polke to-morrow.

Wednesday, 31st Octr.—Left Encampment this morning at half after 7 o'clock—the company under Capt. Hull being attached to the emigration—and at 12 o'clock passed through Independence. At 1 we reached our present encampment two miles south of Independence, and ten miles from the camp of yesterday. After reaching camp in the evening a small quantity of shoes were distributed among the emigrants. Many Indians came into camp during the afternoon much intoxicated.

Thursday Nov 1st—Left camp Independence at a little after 9—an hour or 2 having been allowed the Indians for their religious exercises. At 3 o'clock reached our present encampment on Blue River, sixteen miles. The journey was exceedingly pleasant—the weather being warm and the road very good. Subsistence and forage of good and healthy character, and to be had in abundance. To-morrow we shall cross the state line, and thereafter experience some difficulty in provisioning, the country being almost an entire wilderness.

Friday, Nov. 2nd—This morning broke upon us rainy and disagreeable. The Conductor being anxious, however to complete the journey now so near at an end, gave the word for a move, and at 8 o'clock we were on the road—the rain increasing as we advanced. At 9 we crossed the boundary line, and found ourselves in the heart of a prairie, with scarcely any traces to mark our route. The journey was continued, and at 12 a large portion of the emigrants on horseback became detached from the wagons, and wandered over the prairie four hours in search of the trace of the wagons. It was found at length, and we reached the camp ground set out for, at a little before 3 o'clock—having travelled a distance (it was computed) of twenty-five miles, although we are now but twelve miles from the encampment of yesterday. Our encampment is known as the North fork of Blue River. Subsistence beef and flour. Forage corn.

Saturday, Nov. 3rd—At an early hour we left our encampment at Oak Grove, and travelled until 2 o'clock when we reached a settlement of Wea Indians, on Bull creek, and camped adjoining Bull-town. Our journey was pleasant, and was marked by the anxiety of the Indians to push forward and see their friends. During the evening an attempt was made to enroll the Indians, but not very successfully. They did not seem (or would not) to understand or appreciate the object. Late in the evening several of the chiefs came to Head Quarters, and requested to remain in camp to-morrow, but the journey being so nearly completed, and the scarcity of forage and provisions induced the Conductor to deny their request, and insist upon travelling.

Sunday, Nov. 4th—Left Bull town encampment this morning at 9 o'clock—two hours having been allowed the Indians for devotional exercises. At 2 we crossed the Osage, where the Indians were met and welcomed by many of their friends, and at half after 3 reached Pottawotomie Creek, the end of our destination. The emigrants seemed delighted with the appearance of things—the Country—its advantages—the wide spreading prairie and the thrifty grove—the rocky eminence and the meadowed valley—but particularly with the warm and hearty greetings of those who have tested (and but to become attached to,) the country assigned them by government. The evening was spent in preparing for some settlements of to-morrow. The distance of to-day's travel is computed at twenty miles.

Monday, Nov. 5th—The day was consumed in making settlements with the officers. During the afternoon a considerable number of the Indians, assembled at Head Quarters, and expressed a desire to be heard in a speech. Pe-pish-kay arose and in substance said—That they had now arrived at their journey's end—that the government must now be satisfied. They had been taken from homes affording them plenty, and brought to a desert—a wilderness, and were now to be scattered and left as the husbandman scatters his seed. The agent, Mr. Davis, they knew not, and his absence would not afford them an opportunity of deciding what they might expect from him. The Indians did not think such treatment of a character with that promised them in their treaties. They hoped Judge Polke, their friend, would remain with them and see that justice should be rendered. Judge Polke informed them that considering their request too important to be disregarded, he would return from Independence, whither it was necessary he should go to attest the settlements of the emigration, and remain with them until Mr. Davis's return. He would leave his son (Mr. B. C. Polke) who would, in company with them, visit and select such localities in the country as might please them. They (the Indians) returned for answer that they would reply in the morning. The Council then broke up. Quite an old man died after coming into camp last night. Beef and corn were delivered to the Indians in the afternoon. During the evening a wagon belonging to and owned by Andrew Fuller, a Pottawattamie, containing six Indians, came into camp. They had travelled from Michigan with the intention of becoming citizens of the Western Territory, and borne their expenses for the whole route. They came without any instructions from the agent at Logansport, Ia.

Tuesday, Nov. 6th—We were early preparing to move on our return—the Officers and wagoners generally expressing much anxiety to hasten their departure. The Indians assembled again, and after a repetition of the requests and arguments of yesterday, informed the Conductor that they were willing he should leave them, but they should expect his return. In the meantime they hoped that Judge Polke would interest himself in their affairs. They had confidence in him, and hoped he would not betray it. Immediately after we left the encampment, and proceeded on our return. Much feeling was manifested at our separation. On our way we passed a wagon containing two dead persons. A sick family of Indians had been left at Bull town, two among them had died. They reached the camp of the Indians before night. We arrived at our encampment of Saturday last at 3 o'clock. To-morrow we shall proceed near to West-port.

Wednesday, Nov. 7th—Travelled from Bull town encampment to McLean's Grove, a distance of twenty-five miles. It had snowed the night previous, and continued most of the day, which was very windy and excessively cold. But a small number of the teams kept in company—most of them selecting their own routes.

Thursday, Nov. 8th—Left McLean's Grove and travelled to Westport to breakfast, a distance of nine miles. After Breakfast we continued on our way, and arrived at Camp near Independence at 5 o'clock. Several of the teams were already in camp, and others coming in. To-day we travelled a distance of twenty-one miles.

Friday Nov. 9th—During the day the wagons left behind us came into camp. The settlements with the teams will be commenced to-day and perhaps be concluded to-morrow.

Saturday, Nov. 10th—The settlements with the Teamsters and officers were concluded to-day. To-morrow we set out for home, every thing having resulted as well and as happily as could have been anticipated by the most sanguine.

I believe the foregoing Journal to be correct in all its distances, localities, etc., etc.

J. C. Douglass, Enroll[ing]. Agent.

Source: National Archives Records Group 75, Records of the Bureau of Indian Affairs, Special Files of the Office of Indian Affairs, 1807–1904, National Archives Microfilm Publications Microcopy M574, Roll 14, Case 98, Emigration of the Potawatomi Indians in 1838; *HowNiKan* 9 (June 1987): 5, 7, 15; and *HowNiKan* 9 (July 1987): 14–15.

ANNOTATED BIBLIOGRAPHY

Secondary Sources

Akers, Donna L. "Removing the Heart of the Choctaw People: Indian Removal from a Native Perspective." *American Indian Culture and Research Journal* 23, no. 3 (1999): 63–76. Akers examines Choctaw removal from a Choctaw perspective.

Anderson, Gary Clayton. "The Removal of the Mdewakaton Dakota in 1837: A Case for Jacksonian Paternalism." *South Dakota History* 10, no. 4 (1980): 310–333. This article details the events leading up to and following the 1837 Mdewakaton Dakota removal.

Anson, Bert. "Chief Francis Lafontaine and the Miami Emigration from Indiana." *Indiana Magazine of History* 60, no. 3 (1964): 241–268.

Anson, Bert. "Variations of the Indian Conflict: The Effects of the Emigrant Indian Removal Policy, 1830–1854." *Missouri Historical Review* 59, no. 1 (1964): 64–89. Anson gives an overview of Indian removal policy and its effects on the removed Indians.

Berry, Kate, and Melissa A. Rinehart. "A Legacy of Forced Migration: The Removal of the Miami Tribe in 1846." *International Journal of Population Geography* 9, no. 2 (2003): 93–112. Looks at the immediate and long-term effects of removal on the Miamis.

Berthrong, Donald J. "John Beach and the Removal of the Sauk and Fox from Iowa." *Iowa Journal of History* 54 (1956): 313–354. Berthrong focuses on politics and white pressure for the removal of the Sauks and Foxes from Iowa after 1840.

Blais, M. Jeanne. "The Imposing Alliance: Jackson, Georgia, and Indian Removal, 1825–1832." *Indian Historian* 8 (Winter 1975): 47–53. The alliance between President Jackson and Governor Lumpkin aided removal of Georgia's Indians.

Bollwerk, Elizabeth. "Controlling Acculturation: A Potawatomi Strategy for Avoiding Removal." *Midcontinental Journal of Archaeology* 31, no. 1 (2006): 117–141. Well-written article examining the Potawatomi bands' differing resistance to removal; uses archaeological evidence at three removal-era sites.

Bolton, S. Charles. "Jeffersonian Indian Removal and the Emergence of Arkansas Territory." *Arkansas Historical Quarterly* 62, no. 3 (2003): 253–271. Well-written article on Jeffersonian removal policy and how it shaped Arkansas Territory.

Bragaw, Stephen G. "Thomas Jefferson and the American Indian Nations: Native American Sovereignty and the Marshall Court." *Journal of Supreme Court History* 31, no. 2 (2006): 155–180. Bragaw's article is a well-written history of Jeffersonian removal's influence on Jacksonian removal policy and the Marshall Court.

Burke, Joseph C. "The Cherokee Cases: A Study in Law, Politics, and Morality." *Stanford Law Review* 21, no. 3 (1969): 500–531. A study of decision making in *Cherokee Nation v. Georgia* and *Worcester v. Georgia*, in which the judges considered politics and morality as well as law in their landmark rulings.

Carson, James T. "State Rights and Indian Removal in Mississippi, 1817–1835." *Journal of Mississippi History* 57, no. 1 (1995): 25–41. Chronicles the growth of the states' rights movement among Mississippi politicians and its effects on the Choctaws and Chickasaws.

Cave, Alfred A. "Abuse of Power: Andrew Jackson and the Indian Removal Act of 1830." *Historian* 65, no. 6 (2003): 1330–1353. Examines the Indian Removal Act and how Jackson abused presidential power in carrying out the act.

Clark, Carter Blue. "'Drove Off like Dogs'—Creek Removal." In *Indians of the Lower South: Past and Present.* Ed. John K. Mahon. Pensacola, FL: Gulf Coast History and Humanities Conference, 1975, pp. 118–124. A brief account of the inhumane treatment of the Creeks as a result of Jacksonian removal policy.

Clifton, James A. "The Post-Removal Aftermath." In *The Historic Indian in Ohio.* Ed. Randall Buchman. Columbus: Ohio Historical Society, 1976, pp. 38–46. A good examination of Ohio Indians in the postremoval period.

Cooke, Sarah E., et al. *Indians and a Changing Frontier: The Art of George Winter.* Indianapolis: Indiana Historical Society, 1993. George Winter, painter, was an eyewitness to removal of northern tribes in the 1830s.

Corn, James F. "Conscience or Duty: General John E. Wool's Dilemma with Cherokee Removal." *Journal of Cherokee Studies* 3 (Winter 1978): 35–39. Gen. John E. Wool's humane treatment of the Cherokees angered superiors and local whites, leading to a court of inquiry hearing.

Covington, James W. "Billy Bowlegs, Sam Jones, and the Crisis of 1849." *Florida Historical Quarterly* 58, no. 3 (1990): 299–311. The author uses the delivery of prisoners to the United States for punishment to argue that it was Sam Jones, not Bowlegs, who was the leading authority among the Florida Indians.

Covington, James W. "An Episode in the Third Seminole War." *Florida Historical Quarterly* 45, no. 1 (1966): 45–59. Analyzes the role of the Florida militia in the Third Seminole War.

Covington, James W. *The Seminoles of Florida.* Gainesville: University Press of Florida, 1993. The best comprehensive study of the Florida Indians during the preremoval, removal, and postremoval eras.

Cutter, Donald C. "President Andrew Jackson and the West." *Journal of the West* 31, no. 3 (1992): 38–43. An overview of President Jackson and his western policy, including American Indians and removal.

DeRosier, Arthur H., Jr. "The Choctaw Removal of 1831: A Civilian Effort." *Journal of the West* 6, no. 2 (1967): 237–247. The focus is on challenging the commonly held view that Choctaw civilian agents treated Indians inhumanely.

DeRosier, Arthur H., Jr. "Myths and Realities in Indian Westward Removal: The Choctaw Example." In *Four Centuries of Southern Indians*. Ed. Charles M. Hudson. Athens: University of Georgia Press, 1975, pp. 83–100. Challenges traditional views of Choctaw removal, correcting the myths presented in school textbooks by detailing the reality of Choctaw removal.

DeRosier, Arthur H., Jr. *The Removal of the Choctaw Indians*. Knoxville: University of Tennessee Press, 1970. The most detailed and comprehensive history of Choctaw removal.

Duffield, Lathel F. "Cherokee Emigration: Reconstructing Reality." *Chronicles of Oklahoma* 80, no. 3 (2002): 314–347. Analyzes historical treatments that romanticize removal and challenges scholars to go back to the original documents to create a new interpretation of events.

Edmunds, R. David. "Potawatomis in the Platte Country: An Indian Removal Incomplete." *Missouri Historical Review* 68, no. 4 (1974): 375–392. Lack of communication and planning turned the settlement of the Potawatomis in Missouri into a temporary settlement.

Edmunds, R. David. "The Prairie Potawatomi Removal of 1833." *Indiana Magazine of History* 68, no. 3 (1972): 240–253. Prairie Potawatomi removal from Indiana to west of the Mississippi was hampered by a lack of planning.

Edwards, John Carver. "'Oh God the Horror of That Night Will Never Be Forgot': Ann Margaret McCall and the Creek War of 1836." *Manuscripts* 28 (Spring 1976): 140–145. An inflammatory piece about the Creek War.

Eisenhower, John S. D. *Agent of Destiny: The Life and Times of General Winfield Scott*. Norman: University of Oklahoma Press, 1997. An excellent study of Scott's life, providing good insights into his involvement in removal of the Sauks and Foxes, Seminoles, and Cherokees.

Ellenberg, George B. "An Uncivil War of Words: Indian Removal and the Press." *Atlanta History: A Journal of Georgia and the South* 33, no. 1 (1989): 48–59. Illustrates how four newspapers covered removal differently, based on location, with southern papers supporting Jacksonian removal policy.

Ellisor, John T. "'Like So Many Wolves': Creek Removal in the Cherokee Country, 1835–1838." *Journal of East Tennessee History* 71 (1999): 1–24. Presents the aftermath of the Treaty of Cusseta, which led to Creeks fleeing into Cherokee territory, from which they were removed into the West.

Evans, E. Raymond. "Fort Marr Blockhouse: The Last Evidence of America's First Concentration Camps." *Journal of Cherokee Studies* 2 (Spring 1977): 256–263. Presents history of the Fort Marr blockhouse, used to confine Cherokees prior to removal west.

Fabin, W. W. "Indians of the Tri-State Area, the Potawatomis, the Removal." *Northwest Ohio Quarterly* 40, no. 2 (1968): 68–84. Focuses on later Potawatomi removals after the 1836 treaty, a process that lasted for years.

Finger, John R. "The Saga of Tsali: Legend versus Reality." *North Carolina Historical Review* 56, no. 1 (1979): 1–18. A well-researched article that challenges the legend of Tsali using historical evidence to point out inaccuracies.

Foreman, Grant. *Indian Removal: The Emigration of the Five Civilized Tribes of Indians*. Norman: University of Oklahoma Press, 1989. A detailed but dated study of the removal of the large southeastern tribes, but still the most comprehensive study of the removal of the Creeks, Seminoles, and Cherokees.

Foreman, Grant. *Last Trek of the Indians.* New York: Russell & Russell, 1972. Deals primarily with tribes of the Midwest and Northwest.

Fritz, Henry E. "Humanitarian Rhetoric and Andrew Jackson's Indian Removal Policy." *Chronicles of Oklahoma* 79, no. 1 (2001): 62–91. Examines Andrew Jackson's rhetoric and its relation to his Indian removal policy.

Garrison, Tim Alan. "Beyond 'Worcester': The Alabama Supreme Court and the Sovereignty of the Creek Nation." *Journal of the Early Republic* 19, no. 3 (1999): 423–450. As *Worcester* remained unenforced, Alabama expansionists used the state supreme court to force Indian removal in their state.

Gibson, Arrell Morgan, ed. *America's Exiles: Indian Colonization in Oklahoma.* Oklahoma City: Oklahoma Historical Society, 1976. Reprint of *Chronicles of Oklahoma* 54 (Spring 1976), presenting an overview of Indian removal into Oklahoma, emphasizing the Five Civilized Tribes' experiences.

Gibson, Arrell Morgan. "The Great Plains as a Colonization Zone for Eastern Indians." In *Ethnicity on the Great Plains.* Ed. Frederick C. Leubke. Lincoln: University of Nebraska Press, 1980, pp. 19–37. Analyzes removal of eastern Indians to the Great Plains and the conflicts that arose with whites who wanted their new lands.

Goodyear, Frank H., III. "'Nature's Most Beautiful Models': George Catlin's Choctaw Ball-Play Paintings and the Politics of Indian Removal." *International Journal of the History of Sport* 23, no. 2 (2006): 138–153. Examines Catlin's paintings of Choctaw ball play in the context of Indian removal and how it marginalized Choctaw suffering as a result of Indian removal.

Gray, Susan E. "Limits and Possibilities: White-Indian Relations in Western Michigan in the Era of Removal." *Michigan Historical Review* 20, no. 2 (1994): 71–91. Analyzes the relationship between whites and Potawatomis in Michigan during the removal period.

Green, Michael D. *The Politics of Indian Removal: Creek Government and Society in Crisis.* Lincoln: University of Nebraska Press, 1985. An excellent study of Creek and national politics before the Creek forced removal, necessary for those seeking an understanding of Georgia's successful efforts to remove the last of the Creeks from within its borders.

Grinde, Donald. "Cherokee Removal and American Politics." *Indian Historian* 8 (Summer 1978): 32–42, 56. Brief explanation of the politics and policies influencing Cherokee removal.

Hauptman, Laurence M., and Gordon L. McLester, eds. *The Oneida Indian Journey: From New York to Wisconsin, 1784–1860.* Madison: University of Wisconsin Press, 1999. An excellent collection of essays on Oneida removals by good scholars and Oneida historians.

Hershberger, Mary. "Mobilizing Women, Anticipating Abolition: The Struggle against Indian Removal in the 1830s." *Journal of American History* 86, no. 1 (1999): 15–40. Analyzes the organized opposition to Indian removal by a national women's petition drive in 1829 and its effect on the debate on the Indian Removal Act.

Horseman, Reginald. *The Origin of Indian Removal.* East Lansing: Michigan State University Press, 1970. Provides background on the development of removal as national Indian policy.

Huber, Donald L. "White, Red, and Black: The Wyandot Mission at Upper Sandusky." *Timeline* 13, no. 3 (1996): 2–17. A history of the Wyandot Mission, including the role it played in removal.

Indiana Historical Society. *The Journals and Indian Paintings of George Winter 1837–1839.* Indianapolis: Indiana Historical Society, 1948. Selected paintings and journals kept by George Winter, including those related to removal.

Jahoda, Gloria. *The Trail of Tears.* New York: Holt, Rinehart and Winston, 1975. A popularized treatment of the application of removal policy to tribes east of the Mississippi River.

Kelleher, Michael. "The Removal of the Southeastern Indians: Historians Respond to the 1960s and the Trail of Tears." *Chronicles of Oklahoma* 78, no. 3 (2000): 346–353. Political and cultural changes in the 1960s influenced historians to renew research into Indian issues, including removal.

Keller, Christian B. "Philanthropy Betrayed: Thomas Jefferson, the Louisiana Purchase, and the Origins of Federal Indian Removal Policy." *Proceedings of the American Philosophical Society* 144, no. 1 (2000): 39–66. Traces the development and ultimate failure of Thomas Jefferson's philanthropic removal policy.

Keller, Robert H., Jr. "The Chippewa Treaties of 1826 and 1836." *American Indian Journal* 9, no. 3 (1986): 27–32. Discusses the Chippewa Treaties of 1826 and 1836, including historical background on the treaties and the efforts to resist removal.

Kern, Kevin. "It Is by Industry or Extinction That the Problem of Their Destiny Must Be Solved: The Wyandots and Removal to Kansas." *Northwest Ohio History* 75, no. 2 (2004): 160–168. Argues that the Wyandots suffered less than other tribes in their removal; however, their successful assimilation into white society led to the tribe's dissolution.

Kersey, Harry A., Jr. "The Cherokee, Creek, and Seminole Responses to Removal: A Comparison." In *Indians of the Lower South: Past and Present.* Ed. John K. Mahon. Pensacola, FL: Gulf Coast History and Humanities Conference, 1975, pp. 112–117. A brief survey that looks comparatively at Cherokee legal tactics, Creek national despair, and Seminole armed resistance as responses to Indian removal.

Klopfenstein, Carl G. "The Removal of the Indians from Ohio." In *The Historic Indian in Ohio.* Ed. Randall Buchman. Columbus: Ohio Historical Society, 1976, pp. 28–38. Provides a history of Ohio Indian land cessions and treaties leading up to removal as well as the removal of the Ohio Indians to the West.

Klopfenstein, Carl G. "The Removal of the Wyandots from Ohio." *Ohio Historical Quarterly* 66, no. 2 (1957): 119–136. Demonstrates how the Wyandots resisted removal west but finally removed in 1845.

Klopfenstein, Carl G. "Westward Ho: Removal of the Ohio Shawnees, 1832–1833." *Bulletin of the Historical and Philosophical Society of Ohio* 15, no. 1 (1957): 3–31. Excellent history of Shawnee removal from their unification in Ohio to their final removal west as a result of the 1830 Indian Removal Act.

Lankford, George E. "Trouble at Dancing Rabbit Creek: Missionaries and Choctaw Removal." *Journal of Presbyterian History* 62 (1968): 51–66. Treats U.S. expulsion of two missionaries to the Choctaws during the 1830 treaty negotiations setting into motion Choctaw removal west.

Lass, William E. "The Removal from Minnesota of the Sioux and Winnebago Indians." *Minnesota History* 38, no. 8 (1963): 353–364. Chronicles the removal of the Sioux and Winnebagos from Minnesota, including accounts by accompanying missionaries.

Littlefield, Daniel F., Jr. *The John Drew Detachment.* Resources on Indian Removal No. 2. Little Rock: Sequoyah Research Center, 2006. Historical account of John Ross's removal to the West in 1838–1839.

Littlefield, Daniel F., Jr. *Removal Muster Rolls, Rosters, and Lists.* Resources on Indian Removal No. 1. Little Rock: Sequoyah Research Center, 2006. A bibliography of rolls, rosters, and lists of Choctaws, Muscogees (Creeks), Chickasaws, Seminoles, and Cherokees who removed or were sent to the West.

Loos, John L. "William Clark: Indian Agent." *Kansas Quarterly* 3, no. 4 (1971): 29–38. An account of the life of Indian agent William Clark, who helped carry out the Indian Removal Act of 1830.

Mahan, Bruce. "Moving the Winnebago." *The Palimpsest* 3, no. 2 (1922): 33–52. Discusses the relocation of Iowa Winnebagos west of the Mississippi and the difficulties they faced.

Mahon, John K. *History of the Second Seminole War, 1835–1842.* Gainesville: University Press of Florida, 1967. The most detailed and authoritative study of the Second Seminole War.

Manzo, Joseph T. "Emigrant Indian Objections to Kansas Residence." *Kansas History* 4, no. 4 (1981): 246–254. Demonstrates how emigrating Indians had concerns regarding the new lands in Kansas they were removing to, including the inhospitable environment and new neighboring tribes.

McClurken, James M. "Ottawa Adaptive Strategies to Indian Removal." *Michigan Historical Review* 12, no. 1 (1986): 29–55. Demonstrates how the Jackson and Van Buren administrations tried to press Ottawa removal and how the Ottawas were able to resist removal by becoming landowners and an important part of the local economy.

McLoughlin, William G. "Georgia's Role in Instigating Compulsory Indian Removal." *Georgia Historical Quarterly* 70, no. 4 (1986): 605–632. Places removal in the context of Georgia's view of removal as a states' rights issue and its determination to control all land within its boundaries.

McLoughlin, William G. "The Murder Trial of the Reverend Evan Jones, Baptist Missionary to the Cherokee in North Carolina, 1833." *North Carolina Historical Review* 62, no. 2 (1985): 157–178. Chronicles how anti-removal missionary Evan Jones faced murder charges brought up by whites who wanted Cherokee lands in Georgia.

McLoughlin, William G. "Thomas Jefferson and the Beginnings of Cherokee Nationalism, 1806 to 1809." *William & Mary Quarterly* 32, no. 4 (1975): 547–580. Demonstrates how a threatened Indian removal led to the growth of Cherokee nationalism in the early 19th century.

Meyers, Jason. "No Idle Past: Uses of History in the 1830 Indian Removal Debates." *Historian* 63, no. 1 (2000): 53–65. Demonstrates how both sides of the Indian removal issue used history in debates over removal.

Miles, Tiya. "'Circular Reasoning': Recentering Cherokee Women in the Antiremoval Campaigns." *American Quarterly* 61, no. 2 (2009): 221–243. Recounts Cherokee women's active involvement in the anti-removal debate over a decade before Anglo women's political involvement.

Morris, Michael. "Georgia and the Conversation over Indian Removal." *Georgia Historical Quarterly* 91, no. 4 (2007): 403–423. Examines how Georgia officials helped shape the debate over Indian removal.

Neumeyer, Elizabeth. "Michigan Indians Battle against Removal." *Michigan History* 55, no. 4 (1971): 275–288. Demonstrates how only a small percentage of

Michigan Indians were removed because of the success Michigan Indians had in resisting removal.

Norgren, Jill L., and Petra T. Shattuck. "Limits of Legal Action: The Cherokee Cases." *American Indian Culture and Research Journal* 2, no. 2 (1978): 14–25. Examines the limitations of legal action to protect Indian sovereignty by using the 19th-century Cherokees as an example.

Norwood, Frederick A. "Strangers in a Strange Land: Removal of the Wyandot Indians." *Methodist History* 13, no. 3 (1975): 45–60. A history of the 1843 Wyandot removal from Ohio to the West and the role Methodists played in the removal.

Owens, Robert M. "Jean Baptiste Ducoigne, the Kaskaskias, and the Limits of Thomas Jefferson's Friendship." *Journal of Illinois History* 5, no. 2 (2002): 109–136. Demonstrates how the relationship between the Kaskaskia tribe and the federal government changed from Thomas Jefferson to Andrew Jackson.

Parsons, Lynn Hudson. "'A Perpetual Harrow upon My Feelings': John Quincy Adams and the American Indian." *New England Quarterly* 46, no. 3 (1973): 339–379. Analyzes John Quincy Adams's views on Indian policy, including removal, as it evolved over time.

Paulson, Howard W. "Federal Indian Policy and the Dakota Indians: 1800–1840." *South Dakota History* 3, no. 2 (1973): 285–309. Demonstrates how federal policy toward the Dakota Indians pushed them further westward in the early half of the 19th century.

Perdue, Theda. "Cherokee Women and the Trail of Tears." *Journal of Women's History* 1, no. 1 (1989): 14–30. Analyzes the role of Cherokee women in removal: their attitudes toward the policy, how it affected them, their experiences along the trail, and how they rebuilt their lives in the West.

Perdue, Theda. "The Conflict Within: The Cherokee Power Structure and Removal." *Georgia Historical Quarterly* 73, no. 3 (1989): 465–491. Analyzes the effects of political factionalism on Cherokee removal.

Perdue, Theda, and Michael D. Green. *The Cherokee Removal: A Brief History with Documents.* Boston: Bedford Books of St. Martin's Press, 1995. An excellent introductory study for students of Cherokee removal.

Porter, Kenneth W. "Billy Bowlegs (Holata Micco) in the Seminole Wars (Part I)." *Florida Historical Quarterly* 45, no. 3 (1967): 219–242. A detailed account of Bowlegs's role in events leading to the Third Seminole War and the last Seminole removal.

Porter, Kenneth W. *The Black Seminoles: History of a Freedom-Seeking People.* Rev. and ed. Alcione M. Amos and Thomas P. Senter. Gainesville: University Press of Florida, 1996. This posthumous study of African-descended people among the Seminoles is the most comprehensive to date.

Porter, Kenneth W. *The Negro on the American Frontier.* New York: Arno Press and the New York Times, 1971. A dated but still useful study of African-descended people and American Indians, with primary focus on the tribes of the Southeast.

Portnoy, Alisse. "'Female Petitioners Can Lawfully Be Heard': Negotiating Female Decorum, United States Politics, and Political Agency, 1829–1831." *Journal of the Early Republic* 23, no. 4 (2003): 573–610. Demonstrates how Catharine Beecher organized a national campaign of white women to petition against Indian removal.

Portnoy, Alisse. *Their Right to Speak: Women's Activism in the Indian and Slave Debates.* Cambridge, MA: Harvard University Press, 2005. Examines the role women played in debates over both Indian removal and abolitionism.

Prucha, Francis Paul. "Indian Removal and the Great American Desert." *Indiana Magazine of History* 59, no. 4 (1963): 299–322. Presents a pro-government view of the early debates regarding Indian removal to the Great American Desert.

Prucha, Francis Paul. "Protest by Petition: Jeremiah Evarts and the Cherokee Indians." *Proceedings of the Massachusetts Historical Society* 97 (1985): 42–58. Analyzes Evarts's role in the anti-removal political debates.

Remini, Robert V. *Andrew Jackson and His Indian Wars.* New York: Viking, 2001. An account of Jackson's Indian policy that is more apologetic of Jackson's role than most.

Satz, Ronald N. *American Indian Policy in the Jacksonian Era.* Lincoln: University of Nebraska Press, 1975. A balanced analysis of Andrew Jackson's Indian removal policy.

Satz, Ronald N. "Indian Policy in the Jacksonian Era: The Old Northwest as a Test Case." *Michigan History* 60, no. 1 (1975): 71–93. An examination of removal policy as it applied to the tribes of the Old Northwest.

Scherer, Mark R. "'Now Let Him Enforce It': Exploring the Myth of Andrew Jackson's Response to 'Worcester' v. 'Georgia' (1832)." *Chronicles of Oklahoma* 74, no. 1 (1996): 16–29. Examines the popular misconception regarding Jackson's words and argues that there were not only political but also legal reasons for his inaction regarding the Supreme Court's ruling.

Secunda, W. Ben. "To Cede or See? Risk and Identity among the Woodland Potawatomi during the Removal Period." *Midcontinental Journal of Archaeology* 31, no. 1 (2006): 57–88. Secunda examines removal-period Potawatomis and their split into bands, showing how some bands evaded removal whereas others did not.

Shriver, Phillip R. "Know Them No More Forever: The Miami Removal of 1846." *Timeline* 10, no. 6 (1993): 30–41. Excellent overview of Miami removal and how a small minority stayed in Ohio while the majority of the tribe removed west.

Smith, F. Todd. "After the Treaty of 1835: The United States and the Kadohadacho Indians." *Louisiana History* 30, no. 2 (1989): 157–172. Examines the Caddo removal treaty of 1835 and the aftereffects.

Stein, Gary C. "Indian Removal as Seen by European Travelers in America." *Chronicles of Oklahoma* 51, no. 4 (1974): 399–410. Discusses how Europeans traveling in the United States routinely criticized Indian removal and the American public's lack of criticism.

Stowe, Christopher S. "One Could Not but Feel Melancholy: Ohio Remembers the Wyandot." *Northwest Ohio History* 75, no. 2 (2004): 149–159. Recalls the 1843 Wyandot tribe's removal from Ohio, including Ohio newspaper coverage of the removal.

Strickland, William M. "The Rhetoric of Removal and the Trail of Tears: Cherokee Speaking against Jackson's Indian Removal Policy." *Southern Speech Communications Journal* 47, no. 3 (1982): 292–309. Illustrates how Cherokees spoke out against President Jackson's removal policy.

Stuart, Benjamin F. "Transportation of Pottawattomies: The Deportation of Menominee and His Tribe of the Pottawattomie Indians." *Indiana Magazine of History* 18, no. 3 (1922): 255–265. A sentimental account of the removal of Chief Menominee's band of Potawatomis.

Swindler, William F. "Politics as Law: The Cherokee Cases." *American Indian Law Review* 3, no. 1 (1975): 7–20. Examines the Marshall Court's handling of cases involving the Cherokee Nation and removal.

Syndergaard, Rex. "The Final Move of the Choctaws, 1825–1830." *Chronicles of Oklahoma* 52, no. 2 (1974): 207–219. Examines the policies behind the last removal of the Choctaws to the West.

Trennert, Robert A. "The Business of Indian Removal: Deporting the Potawatomi from Wisconsin, 1851." *Wisconsin Magazine of History* 63, no. 1 (1979): 36–50. Demonstrates how the Ewing family, contractors for Wisconsin Potawatomi removal, profited greatly in removal at the expense of the welfare of the Potawatomi.

Valone, Stephen J. "William Seward, Whig Politics, and the Compromised Indian Removal Policy in New York State, 1838–1843." *New York State History* 82, no. 2 (2001): 106–134. Analyzes the success of anti-removal forces in saving some tracts of tribal land.

Vipperman, Carl J. "'Forcibly if We Must': The Georgia Case for Cherokee Removal, 1802–1832." *Journal of Cherokee Studies* 3 (Spring 1978): 103–110. A study of the relationship between Georgia's arguments for claiming Cherokee lands in its borders and the earlier Yazoo Land Act.

Williams, David. "Gold Fever, the Cherokee Nation and the Closing of Georgia's 'Frontier.'" *Proceedings and Papers of the Georgia Association of Historians* 11, no. 2 (1990): 24–29. Analyzes a major event in Georgia's drive to rid the state of its Indian population.

Young, Mary. "The Exercise of Sovereignty in Cherokee Georgia." *Journal of the Early Republic* 10, no. 1 (1990): 43–63. An interesting analysis of the role of Georgians who opposed the prevailing sentiment for forcible eviction of the Cherokees and confiscation of their property.

Young, Mary. "Indian Removal and the Attack on Tribal Autonomy: The Cherokee Case." In *Indians of the Lower South: Past and Present.* Ed. John K. Mahon. Pensacola, FL: Gulf Coast History and Humanities Conference, 1975, pp. 125–142. A thoroughly documented analysis of the role of the federal government as well as Georgia in the destruction of the Cherokee Nation.

Young, Mary. "Indian Removal and Land Allotment: The Civilized Tribes and Jacksonian Justice." *American Historical Review* 64, no. 1 (1958): 31–45. Authoritative account of removal and allotment.

Young, Mary E. *Redskins, Ruffleshirts and Rednecks: Indian Allotments in Alabama and Mississippi, 1830–1860.* Norman: University of Oklahoma Press, 1961. The most authoritative study of fraud in Indian land sales in the Southeast.

Published Primary Sources

Journals

Foreman, Grant. "Journey of a Party of Cherokee Emigrants." *Mississippi Valley Historical Review* 18, no. 2 (1931): 232–245. Reprints the journal of occurrences kept by Dr. Clark Lillybridge during the removal of a contingent of Treaty Party Cherokees in 1837.

Indiana Historical Society. "Removal of Indians from Ohio: Dunihue Correspondence of 1832." *Indiana Magazine of History* 35, no. 4 (1939): 408–426. Reprints correspondence of the Dunihue family relating to removal of Indians from Lewistown, Ohio.

Litton, Gaston. "Journal of a Party of Emigrating Creek Indians, 1835–1836." *Journal of Southern History* 7, no. 2 (1941): 225–242. Edited transcription of the journal of occurrences kept by Dr. Clark Lillybridge during the removal of a party of Treaty Party Cherokees.

Oklahoma Chapter, Trail of Tears Association. *Cherokee Removal: The Journal of Reverend Daniel S. Butrick, May 19, 1838–April 1, 1839.* Park Hill: Oklahoma Chapter, Trail of Tears Association, 1998. An excellent source on conditions in the Cherokee preremoval holding camps; indispensable for the study of the Taylor contingent of removing Cherokees.

Polke, William. "Journal of an Emigrating Party of Pottawattomie Indians, 1838." *Indiana Magazine of History* 21, no. 4 (1925): 315–336. Reprints the journal kept by officials attending the Potawatomis on their 1838 trek from Twin Lakes, Indiana, to the Osage River in the western territory.

Polke, William. "Removal Journal Part I." *HowNiKan* 9, no. 6 (1987): 5, 7, 15. Reprints the journal kept during removal of Potawatomis from Twin Lakes, Indiana, to Kansas in 1838 on their infamous Trail of Death.

Polke, William. "Journal of Removal—Part II." *HowNiKan* 9, no. 7 (1987): 14–15. Reprints the journal kept during removal of Potawatomis from Twin Lakes, Indiana, to Kansas in 1838 on their infamous Trail of Death.

Proffit, George H. "Removal Journal—The Trail of Death." *HowNiKan* 9, no. 8 (1987): 6–8. Reprints the journal of emigration kept by Proffit during the removal of Potawatomis from near Monticello, Indiana, to Kansas in 1837.

Smith, Dwight L., ed. "The Attempted Potawatomie Removal of 1839." *Indian Magazine of History* 45, no. 1 (1949): 51–80. Reprints correspondence of William Polke regarding Potawatomi removal from Indiana.

Smith, Dwight L., ed. "Continuation of the Journal of an Emigrating Party of Potawatomie Indians, 1838 and Gen William Polke Manuscripts." *Indiana Magazine of History* 44, no. 4 (1948): 393–408. Journal chronicles events related to the Potawatomis after their arrival in Kansas, 1838.

Smith, Dwight L., ed. "Jacob Hull's Detachment of the Potawatomie Emigration of 1838." *Indiana Magazine of History* 45, no. 3 (1949): 285–288. Journal of occurrences of Potawatomis removing from Logansport, Indiana, to the Osage River in the western territory.

Winter, George. "George Winter Meets the Potawatomi." *HowNiKan* 8, no. 7 (1986): 6–7. Excerpts from Winter's journal during his summer 1837 visit to the Potawatomis of Indiana.

Winter, George. "George Winter's Journal, Part II." *HowNiKan* 8, no. 8 (1987): 6–7. Excerpts from Winter's journal during his summer 1837 visit to the Potawatomis in Indiana.

Letters and Other Writings

Boudinot, Elias. *Cherokee Editor: The Writings of Elias Boudinot.* Ed. Theda Perdue. Knoxville: University of Tennessee Press, 1983. Necessary for an understanding of Boudinot's role in the Cherokee removal.

King, Duane H., and E. Raymond Evans, eds. "The Trail of Tears: Primary Documents of the Cherokee Removal." *Journal of Cherokee Studies* 3 (Summer 1978): 131–185. A somewhat dated but still useful attempt to create a source book on Cherokee removal.

Payne, John Howard. "The Cherokee Cause." *Journal of Cherokee Studies* 1 (Summer 1976): 17–22. Reprints the 1835 letter by John Howard Payne defending the Cherokee Indians against removal.

Ross, John. *The Papers of Chief John Ross.* 7 vols. Ed. Gary E. Moulton. Norman: University of Oklahoma Press, 1984. Contains Ross's letters and other documents covering the period 1807–1866; indispensable to any study of Cherokee removal.

Rozema, Vicki. *Voices from the Trail of Tears.* Winston-Salem, NC: John F. Blair, 2003. A collection of documents related to Cherokee removal.

Sturgis, Amy H. *The Trail of Tears and Indian Removal.* Westport, CT: Greenwood Press, 2007. A recent study and source book on Cherokee removal.

Whalen, Brett E., comp. "A Vermonter on the Trail of Tears, 1830–1837." *Vermont History* 66, nos. 1–2 (1998): 31–38. An account of William Beattie and Muscogee (Creek) removal.

Congressional Serial Set

Choctaw Indians, contracts for removal. H. Doc. 107. 27th Cong., 2nd sess. Serial 465. Proposals for subsistence for the Choctaws removing in 1840s.

Claims against the Pottawatomie Indians. Letter from the Secretary of War, transmitting the information called for by the resolution of the House of Representatives of the 11th ultimo, relating to the settlement of claims of citizens of the United States against the Pottawatomie Indians. H. Doc.143. 27th Cong., 2nd sess. Serial 403. Documents and letters regarding Potawatomi removal.

Correspondence on the Emigration of Indians, 1831–1833. S. Doc. 512 [5 vols.]. 23rd Cong., 1st sess. Serial 244–248. Correspondence related to all tribes who removed during the first few years after the Indian Removal Act.

Frauds upon Indians—Right of the President to withhold papers. H. Rept. 271. Serial 421. Information collected by Lt. Colonel Hitchcock during his investigation into removal subsistence fraud.

Letter from the Secretary of War, transmitting copies of the proceedings of a court of inquiry, convened at Frederick-town, in relation to the operations against the Seminole and Creek Indians, &c. H. Doc. 78 (25–2). Serial 323. Documents and evidence used in the court of inquiry against Generals Scott and Gaines.

Letter from the Secretary of War transmitting documents in relation to hostilities of Creek Indians. H. Doc. 276. 24th Cong., 1st sess. Serial 292. Correspondence and reports related to the so-called Creek War of 1836 and Creek removal; includes letters written by disbursing officers.

Message from the President of the United States, transmitting Information in relation to Alleged Frauds on the Creek Indians in the Sale of their Reservations. H. Doc. 452. 25th Cong., 2nd sess. Serial 331. Contains documents and testimony regarding fraud committed against the Creeks during the sale of reservation lands in the East.

American State Papers

Causes of hostilities of Creek and Seminole Indians in Florida, and instructions to and correspondence with agents and other persons contracted for their removal to the West. *American State Papers: Military Affairs* 690. 24th Cong., 1st sess. Documents and correspondence regarding the removal of the Creeks and Seminoles.

Causes of Hostilities of Creek and Seminole Indians in Florida; instructions to Brevet Major General Thomas S. Jesup and other officers of army for their removal to the West, and correspondence with governors of States and agents.

American State Papers: Military Affairs 691. 24th Cong., 1st sess. Documents and correspondence regarding the subsistence of the Creeks and Seminoles removing west.

Military orders and operations against Seminole Indians in Florida and their removal west of Mississippi River. *American States Papers: Military Affairs* 638. 24th Cong., 1st sess. Military reports regarding the Second Seminole War and removal of the Seminoles.

Unpublished Primary Sources

National Archives Microfilm Publications

"Census of Creek Indians Taken by Parsons and Abbott, 1832." Microcopy T275, RG75. 1 roll. Census arranged by town, listing heads of households entitled to allotments in Alabama, enumerating males, females, and slaves in each household.

"Census Roll of Cherokee Indians East of the Mississippi and Index to the Roll, 1835." Microcopy 496. 1 roll. A census of the Cherokees prior to the Treaty of New Echota, providing for their removal, listing heads of families, numbers in households, occupations, and other information.

"Cherokee Land 1823." Microcopy T135. 1 roll. Map of Cherokee land, segregated from Claim 8568, RG 217, Entry 525.

"Correspondence of the Eastern Division Relating to Cherokee Removal, April 1838–December 1838." Microcopy M1475, RG393. 2 rolls. Contains documents related to Gen. Winfield Scott's command during the forced removal of the Cherokees.

"Documents Relating to the Negotiation of Ratified and Unratified Treaties with Various Indian Tribes, 1801–1869." Microcopy T494, RG11. 10 rolls. Often contains useful information about treaty negotiations not available in other resources, providing insights into how well the negotiators conducted themselves.

"Letters Received by the Office of Indian Affairs, 1824–1881." Microcopy M234, RG75. 962 rolls. Arranged by agency or jurisdiction and then by year, includes ordinary agency correspondence as well as segregated files relating to removal of the tribes under the agency.

"Letters Sent by the Office of Indian Affairs, 1824–1881." Microcopy M21, RG75. 166 rolls. Outgoing correspondence complements incoming correspondence in Letters Received (Microcopy M234), especially rolls 1–65 for the removal period 1824–1860.

"Records of the Cherokee Indian Agency in Tennessee, 1801–1935." Microcopy M208, RG75. 14 rolls. Contains correspondence and other records covering the period of early removals to the Treaty of New Echota.

"Records of the Michigan Superintendency of Indian Affairs, 1814–1852." Microcopy M1, RG75. 71 rolls. Correspondence and other records related to a number of tribes in the Old Northwest during the removal period.

"Records of the Southern Superintendency of Indian Affairs, 1832–1870." Microcopy M640, RG75. 22 rolls. Contains correspondence of the Western Superintendency (agency's name 1832–1851) regarding Choctaws, Creeks, Cherokees, Senecas, mixed bands of Senecas and Shawnees, and, later, Quapaws, Seminoles, and Chickasaws.

"Records of the Wisconsin Superintendency of Indian Affairs, 1836–1848, and Green Bay Subagency, 1850." Microcopy M95, RG75. 4 rolls. Contains correspondence, transcriptions of Indian talks, and other types of documents.

"Report Books of the Office of Indian Affairs, 1838–1885." Microcopy M348, RG75. 53 rolls. Includes copies of communications sent from the office to members of the cabinet regarding Indian affairs, covering various aspects of issues, including removal, especially rolls 1–11 for the period 1838–1860.

"Special Files of the Office of Indian Affairs, 1807–1904." Microcopy M574, RG75. 85 rolls. Documents relating to claims and other issues arising from removal of Cherokee, Chippewa, Creek, Delaware, Kickapoo, Ottawa, Sauk and Fox, Miami, Ottawa, Potawatomi, Seminole, Seneca, Winnebago, and other tribes.

National Archives Loose Documents

Records of the Accounting Officers of the Department of the Treasury, RG 217. Records of the Office of the Second Auditor, Entry 524: "Claims Settled under the Chickasaw Treaty, 1833–71." Correspondence, receipts, commutation vouchers, and other records justifying disbursements by the Office of Indian Affairs related to Chickasaw removal.

Records of the Accounting Officers of the Department of the Treasury, RG 217. Records of the Office of the Second Auditor, Entry 525: "Indian Affairs, Settled Accounts and Claims, 1794–1894." Correspondence, receipts, journals, and other records submitted by agents, removal conductors, and disbursing agents to justify disbursements during the removal process; indispensable in documenting day-to-day events.

Records Relating to Indian Removal, RG 75. Records of the Bureau of Indian Affairs. Preliminary Inventory 163, Entries 198–300. A massive collection of loose documents including Records of the Commissary General of Subsistence (Entries 198–216), which contains record categories of Cherokee, Chicago Agency, Choctaw, Creek, Florida, Kickapoo, Ohio, Ottawa, Potawatomi, Quapaw, St. Louis Superintendency, Seminole, Western Superintendency, and Winnebago; Cherokee Removal Records (Entries 217–251); Chickasaw Removal Records (Entries 252–257); Choctaw Removal Records (Entries 258–284); Creek Removal Records (Entries 285–300); and Other Removal Records (Entry 301), containing records of Apalachicola, Seminole, Kickapoo, New York, Ottawa, Potawatomi, Quapaw, and Wyandot removals.

INDEX

Abercrombie, Charles, 2:205, 2:209, 2:211
Abert, J. J., 2:191; letter to Lewis Cass, 2:194–196
aboriginals, 2:52, 2:113, 2:126
Abraham, 1:1–3, 1:4–5, 1:54, 1:78, 1:100–101
acculturation, 1:26, 1:28, 1:65, 1:116, 1:118, 1:271
acquisition of property, 1:65, 1:84, 1:113, 1:145, 2:7, 2:9, 2:38, 2:40, 2:44, 2:113, 2:127–128
Adair, Walter S., 2:82
Adams, John Quincy, 1:36, 1:86–87, 1:102, 1:227, 1:259–261
Aehaia, Epenetus, 2:247
African-descended people, 1:1–2, 1:35, 1:52–54, 1:58, 1:91, 1:101, 1:114, 1:115, 1:284, 2:168–175; and removal, 1:3–6
agriculture, 1:38, 1:139, 1:143, 1:164–165, 1:195, 2:20, 2:22, 2:40–41, 2:49, 2:52, 2:65, 2:129
Alabama, 1:32–33, 1:38–44, 1:59–60, 1:70–75, 1:84–87, 1:96, 1:102–104, 1:109–110, 1:112–114, 1:125–127, 1:146–149, 1:174–175, 1:197–200, 1:224–227, 1:249–252, 2:18–19, 2:23, 2:30, 2:52, 2:59, 2:68, 2:82–83, 2:85, 2:169, 2:172, 2:175, 2:203–204, 2:219, 2:238–239, 2:255, 2:261–262; and Indian removal, 1:6–10
Alabama Creeks, 1:86, 1:197

Alabama Emigrating Company, 1:59, 1:148, 1:199, 1:222, 1:252
Albany, 1:157, 1:169–171, 1:239
Allegany reservation, 1:157–58, 1:173, 1:229, 1:238, 1:239, 1:242–243
Allen, John, 1:237, 1:268
Allen, Thomas, 2:45
Alligator. See Hulbutta Tustenuggee
allowances, personal, 2:138–139
American Board of Commissioners for Foreign Missions (ABCFM), 1:67, 1:269–270
American settlements, 1:22–23, 1:39, 1:60, 1:62, 1:107, 1:165, 1:202, 1:228
Anderson, Richard, 2:171
Anglo-Americans, 2:67–68, 2:70
Anishinaabeks, 1:166, 1:196
Anosta, Atalah, 2:83
anti-removal sentiment, 1:24, 1:27, 1:105, 1:112, 1:116, 1:127–128, 1:173, 1:192, 1:206, 1:245, 1:247, 1:264, 1:270, 2:75–86, 2:245
Anti-Treaty Cherokees, 1:246
Anti-Treaty Party, 1:245
Apalachicolas, 1:70, 1:76–77, 1:208, 1:211–213; removal, 1:11–12
Arbuckle, Matthew, 2:218
Arkansans, 1:15, 1:40, 1:47, 1:94, 1:233
Arkansas, 1:35, 2:18, 2:48–49, 2:65, 2:67, 2:83, 2:89, 2:169–175, 2:179, 2:183, 2:196–197, 2:203, 2:212–217, 2:222–223, 2:229; and Indian removal, 1:13–16

Arkansas River, 1:2, 1:13–14, 1:78, 1:94, 1:146—147, 1:252, 1:258, 2:239–243
Armstrong, Francis, 1:48
Armstrong, Robert, 1:17
Armstrong, William, 1:16–19
army disbursing agents, journals of, 2:196–203, 2:219–224
Articles of Agreement and Cession, 2:1–4
Articles of Convention and Agreement, 1:44
Ash-kum, 2:273, 2:276
Atkinson, Henry, 1:20, 1:23

Bailey, David, 2:177
Baptists, 1:115, 1:132
Barbour, James, 1:86, 1:200, 2:7
Barnett, Tony, 1:4, 1:54, 1:214
Bateman, Capt., 2:210–211
Battle of Horseshoe Bend, 1:31
Battle of Lake Okeechobee, 1:35
Battle of New Orleans, 1:31
Battle of Stillman's Run, 1:22, 1:206, 1:224
Baylor, J. R., 1:30
Bayou Mason, 2:180–182
Beattie, William, 1:12
Bell, John (U.S. Secretary of War), 1:16, 1:17, 1:19, 1:103–104, 1:260
Bell, John A. (Cherokee chief), 1:42, 1:60
Benge, John, 1:10, 1:42, 1:43, 2:86
Big Raft, 1:94–95
Big Town, 1:11, 1:12
Big Warrior, 1:160
Black Hawk, 1:20–21
Black Hawk's band, 1:22
Black Hawk War, 1:20, 1:21–24, 1:34; 1:98, 1:121, 1:122, 1:134, 1:203, 1:224, 1:263
Black Seminole, 1:2, 1:35
Bloody Fellow, 1:231–232
Blount, John, 1:11–12
Blount, William, 1:232
Boudinot, Elias, 1:19, 1:24–26, 1:28, 1:187–192, 1:245, 1:269–271, 2:50, 2:52–53, 2:75, 2:84, 2:86, 2:91, 2:97, 2:99, 2:101, 2:258–259; editorial by, January 28, 1829, 2:50–52; editorial by, June 17, 1829, 2:52–53; editorial by, June 19, 1830, 2:53–55
Bourbon County, 2:2
Bowlegs, Billy. See Hulbutta Micco
Boyd, Daniel, 1:12

Brazos River Reserve, 1:29–30
Brish, Henry C., 1:218, 1:220, letters of, 2:175–179
Britons, 2:145
Broglie, Duc de, 2:57
Brothertons (also spelled Brothertowns), 1:97, 1:136, 1:159, 1:162, 1:182, 1:228, 2:46, 2:156, 2:160, 2:162; removal, 1:26–27
Brown, Jacob, 1:48–49, 1:130, 2:197
Brown, James, 1:42, 2:86
Buck, John, 2:137
Buell, James H., 2:267
Buffalo, New York, 1:156–158, 1:229, 2:113, 2:124, 2:131, 2:132, 2:148, 2:156, 2:161
Buffalo Creek reservation, 1:173, 1:238–239, 1:242, 2:113, 2:124, 2:125, 2:127, 2:137, 2:154, 2:161. See also Treaty of Buffalo Creek
Bushyhead, Jesse, 1:42
Butler, Elizur, 1:89, 1:187, 1:197, 1:270
Butrick, Daniel S., 1:27–28, 1:187, 1:270; journal of, 2:245–261
Buzzard Roost, 1:57, 2:23

Caddos, 1:94–95, 1:149, 1:181, 1:200, 1:205; removal, 1:29–30; treaty, 1:29
Caldwell, Billy, 1:30–31
Caldwell's Band of Potawatomis, 1:31
Calhoun, John C., 1:47
Canby, E. R. S., 1:35, 1:93
Cannon, B. B., 1:41, journal of 1837 Cherokee emigration party, 2:229–238; route, 1:42–143
Cape Girardeau, 1:41, 1:62, 1:188
Carroll, William, 1:25, 1:31–33, 1:39, 1:67, 1:90, 1:205, 1:233, 1:245
Cass, Lewis, 1:21, 1:24, 1:33–34, 1:51, 1:68, 1:72, 1:90, 1:136, 1:177, 1:179, 1:187, 1:191, 1:204, 1:228; letter to, 2:194–196; report from (1831), 2:34–42
Catholics, 1:177, 2:265
Catlin, George, paintings by, 1:53, 1:142, 1:150
Cattaraugus reservation, 1:157, 1:173, 1:238–239, 1:242–243, 2:113
Cavallo, John (Gopher John), 1:2, 1:5, 1:34–35, 1:52–53, 1:58, 1:91, 1:101, 1:114, 1:115, 1:214

census, 2:105, 2:142, 2:156
Cherokee "civilization," 1:24, 1:38;
  defense of, 2:50–52
Cherokee Nation v. Georgia, 1:36–37,
  1:67, 1:89, 1:192, 1:262, 1:270, 1:272,
  2:23
Cherokee Phoenix, 1:24–25, 1:38, 1:65,
  1:90, 1:187–88, 1:190, 1:192, 1:245,
  1:269, 1:270; letter to, 2:47–50. *See
  also* Boudinot, Elias, editorials
Cherokees, 1:6–10, 1:13–16, 1:24–26,
  1:27–28, 1:67, 1:84–91, 1:101,
  1:155–116, 1:185–194, 1:198–200,
  1:206–208, 1:231–234, 1:240–241,
  1:245–246, 1:262–267, 1:271–273,
  2:1, 2:17–19, 2:23–25, 2:31–33,
  2:47–48, 2:50–55, 2:59–63, 2:65–69,
  2:86, 2:168, 2:169, 2:219, 2:229,
  2:238–239, 2:241–242, 2:245–261,
  2:261–262; Boudinot removal
  response, 2:97–107; defense of
  civilization, 2:50–52; journal of 1837
  emigration party, 2:229–238;
  journal of 1838 emigration party,
  2:238–245; memorial and protest
  by, 2:75–86; removal, 1:9, 1:32,
  1:37–43, 1:54, 1:60, 1:154, 1:205,
  1:225–227, 1:257, 1:262. *See also*
  Eastern Cherokees; Treaty Party;
  Western Cherokees
Chicago, 1:31, 1:17, 1:224
Chickasaw Commission, 1:46,
  1:109–110, 1:249
Chickasaws, 1:5, 1:6–10, 1:16–19, 1:32,
  1:55–56, 1:56–58, 1:66–67, 1:109–110,
  1:125–127, 1:130, 1:142–143,
  1:231–234, 1:236–238, 1:243, 1:244,
  1:246–250, 1:255, 1:264–266, 2:14,
  2:17, 2:19, 2:22, 2:29, 2:67, 2:168,
  2:172–173, 2:206–207, 2:222; letter of
  chiefs to Andrew Jackson, 2:71–75;
  removal, 1:14–15, 1:44–46
childrearing, 1:268
Chippewas, 1:165–168, 1:206. *See also*
  Saginaw Chippewa removal
Choctaws, 1:5, 1:6–10, 1:13–16, 1:29,
  1:30, 1:44, 1:45, 1:55–56, 1:66–67,
  1:79–81, 1:110, 1:122, 1:125,
  1:127–129, 1:130, 1:134, 1:142–143,
  1:149–150, 1:243–245, 1:246–250,
  1:264, 1:265, 1:237, 1:240, 2:14–15,

2:17, 2:18–19, 2:22, 2:29, 2:43, 2:67,
  2:168–171, 2:179–186; journal of
  1832 emigration party, 2:179–186;
  removal, 1:6, 1:46–50. *See also*
  Mississippi Band of Choctaw Indians
Choctaw Agency, 1:13, 1:16, 1:45, 1:93,
  1:131, 1:145, 1:214, 2:199, 2:202
cholera, 1:12, 1:15, 1:40, 1:45, 1:46,
  1:49, 1:80, 1:135, 1:180, 1:224, 1:264,
  2:181, 2:191
cholera infantum, 1:71, 1:74
Christian community, appeal to, on
  condition and prospect of the New-
  York Indians, 1:230, 2:126–167
church, 1:103, 1:144, 1:150, 1:160,
  1:260, 2:146, 2:152. *See also by
  denomination*; missionaries; religion
Chuwalookee, 1:42
cities: benefits and dangers of, 2:30,
  2:144, 2:146, 2:151, 2:161; eastern in
  which support sought for Indian
  "civilization," 1:24, 1:187, 1:190,
  1:269, 2:270; Indians brought to,
  1:21, 1:23, 1:121, 1:158
citizenship: Cherokee Nation, 1:38,
  1:87, 2:93, 2:257; for Indians, 1:82;
  U.S., 1:26, 1:82, 1:229, 1:275, 2:93,
  2:95; in *Worcester v. Georgia*, 1:39
"civilization" programs, 1:24, 1:27, 1:38,
  1:62, 1:68, 1:103, 1:107, 1:176–177,
  1:204, 1:270, 2:5, 2:7, 2:9–14, 2:17,
  2:29–30, 2:43, 2:49, 2:65–66, 2:76,
  2:100, 2:115–118, 2:122, 2:129,
  2:143–146, 2:160–161, 2:164,
  2:166–167
Clarendon, 1:13, 1:45, 1:49
Clark, William, 1:21, 1:33, 1:50–51,
  1:119–120, 1:128, 1:133–134, 1:202
Clay, Henry, 1:32, 1:105, 1:259, 1:260
Clinch, D. L., 1:76, 1:77, 1:100, 1:208,
  1:210, 1:212
Coacoochee, 1:2, 1:34–35, 1:51–53,
  1:78, 1:93, 1:101, 1:114, 1:122, 1:209,
  1:214
Coe Hadjo, 1:2, 1:34, 1:51, 1:53–54,
  1:114, 1:213–214
Coffee, John, 1:32, 1:55–56, 1:57, 1:66, 1:67,
  1:113, 1:128, 1:129, 1:233, 1:244, 1:247
Colbert, Levi, 1:56–58, 1:109, 1:236,
  1:265, 1:266. *See also* Treaty of
  Pontotoc

Cole, Robert, 1:79, 1:128

Collins, R. D. C., 1:16–17, 1:130

colonies, American, 1:12, 1:84, 1:251, 2:22, 2:60–61, 2:66, 2:139, 2:143–145, 2:154, 2:162

Colston, Daniel, 1:42

Columbus: Georgia, 1:11, 1:70, 1:73, 1:96, 1:197–199; Mississippi, 1:147, 1:198; Ohio, 1:83

Columbus Land Company, 1:126

Comanches, 1:30, 1:77

communities, 1:3, 1:26, 1:61, 1:65, 1:137–140, 1:154, 1:164–166, 1:171, 1:174–177, 1:195–196, 1:201–203, 1:228–232, 1:239, 1:262, 1:265–266, 1:272–273

Confederate Indian forces and sympathizers, 1:93, 1:161, 1:219, 1:255

confederations: Cherokee, 1:64, Creek, 1:11; Iroquois, 1:156, 1:158–159, 1:217, 1:242, 1:267; Peoria, 1:172; Tecumseh, 1:122; Three Fires, 1:176, 1:195

Congregationalists, 1:25, 1:27–28, 1:186, 1:269, 1:271

Continental Congress, 1:24, 1:61; 1:151

contractors, 1:18, 1:59, 1:81, 1:180, 1:222, 1:252, 2:204–206, 2:209–210, 2:224

contracts, 1:12, 1:16–18, 1:42, 1:59, 1:141, 1:147, 1:193, 1:198–199, 1:223, 1:253, 1:256, 2:63, 2:77, 2:123, 2:126, 2:243

corn, 1:15, 1:22, 1:80–82, 1:133, 1:168, 1:263, 1:265, 1:267, 2:17

cotton, 1:3, 1:7, 1:15, 1:47, 1:48, 1:57, 1:125, 1:127, 1:142, 1:143, 2:17

Cowaya, John. See Cavallo, John

Crawford, Hartley, 1:17, 1:18, 1:257–258, 2:137

Crawford County, Ohio, 1:273–274

Creeks, 1:3, 1:5, 1:6–10, 1:11, 1:14–17, 1:32, 1:53, 1:55, 1:68, 1:69–71, 1:72–74, 1:75–82, 1:84–88, 1:93, 1:96, 1:112, 1:114, 1:126, 1:160–161, 1:186, 1:198–199, 1:207, 1:210, 1:212, 1:224, 1:231, 1:250, 1:254, 2:1; removal, 1:146–149. See also McIntosh Creeks; Muscogees (Creeks); Poarch Band of Creek Indians

Creek War: of 1813, 1:111, 1:174: of 1836, 1:8, 1:70, 1:73, 1:87, 1:96,

1:147, 1:174, 1:199, 1:224, 1:225, 1:251–252, 1:263–264, 2:81

crimes, 1:70, 1:232, 1:244, 1:257

Cudjo, 1:4, 1:54, 1:214

cultivation, soil, 2:9, 2:12, 2:20, 2:22, 2:48–49, 2:81, 2:117–119, 2:122, 2:129, 2:144, 2:156

Currey, Benjamin, 1:39–40, 2:82–83, 2:91

Cussetas. See Kasihtas

Daniel, Moses, 1:42

Danville, Illinois, 1:177–178, 2:225–227

Davis, William A., 2:84

Deas, Edward, 1:41–42, 1:59–60; journal of 1837 Creek emigration party, 2:219–224; journal of 1838 Cherokee emigration party, 2:238–245

debts, tribal, 1:44, 1:57, 1:62, 1:72, 1:85, 1:107–108, 1:125, 1:139, 1:220, 1:250–251

Delawares, 1:78, 1:103, 1:107, 1:117–118, 1:209, 1:273, 1:275; removal, 1:60–63. See also Munsee Delawares

Democrats, 1:19, 1:33, 1:153, 1:197, 1:198, 1:256–257, 1:259–261, 1:270

Detroit, 1:33, 1:164, 1:222

diet during removal, 1:73, 1:134–135, 1:178–179

Drane, G. S., 1:42, 1:226

Drane Contingent of Cherokees, 2:261–263

Drew, John, 1:43, 1:193

Dutch Reformed church, 1:204

DuVal, William, 1:70

Eastern Band of Cherokees v. The United States and the Cherokee Nation, 1:65

Eastern Cherokees, 1:64–65; 1:188, 1:204, 1:233

Eaton, John Henry, 1:32, 1:33, 1:55, 1:66–67, 1:72, 1:83, 1:113, 1:128–129, 1:241, 1:244, 1:247, 1:251, 2:52

Econchatimico, 1:11

Ecore Fabre, 1:13, 1:14, 1:48–49, 1:129

Eel River, 1:139, 2:18, 2:21

Elk River, 2:179, 2:220

Ellsworth, Henry L., 1:1, 1:53, 1:68–69, 1:106, 1:133, 1:204–205

Emathlachee, 1:11

emigration, 1:7–8, 1:25, 1:49, 1:53, 1:57,
    1:72, 1:83–84, 1:111–112, 1:146–147,
    1:161, 1:196, 1:199–200, 1:221, 1:225,
    1:250, 1:274, 2:15–16, 2:18–19, 2:32,
    2:47–48, 2:82–83, 2:127–129, 2:133,
    2:164, 2:194–196, 2:219–220, 2:224,
    2:238–239, 2:241, 2:263–267,
    2:269–273, 2:276. *See also* Alabama
    Emigrating Company; Sanford
    Emigrating Company; *individual tribes
    and their removal*
Eneah Emathla (Neamathla), 1:11,
    1:12, 1:69–71, 1:73, 1:96, 1:199, 1:207
Eneah Micco (Neamicco), 1:70,
    1:72–74, 1:96, 1:199, 1:251
enforcement, 1:22, 1:34, 1:119, 1:168,
    1:272, 2:23, 2:33, 2:54
England, 1:85, 1:164, 1:231, 2:64, 2:118,
    2:143, 2:162–163
Episcopal church, 1:175
Erath, George, 1:29
Erie Canal, 1:139, 1:156–158, 1:242
escaped slave advertisements, 2:168–175
Evarts, Jeremiah, 1:27, 1:67, 2:55–70
Everglades, 1:99, 1:215, 1:216, 1:234,
    1:235

factionalism, tribal, 1:79, 1:170–171,
    1:230, 1:239, 1:242
Fanning, Alexander, 1:51
farmers, 1:7, 1:11, 1:113, 1:143–144,
    1:160–161, 1:168, 1:171, 1:198, 1:233,
    1:267, 2:89, 2:253
federal government, 1:36–37, 1:62–63,
    1:75–76, 1:87–89, 1:97–98, 1:107–108,
    1:140–141, 1:146–147, 1:151–153,
    1:154, 1:158–160, 1:162–163,
    1:195–196, 1:209–211, 1:218–219,
    1:231–232, 1:272–274
First Seminole War, 1:1, 1:69, 1:76,
    1:208
Five Civilized Tribes, 1:46–47, 1:106,
    1:144
flatboats, 1:10, 1:40, 1:41, 1:43, 1:193,
    1:212, 1:241, 2:220
Florida and Indian removal, 1:75–79
Folsom, David, 1:79–81
food, 1:81–82
Forsyth, John, 1:104, 2:24
Fox Indians. *See* Sauk and Musquakie
    (Fox)

Fox River, 1:26, 1:97, 1:135–136, 1:162,
    1:182, 1:228
Franklin, J., 2:4
Franklin, State of, 1:232
Franklin, Tennessee, 1:66, 1:128, 1:143,
    1:243, 1:247
French and Indian War, 1:61, 1:122
Fuckalusti Harjo, 2:203
Fuller, Andrew, 2:278
Fulsom, David, 2:184
Fulton, John T., 2:178

Gadsden, James, 1:11, 1:76, 1:204, 1:211
Gaines, Edmund P., 1:2, 1:86, 1:186,
    1:224
Gallatin, Albert, 1:31, 2:4
gambling, 2:170, 2:250–253, 2:256
Gardiner, James B., 1:83–84, 1:217,
    1:219–221, 2:187–190
Garland, John, 1:79–80
Garland, Samuel, 1:127–128
Gasconade River, 2:192, 2:236
Gates, William, 1:52
General Allotment Act, 1:106
Georgia: act of 1828 to appropriate
    Cherokee territory within state,
    2:23–24; and Indian removal,
    1:84–91; legislature, 1:28, 1:36–38,
    1:89, 1:103–104, 1:190, 1:197, 1:271;
    penitentiary, 1:88, 1:270–271,
    2:31–32, 2:79, 2:250
Georgia Committee Report, 2:24–27
Georgia Compact, 1:31, 1:84, 1:102,
    1:124, 1:127, 1:227, 1:262, 2:1–4
Georgia Guard, 1:38, 1:89–90, 1:188,
    1:190, 1:197–198, 1:265, 2:31, 2:80,
    2:82, 2:255
Gilmer, George R., 1:32, 1:40, 1:90,
    1:197–198, 2:34
Glasgow & Harrison, 1:16, 1:17
gold, 1:32, 1:38, 1:88, 1:187, 1:192,
    1:197, 2:31, 2:34, 2:79, 2:105–107,
    2:256
Gopher John. *See* Cavallo, John
governance, 1:152, 1:169, 1:171, 1:229,
    1:239, 1:243, 1:260
Green Bay, 1:97, 1:135–137, 1:159,
    1:162, 1:183, 1:228

Halleck Tustenuggee, 1:35, 1:92–94,
    1:101, 1:214, 1:235

Harkins, George, 1:129, 1:150, 1:244

Harris, Carey A., 1:113, 1:233, 1:256, 2:224

Harris, Joseph W., 1:40

Harrison, William Henry, 1:19, 1:62, 1:107–108, 1:202, 1:257, 1:260

Haughton, Richard, 2:170

Heckaton, 1:94–95, 1:181, 1:200

Henry (McHenry), Jim, 1:70, 1:71, 1:73, 1:95–97, 1:199, 1:224

Hernandez, Joseph M., 1:34, 1:51–52, 1:54

Hichitis, 1:11, 1:69, 1:70, 1:72, 1:95, 1:96, 1:199

Hicks, Elijah, 1:42, 2:82, 2:86

Hicks, George, 1:42, 2:256

Hilderbrand, Peter, 1:42

Hitchcock, Ethan Allen, 1:6–19, 1:79, 1:207, 1:209, 1:260

Ho-Chunk Indians, 1:22; removal, 1:97–98, 1:159, 1:162–163, 1:203, 1:206. *See also* Winnebagos

Hogan, John B., 1:73

Hog Creek Shawnees, 1:83, 1:218, 1:222, 1:273, 2:186

Honey Creek, 1:25, 1:189, 1:191

Hopewell Treaty, 1:104, 1:231–232

Horse, John. *See* Cavallo, John

Hulbutta Micco (Billy Bowlegs), 1:1, 1:3, 1:26, 1:99–100, 1:215–216, 1:234–236

Hulbutta Tustenuggee (Alligator), 1:2, 1:35, 1:52–53, 1:77, 1:100–101, 1:208, 1:213

humanity, 2:8, 2:14, 2:16, 2:26, 2:30, 2:41, 2:50, 2:78–79, 2:81, 2:84, 2:114–115, 2:117–118, 2:122

Humboldt, Baron, 2:57

Humphreys, Gad, 1:70

hunters, 2:20, 2:26, 2:30, 2:40, 2:43, 2:51–52, 2:203; bounty, 1:235; Caddo, 1:29; gold, 1:192; slave, 1:12, 1:101, 1:214

Illinois, 1:20, 1:21–24, 1:31, 1:41, 1:50, 1:97, 1:119, 1:122, 1:133–134, 1:168–169, 1:172, 1:202–203, 1:224, 2:18, 2:186, 2:190, 2:225–226

Indiana and removal, 1:107–109

Indian Removal Act, 1:3, 1:6, 1:9, 1:32, 1:34, 1:38, 1:62, 1:66, 1:68, 1:76, 1:102–106, 1:111–112, 1:153, 1:154, 1:259, 2:27–29

Indian Territory, 1:106–107

Indian Vaccination Act, 1:135, 1:166

Indian women: during removal, 1:262–267; roles and removal, 1:267–269

Iroquois, 1:156, 1:158–159, 1:170–172, 1:217, 1:238–239, 1:241–243, 1:267

Ishtehotopa, 1:46, 1:109–110, 1:238, 1:264, 2:75

Jackson, Andrew, 1:6, 1:8, 1:10, 1:11, 1:16–19, 1:21, 1:23, 1:25, 1:31–32, 1:33, 1:39, 1:41, 1:47, 1:55, 1:66–67, 1:102–105, 1:111–113, 1:143, 1:153–154, 1:187, 1:220, 1:224–225, 1:233, 1:243–244, 1:247, 1:256–258, 1:259–260, 2:113, 2:127; letter from Chickasaw chiefs to, 2:71–75, second annual presidential message, 2:29–31

Jacksonian Era, 1:34, 1:43, 1:56, 1:68–69, 1:106–107, 1:113, 1:129, 1:155, 1:167, 1:197, 1:205, 1:245, 1:258, 1:261

Jacksonville, 1:13, 1:178–179

jail, 1:23, 1:71, 1:96, 1:235, 1:237, 2:32, 2:82, 2:168–175

Jarvis, Nathan, 1:54

Jefferson, Thomas, 1:6, 1:13, 1:102, 1:108, 1:151, 1:153, 1:201; "civilization" program, 1:62

Jefferson Barracks, 1:20, 1:23, 1:121

Jesup, Thomas S., 1:2, 1:5, 1:52, 1:54, 1:70, 1:73, 1:77–78, 1:114, 1:208–209, 1:224–225, 1:252, 1:254–255

Jim Boy. *See* Tustenuggee Emathla

Johnson, Joseph, 1:26

Jones, Evan, 1:27–28, 1:115–116, 1:269–270

Jones, Sam, 1:99–100, 1:234

journals of emigration parties, 2:179–186, 2:186–194, 2:196–203, 2:203–219, 2:219–224, 2:224–228, 2:229–238, 2:238–245, 2:245–261, 2:263–279

Jumper, John, 1:2, 1:53, 1:77, 1:78, 1:100, 1:208–209, 1:213, 1:215, 1:235–236

jurisdiction, 1:6, 1:32–33, 1:36–39, 1:79, 1:89, 1:103, 1:112, 1:147, 1:187, 1:192,

1:243, 1:245, 1:250, 1:270, 1:272, 2:1, 2:3, 2:26, 2:35–36, 2:43, 2:47, 2:53, 2:68, 2:78, 2:80, 2:92, 2:113, 2:126
justice, 1:26, 1:36–37, 1:39, 1:68, 1:89, 1:109, 1:147, 1:179, 1:251, 1:262, 1:264, 1:272, 2:7–9, 2:13–14, 2:34, 2:36, 2:49–50, 2:54–55, 2:58, 2:63–65, 2:70, 2:82, 2:85, 2:91, 2:96, 2:122, 2:140–141, 2:252

Kansas, 1:23, 1:31, 1:53, 1:62–63, 1:108–109, 1:119–122, 1:137, 1:140, 1:161–162, 1:164–166, 1:172, 1:185, 1:203, 1:274–275, 2:114, 2:127, 2:194
Kansas-Nebraska Act, 1:63, 1:117, 1:275
Kansas territory and Indian removal, 1:117–118
Kasihtas (Cussetas), 1:70, 1:73, 1:96, 1:199, 1:251–252
Kaskaskias. See Peoria-Kaskaskia-Piankeshaw-Wea removal
keelboats, 1:40–41, 1:146–147, 1:198, 1:212–213, 1:241, 2:197
Kennekuk, 1:119–120, 1:122, 1:133–134, 1:168–169
Keokuk, 1:120–122
Kickapoos, 1:133–134, 1:168–169, 1:172; removal, 1:122–123
Kingsbury, G. P., 1:17
Kishko, 1:119

land cession treaties, 1:33, 1:51, 1:176, 1:238, 1:242, 1:273
land speculation, 1:6, 1:32, 1:44, 1:70, 1:72, 1:143–144, 1:174, 1:195, 1:197–198, 1:238, 1:242, 1:244, 1:248, 1:253, 1:256, 1:266; and Indian removal, 1:124–127
Lane, J. F., 1:81, 1:84, 1:221, 2:187, 2:193
languages, Indian, 1:25, 1:27, 1:64–65, 1:72, 1:89, 1:115, 1:139, 1:140, 1:159, 1:230, 1:269–270, 2:131, 2:172, 2:174, 2:262
LeFlore, Greenwood, 1:47–48, 1:66, 1:79–80, 1:127–129, 1:149, 1:244
legislation, removal, 1:6, 1:27, 1:87, 1:102–106, 1:108, 1:112, 1:135, 1:140, 1:187, 1:262, 2:27, 2:36, 2:44, 2:49, 2:58, 2:76–77, 2:79, 2:94, 2:101, 2:165; Great Society, 1:145

Lewis, Meriwether, 1:50
Lillybridge, Clark, 1:40
Little Rock Office of Removal and Subsistence, 1:130–131
Little Turtle, 1:15, 1:184
Longhouse religion, 1:113, 1:127
Louisiana, 1:29, 1:48–49, 1:95, 1:106, 1:125, 1:181, 1:225, 2:66
Louisiana Purchase, 1:6, 1:13, 1:50, 1:103, 1:181, 1:201
Lowrey, George, 1:4, 1:190

Makataimeshekiakiak. See Black Hawk
Manypenny, George, 1:117
marriages, 2:74, 2:118; intermarriage, 1:268, 2:195
Marshall, John, 1:36, 1:39, 1:89, 1:173, 1:262, 1:270–273
Martin, John, 1:90, 2:80, 2:86
Mashpees, 1:154–155; Revolt, 1:154
Maumee River, 1:164
McCauley, Clay, 1:79, 1:209–210
McCoy, Isaac, 1:67, 1:106, 1:115, 1:119, 1:132–133, 2:176–177
McHenry, Jim. See Henry, Jim
McIntosh, Roley, 1:71, 1:255
McIntosh, William, 1:7, 1:70, 1:72, 1:76, 1:85, 1:146, 1:160, 1:161, 1:186, 1:210–211, 1:227
McIntosh Creeks, 1:197–198, 1:204
McKenney, Thomas, 1:56; removal report, 2:14–23
Mecina, 1:122, 1:133–134, 1:168–169
medicine and disease, 1:134–135
Memphis, 1:13–15, 1:42, 1:44–45, 1:49, 1:59–60, 1:110, 1:147–149, 1:198–199, 1:222, 1:233, 1:252–253, 1:255, 1:266
Menominee (chief), 1:109, 1:177
Menominees, 1:26, 1:97, 1:159–160, 1:162–163, 1:182–183, 1:228–229, 2:203–204, 2:209–212, 2:222, 2:240; removal, 1:135–137; statement concerning treaties, 2:46–47, 2:128–129, 2:148
merchants, 1:9, 1:19, 1:44, 1:46, 1:80, 1:108, 1:126, 1:185, 1:233, 1:244
Mesquakie (Fox) Indians. See Sauk and Mesquakie (Fox)
Methodists, 1:96, 1:106, 1:118, 1:119, 1:154, 1:159, 1:273, 1:275
Metoxin, John, 1:137, 1:238

Mexican War, 1:29–30, 1:207
Mexico, 1:35, 1:252–253
Miamis, 1:107–108, 1:152, 1:184–185,
    1:228, 1:235; removal, 1:137–140
Miccosukees, 1:69, 1:92–93, 1:99,
    1:140–141, 1:215–217, 1:234, 1:236
Miccosukee Seminole Nation,
    1:140–141, 1:236
Michigan, 1:33–34, 1:106, 1:124, 1:139,
    1:151, 1:166, 1:176, 1:195–196, 1:205,
    1:222
Michigan Ottawas, 1:164–166
Miconopy, 1:1–3, 1:34, 1:51, 1:54,
    1:77–78, 1:99, 1:100, 1:114,
    1:141–142, 1:208, 2:213–214
migrations, 1:22, 1:47, 1:136–137, 1:140,
    1:172
minko, 1:46, 1:56, 1:109–110, 1:236,
    1:238, 1:264
missionaries, 1:24, 1:27–28, 1:47, 1:50,
    1:61–62, 1:66, 1:106, 1:115–116,
    1:122, 1:129, 1:132, 1:138, 1:150,
    1:187, 1:196–198, 1:269–271, 2:8,
    2:25, 2:51, 2:79, 2:113–114,
    2:126–127, 2:132, 2:146, 2:176, 2:245,
    2:252–253, 2:255. See also by
    denomination; church; religion
Mississippi (state), 1:6, 1:9, 1:32, 1:44,
    1:47–48, 1:56, 1:57, 1:79, 1:84, 1:102,
    1:112, 1:125, 1:127, 1:128–129, 1:237,
    1:243–244, 1:266; and Indian
    removal, 1:142–143
Mississippians, white, 1:47, 1:50,
    1:142–143
Mississippi Band of Choctaw Indians,
    1:7, 1:50, 1:144–146
Mississippi River, 1:22–23, 1:40,
    1:42–43, 1:73, 1:77, 1:94, 1:130,
    1:205, 1:212
Mississippi Swamp, 1:14, 1:42, 1:45,
    1:49, 1:252, 1:255, 1:264
Monmouth, 1:149, 1:254–255, 1:264
Monroe, James, 1:47, 1:102, 1:111,
    1:270; pro-removal presidential
    message, 2:4–6
Montgomery, Alabama, 1:8, 1:71, 1:73,
    1:96, 1:148, 1:199, 1:254
Montgomery, Hugh, 2:83, 2:183
Mooney, James, 1:64
mountains, 1:29, 1:64–65, 1:93, 1:157,
    1:231, 1:233, 2:7, 2:49, 2:69, 2:92,

2:105–106, 2:121, 2:202, 2:217, 2:220,
    2:222, 2:230
Mouth of Cache, 1:13, 1:45, 1:49
Mulatto King, 1:11
Munsee Delawares, 1:227–228
Munsees, 1:62, 1:136, 1:228–229, 2:44,
    2:128, 2:160, 2:162. See also
    Stockbridge-Munsees
Muscle Shoals, 1:10, 1:43, 1:231, 2:221
Muscogees (Creeks), 1:5, 1:11–12, 1:14,
    1:46, 1:58–60, 1:67–70, 1:72, 1:96,
    1:114, 1:126, 1:130, 1:146–148,
    1:209–211, 1:240, 1:250, 1:252–253;
    journal of 1836 emigration party,
    2:203–219; journal of 1836 emigration
    party, 2:219–224; removal, 1:4, 1:7,
    1:14, 1:59, 1:146–149. See also Creeks
Mushulatubbee, 1:47, 1:79–80,
    1:128–129, 1:149–150, 1:244

Nas-wa-kay, 2:225–226
National Party, 1:39, 1:188, 1:245
Neamathla. See Eneah Emathla
Neamicco. See Eneah Micco
Neapope, 1:20, 1:21, 1:169
negro-Indians, 1:5
Ne-ta-ki-jah, 2:170
New Orleans, 1:4, 1:12, 1:31, 1:52, 1:71,
    1:73, 1:96, 1:99, 1:101, 1:111, 1:130,
    1:148, 1:213–215, 1:254
newspapers, 1:83–84, 1:115, 1:154,
    1:224, 1:240. See also Cherokee Phoenix
Nitakechi, 1:48, 1:80, 1:128–129, 1:144,
    1:149, 1:244
Northwest Ordinance, 1:151–153
nullification, 1:112–113, 1:127, 1:243,
    1:270, 1:272, 2:24, 2:29; and removal,
    1:153–155

Oath Act, 1:28
Occom, Samson, 1:26
Ogden, David A., 1:157
Ogden Land Company, 1:124, 1:136,
    1:137, 1:156–159, 1:169–171,
    1:228–229, 1:238–239, 1:241–243,
    2:113, 2:123, 2:127–128, 2:130, 2:141,
    2:143, 2:165
Ohio (state), 1:24, 1:33, 1:50, 1:61, 1:83,
    1:84, 1:124, 1:152, 1:217–218, 273,
    2:175, 2:186. See also Shawnee
    removal from Ohio

Ohio Indians, 1:25, 1:61, 1:81, 1:83,
    1:107, 1:124, 1:132, 1:139, 1:152,
    1:222, 1:274, 2:18, 2:21, 2:34, 2:41;
    journal of 1832 emigration party,
    2:186–194
Ohio Ottawas, 1:164–166
Ohio River, 1:40–41, 1:139, 1:146,
    1:152, 1:274
Oklahoma Creeks, 1:175
Old Fields, 1:42
Old Settlers, 1:26, 1:189, 1:193
Omnibus Treaty, 1:172, 1:219
Oneidas, 1:26–27, 1:97, 1:136,
    1:159–160 1:162, 1:182, 1:217, 1:228,
    1:242
Opothleyohola, 1:70, 1:72, 1:86, 1:96,
    1:160–162, 1:186, 1:250, 1:253
orphans, 1:19, 1:44, 1:46, 1:126, 1:249,
    1:267
Osages, 1:16, 1:94, 1:130, 1:181,
    1:200–201
Oscen Tustenuggee, 1:235
Osceola, 1:2, 1:51, 1:54, 1:77–78, 1:100,
    1:114, 1:141, 1:208–209, 1:212–214
Oshkosh, 1:136, 1:162–163
Ottawas, 1:24, 1:83, 1:97, 1:132,
    1:163–167, 1:169, 1:195, 1:206,
    1:218–219, 1:221; removal, 1:163–167.
    See also Michigan Ottawas; Ohio
    Ottawas
Overton, John, 1:31

Panoahah, 1:122, 1:123, 1:168–169
paper money, 1:115
papers, treaty, 1:53, 1:53, 1:248
Parker, Ely S., 1:169–171, 1:229, 1:239
Parker, Nicholson, 1:171–172, 1:229,
    1:239
Pass Christian, Mississippi, 1:8,
    1:148–149, 1:254, 1:265
Penn, William, 1:61
Penn, William (pseudonym of Jeremiah
    Evarts), essays, 2:55–70
Peoria-Kaskaskia-Piankeshaw-Wea
    removal, 1:172–173
Peorias. *See* Peoria-Kaskaskia-
    Piankeshaw-Wea removal
Pepper, Abel C., 1:108, 2:24;
    Potawatomi response to, 2:107–113
Piankeshaws. *See* Peoria-Kaskaskia-
    Piankeshaw-Wea removal

Pierce, Maris Bryant, 1:173–174, 1:229,
    1:230
Poarch Band of Creek Indians, 1:9,
    1:149, 1:174–175
Pokagon, Leopold, 1:177, 1:179
Pokagon Band of Potawatomi, 1:176,
    1:179–180
politics, 1:31, 1:34, 1:37, 1:90–91, 1:96,
    1:104, 1:135, 1:149, 1:154–155, 1:162,
    1:172, 1:199, 1:227, 1:231, 1:251,
    1:257
Polke, William, 1:178, 2:263
population: African-descended, 1:5;
    Indian, 1:3, 1:4, 1:8, 1:50, 1:75, 1:121,
    1:210, 1:232–233, 2:17, 2:56–57,
    2:105–106, 2:120–122, 2:156,
    2:158–159; Little Rock, 1:131;
    unfavorable mixing, 2:106, 2:141,
    2:144, 2:151; white American, 1:3,
    1:38, 1:102, 1:152, 1:158, 1:202, 1:242,
    2:10, 2:29–31, 2:44, 2:48–49, 2:67,
    2:69, 2:100, 2:121, 2:147–149, 2:156
postremoval, 1:16, 1:93, 1:207, 1:237,
    1:264, 1:269
Potawatomis, 1:24, 1:31, 1:97,
    1:107–109, 1:120, 1:132–133,
    1:135–136, 1:166, 1:169, 1:175–180,
    1:195, 1:223, 1:225–226, 1:266,
    2:107–108, 2:224, 2:263, 2:279;
    journal of 1838 emigration party,
    2:263–279; removal, 1:175–180
Potawatomis of Wabash response to
    Pepper, A. C., 2:107–113
pre-emption claims, 2:78, 2:125, 2:149,
    2:155, 2:159, 2:161, 2:163, 2:165
Presbyterians, 1:137, 2:248, 2:256
prison and prisoners, 1:23, 1:28, 1:52,
    1:54, 1:71, 1:73, 1:93, 1:100, 1:114,
    1:120, 1:141, 1:148, 1:178, 1:214,
    1:266, 1:270–271, 2:82, 2:111, 2:246–
    248, 2:251, 2:260
Proffit, George H., removal journal,
    2:224–228
pro-removal sentiment, 1:3, 1:28, 1:80,
    1:102, 1:114, 1:128, 1:142, 1:187,
    1:204, 1:206, 1:208, 1:229, 1:233,
    1:249, 1:260

Quakers, 1:105, 1:173, 1:220, 1:239,
    1:242, 2:114, 2:127, 2:132, 2:135,
    2:140, 2:142–144

Quapaws, 1:16, 1:94–95, 1:130, 1:172,
1:200–201, 1:205; removal, 1:181–182
Quinney, John W., 1:182–183, 1:228

Raines, Austin J., 1:16–17
Red Jacket, 1:157–158, 1:160, 1:238,
1:242, 2:117, 2:139
Red River, 1:6, 1:14, 1:29–30, 1:80,
1:94–95, 1:150, 1:181, 1:200, 1:205,
1:244–245, 2:170, 2:199
Red Stick War, 1:69, 1:76, 1:189, 1:211,
1:253
refugees, 1:12, 1:65, 1:148
religion, 1:119–120, 1:159, 1:162, 1:177,
1:293, 2:30, 2:38, 2:40, 2:50, 2:51,
2:78, 2:122, 2:143, 2:250, 2:251, 2:258.
See also by denomination; church;
missionaries
Revolutionary War, 1:84, 1:85, 1:113,
1:152, 1:159, 1:217, 2:113, 2:126,
2:148
Reynolds, John, 1:22, 1:169, 1:224
Richardville, Jean Baptiste, 1:137–139,
1:184–185
Ridge, John, 1:4, 1:19, 1:24–25,
1:185–189, 1:246, 2:84, 2:95
Ridge, Major, 1:25, 1:189–191,
1:245–246, 2:95, 2:257
Rock River, 1:20, 1:22, 1:168, 1:202–203,
1:224
Rock Roe, 1:14, 1:49, 1:59, 1:71, 1:73,
1:148, 1:161, 1:253, 2:179, 2:183,
2:211
Rollins v. Cherokees, 1:65
Ross, John, 1:4, 1:10, 1:25, 1:28, 1:38,
1:39, 1:42–43, 1:54, 1:64, 1:85, 1:90,
1:114, 1:116, 1:188, 1:190,
1:191–194, 1:207, 1:213, 1:227,
1:233, 1:245–246, 2:75, 2:80;
Boudinot response to "Letter to a
Friend," 2:97–107, 2:261–262; letter
(1836), 2:86–97
Ross, Lewis, 1:42, 2:86

Sabbath, 2:247–251, 2:272, 2:274
Saginaw Chippewa removal, 1:195–197
Sanderson, James S., 1:52
Sandusky River, 1:83, 1:217, 1:219,
1:221
Sanford, John W. A., 1:12, 1:73, 1:89,
1:197–200

Sanford Emigrating Company, 1:12,
1:59, 1:71, 1:73, 1:147, 1:198–199
Sarasin, 1:95, 1:181, 1:200–201
Sauganash. *See* Caldwell, Billy
Sauk and Mesquakie (Fox) Indians,
1:20–23, 1:82, 1:97, 1:106, 1:120–121,
1:135–136, 1:163, 1:168–169, 1:172,
1:206; removal, 1:201–204
Saukenuk, 1:20, 1:22, 1:168, 1:203
Schermerhorn, John F., 1:1, 1:25, 1:32,
1:39, 1:53, 1:68, 1:90, 1:95, 1:106,
1:133, 1:188, 1:192, 1:200, 1:204–205,
1:242, 1:245; 2:81, 2:85, 2:90–94, 2:96,
2:158–259
Schoolcraft, Henry Rowe, 1:166,
1:205–206
schools, 1:11, 1:24–25, 1:33, 1:82, 1:118,
1:144–145, 1:160, 1:170–171, 1:173,
1:175, 1:181, 1:184–185, 1:187–188,
1:190, 1:258, 2:235
Scott, Winfield, 1:10, 1:17, 1:18, 1:41,
1:65, 1:206–208, 1:226, 2:245,
2:261–262
Second Creek War. *See* Creek War of
1836
Second Seminole War, 1:2, 1:12, 1:35,
1:54, 1:67, 1:68, 1:99, 1:206,
1:208–210, 1:212–214, 1:223–225,
1:234–235
self-governance, Indian, 1:37, 1:57,
1:272, 2:88
self-interest, 1:138, 2:55, 2:102
Seminoles, 1:2–6, 1:11–12, 1:16–17,
1:34–35, 1:51–55, 1:67–71, 1:74–79,
1:92–94, 1:99–101, 1:112–114,
1:140–142, 1:204–217, 1:223–225,
1:234–236, 1:240–241, 1:265–266;
journal of 1836 emigration party,
2:196–203; removal, 1:1, 1:11, 1:14,
1:51, 1:67, 1:210–216
Seminole Tribe of Florida, 1:216–217
Seminole Wars, 1:75–76. *See also* First
Seminole War; Second Seminole
War; Third Seminole War
Senecas, 1:16, 1:81, 1:83, 1:130,
1:156–158, 1:170–171, 1:173–174,
1:205, 1:217–222, 1:229–230,
1:238–239, 1:241–242; removal,
1:217–219; of Sandusky, 1:217, 1:220,
2:175, 2:177, 2:186. *See also*
Tonawanda Senecas

Senecas of Ohio; Brish letters about removal, 2:175–179

Shawnee removal from Ohio, 1:219–222; journal of 1832 emigration party, 2:186–194

Shawnees, 1:16, 1:31, 1:61, 1:63–64, 1:78, 1:81–82, 1:107, 1:117–118, 1:124, 1:130, 1:205, 1:209, 1:217–222, 1:231, 1:273–274. *See also* Wapakoneta Shawnees

Sherman, William T., 1:52

Situwakee, 1:42, 1:116

slavery, 1:3, 1:75, 1:77, 2:3, 2:39, 2:57, 2:71, 2:166, 2:168–169, 2:171, 2:174–175, 2:243. *See also* escaped slave advertisements

Smith, Archilla, 2:84

Smith, Benjamin, 1:57

soldiers, 1:23, 1:31, 1:41, 1:47, 1:50–51, 1:78, 1:81, 1:109, 1:139, 1:152, 1:185, 1:207, 1:209, 1:213, 1:241, 1:265, 2:81, 2:88, 2:207, 2:215, 2:245–251, 2:255

Southern and Northern Methodist Episcopal church, 1:118

sovereignty: American, 1:33; Indian, 1:27, 1:37–38, 1:65, 1:89–90, 1:105, 1:141, 1:192, 1:262, 1:270, 1:272–273, 2:34, 2:59, 2:70, 2:78, of states, 1:103–104, 1:153, 2:24–27, 2:154, 2:256

Spencer, John, 1:17–18

Sprague, John T., 1:92, 1:199, 1:222–223, 1:252; journal of 1836 Creek emigration party, 2:203–219

Sprague, Peleg, 1:104

St. Augustine, 1:35, 1:52, 1:54, 1:92, 1:213–214

St. Francis County, Arkansas, 1:171–172

St. Francis River, 1:13–14, 1:45, 2:234

St. Louis, 1:16, 1:20, 1:23, 1:50–51, 1:94, 1:119–121, 1:139, 1:177, 1:201, 1:218, 1:274

state militias and removal, 1:223–227

steamboats, 1:7–8, 1:10, 1:14–15, 1:23, 1:40–43, 1:45, 1:49, 1:59, 1:71, 1:139, 1:146–149, 1:198–199, 1:212–215, 1:218, 1:226–227, 1:265–266, 2:175, 2:179, 2:187, 2:197, 2:203, 2:261

Stephenson, J. R., 1:81, 2:218

Stockbridge-Munsees, 1:26–27, 1:137, 1:159–160, 1:162, 1:182; removal, 1:227–229. *See also* Munsees; Stockbridges

Stockbridges, 1:97, 1:136–137, 1:228–229

Stokes, Montfort, 1:1, 1:53, 1:68, 1:106, 1:133, 1:204–205

Stokes Commission, 1:1, 1:53, 1:95, 1:132–133, 2:186

Strong, Nathaniel Thayer, 1:229–230; "Appeal to Christian Community," 2:126–167

Swan Creek, 1:195–196, 1:205, 1:228

Tampa Bay, 1:2, 1:4, 1:34, 1:51–52, 1:77, 1:100, 1:208, 1:212, 1:214, 1:234

Tapanahoma, 1:79, 1:128

Taylor, Richard, 1:42, 1:90, 2:81

Taylor, Zachary, 1:78, 1:100, 1:209

teachers, 1:115, 1:185, 2:16–17, 2:89, 2:120, 2:146, 2:245, 2:250

Tennessee, 1:10, 1:17, 1:28, 1:31–32, 1:38, 1:41, 1:66, 1:90, 1:103, 1:111, 1:189, 1:225–226, 2:18, 2:80–81, 2:229; and Indian removal, 1:231–234

Tennessee River, 1:9–10, 1:40–41, 1:43, 1:57, 1:146–147, 1:193, 1:226, 2:2, 2:17, 2:219–220

Terrell, John, 1:247–249

territories, 1:13–14, 1:22–24, 1:36, 1:47, 1:50–51, 1:61–63, 1:67, 1:76, 1:105–107, 1:117–118, 1:132–133, 1:151–152, 1:156–157, 1:178, 1:202, 1:271–274

Third Seminole War, 1:75, 1:79, 1:99–100, 1:209–210, 1:215–216, 1:22579, 1:234–236

Thomas, William H., 1:65

Thompson, Wiley, 1:54, 1:100

Three Fires Confederation, 1:176, 1:195

Tishomingo, 1:236–238

Tonawandas, 1:158, 1:169–171, 1:238–239, 1:242–243

Tonawanda Senecas, 1:238–239

townships, 1:11–12, 1:26–27, 1:40, 1:60–62, 1:69–70, 1:72, 1:85–86, 1:96, 1:115, 1:182–183, 1:186–187, 1:190, 1:231–232, 1:250–252, 1:254, 1:274–275

trade, 1:3, 1:5, 1:16, 1:31, 1:56, 1:97, 1:106–109, 1:138–139, 1:162, 1:164–165, 1:184–185, 1:196, 1:199–202, 1:216, 1:221, 1:250–251

traders, 1:69, 1:108, 1:138–139, 1:162
Trail of Tears, 1:43, 1:193, 1:240–241;
    National Historic Trail legislation,
    1:241
Treasury. *See* U. S. Department of the
    Treasury
treaty commissioners, American,
    1:23–24, 1:34, 1:47, 1:203, 1:273
Treaty of Buffalo Creek, 1:158, 1:170,
    1:171, 1:173, 1:229, 1:238, 1:241–243
Treaty of Chicago, 1:31
Treaty of Dancing Rabbit Creek, 1:6–7,
    1:32, 1:48, 1:55, 1:66, 1:80, 1:125,
    1:129, 1:130, 1:143–144, 1:149,
    1:243–245
Treaty of Doak's Stand, 1:13, 1:47,
    1:127, 1:142–143
Treaty of Doaksville, 1:44, 1:57, 1:249
Treaty of Fort Jackson, 1:9, 1:85, 1:149,
    1:174
Treaty of Franklin, 1:44, 1:55, 1:57,
    1:66, 1:143, 1:244, 1:247, 1:249, 1:265,
    2:29
Treaty of Greenville, 1:61, 1:107, 1:164,
    1:176, 1:184
Treaty of Indian Springs, 1:7, 1:72, 1:85,
    1:86, 1:146–147, 1:160, 1:198
Treaty of Moultrie Creek, 1:1, 1:11,
    1:69–70, 1:76, 1:141, 1:211, 1:266
Treaty of New Echota, 1:4, 1:10, 1:25,
    1:32, 1:39, 1:60, 1:65, 1:186, 1:188,
    1:191–192, 1:205, 1:225, 1:233, 1:245,
    1:245–246, 1:271, 2:75, 2:97
Treaty of Payne's Landing, 1:1, 1:5,
    1:11, 1:53–54, 1:68, 1:77, 1:101, 1:204,
    1:212, 1:246–250
Treaty of Pontotoc, 1:5, 1:9, 1:32, 1:44,
    1:56–57, 1:109, 1:126, 1:143, 1:148,
    1:236, 1:238, 1:246–250, 1:265
Treaty of Prairie du Chien, 1:51
Treaty of Washington, 1:8, 1:32, 1:47,
    1:87, 1:125, 1:147, 1:174, 1:186, 1:197,
    1:250–251, 1:253, 1:266, 2:72, 2:74–75
Treaty Party (Cherokee), 1:4, 1:25–26,
    1:28, 1:32, 1:39–42, 1:90, 1:188–189,
    1:191–193, 1:245, 1:257, 1:271
Troup, George, 1:85–87
Troy, Missouri, 1:218, 2:175
Tuckabatche Hadjo, 1:251–253
Tukose Emathla (John Hicks), 1:70,
    1:141

Turner, Nat, 1:3
Tuski Hajo, 1:11
Tustenuggee Emathla (Jim Boy), 1:70,
    1:73, 1:96, 1:161, 1:174, 1:225,
    1:253–255
Twin Lakes Indians, 1:109, 1:178–179,
    1:225–226, 2:263
Tyler, John, 1:18–19, 1:207, 1:257,
    1:260–261

United Brethren, 2:256
United Nation of Senecas and
    Shawnees, 1:204, 1:218, 1:221, 2:186
Upper Sandusky, 1:273–274
U.S. Army, 1:4–5, 1:23, 1:30, 1:31, 1:35,
    1:41, 1:52, 1:54, 1:70, 1:73, 1:96,
    1:100, 1:111, 1:122, 1:161, 1:214,
    1:223, 1:227, 1:254
U.S. Department of the Treasury, 1:18,
    1:170, 1:207, 2:2, 2:140, 2:147, 2:152,
    2:157

Van Buren, Martin, 1:19, 1:109, 1:173,
    1:226, 1:242, 1:256–258, 1:260, 2:259;
    first annual presidential message,
    2:43–45
Van Horne, J., journal of 1832 Choctaw
    emigration party, 2:179–186; journal
    of 1836 Seminole emigration party,
    2:196–203
Vann, "Rich" Joe, 1:215
Vesey, Denmark, 1:3
Vicksburg, Mississippi, 1:7, 1:48–49,
    1:80; 2:179
villages, 1:7, 1:20, 1:22, 1:62, 1:101,
    1:109, 1:114, 1:119, 1:139, 1:165,
    1:177, 1:202–203, 1:217, 1:225, 1:273,
    2:17, 2:146, 2:151, 2:163, 2:176, 2:189,
    2:195–196, 2:206, 2:253, 2:265–266,
    2:269, 2:275
violence, 1:12, 1:21–24, 1:41, 1:50, 1:61,
    1:63, 1:72, 1:113, 1:126, 1:138, 1:148,
    1:166, 1:194, 1:202, 1:232, 1:263–264

Walking Purchase Treaty, 1:61
Wapakoneta Shawnees, 1:83, 1:218,
    1:220–221, 2:186
war, 1:2–5, 1:15–24, 1:29–35, 1:53–56,
    1:64–73, 1:75–79, 1:83–87, 1:92–94,
    1:96–101, 1:113–114, 1:121–122,
    1:133–136, 1:198–217, 1:222–225,

1:232–236, 1:251–255, 2:4–7, 2:14,
2:22, 2:25, 2:34, 2:39, 2:41–44, 2:52,
2:59, 2:81–82, 2:91, 2:109–110,
2:135–136, 2:148, 2:160, 2:162–163
Ward, William, 1:48, 1:144
Washington, George, 1:152, 1:232, 2:51
Waterloo, 1:10, 1:40–42, 1:147, 1:226
Wea removal. *See* Peoria-Kaskaskia-
Piankeshaw-Wea removal
Webster, Daniel, 1:33
Western Cherokees, 1:9, 1:32, 1:38,
1:39, 1:43, 1:60, 1:68, 1:193, 1:204
Whig Party, 1:18–19, 1:27, 1:84, 1:206,
1:258, 1:259–261, 1:270
Whiteley, R. H. K., 1:41–42
Wichita Agency, 1:30
Wildcat. *See* Coacoochee
Winnebagos, 1:22, 1:26, 1:82, 1:136,
1:159, 1:162, 1:169, 1:203, 1:206,
1:228, 2:47, 2:128–128; removal, *see*
Ho-Chunk removal

Wirt, William, 1:36, 1:89, 1:261–262
Wisconsin, 1:20, 1:23, 1:26–27, 1:97–98,
1:106, 1:124, 1:136–137, 1:151,
1:159–160, 1:162–163, 1:169, 1:176,
1:180, 1:182–183, 1:228–229
women: during removal, 1:262–267;
roles and removal, 1:267–269
Worcester, Samuel A., 1:24–25, 1:27–28,
1:39, 1:89, 1:115, 1:197, 1:232,
1:269–271
Worcester v. Georgia, 1:25, 1:36, 1:39,
1:89, 1:153–154, 1:191, 1:192,
1:271–273
Worth, William J., 1:52, 1:93, 1:99,
1:223, 1:234
Wyandots, 1:117–118, 1:273–275, 2:18;
removal, 1:273–275

Yaha Hadjo, 1:2
Young, John S., 1:40
Yuchis, 1:70–71, 1:73, 1:96, 1:199

ABOUT THE EDITORS

Editors

Daniel F. Littlefield, Jr. is Director of the Sequoyah National Research Center at the University of Arkansas at Little Rock. He is the author or editor of more than twenty books in Native American studies.

James W. Parins is Professor of English and Associate Director of the Sequoyah National Research Center at the University of Arkansas at Little Rock. He is an internationally known biographer of American Indians and an author and editor of nearly twenty books in Native American studies.